KNOWING POETRY

KNOWING POETRY

Verse in Medieval France from
the *Rose* to the *Rhétoriqueurs*

ADRIAN ARMSTRONG
& SARAH KAY

with the participation of
Rebecca Dixon, Miranda Griffin,
Sylvia Huot, Francesca Nicholson,
and Finn Sinclair

CORNELL UNIVERSITY PRESS
Ithaca & London

This book is the outcome of a research project entitled "Poetic Knowledge in Late Medieval France," funded by the British Arts and Humanities Research Council (AHRC). The authors gratefully acknowledge this assistance.

Arts & Humanities
Research Council

First published 2011 by Cornell University Press
Printed in the United States of America

Library of Congress Cataloging-in-Publication Data

Armstrong, Adrian.
    Knowing poetry : verse in medieval France from the rose to the rhétoriqueurs /
Adrian Armstrong and Sarah Kay ; with the participation of Rebecca
Dixon...[et al.].
        p. cm.
    Includes bibliographical references and index.
    ISBN 978-0-8014-4973-4 (cloth : alk. paper)
    1. French poetry—To 1500—History and criticism.   2. Knowledge, Theory
of, in literature.   I. Kay, Sarah.   II. Dixon, Rebecca.   III. Title.
    PQ151.A67 2011
    841'.109—dc22   2010052646

Cloth printing   10 9 8 7 6 5 4 3 2 1

Contents

Illustrations

Preface and Acknowledgments

This book is the outcome of a research project on the relationship between poetry and knowledge in France in the period approximately 1270 to 1530. Titled "Poetic Knowledge in Late Medieval France," the project was funded by the British Arts and Humanities Research Council (AHRC) over a total of four and a half years from January 2005 to June 2009. The grant made it possible for us to sustain dialog with other scholars by means of seminars, visits, and a conference, and, crucially, to employ two full-time postdoctoral research associates. During the life of the project we thus benefited from having four co-workers succeed one another in these two positions: Rebecca Dixon, Miranda Griffin, Francesca Nicholson, and Finn Sinclair. Originally led by two senior scholars, Adrian Armstrong and Sarah Kay, at the Universities of Manchester and Cambridge, respectively, the team was fortunate to prevail upon a third senior figure, Sylvia Huot, to represent Cambridge when Sarah Kay moved to Princeton. We warmly thank her for agreeing to join the project and for devoting so much care and time to it at a point when her research plans were poised to move in another direction entirely.

As part of their roles, our research associates had the task of editing selected papers from among the project's seminars and its conference (Princeton, November 2006). *Poetry, Knowledge, and Community* appeared in 2009, edited by Rebecca Dixon and Finn Sinclair, whose comments and reflections frame the contributions to our field of inquiry from the wider scholarly community. In addition to articles published by all team members within the general field of "Poetic Knowledge in Late Medieval France," each of the project's senior scholars produced monographs: Kay's *Place of Thought* (2007) was followed by Huot's *Dreams of Lovers and Lies of Poets* (2010), Armstrong's *Virtuoso Circle* (2012), and Kay's *Parrots and Nightingales* (forthcoming). The present book, written by the original leaders of the project, presents the outcome of our thinking about the role of poetry in transmitting and shaping knowledge in late medieval France.

This brief outline is offered by way of explanation for the rather unusual circumstances—at least as far as the humanities are concerned—in which this book was written. Its authors, Adrian Armstrong and Sarah Kay, wrote in close collaboration, and we assume joint responsibility for the whole work. The research associates participated by contributing notes and brief synopses on their reading, and joining in collective discussions. Their input was then recast by us for integration into the arguments of particular chapters, then submitted back to the entire team for comment. It was an enormous privilege to have Sylvia Huot intimately involved in all these conversations. Participation of all these team members is acknowledged on our title page. When we had drafted an entire typescript, we held a two-day seminar in Cambridge in March 2009 at which it was reviewed and critiqued by a panel of scholars whose expertise overlapped or bordered our own. François Cornilliat, Noah Guynn, Neil Kenny, Jean-Claude Mühlethaler, and David Wallace were unstintingly generous with their time, knowledge, and insight. We thank them all for their collegiality and for their many suggestions for improvement, which we have sought to implement within the space at our disposal. More broadly, we are indebted to all our many generous interlocutors in our seminars and conference. Our warm thanks go, too, to Peter Potter at Cornell University Press for his consistent support for this volume, even when some of the anonymous reports were less than rhapsodic, and to those readers for so perceptively helping us to identify and rectify some of its shortcomings.

We also acknowledge the support of several institutions, first among them the AHRC for providing the funding that not only enabled us to pursue this research but also nurtured the careers of young postdoctoral researchers through several lean years of the job market. The Universities of Manchester and Cambridge have provided administrative support and a collegial environment. Princeton University funded our conference and enabled transatlantic meetings to take place. The School of Advanced Study at London University conferred on Sarah Kay a visiting research professorship to support her research on Occitan. Adrian Armstrong had additional leave from the AHRC for exploratory studies on the *rhétoriqueurs* at a vital early stage. We also gratefully acknowledge contributions toward the cost of publication from Princeton University and the University of Manchester, and help with compiling the index from Sarah Beytelmann.

The most exciting feature of working on this book has been realizing that we could achieve collectively a breadth of understanding that neither of us could have arrived at independently, and this volume is genuinely the outcome of a team effort.

KNOWING POETRY

Introduction

"No rhymed story is true," "for a history can scarcely be told in rhyme without lies being added for the sake of the rhyme."[1] From the early thirteenth century, when prose is first pioneered as a medium for writing history in the vernacular, prose writers denigrate verse in terms like these as artificial, unreliable, and falsifying.[2] Rather than subjecting their material to the distortions of meter and rhyme, authors of prose texts protest, they present it in an unvarnished form. The identification of prose with factual accuracy and instructional value becomes rapidly established.[3] Throughout the remainder of the Middle Ages, treatises on topics as diverse as falconry, rhetoric, and warfare all tend to be written in prose. Although some narrative verse continues to

---

1. "Nus conte rimés no es verais," in Nicolas de Senlis, *Chronique dite Saintongeaise,* ed. de Mandach, 256; "Quar enviz puet estre rimée / Estoire ou n'ai ajostée / Mançongne por fere la rime," cited from Meyer, "Prologue en vers français," 498, vv. 105–7. Is the second author unaware that, given he is writing in verse, his claims are a paradox like those of the Cretan liar? Pronouncements on the alleged falsity of verse have been much reviewed; see, for example, Hult, "Poetry and the Translation of Knowledge."

All primary works are cited from the editions listed in the bibliography. All translations from both primary and secondary works are our own unless otherwise indicated.

2. As is shown by Beer, *Early Prose,* prose was earlier used in the vernacular for charters, sermons, and Bible translations. See also Woledge and Clive, *Répertoire;* Brunel, *Les plus anciennes chartes.* The move to prose is simultaneous in France, Italy, and Spain; Galderisi, "Vers et prose," 750–51.

3. Beer, *Early Prose,* 127; also Morse, *Truth and Convention,* 98–99.

be composed into the fifteenth century,[4] the verse narrative genres from the early Middle Ages are increasingly sucked into this promotional machine, rewritten in prose, or else supplanted by their prose equivalents. Thus verse romances are often recast as prose romances, the *fabliau* cedes to the *nouvelle,* and *chansons de geste* are "de-rhymed," often in massive historical compilations.[5] Historiography, in which factuality, narrative, and instruction all combine, for the most part adheres staunchly to the new medium. The majority of late medieval chronicles are written in prose, although, as with other forms of narrative, there are important exceptions (see chapter 2).

The "rise of prose" has become a literary-historical topos. Wlad Godzich and Jeffrey Kittay chart the phenomenon in medieval France in terms of what they call a "crisis of authority." The legitimating effect of bodily presence (that of the *jongleur* in oral performance) becomes eroded in favor of the self-sufficiency of the prose text, at the same time that feudal relations give way to the impersonal regime of the state; the "emergence of prose" is thus, for them, a corollary of the passage to modernity.[6] Gabrielle Spiegel offers a more local and focused explanation. Prose was cultivated, she believes, by the earliest patrons of prose historiography, the aristocracy of Flanders and Artois. They embraced a form associated with documentary truth for narratives whose content was largely legendary as a means of promoting their Carolingian heritage, thereby stressing their dynastic superiority to the Capetian dynasty and affirming their autonomy in the face of Philippe Auguste's centralizing policies.[7] However it is explained, the advent of vernacular prose writing certainly transformed the economy of representation in ways that have been widely discussed.[8]

Not the least of its effects, however, is to give heightened definition to verse. In much the same way that the establishment of color photography did not eliminate black and white but instead defined it as a category and endowed it with a whole new meaning, the widespread use of prose redefined the status of verse; for example, the octosyllabic rhyming couplet, which, as the *degré zéro* of versification in the twelfth century and the form least likely to be sung, had functioned as the "prose" of the early Middle Ages, became much more visibly a verse form. Despite the "rise" of color, photographs and even cinema

4. Witness the recasting of the Mélusine legend in rhyme by Coudrette *after* the prose version of Jean d'Arras, Coudrette's being the more successful; Galderisi, "Vers et prose," 762.

5. On *dérimage,* see Doutrepont, *Mises en prose;* Jones, *Philippe de Vigneulles,* 116–20.

6. Godzich and Kittay, *Emergence of Prose.*

7. Spiegel, *Romancing the Past.*

8. See the essays in *Le Choix de la prose;* Hult, "Poetry and the Translation of Knowledge"; Mühlethaler, "Vers statt Prosa"; Griffin, *The Object and the Cause,* 5–7.

films have continued to be produced in the medium of black and white, which connotes its own authenticity, albeit one that differs representationally from color. Similarly with verse: rather than succumb to the view that prose has cornered the market in truth or knowledge (terms we will examine later in this introduction), we contend that verse in France takes on a whole new life as a medium of reflection and enlightenment in the wake of the increasing predominance of prose.

We specify "in France," as opposed to "in French," because this tendency can be observed particularly clearly in texts composed in Occitania, within the boundaries of modern-day France but in a language distinct from French. We also recognize, of course, that French poetry was a medium of knowledge elsewhere in Europe and beyond, particularly in England. So although grounded "in France," our study refers more broadly to the French-speaking world. The formulation "in France" also enables occasional reference to the Latin language culture of the Middle Ages, which continued to be the repository of authority for many medieval writers, though (perhaps surprisingly) not consistently so for authors of this period. Vernacular translations of Latin learned works were usually rendered in prose; otherwise the relationship in this period between Latin and vernacular writings is fluid, with some verse genres (such as encyclopedias) being more much closely linked with Latin than others (such as lyric poetry), and vernacular traditions in both Occitan and French having more coherence within themselves than in their relation to Latinity.

From the continuation (ca. 1270) by Jean de Meun of the *Roman de la rose* to Jean Bouchet, last of the *grands rhétoriqueurs* (most of whose significant work was produced by about 1530), there is a prolific production in France (or in French) of verse texts transmitting encyclopedic, political, philosophical, moral, and other epistemic contents. New verse genres appear: the *dit,* which increasingly takes on philosophical, political, and even scientific themes, owing in large measure to Jean de Meun's influence; new stanzaic or lyric forms, whose capacity for conveying and inflecting subject matter increases dramatically with the political and social involvement of poets from Deschamps onward; and a range of urban theatrical genres from farces to Passion plays exploring social, political, and theological ideas. Not all the verse composed in France in this period shares this epistemic ambition, but the late medieval verse texts most obviously marked by such ambition typically have a markedly anti-prosaic character, rejoicing in elaborate metrical and rhetorical forms that inflect how their content is perceived. It is also striking that the genres most resistant to prose—lyric and drama—are almost always transmitted in manuscripts that are specific to the genre concerned: lyric anthologies or songbooks on the one hand, and theatrical manuscripts of various kinds on the other.[9]

Ultimately and paradoxically, then, a direct consequence of the so-called rise of prose is the forging of a new relationship between poetry and knowledge in which poetry not only transmits what we can reasonably call "knowledge," but also, through its own reflective and self-reflective procedures, shapes that knowledge and determines how it is received. It is this intimate connection between verse production and knowledge in the period from about 1270 to about 1530 in France (or in French) that is the subject of this book.

Recognizing that poetry relates directly to the production and transmission of knowledge has hitherto been the hallmark of scholarship on the periods that flank the later Middle Ages on either side and are often termed "renaissances": the Renaissance that inaugurates the early modern period, and the so-called twelfth-century renaissance. Both periods are often associated with humanism (albeit in varying acceptances of the term), and characterized by a flowering of classical learning, the cultivation of Latin poetry, the reevaluation of rhetoric, and an association between poetry and Neoplatonist philosophy (which again takes divergent forms from the earlier to the later Renaissance). In both of these alleged revivals of antiquity, the production of knowledge is inseparable from poetic activity. In the twelfth century, the most ambitious writings of this kind (for example, poetry on cosmic themes by Bernard Silvester and Alan of Lille) are in Latin; but although uniquely philosophical vernacular poems (such as Simun de Freine's *Roman de Philosophie,* which reworks Boethius's *Consolation of Philosophy* in heptasyllabic couplets) are rare, courtly poetry in general bears witness to the vibrancy of clerical culture.[10] In the early modern Renaissance, although poetry takes divergent paths, verse production often likewise has an important cognitive or conceptual dimension, and can have explicitly philosophical, scientific, or political content (as in the work of Scève, Sponde, or d'Aubigné).[11]

The late Middle Ages have sometimes seemed lackluster by comparison with these two moments of self-conscious brilliance, a lull between periods in which poetry, philosophy, and rhetoric interacted intensively.[12] The very didactic character of late medieval poetry can provoke a perverse resistance

9. Runnalls, "Towards a Typology"; Taylor, *Making of Poetry,* 55–81.

10. Brooke, *Twelfth-Century Renaissance;* for the impact of clerical culture on vernacular writing, see Hunt, "Aristotle, Dialectic"; Kay, *Courtly Contradictions.*

11. E.g., Staub, *Le Curieux Désir;* Fragonard, *La Pensée religieuse;* Miernowski, *Dialectique et connaissance;* Pantin, *La Poésie du ciel;* Banks, *Cosmos and Image.*

12. Champion, *Histoire poétique,* 1:x: "Il y a trop de prose dans cette poésie, de trop longs développements aussi."

in modern readers to what it has to teach. Although some individual writers (such as Jean de Meun, Christine de Pizan, and Jean Gerson) have of course been studied from the standpoint of their learning, critics have been more inclined to see late medieval literature as peddling moralizing and edifying banalities than as participating in the production and transmission of knowledge.[13] And the specific contribution made by verse has been overlooked. For instance, the survey of fourteenth- and fifteenth-century didactic and instructional writings in the authoritative *Grundriss der romanischen Literaturen des Mittelalters* does not specify the form of individual texts, assumes for the most part that they are in prose, and ignores the possibility that there might be any significant distinction between prose and verse.[14] We are fortunate that interest in the later Middle Ages has boomed in recent years, generating a significant number of editions and studies of individual poets and poetic movements. With so many sources now available, a work of synthesis becomes at once possible and highly desirable.[15] It was in order to undertake such a synthesis that we embarked on this research project on poetry and knowledge in late medieval France, whose collaborative nature (see the preface) has enabled us to chart the scale of the interaction between poetry and knowledge in this period.

Medieval writers manifest awareness in many ways that the rise of prose is, at the same time, a reinvigoration of verse. In the early Middle Ages, the Latin term *prosa* was often used to refer to medieval Latin rhythmic verse so as to distinguish it from classical metrical verse. Strophic verse, Latin and vernacular, was standardly laid out on the page as if it were prose, line-by-line recording being reserved for narrative verse until the establishment of the *formes fixes* (*ballades* and *rondeaux* were copied line by line).[16] In the early thirteenth century, French prose works are defined only as being "without rhyme" (*sans rime*). The word "prose" in opposition to verse first makes its appearance in French in Brunetto Latini's prose encyclopedia the *Livres dou Tresor* (ca. 1260), in a section headed "De dui maniere dou parler, en prose ou en rime" (Of two

---

13. Kay's *Place of Thought* argues *passim* that medieval texts commonly considered "didactic" are philosophically and aesthetically interesting.

14. See volume 8, part 1. The review of late medieval didactic literature was left incomplete.

15. For example, reliable editions of George Chastelain's verse have only begun to be produced since the 1990s; Hesketh's edition of the *Lumere as lais* appeared in 1996–1998; Armstrong's edition of Bouchet's *Jugement poetic de l'honneur feminin* appeared only in 2006; a critical edition by Ricketts of the *Breviari d'amor* has been in the process of publication during the course of this project; and at last a new edition of the *Ovide moralisé* is under way. Modern editions of the two versions of the Occitan *Leys d'amor* are sorely needed.

16. Bourgain, "Chansonniers lyriques latins," 64; Hasenohr, "Traductions et littérature."

forms of expression, prose and verse).[17] When Brunetto says that prose is like an open road, whereas verse is a steep and narrow pathway,[18] the biblical metaphor weighs heavily in favor of verse against Brunetto's own chosen form. Prose may be more accessible, but its poetic alternative promises greater edification. The spare, expository prose of the thirteenth century is supplemented by the more elaborate prose styles cultivated in the fifteenth, which may even embrace rhyme, as recommended by Jacques Legrand in his *Archiloge Sophie* (ca. 1400).[19] Nevertheless, the new sense that verse offers a surplus, rather than a deficit, with respect to prose continues into the sixteenth century. Pierre Fabri's 1521 two-part *Grand et vrai art de pleine rhétorique* deals first with prose rhetoric and then with verse, of which Fabri says that it is more pleasing than prose and also, in the case of religious verse, that understanding both improves and is improved by the quality of poetry.[20]

Verse writers also recognize a renewed relationship with knowledge in their medium. (For full discussion of the knowledge that poetry conveys about itself, see chapter 5.) From the early troubadours on, Occitan writers pun on the word *vers,* which in Occitan means both "true" and "verse." In his verse encyclopedia the *Breviari d'amor* (1282–ca. 1284), the late troubadour Matfre Ermengaud of Béziers frequently invokes this pun when alleging the truthfulness of his citations from other troubadours. Following a quotation from Aimeric de Peguilhan, for example, he comments:

Ben es vers senes falhensa
Segon quez a dig N'Aimerics. (29402–3)

(It is indeed true without mistake [*or,* a poem without fault], according to what Sir Aimeric said.)

The pun is made explicit in the definition of the *vers* offered by the *Leys d'Amors* (Laws of Love), of which two versions were drawn up in Toulouse

17. Speer and Foulet, "Is *Marques de Rome* a Derhymed Romance?"; Brunetto Latini, *Li Livres dou tresor,* 3.10; ed. Baldwin and Barrette, 301–2.
18. "La voie de prose est large & pleniere, si come est hore la commune parleure des jens, mais le sentier de rime plus estrois & plus fors, si come cellui qui est close & fermé de murs & de palis," 301.
19. Jacques Legrand, *Archiloge Sophie,* 141; more generally, see Rasmussen, *La Prose narrative.*
20. "Pour aulcun cas est plus plaisant que la prose, car les propositions et mesures delectent plus l'entendement que simple prose; et aussi a celle fin que les deuotz facteurs du champ royal du Puy de l'immaculée Conception de la Vierge ayent plus ardant desir de composer, de tant qu'ilz en congnoissent la maniere, par laquelle leur deuotion croistra" (Fabri, *Le Grand et vrai art de pleine rhétorique,* 2:2).

by Guilhem Molinier between 1341 and 1356 for the provocatively named
Conservatory of Joyous Knowledge, the Consistori de Gai Saber:

> Vers es us dictatz en romans,
> de sen quar es verays tractans.[21]

(*Vers* designates a vernacular genre [*or*, a vernacular composition is true], because
it deals wisely with the truth.)

In opposition to the trumpetings of prose, the claim is thereby lodged that a
text may be true not just *although* it is in verse but *because* it is. Poetic treatises
in medieval Occitan are composed from as early as the turn of the thirteenth
century. In the earliest of these, the *Razos de trobar* (Treatise on Composing
Poetry), Raimon Vidal promotes poetry as a form of moral memory and an
inspiration to courageous acts.[22] The *Razos de trobar* were extremely influential, inspiring a series of thirteenth-century imitations and adaptations, most
of which, like it, were addressed to nonnative speakers of Occitan.[23]

The most comprehensive and important Occitan poetic treatise, however,
is Guilhem Molinier's Toulouse-based *Leys d'amors,* which, evolving through
the mid-fourteenth century, falls squarely within our period of study. Its
purpose was to educate aspiring troubadours in all aspects of composition,
thereby enabling them to avoid moral as much as linguistic or stylistic flaws.
In the second prose redaction, poetry is presented as a branch of philosophy,
for poetry follows the laws of Love, and Love is the mother of philosophy.[24]
Writers, says Molinier, often depict philosophy as a lady of great worth and
nobility, able to encompass both earth and heaven (seemingly a reference to
book 1 of Boethius's *Consolation of Philosophy*). Philosophy is also like a fountain from which flow many delicious rivers, the arts and sciences, which flow
out on to the entire world; there are those who drink from one river and
those who drink from another (an image found in several encyclopedias).[25]
Isidore, Molinier continues, said that philosophy is the knowledge of human
and divine things, and that it leads to a better life. The *Leys* thereby place lyric
poetry on a par with some of the most revered authorities of the Middle Ages.
Grandiose though these claims are, they are modest beside those lodged by

21. Ed. Anglade, 2:175.
22. Ed. Marshall, *B* text, lines 27–31.
23. Ibid., xcvi.
24. Ed. Anglade, 1:71. See also Anglade's notes to this passage in volume 4 and his source
study, 4:52–70.
25. Cf. Brunetto Latini, *Livres dou tresor,* 1.1.

Matfre Ermengaud in the *Breviari d'amor,* a text clearly known to Molinier. Matfre uses quotations from the love poetry of the troubadours to argue for the necessity of sexual love in the divine plan, not only in order to ensure the perpetuation of the species, but also as the tree of knowledge of good and evil, and thus the means to understanding damnation and salvation. In Occitania, then, poetry is identified as a privileged source of ethical, philosophical, and theological knowledge (see chapter 4). Although in the later Middle Ages, Occitania is more closely linked with Catalonia and Italy than with northern France, we include it in this study because of this precocious and explicit exploration of the importance of poetry to knowledge and vice versa.

Vernacular treatises in French appear much later than in Occitan, not before the end of the fourteenth century with Eustache Deschamps's *Art de dictier* (1392). They are collectively known as the *arts de seconde rhétorique,* a phrase already used in the *Leys* to designate the rhetoric applicable to verse rather than to prose in a passage that adapts and modifies the verse-prose distinction in Brunetto Latini's *Tresor.*[26] Though not having such exalted aspirations as their Occitan forebears, these French *arts* imply strong claims about the value of vernacular verse as they experiment with various alliances between poetry and the liberal arts.[27] Deschamps influentially categorizes poetry as a form of music, and thus by implication as not merely an expressive or reflective discipline from the *trivium* of grammar, rhetoric, and dialectic, but a real-world science on the same level as the other branches of the *quadrivium* (mathematics, geometry, and astronomy, in addition to music itself).[28] Poetry was thereby presented not just as a way of talking about reality but also as a structuring element within it, able to contribute its own understanding of how the world is ordered. Although northern French writers came later than Occitan ones to identify poetry as a major branch of rhetoric, their conclusions were no less far-reaching. The French term *rhetorique* comes to mean "poet," as when Eustache Deschamps mourns the death of Machaut as a "noble retorique."[29] When Fabri says of rhetoric that it is "la royne de la pensee des hommes, qui tourne les couraiges, suadant et dissuadant en tel fin qu'il plaist" (the queen of men's thinking, directing their hearts, persuading or dissuading them to whatever end it wishes, 2:1), poetry is included in his praise. Poetry does not

---

26. Ed. Anglade, 2:13.

27. Primarily *Recueil d'arts de seconde rhétorique,* ed. Langlois; *Instructif de seconde rhétorique,* in *Le Jardin de Plaisance et Fleur de Rhétorique,* ed. Droz and Piaget, vol. 1, fols. a$_{ii}$v–c$_{iii}$r.

28. E.g., Dragonetti, "La Poésie…ceste musique naturele"; Cornilliat, Mühlethaler, and Duhl, "La Poésie parmi les arts," 30–36.

29. *Œuvres complètes, Ballade* 123, 1:243–44.

simply present reality to its audience; it also directs the way they feel and act toward it.

Verse and *Poetrie*

The *arts de seconde rhétorique* are above all celebrations of *metrical* complexity, and it is no doubt here that their kinship with other *numerical* or "scientific" arts is most palpable. But some later medieval French writers, taking up the classical term *poeta,* also promote a new concept of *poetrie* broadly understood as a style of writing that relies on *figural* complexity, and is potentially expressive of *philosophical* meaning; rhetoric thereby becomes associated with dialectic and even with theology.[30] The features that typify *poetrie* are the use of classical myths, sustained personification, or forms of extended metaphor: devices constitutive of what we might call allegory. Texts that use these figures place demands on their readers because it takes time and thought to interpret them; but they also reward their readers with more knowledge or moral insight than could be gleaned on first reading. Thus the Middle French words *poetrie, poesie, poete,* and *poetique* do not mean the same as their modern equivalents but something closer to "allegory," "allegorist," "allegorical."

To what extent is *poetrie* to be equated with verse? Latin theorists, vernacular treatises, and practicing poets do not always agree about the answer to this question, reminding us that distinctions in literary history are not always clear-cut. The Latin work that exercised the greatest influence in France in the late Middle Ages was Boccaccio's *Genealogia deorum gentilium* (1360, revised up to 1374), which resoundingly endorses poetry as a vehicle of knowledge: "Poetry [*poetria*]...constitutes a stable and fixed science [*scientia*] founded upon things eternal, and confirmed by original principles; in all times and places this knowledge is the same, unshaken by any possible change" (*Genealogy* 14.25–26). Poetry is not to be identified with versification or rhyme; it can be in verse or prose, or indeed both at once (as is, for example, the Bible); and it increases in value the more it is embellished by the poet's craft. Many manuscripts of Boccaccio's *Genealogia* circulated in France in the fifteenth century, feeding the predilection of French poets for elaborately allegorical *prosimetra*.[31]

A work that contributed to this diffusion was the already mentioned Jacques Legrand's *Archiloge Sophie.* This is a partial French adaptation (two

---

30. Cornilliat, Mühlethaler, and Duhl, "La Poésie parmi les arts," 37–47.
31. Mombello, "I manoscritti"; Bozzolo, *Manuscrits des traductions françaises.*

books out of a projected ten) of Legrand's earlier *Sophilogium,* a compendium
of extracts from Latin learned texts including Boccaccio's *Genealogia.* Marc-
René Jung examines the *Archiloge* closely, concluding that for Legrand, the
defining feature of *poetrie* is not the presence of verse as a form but the use of
allegory or metaphor.[32] In the course of describing various liberal arts, the
Archiloge implies a separation between versification and *poetrie* by devoting
different chapters to each;[33] it defines *poetrie* as "science qui aprent a faindre
et a faire fictions fondees en raison et en la semblance des choses desquelles on
veult parler" (a science that teaches how to contrive and create fictions based
on reason and on the appearance of the things of which one wishes to speak,
149). This injunction to compose what sounds like allegory in any medium
is, however, framed by Legrand against the competing one—expressed only
five lines later—that "poetrie est science qui aprent a versifier et a ordonner
ses moz et ses paroles par certaine mesure" (poetry is a science that teaches
how to versify and arrange one's words and utterances according to a definite
meter, 149).[34] Clearly the notion of *poetrie* is a controversial one, and the *Archiloge* (like the *arts de seconde rhétorique,* to which it is related) is involved in a
polemic about how to situate it among the disciplines. Legrand asserts (against
the Persian philosopher Al-Farabi, ca. 870–950) that *poetrie* is a subsection of
rhetoric, not logic, because its purpose is not to formulate arguments but to
represent the world, albeit in a contrived and many-layered fashion.

The controversies of the theorists correspond to a certain degree of confusion among practitioners, which has been skillfully documented by Glending
Olson. Drawing on a wide range of mainly vernacular texts in French and
English from the fourteenth and fifteenth centuries, Olson proposes that the
late medieval term "poet" should be understood in opposition to that of a
"maker" or *faiseur.*[35] A "poet" composed texts that could be in either verse or
prose, the defining feature of which was that they were edifying or instructive in some way. Some medieval writers reserve the term for the ancients;

32. Jung, "Poetria."
33. Langlois's introduction to the chapter "Des rimes," reprinted in *Recueil d'arts de seconde
rhétorique,* notes that Legrand regards verse and *poetrie* as different.
34. Jung, "Poetria, 58–59: "Poetrie est science qui aprent à faindre et à faire fictions fondees
en raison et en la semblance des choses desquelles on veult parler, et est ceste science moult
necessaire à ceulz qui veulent beau parler, et pour tant poetrie, à mon avis, est subalterne de
rethorique. Bien est vray que aucuns dient l'opposite, come Alpharabe, en son livre *de la Division des sciences,* lequel dit que poetrie est la derreniere partie de logique, et dit oultre plus que
poetrie est science qui aprent à versifier et à ordonner ses moz et ses paroles par certaine mesure;
mais, à mon avis, ceste opinion n'est pas raisonnable, car poetrie ne aprent point à argüer" (BnF,
ms fr. 24232, fol. 61v).
35. Olson, "Making and Poetry."

alternatively, *poetrie* could be equated simply with "classical lore."[36] Olson draws attention to the use of the rubrics "balade sur la poeterie" (Deschamps) and "balade pouetique" (Christine de Pizan) to designate *ballades* on mythological subjects.[37] In other cases, *poetrie* implies a separation between literal and allegorical levels, associating what medieval writers sometimes referred to as the "integument" or outer covering with the inner kernel or "cortex" (compare Raison in the *Roman de la rose*, who refers to the "integumenz aus poetes").[38] *Poete* is always a term of commendation; *faiseur*, by contrast, is either neutral or a superordinate term that includes *poete*. It could refer to a composer of verse, often lyric poetry, that had little or no significance beyond the literal; such verse could be diverting, soothing, or otherwise therapeutic (and thus not without positive value), but was not intellectually demanding.[39] *Faiseur*, however, also had the technical meaning of "versifier," and thus it was possible for a *faiseur* to compose work that was also *poetique*. *Poetrie*, then, is a mode that bisects the category of verse, dividing off serious from nonserious verse, and allowing the former to be placed in the same category as prose characterized by the same figures and epistemic ambition.

Although *poetrie* and verse could be distinguished in a variety of ways, in practice the two coincide, at least in the earlier part of our period. Even if, when Deschamps calls Machaut a "noble poete," he has in mind Machaut's use of personification and mythology rather than his command of meter and rhyme, the fact remains that Machaut's output is almost exclusively in verse.[40] Evrart de Conty (ca. 1330–1405) in the prologue to his *Eschez amoureux moralisés* states that he will expound his model in prose because "some of the things contained in rhyme appear obscure or abstruse at first sight" (aucunes choses que la rime contient qui semblent estre obscures et estranges de prime face), whereas "prose is more transparent than verse" (prose est plus clere a entendre que n'est rime), a formulation that appears to invest rhyme with the same indirection and need for interpretation as other authors attribute to allegory.[41] (The *Eschez amoureux* of 1370–1380 is a verse text recasting the *Roman de la rose* as a game of chess; Evrart's commentary on it was composed around

36. Ibid., 278.
37. Deschamps, *Œuvres*, 1:251; Christine de Pizan, *Œuvres poétiques*, ed. Roy, 1:90.
38. *Le Roman de la rose*, ed. Lecoy, 7132–38: "et qui bien entendroit la letre / le sen verroit en l'escriture, / qui esclarcist la fable occure./ La verité dedenz reposte / seroit clere, s'el iert esposte:/ bien l'entendras, si bien repetes / les integumenz aus poetes."
39. Olson, *Literature as Recreation*.
40. Deschamps, *Ballade* 447, v. 3 (*Œuvres* 3:259–60). First discussed by Brownlee, *Poetic Identity*, 7–20; more recently by Huot, "Reading the Lies of Poets."
41. Évrart de Conty, *Li Livre des eschez amoureux moralisés*, ed. Roy and Guichard-Tesson, 2.

1400.) Evrart proceeds to liken the author of the *Eschez* to the *poetes* of antiquity on three counts. First, the meaning of the *Eschez* is moral and improving. Second, the text is allegorical, or as he puts it, the author speaks "en faignant et fabuleusement" (by means of contrivance and fabulation), and is not to be understood "a la lectre" (literally). And third, the author has chosen to write in verse:

> Item il resamble aux poetes car il fait son livre par rimes et par vers; et de ceste maniere de parler par rimes et par vers ou mectres, usent communement en leurs faiz les poetes, pour plus sutillement et plaisaument dire ce qu'ilz veulent, car en rime et en mectre est la parole assise et mesuree par musical mesure, c'est a dire par nombres ressamblables a ceulx dont les consonances musicaulx dependent, en laquel musical consonance se delite moult l'ame humaine naturelement, come Aristote dit ailleurs. (2–3)

> (Additionally, he resembles the poets because he composes his book in rhyme and meter, and poets in their compositions commonly make use of this manner of speaking in rhyme and meter in order to convey their meaning more subtly and pleasingly, because in verse one's words are placed and measured by the same principles as in music, that is, by numbers resembling those on which musical harmonies depend, in which the human soul naturally delights, as Aristotle says elsewhere.)

Although some of the ancient texts Evrart mentions as examples of covert fictions are predominantly in prose, *poetes* "commonly" have recourse to verse, and all the vernacular "poetic" works he cites (25) are in verse. (They include the *Roman de Renart,* the *Rose,* and the 1332 *Prise amoureuse* by Jean Acart de Hesdin.) His ideal, Sylvia Huot concludes, is that "rhyme, metrics, language and didactic import work together in their impact on the reader."[42]

Thus, although not all vernacular verse qualified as *poetrie,* for most of the fourteenth century vernacular *poetrie* was overwhelmingly in verse. Their separation seems not to have come about until very late in the century, an intriguing early example being Philippe de Mézières's *Songe du vieil pelerin* of 1386–1389, a work of political and historical reflection embellished with long and improbable allegories, which may first have been written in verse although only the prose version survives.[43] The French author who most clearly consecrates the composition of *poetrie* exclusively in prose is Christine de Pizan.

---

42. Huot, "Reading the Lies of Poets," 48.
43. Di Stefano, "Nota sul Songe du Vieil Pelerin."

After completing her long verse *dits* the *Livre de la Mutacion de Fortune* and *Livre du Chemin de long estude* in 1403, she shifts away from verse for the *Livre de l'Advision Cristine* and *Livre de la Cité des dames,* texts that adapt all the armory of medieval allegory from her verse *dits*—mythography, personification, sustained metaphors—into prose. Never unassuming in her choice of models, Christine in her prose biography of Charles V (1404) cites the Old Testament and the parables of Jesus as examples of *poesie,* which she defines, following Boccaccio, as "toute narracion ou introduction apparaument signifiant un senz, et occultement en segnifie un aultre ou plusieurs...dont la fin est vérité" (every narrative or presentation that overtly has one meaning and covertly another or several others,...the purpose of which is truth), specifying that the "dress" (*revestemens*) assumed by the text's teaching could be far removed ("d'estranges guises") from its purport.[44] But although Christine thus cements the theoretical divorce between *poetrie* and verse, the association between them persists, and allegorical and mythographic texts at least partly in verse continue to be produced throughout the fifteenth century and at least to the end of the period covered in this book (1530).

In this study we have decided to maintain verse rather than *poetrie* as our focus, not only because of the clear association between *poetrie* and verse, but also because we are persuaded—despite the pretensions of *poetrie*—that many verse texts that are not allegorical possess epistemic value. Allegory is not, for example, a necessary component of encyclopedias, yet one can hardly doubt the commitment of these texts to conveying knowledge to their readers; and even verse texts of a more obviously diverting character can have a therapeutic or consolatory effect on their hearers' minds.[45] Moreover, as we have already said, a thoroughgoing assessment of the value of verse production *as knowledge* in the later Middle Ages is long overdue. Although some of our findings may be applicable to prose texts, and some may not be applicable to all verse texts, we confine ourselves to texts that are substantially in verse and concentrate on how this fact contributes to their overall import. Henceforth we will use the word "poetry" to refer to texts in verse and have recourse to the term *poetrie* when we want to designate the medieval notion.

44. "Si est assavoir que comme en general le nom de poesie soit pris pour fiction quelconques, c'est-à-dire pour toute narracion ou introduction apparaument signifiant un senz, et occultement en segnifie un aultre ou plusieurs, combien que plus proprement dire celle soit poesie, dont la fin est vérité, et le procès doctrine revestue en paroles d'ornemens delictables et par propres couleurs, lesquelz revestemens soient d'estranges guises au propos dont on veult, et les couleurs selon propres figures..., car, si comme il appert, l'ancien Testament fu tout fait par figures, meismement aussi Jhesu-Crist si parla par figures." *Livre des fais et bonnes meurs du sage roy Charles V,* ed. Solente, 2:176–77.

45. Olson, *Literature as Recreation,* 105, 128–63; Dixon, "Conclusion."

The Late Medieval Tradition and the Poetics of Mediation

The specific time span on which we have chosen to focus calls for further comment. The roughly 260 years that separate Jean de Meun from Jean Bouchet are not usually seen as constituting a period in their own right. In linguistic terms, we range over two or even three periods of the language, given that our starting date of around 1270 falls within the Old French period, the fourteenth and fifteenth centuries are thought of as Middle French, and some scholars see sixteenth-century French as constituting a different period again.[46] In literary terms, late medieval poetry is often seen as beginning with Machaut, whose main literary output dates between approximately 1340 and 1377, and as ending before Bouchet, perhaps with Molinet (fl. 1464–1507) or with Jean Lemaire de Belges (fl. 1498–1515).

There are, however, a number of prima facie justifications for regarding our period as a unity. (Its coherence will be demonstrated at greater length in the following chapters.) The period is dominated by the constantly renewed poetic engagement with theological and philosophical themes; a handful of ambitious key texts (the *Roman de la rose,* the *Ovide moralisé,* Boethius's *Consolation*) exert an urgent and unceasing fascination. Such preoccupations are symptomatic of a more general sense that vernacular literary production constitutes, in itself, a significant artistic and intellectual pursuit. Poets are intensely aware of contributing to the development of a literary tradition. They respond to one another's writings, at once vying and paying tribute, jockeying for position with their contemporaries and creating genealogies of antecedents that stretch back to the past. When Amors in the *Rose* compares Guillaume de Lorris with Gallus, Catullus, and Ovid (10492), he is epitomizing what will be the implicit procedure of succeeding generations.[47] This is precisely not the spirit of "renaissance," because there is no sense here of an ideal ambition to resurrect the past *tel quel.* Renaissance poetics tend to value the inspirational, even antirational qualities of poetry and the qualities of the solitary poet in himself rather than the tradition in which he stands; late medieval poets, on the contrary, are confident in their own powers of mediation in a trajectory that, while it connects them to their forebears, also holds them at a distance. For them time, and not immediacy, is of the essence. Poetry in this period sees itself crucially as caught up in history rather than

---

46. Marchello-Nizia, *Langue française,* 4–6.
47. See Bagoly, "'De maincts aucteurs une progression'"; Gally, *L'Intelligence de l'amour,* 35–37. The same idea of a tradition is treated in different modes in Italian and English literature; Wallace, *Chaucerian Polity,* 80–82, 377–78 (n. 81).

abstracted from it, a fact that is reflected in the prominence accorded historical and political themes that are relatively absent from Renaissance poetry, or
at least from that of the Pléiade. Even if, in the latter end of our period, the
weight of the medieval poetic tradition induces a melancholic dread that all
has already been said, this is still a tribute of a kind to the fullness that has
been achieved.[48] Poets' awareness of the development of metrical forms, and
of contributing to the history of rhetoric through composition of their own
poetic treatises (as mentioned earlier), is further evidence of a specifically late
medieval literary-historical self-consciousness. It continues through the *grands
rhétoriqueurs* with Bouchet, whereas after him there is a break with medieval
strophic patterns and a cultivation of new genres with a more or less classical
ancestry.

Educationally speaking, the period 1270–1530 is the age of the university
rather than of the schools that characterize the twelfth and early thirteenth
centuries on the one hand and the early modern Renaissance on the other.
Although the University of Paris was inaugurated as early as the mid-twelfth
century, its preeminence as a center of learning is not achieved until the foundation of the Sorbonne as its faculty of theology in the mid-thirteenth, and
its imprint on literature is not perceived until the 1260s and 1270s with Rutebeuf and Jean de Meun. At the other end of our period, 1530 was the year in
which Francis I founded the Collège des Lecteurs Royaux (later to become
the Collège de France) in a deliberate bid to end the Sorbonne's monopoly of
learning.[49] Our roughly 260-year time span, then, is one dominated by scholasticism, a set of intellectual practices to which the Renaissance—especially
Rabelais—gave a bad name which has tended to stick, despite its continuing
development and importance to early modern academic philosophy.[50] Rabelais is certainly right that scholasticism is the antithesis of renaissance, but this
is precisely because late medieval intellectuals and educators believed in the
value of the mediation that contemporary learning had to offer. Perhaps they
would have been as mistrustful of the concept of immediacy as Rabelais was
of that of authority. The late Middle Ages are a time when scholars aspired,
if not to absolute knowledge, to as much knowledge as was possible within
human limitation, and when they worked institutionally, systematically, and
often with exquisite sophistication to achieve it. Hence it is also the age of the

48. Cerquiglini-Toulet, *La Couleur de la mélancolie.*
49. Knecht, *Renaissance Warrior and Patron,* 306–7, 560. Initially the Collège had no building, consisting simply in the creation of lectureships in Greek and Hebrew (and later Latin).
50. Langer, *Divine and Poetic Freedom,* 11–19, notes the continuing centrality of scholasticism in many areas of intellectual life; Schmitt, *Aristotle and the Renaissance.*

summa, the drive for comprehensiveness, the quest for universality. Unlike in the earlier and later renaissances, more fascinated, as we have said, by forms of Neoplatonism, intellectual inquiry in this period is dominated by versions of Aristotelianism that invite an anthropocentric view of knowledge grounded in individual experience, founded on the form of individual things, and yet pitched at a universal level. The Aristotelian concept of "form" as the vehicle of intelligibility may lie behind some of the intricate formal experiments of the period, which, although they can strike some modern readers as a merely sterile exercise, clearly carried the potential for meaningfulness and even for knowledge at the time.

Many writers in this period appear to have benefited from a university education. Book production increases dramatically, the secular trade booming to meet the growing body of educated readers.[51] The format of books also changes to render them easier to consult. Rubrics, tables, indexes, *notae,* running headers all make it easier for texts to deliver up knowledge to their readers.[52] All these features were, of course, accelerated by the advent of printing, which reached France in 1470 and thus decisively influenced approximately the final quarter of our period. Scholasticism, interpreted retrospectively as stifling, was experienced as empowering, and this is perceptible in the period's poetry, whether or not it is explicitly about scholastic thought. Jacqueline Cerquiglini-Toulet provides a wonderful example of such empowerment in her study of the effects, in Machaut's poetry, of the scholastic concept of *subtilitas.*[53]

Knowing, Knowledge, and Truth

What kinds of knowledge are found in verse texts, and what extra dimensions does the fact that they are in verse contribute to the kinds of knowledge they purvey? Clearly this poses other, far-reaching questions about what we mean by "knowledge" and related concepts such as "learning" and "truth." We have sought to keep an open mind on these questions; working as a team in any case favors methodological eclecticism. Dialogue with francophone colleagues has provided the constant stimulus of obliging us to choose between the various French translations of "knowledge" as *savoir, connaissance,*

---

51. Rouse and Rouse, *Manuscripts and Their Makers.*
52. Parkes, "Influence of the Concepts of *Ordinatio* and *Compilatio*"; Huot, *Romance of the Rose* and "'Finding–Aids'."
53. Cerquiglini-Toulet, "*Un engin si soutil.*" See also Corbellari, *La Voix des clercs;* Bolduc, *Medieval Poetics of Contraries.*

or *science*. Usually we render the title of our project in French as *poésie et savoir*, not only because this offers the broadest understanding of "knowledge" but also because the verbal character of *savoir* foregrounds it as an activity (knowing) performed in and through poetic texts. Confronting the fracture between knowledge as content (*connaissance*), including prestige or abstruse contents (*science*), and knowledge in act (*savoir*) is a salutary reminder that not all knowledge needs to be present to the mind in order to have an informing or determining role. *Savoir* may indeed consist primarily in a *savoir faire*: the mastery of art as technique rather than a magisterial learning. While continuing to accept that knowledge can take the form of substantive *connaissance* (as when, for example, an encyclopedia details the makeup of the world), we are alert to those processes of *savoir* that are not, and sometimes cannot be, translated into content of this kind.

The medieval terminology of knowledge is likewise conceptually divided. It is striking how many of the personifications that characterise *poetrie* belong in this lexical field, and are thereby elaborated and dramatized. Unlike in the *Rose,* where only one character's name—Raison—designates a strictly mental capacity (moreover the personification is not represented in an altogether consistently rational guise), in later *dits* and *prosimetra* figures proliferate with such names as Cognoissance, Avis, Sagesse, Sapience, Science, and Entendement.[54] The constellations in which these characters are positioned constantly refocus the nature of human understanding and of the knowledge that is available to it. Sometimes the context is religious, as in Guillaume de Deguileville's *Pèlerinage de vie humaine,* where Raison is inferior to Grace Dieu even if she is better than Rude Entendement, or Alain Chartier's *Livre de l'Esperance,* where Entendement dialogues with Foi and Esperance (a third part featuring Charité was seemingly never written). At other times knowledge is more social or political, as in Machaut's *Jugement dou roy de Navarre,* where Cognoissance (knowledge, discernment) is teamed with Avis (right judgment) and other qualities desirable in a ruler such as Prudence. Perhaps the author whose schemes offer the greatest scope for reflection on the powers and limitations of knowledge is Christine de Pizan. In her *Livre du Chemin de long estude,* Raison presides over a court made up of the Influences, or Destinies, that rule the world. Accorded the most prestige of the

---

54. Mühlethaler, "Les poetes que de vert on couronne," notes that from the thirteenth century, *sagesse* starts replacing *sapience* as the generic term, the latter being increasingly restricted to divine wisdom. *Sophie* appears in the late fourteenth century, associated with *sapience,* but by the sixteenth century it has come to mean "sagesse humaine"; *science* applies to any kind of learning.

four, Sagesse comments lengthily on her fellows Richesse, Noblesse, and Chevalerie. As Miranda Griffin has shown, knowledge in this text and in the *Mutacion de Fortune* is presented as a good in more than one sense. Like other earthly goods, knowledge is subject to fortune and its Destinies; yet it also has the capacity to console and fortify against fortune.[55] As a result of this paradoxical status, knowledge is sometimes assimilated to a form of wealth and sometimes opposed to it. As knowledge is also inevitably compromised in worldly contingency, it also always has to be exercised ethically; for this reason, Christine favors figures representing wisdom (Sagesse, Sapience) rather than knowledge alone. Finally, it is important to Christine's concept of knowledge that there are always parts of it that will remain closed off to her. In both the *Chemin de long estude* and the *Mutacion de Fortune,* knowledge is figured as a series of paths only some of which she can travel. Although knowledge is universal, our capacity for it is relative, partial, and contingent. Another fracture in the field of knowledge, then, results from much of it lying beyond our scope, where it is destined to remain unknown.[56]

In analyzing the ruptures and discontinuities in the field of knowledge, we have drawn discreetly on modern thinkers. Lacan's topology of symbolic, imaginary, and real has proved illuminating, since it maps these fractures by proposing a series of different sites for "knowledge" and for "truth." Lacan insists that some proportion of knowledge (*savoir*) is unconscious and permanently unavailable except insofar as it inflects what we think we know. He retains a refreshingly iconoclastic attitude toward *connaissance,* which he sees as always to some extent contaminated with *méconnaissance.*[57] In his Seminar 15 he also punningly aligns it with the verb *déconner* (to fool around), suggesting that *il déconnait* (he was fooling around) could be read as *il déconnaît,* a present-tense form of a nonexistent derivative of the verb *connaître* which Lacan invents in order to point to a degree of tomfoolery (*déconnaissance*) in all pretensions to knowledge (*connaissance*).[58] It is useful to be reminded of the unconscious distortions that knowledge presents us with when we are considering texts in which love or desire plays a part, especially when they are associated with a quest for enlightenment as in the *Rose* and its descendants. The lover in the *Rose* is a good example, indeed, of such imbecility, since he shows little interest in anything but *con* and is incapable of anything

55. Griffin, "Material and Poetic Knowledge"; Kay, *Place of Thought,* chap. 6.
56. Kelly, *Christine de Pizan's Changing Opinion.*
57. Lacan, "Le Stade du miror," in *Écrits,* 93–100.
58. *Le Séminaire de Jacques Lacan Livre XV (L'Acte psychanalytique),* séance 2, which took place on November 22, 1967. See Kay, "Poésie, vérité" and "Knowledge and Truth."

but *déconner* regardless of the *connaissances* that are heaped on him. Yet for all his skepticism about knowledge, Lacan is never dismissive of the concept of truth, only of the illusion that it is readily available. Truth is what causes us to speak, even if it is not to be found in what we say. At the cost of simplification, for Lacan truth is of the real, *savoir* is in the symbolic unconscious, and *connaissance* belongs in the imaginary. His dispersal of the cognitive processes across different psychic domains provides a fruitful way of capturing their disjunction (and potential dysfunction) in poetic texts.[59]

We have been struck that knowledge, when it is explicit (in didactic works, for example), often needs to be duplicated: to know is not enough, one must know that one knows; the conviction that what one knows is "true" results from this secondary act of validation. Such reduplication gives rise to a different kind of fracture in the epistemic field, and a theorist who has helped to advance our thinking on this point is Jean-François Lyotard. Although Lyotard does not address medieval literature as such, his *Condition postmoderne* uncovers strategies to which thinkers prior to postmodernity have had recourse in order to legitimize knowledge and thereby raise it to the level of "knowing that one knows," strategies that lend themselves well to describing the mechanisms we encounter in didactic texts. Lyotard points out how, in each case, the very processes by which knowledge is ratified end up eroding it, and how, as a result, the concepts of both "knowledge" and "truth" are destabilized.

In describing modern political myths, for example, Lyotard draws attention to the way a narrative may be supplemented with overt exhortation; medieval equivalents to this are found when a moral is appended to an exemplum, or an allegoresis to an allegory. The gap between the place where knowledge is claimed to reside (the exemplum or allegory) and the place where it is rendered explicit (the moral or allegoresis) is potentially corrosive. It is enough for the reader to sense this gap as a divergence (for instance, to perceive the moral as arbitrary or inappropriate) for the procedure to backfire; the very fact of trying to validate the "knowledge" in the exemplum by claiming to formulate it in the *moralité* runs the risk of *in*validating it. Another practice of legitimation that Lyotard critiques also has close parallels in medieval usage, namely the processes of citation and compilation. Here, in Lyotard's account, the knowledge in the text that is cited or included in the compilation is validated by virtue of being incorporated in a second, framing discourse. The risk inherent to this procedure is that it implicitly demotes the text that has

59. Armstrong, "Yearning and Learning."

been cited or compiled, which now appears to have lacked authority until it was taken up by the host text. Many late medieval texts, notably the *dit* (as Cerquiglini-Toulet has defined it), depend precisely on compiling discourses in this way.[60] *La Condition postmoderne* enables us to inquire into the relation to knowledge of such compilations. When, for example, passages from Boethius are incorporated into yet another *dit amoureux,* does this confirm the unshakable authority of Boethius, or does it rather lend to it a pliancy, an indeterminacy even, whereby the value of Boethian "knowledge" becomes dependent on the epistemic value of its new frame? Lyotard's critique is helpful, then, as a way of exposing the different rhetorical means (he calls them "language games") by which late medieval texts seek to ratify knowledge as something known, known to be known, known to be worth knowing, and thereby true.

Neither Lacan nor Lyotard endorses the idea that knowledge has truth-value and, broadly speaking, this is a position that we share. We take it, that is, that truth is an effect of a structure, or of a mode of enunciation; we do not hold a brief for truth as a content that can be formulated. This position runs counter to some medieval—and modern—opinion; to claim that one knows something is not generally held to be reconcilable with conceding that it may not be true. The Middle Ages, however, did not equate "facts" (*vera,* true things) with "truth" (*veritas*), as Jeanette Beer has shown apropos of medieval asseverations of truthfulness.[61] Truth might reside in an authority without being attested in reality; it could be "judged as if it were fable."[62] For theologians, and in particular for proponents of negative theology, Truth is likewise an absent cause. The rhetoric of truth-assertion in various contexts is thus capable of holding the concept of truth at a distance from that of knowledge. It is our contention in this book that poetry, by virtue of its form, can lay claim to truth that is independent of its content. To recall an earlier point of this introduction, this is effectively what is at stake in the idea that poetry is true *because* it is poetry and not *despite* it. The poetic form stakes out a relation to truth that is different in nature from the truth-claims of prose—indeed also from those of rhetoric, for which truth is an effect of form regardless of what that form might be.

The writer who has done the most to conceptualize poetic form as itself expressive of truth or knowledge is Giorgio Agamben. In *Stanzas* he privileges the poetic form of medieval verse specifically as a means of overcoming what he sees as the rupture posited by Western thought between poetry and

60. Cerquiglini-Toulet, "Le Clerc et l'écriture."
61. Beer, *Narrative Conventions.*
62. Ibid., 22; see also Huot, *Dreams of Lovers.*

philosophy whereby "poetry possesses its object without knowing it while philosophy knows its object without possessing it" (xvii).[63] Drawing on the etymology of the word *stanza* as "a resting place," Agamben describes the metrical stanza in a flurry of aphorisms as a place where non-knowledge and non-possession meet; medieval poetic form, he contends, enables modes of knowledge and possession that do not have any positive content, except for an explosive release of joy. From this negative perspective, the stanza critiques the Western schism between a poetic word that "enjoys the object of knowledge by representing it in beautiful form" but is unaware of what it is doing, and a philosophical word that adduces knowledge but is incapable of enjoying it (xvii). In a later chapter Agamben attempts to explain this paradoxical enjoyment in (non-)knowledge by proposing that the form of poetry bears the imprint of the phantasm, a concept that, following medieval Aristotelianism, is intermediary between sense perception and intellectual abstraction.[64] Poetic form, then, retains the trace of sensual enjoyment while at the same time offering purchase to knowledge, thereby averting the divorce of knowledge from the joy of its contents. Returning in his later book *The End of the Poem* to the related theme of the relationship between poetry and life, Agamben again privileges medieval poetry as lodging an originary truth that prose narrative seeks in vain to recapture. The prose commentaries, or *razos,* of troubadour songs are, he argues, unable to go beyond the knowledge of the poetic texts they seek to explicate. Poetry encapsulates, disseminates, and serves as an inviolable guarantor of a truth and an experience that inhere in the poetic form rather than reflecting the actual lived experience of poet or protagonist.

We see no need to restrict Agamben's arguments solely to stanzaic forms. Taken in relation to medieval verse in general, his theories are exciting to us because they suggest that medieval poetry is an exceptional moment in the history of thought as well as of literature: a moment in which knowledge in some way inheres in form and does not require recourse to metalanguage. Verse literature may be teaming with what Lyotard terms "strategies of legitimation"; but it also has, via its form, the means to sidestep them. Put more strongly, poetic form itself acts as a mode of legitimation that, because it is immanent to the texts concerned, does not fall casualty to the slippages Lyotard diagnoses.

While our thinking about what we can understand by "knowledge" has been nourished by theoretical reading, we have also found heuristically useful a set of broad-brush distinctions between different kinds of knowledge, which we term "referential knowledge," "textual knowledge," and "ideological

---

63. This position, embraced by Alain Badiou, is critiqued by Kay in "Poésie, vérité."
64. *Stanzas,* chap. 16.

knowledge."[65] The first of these is sometimes equivalent to factual knowledge (such as was laid claim to, as we said at the outset, by prose). The historical and encyclopedic tendencies of late medieval poetry often assume knowledge of this kind. But given the theological or philosophical ambition of many such texts, the word "referential" in our usage takes on the broader sense of a knowledge that seeks to equate itself to the world. For example, encyclopedias seek to acquaint their readers with the Trinity, the orders of angels, and the value of prayer as well as with the humors, planets, and various species of animals, so their descriptions differ in the extent to which they can be said to have "referents." We thus include, under the heading of referential knowledge, speculation of various kinds about how the cosmos is constituted. By textual knowledge, we understand the self-conscious expertise with which writers manipulate language, negotiate generic restraints, or respond to their fellow poets. Considered from a formalist perspective, literary form and the forms of material transmission inevitably inflect content: our task has been to disengage the value *as knowledge* of this inflection, and also the extent to which literature constitutes itself as an *object* of knowledge. Finally, under the heading of ideological knowledge, we consider the social, religious, or political presuppositions of poetic texts. Such knowledge, which is often implicit or even unconscious, conditions how poets represent their relationship to the world; it complements referential knowledge by inducing attitudes to the way we believe the world is constituted, for example, by exhorting readers to cultivate the virtues, condemn idolatry, or uphold the Burgundian cause. Whereas textual knowledge is often conveyed by various forms of *intertextuality,* ideological knowledge can exploit *interdiscursivity,* the inevitable overlaps that exist between discourses within texts and those used to mediate a sense of social knowledge.[66]

This threefold schema has its shortcomings. What knowledge is free from ideology? What knowledge that is expressed in texts is not in some measure already textual knowledge? What knowledge about texts is entirely separate from knowledge about other entities that exist in the world? But while critiquing and refining these distinctions, we have continued to find them useful, and they subtend the organization of chapters 4–6.

The Organization of This Book

Here, then, is a brief outline of the chapters that follow. The first three investigate the ways in which poetry and knowledge come to be associated in the

---

65. Armstrong, "Prosimètre et savoir."
66. The term *interdiscorsività* is coined by Segre, *Teatro e romanzo,* 111.

later Middle Ages in France. Together they advance our understanding of our two key terms and the historical specificity of relations between them in this period. After the advent of prose, the persistence of verse and its association with oral performance may seem conservative, but in fact, as chapter 1 shows, new institutions develop in which often very ambitious verse texts (mystery plays, for example) publicly enact vital fields of knowledge such as religious teaching. The capacity of verse to transmit knowledge is enhanced by the way it is visibly anchored in the bodies of performers and physically shared by the audience. Chapter 2 then examines the connection between verse and history that is established institutionally through patronage, thematically through the treatment of historical issues in poetry, and more generally through the attention paid by poetry to experience and memory. Although the body of a performer may be absent, and the content of knowledge sometimes defi-cient, verse form serves as an index of certain kind of truth and a placeholder of subjectivity. The focus then passes, in chapter 3, to the association forged between poetry and thought by learned poetry. The legacy of the *Rose,* the *Ovide moralisé,* and the *Consolation of Philosophy,* severally and in conjunction, makes verse seem the appropriate medium for inquiring into the interconnec-tions between corporeal nature, contingency, and philosophy. This concludes the first half of our book, in which the groundwork is laid for situating the relationship between verse and knowledge in this period.

The three later chapters each examine the historical development of a par-ticular kind of knowledge in relation to its poetic expression. Chapter 4 tack-les the relationship between poetry and the world, analyzing the structure of late medieval encyclopedias, charting the collapse of verse encyclopedias and the rise of encyclopedic verse, and probing their hesitations about the relation of parts of knowledge to the whole along the problematic axes of hermeneu-tics and ontology. Chapter 5, as already indicated, is about how poetry reflects a knowledge of itself. As well as analyzing explicit statements about poetic quality, we evaluate the implicit significance of practices such as quotation, lyric insertion, and *prosimetrum.* Chapter 6 is about the forms of social, politi-cal, or religious knowledge that poetry conveys through its relation to its audi-ence. Any text presupposes or founds some kind of community: in this period, the persistence of poetry in certain circles (both urban and courtly), and its role in founding or maintaining "textual communities" (in Brian Stock's phrase), mean that it often encodes or challenges group ideologies.[67] Our study of the

---

67. Stock, *Implications of Literacy.* In this respect, verse in the late Middle Ages plays the converse role to that of early-thirteenth-century prose, which, according to Spiegel in *Romanc-ing the Past,* served to forge a sense of identity among northern baronial houses resistant to Capetian power.

transmission of late medieval texts suggests that this domain of knowledge is the one most likely to shift from one manuscript or print context to another, and also the domain most likely to absorb or inflect the others, and for this reason it seems appropriate to study it last.[68]

Finally, in the conclusion we review the larger questions of periodization and the role of literature in an evolving economy of knowledge. Here we summarize the book's overall argument, which is that despite, or rather because of, the rise of prose and its claim to epistemic transparency, verse in late medieval France develops a new relationship both to its own forms and to its capacity for knowledge. This happens, we contend, by virtue of the way in which verse is grounded, or situated, in relation to knowledge in this period. A sense of being situated (as opposed to unanchored or ungrounded) is inherent in versification because of its association with performance, its echo of bodily pulse and reliance on repetition: its situation, that is, in relation to the body and its experience of time. To this degree it could be said that verse carries its own situation around with it, an observation that would hold true of any period. But in late medieval France, the situation of verse is thrown into relief by its new relationship with prose, and takes on a particular historical coloration as a result of its institutional contexts and the literary and reflective traditions in which it finds itself. Poetry in this period is *knowing:* knowing about temporality, subjectivity, the body, and the processes of (not necessarily conscious) thought. And it lends itself particularly to transmitting and shaping knowledge about the world, poetry itself, and its implication in society.

68. Armstrong, "Manuscript Reception."

PART I

SITUATING KNOWLEDGE

CHAPTER ONE

Persistent Presence

Verse after Prose

The purpose of the following three chapters is to examine the circumstances that enabled poetry, despite the pretensions of prose, to take on this second life as a medium of knowledge in the later Middle Ages. We do not set out to map knowledge as a content of texts, nor to analyze how verse texts shape this knowledge, since these issues are addressed in the final three chapters. Instead we seek to explain how and why knowledge and verse are associated and what this means for each of them. In part we do so by paying attention to the historical contexts in which verse was produced. But also, as these chapters develop, we uncover other aspects of the ways verse situates itself in this period and what connotations it thereby comes to bear. As the scope of each chapter is potentially vast, we have been obliged to be sparing in our choice of examples.

Concentration on the spread of prose has diverted the attention of literary historians away from the persistence of verse and the mutations it underwent in the face of the competition posed to it by prose. In particular, scholarly concern with *mise en prose,* a process defined by *dérimage* or the loss of the distinctive features of verse, has tended to obscure the importance of another process affecting late medieval verse: that of *mise en scène,* or at least of *mise sur scène,* the act of staging in which the structures of verse are preserved, sometimes via a generic mutation from a narrative form to a more theatrical one. The "persistent presence" of this chapter's title refers both to the ongoing importance of verse after the advent of prose and to the inventive reaffirmation of live performance as a means by which verse works were made physically present to an audience.

The "Rise of Prose" and the "Rise of Literacy"

Godzich and Kittay's anthropological-semiotic study has the most to say about the impact of prose on verse. Verse is initially effective, they contend, as an oral performative medium in which deixis, or reference to the world, is realized through the person of the performer. The semiotics of verse texts remain indexed to performance even when the texts themselves are written down; the absence of oral performance is a factor precipitating the collapse of confidence in the capacity of verse adequately to convey knowledge of the world. When verse survives alongside prose in later medieval texts, according to Godzich and Kittay, its values remain traditional; the semiotics of personal presence and authority cannot instantly be jettisoned. But verse continues to be regarded as inferior to prose when it comes to rendering reality in the way that social changes increasingly require, namely as impersonal and objective, and as no longer dependent on reference to what is immediately present. In the longer term, therefore, verse finds itself "at the mercy of prose" and is forced to discover ways to "rebel and resist" (203). Given that prose has over-taken verse in affording its readers the sense of communicating to them the world as it really is, the only option open to verse is to offer something not of this world. The solutions that it contrives, they propose, are to stress the value of poetry as an autonomous tradition, to promote lyric poetry, and to revive the association between poetry and myth, by which they mean the legacy of the Greco-Roman world. All of these modifications to the role of verse, as Godzich and Kittay frame them (203–5), postdate the Middle Ages. In short, on their account the continued use of verse in the Middle Ages is solely con-servative; its mutation to confront the challenge posed by prose comes with the Renaissance.

While suggestive on matters of detail and seductive as a broad-brush nar-rative, Godzich and Kittay's account does not always stand up against the very texts they adduce as evidence. Their reading of Jean Molinet's *Ressource du petit peuple* (1481) is symptomatic.[1] A *prosimetrum* allegory reflecting on the difficulties facing the Burgundian Netherlands after the death of Duke Charles the Bold, the *Ressource* is presented as the vision of a first-person witness-narrator, identified in the text as the *acteur*. The *acteur* sets the scene by recounting the suffering that Tirannie (Tyranny) and her followers inflict upon Justice and the Petit Peuple (Ordinary People); Verité (Truth) and Jus-tice deliver invectives, laments, and pleas in verse, interspersed with narrative

---

1. Godzich and Kittay, *Emergence of Prose,* 46–76.

elements and with didactic prose discussions between Verité and Conseil (Counsel); in a final verse section, the *acteur* hopes for an end to the current disorder. Godzich and Kittay propose a variety of ways in which the successive speakers of the *Ressource* lay claim to authority. While verse remains tied to specific contexts of utterance, they contend, prose represents itself as independent of such contexts. It lays claim to be "that which is out of quotes, that which is not for attribution, that which frames [the discourse of another, in either verse or prose] but is not framed itself" (72). It thus "does not need to formulate a claim to authority as such," for "more is to be gained by leaving the determination of the source of authority suspended" (65).

These claims for the differing status of verse and prose are vitiated in a number of ways. Most important, the figure of the *acteur* has been misinterpreted. The term had long been used to denote first-person narrators, in verse as well as prose, whether or not these narrators played a significant role as protagonists within the stories they told. It was also ambivalent, potentially denoting a text's author as well as its narrator. Many late medieval narratives play on precisely this ambivalence, encouraging but not authorizing readers to conflate author and narrator.[2] Besides displaying no awareness of this standard usage, Godzich and Kittay are led astray by the edition they use, which is based on a manuscript that uses headings to identify the narrator's voice as *l'acteur* everywhere except the opening prose section. Consequently, they assume that the heading *l'acteur* denotes a voice different from that of the opening prose, which they identify as "Molinet" (seemingly assuming the author's direct presence in his allegorical fiction). On this fragile basis they characterize the *acteur* as a factitious voice, a device that ascribes written prose to a speaking subject that is not present but must nevertheless be assigned (60–65). The *acteur's* insubstantial quality, it is alleged, leads Molinet's audience to suppose "that it is the recipient of an immediate, rather than mediated, semiotic matter" (66). On the contrary: the *acteur* was a perfectly familiar figure to the late medieval audience and was often represented in manuscript illustrations even when he was little more than a passive witness of events.[3] As such, the *acteur* makes mediation of the allegorical action an *overt* rather than *covert* process.

The misdiagnosis of the *acteur* is exacerbated by a limited understanding of the different roles that prose and verse may play, even within the modest

2. Studies include Chenu, "Auctor, Actor, Autor"; Winn, "In Pursuit of the *Acteur*"; Brown, "Rise of Literary Consciousness." *L'Acteur* is frequently used in manuscript rubrics to identify the first-person narrator of the *Roman de la rose,* sometimes in contrast with *L'Amant,* which designates the fictional protagonist; Huot, "'Ci parle l'aucteur.'"

3. Armstrong, *Technique and Technology,* 46–48, discusses the *acteur's* presence in the illustrations of another *prosimetrum* by Molinet, *Le Naufrage de la Pucelle.*

corpus of Molinet's six *prosimetrum* compositions. Certainly the *Ressource* is typical of these works in that verse is primarily employed where one or several characters "speak," or in some cases "sing," within the fiction. But Molinet uses verse for narrative as well as direct speech, both in the *Ressource* and in all but one of his other *prosimetrum* pieces.[4] Verse also has a set of important functional roles in these texts: it may condense arguments made in the preceding prose section, or convey particular kinds of affective intensity, whether pathos, righteous anger, or exultation.[5] This example is indicative of the extent to which the binaries that Godzich and Kittay seek to map onto verse and prose—oral/written, personal/impersonal, situated/decontextualized—are sometimes overly schematic and insufficiently contextualized themselves.[6]

Overall, Godzich and Kittay's contention that verse lingers through the late medieval period as the remainder of a declining episteme parallels traditional accounts of the decline of orality in favor of literacy. Indeed, it presupposes such accounts insofar as they envisage verse as belonging truly to an oral culture, even though eventually it is committed to writing. These accounts have, however, been successfully countered by Joyce Coleman who, in her book *Public Reading and the Reading Public in Late Medieval England and France,* argues forcefully against recognizing any "decline" of the phenomenon of orality consequent on the "rise" of literacy. Deliberately leaving out of account the large swathes of literature (such as theater) that were expressly composed for live performance, Coleman shows how, far from superseding orality, the spread of writing instead generated new forms of it. Regardless of their ability to read, people regularly had texts read to them (for example, at mealtimes); rather than read privately, they might choose to read aloud to one another in small groups.[7] This culture of reading aloud, which she terms "aural" to distinguish it from earlier kinds of orality, was a social staple of the later Middle Ages. Not all late medieval verse, of course, needs to be seen as

---

4. The exception is *L'Arbre de Bourgonne* (Molinet, *Les Faictz et dictz,* 1:232–50, Molinet's only other *prosimetrum* piece to be cited by Godzich and Kittay (161–68); Armstrong, "Prosimètre et savoir," 131.

5. Thiry, "Au carrefour." *Le Prosimètre à la Renaissance,* ed. Dauvois, documents the variety of *prosimetrum.*

6. They further see Verité's use of invective as incongruous, since in their view truth "ought to...speak dispassionately" (59). For Molinet and his contemporaries, however, rhetorical ornament and affect do not compromise truth, and may enhance it; Thiry, "La Poétique des grands rhétoriqueurs"; Cornilliat, *"Or ne mens."* Eulogies in medieval French literature were not normally reserved for the dead, as Godzich and Kittay claim (70); nor was the *Ressource* composed during "the 95th year of the Hundred Years War [1337–1453]" (47).

7. Bouchet, *Le Discours sur la lecture,* 55, considers that aural reception and silent reading coexisted during the fourteenth and fifteenth centuries, with the latter becoming predominant after 1400.

exclusively associated with oral (or aural) reception. In response to the spread of writing, it develops specific new literary forms. This is precisely the argument of Sylvia Huot's influential *From Song to Book,* for example, which explains the rise of the "lyrico-narrative" mode as one in which formerly oral song comes to be "performed" by the written page. But in this chapter we develop Coleman's insight to show how, just as forms of aurality arose in the context of the spread of literacy, so the growth of prose as a written medium created new environments in which to exploit and redefine the "presentness" traditionally associated with performed verse. The "persistence" of verse is to be understood as its constant reinvigoration and restaging, not merely as its survival as some pallid remainder in the face of the triumph of prose.

Conservation and Transformation of Verse

Instead of assuming that a rise in prose entails a decline in verse, let us instead begin by asking what kinds of verse texts survive alongside prose and may be seen as responding to it. There are several verse genres that, despite their formal innovations, remain in some sense "the same" from the early to the later Middle Ages in France. The most obvious are drama and lyric, both of which elaborate a plethora of new forms while at the same time maintaining the essentials of French (or Occitan) versification: rhyme schemes, stanzaic forms, and standard line lengths. There will be very little prose theater composed in the medieval period (and none before the fifteenth century) and no prose lyric whatever until very much later (unless the prose in *prosimetrum* can be regarded as a form of prose poetry; see chapter 5). Verse also persists in texts on nonfictional, nonnarrative topics from a wide variety of domains (scientific, moral, philosophical, devotional, historical, satirical). While verse on such topics is more strongly challenged by prose than are lyric or theater, it is still thriving at the end of our period, for example, in the hands of the *grands rhétoriqueurs.* When, however, authors from the late thirteenth century onward choose to write such texts in verse, even if they do so in imitation of a model or in conformity with local custom, they are making a very different choice from their predecessors in the late twelfth century—one whose conservatism needs to be reread in the light of the new context(s) that surround(s) it.

Authors often, not surprisingly, choose to write in the same form as the texts they take as their models, and in this respect antecedent tradition is bound to exercise a conservative effect. The *Roman de la rose,* for example, is responsible for attracting huge swathes of late medieval literature to adopt the form of verse. There is nothing remarkable in Guillaume de Lorris's love allegory being in octosyllabic couplets: so are many early-thirteenth-century texts that experiment with the verse narrative traditions of the twelfth. Guillaume's *Rose* is, among other things, a playful variant of the verse quest romance, in which the hero's adventures are crowned (or not) by social integration and love. Maintaining this romance association by prolonging the quest for the rose, Jean de Meun's continuation shows how continuity can at the same time be utterly transformative. In his hands the octosyllabic couplet takes on an altogether different content, that of lively philosophical exchange. The figures encountered on the quest reveal themselves to be mouthpieces of contrasting intellectual traditions engaged in dialogue with one another as much as (indeed more than) with the protagonist. Jean's fictional plot and, as David Hult has shown, often punning rhymes make his text a dynamic—or explosive—fusion of the world of university thought with vernacular literary form.[8]

Without precedent, the *Roman de la rose* did not fail to inspire emulation. The same loci, personified abstractions, and dream-vision framework are used repeatedly over the next two and a half centuries to couch more or less serious reflection in the medium of verse. Texts that imitate the *Rose,* even when devoted to subjects that might have been expected to use prose, nonetheless continue the tradition of octosyllabic couplets. The expanded *Pèlerinage de vie humaine* of Guillaume de Deguileville is a case in point. Deguileville's original poem of 1330–1332 recasts the *Rose* as an allegory of the Christian life in which the pilgrim is assailed by sins but finds salvation in the Church. Even though the revised redaction of 1355 is much more critical of the *Rose* than the earlier one, and even though the third poem of the new trilogy is essentially a life of Christ (a topic far more commonly worked in prose), the text remains formally in the shadow of the *Rose;* it is not until much later, in 1464, and with the intervention of new revisers, that parts of the trilogy are de-rhymed.[9] The formal attraction exerted by a model maintains the identical versification in octosyllabic rhyming couplets from Guillaume's *Rose,* to Jean's continuation, to Deguileville's first redaction, to the expanded trilogy, despite the radical transformation of subject matter and ethos between the beginning and the end of the chain. The *Rose* itself is not de-rhymed until 1500 by Molinet, and Molinet's work is not so much a *mise en prose* as a "moralization," as Molinet

---

8. Hult, "Poetry."

9. Boulton, "Digulleville's *Pèlerinage de Jésus Christ.*" Most explanations for Deguileville's *mise en prose* assume it to be part of the general movement into prose of verse romance, overlooking how far from romance the second redaction had moved. Stephanie Kamath (personal communication) points out that a better model might be Evrart de Conty's *Eschez amoureux moralisés,* which also belongs in the tradition of the *Rose* but adopts the form of scholastic prose.

contributes exegetical material on the model of Evrart de Conty's *Eschez amoureux moralisés*.[10] Molinet's reworking did not inhibit the *Rose* from continuing to circulate as a verse text at least until the end of our period; Clément Marot, for example, edited the verse *Rose* for publication in 1526.

It may also be the case that some regions are more likely to retain verse than others, and might in this respect be described as more conservative; this seems to be the case with Anglo-Norman and Occitania, the linguistic areas that were most innovative in the twelfth century. Yet their late-thirteenth-century verse encyclopedic works are highly creative (see chapter 4), while the establishment of lyric poetry as an object of study by the Consistori de Gai Saber at Toulouse is less an instance of the persistence of verse than of its utter transformation by the contemporary institutions of scholasticism (see the discussion later in this chapter and chapter 5).

Whether the conservative impulse is generic or regional, throughout the later Middle Ages we find repeatedly that traditional verse forms exercise a powerful influence on writers, but that the meaning associated with them is liable to change. In our introduction we used the analogy of the development from black and white to color film to suggest how an older medium (black and white photography, verse literature) can take on new meanings when a new one (color, prose) develops alongside it. This analogy is useful for grasping how apparent continuity may be better described as a shift toward self-consciousness or reflexivity. Modern black and white photography can summon up the memory of an earlier style (such as 1930s urban realism) while also reflecting the distance between those days and the present, a dual focus that is all the more visible because black and white is no longer the "default" photographic medium. Similarly, the form used by Deguileville both recalls the *Rose* and takes the measure of his distance from it, a distance made explicit in his repudiation of Jean de Meun in the second verse redaction of the 1350s.[11]

Verse and Its Institutions

Previous discussions of the "rise of prose" have looked for connections between it as a literary phenomenon and its historical context. For Godzich and Kittay, prose is the medium appropriate to the emergent modern state. By contrast with this account, which forms part of a Hegelian grand narrative

---

10. Dupire, *Jean Molinet,* 72–78. On the moralization, see Devaux, "De l'amour profane à l'amour sacré"; Regalado, "Le *Romant de la Rose moralisé*."

11. Huot, *Romance of the Rose,* 225–29.

about the development of Western culture, Gabrielle Spiegel in *Romancing the Past* situates the "rise of prose" as a response to quite specific political circumstances: the resistance of the northern barons to the erosion of their privileges in the latter part of Philippe Auguste's reign. As a result of their successful ideological manipulation, in her view, the medium of prose became accepted as the form for truthful historical narration and was taken up by royal historiographers in a bid to counterassert Capetian legitimacy.

We have reservations about Spiegel's account. As Ian Short pointed out in his review of *Romancing the Past,* there is a potential circularity in her argument, not least in the assumption that "reality" shapes "literature" more than the other way around (a prejudice that Kittay and Godzich, to their credit, avoid). The sharpness of Spiegel's focus enables her to examine in depth a limited set of texts and their context but also binds her to explain one in terms of the other without reference to the broader literary scene. If prose is an effective tool of propaganda to the northern barons, why do the anti-centralizing epics of revolt continue to be written in verse, and why are many early prose works (the Occitan *vidas* and *razos,* for example) lacking in any dimension of propaganda? Short also critiques Spiegel for taking the pronouncements of prose writers at face value. The earliest known denunciation of verse historiography—Nicolas de Senlis's much-quoted "nus contes rimés no est verais" (no rhymed tale is true)—may, Short suggests, more properly be interpreted as stigmatizing the reliability of the tale in question rather than the use of verse as such. Nevertheless, Spiegel's interest in the ideological investment of particular historiographical texts certainly prompts, as its converse, a questioning of the institutional affiliations of verse. If we suppose that prose is associated with the "will to power" of certain groups, what are the politics of continuing to compose in verse?

The persistence—by which we also mean the transformation—of verse belongs simultaneously in numerous different and seemingly incompatible contexts. The period of the later Middle Ages in France culminates in the consolidation of central authority and the decline in prestige of regional courts. There is, however, no sign of an exclusive linking between the epistemic use of verse and either the French monarchy or rival centers of patronage.[12] The careers of Machaut, Froissart, and Christine de Pizan, to take just three examples, show that there was a rich culture of patronage available, including various royal houses, dukes, and other magnates. Poetry could equally be supported by urban communities, whose assorted professional organizations

---

12. Though major centers did sustain a significant volume of verse production. Later Capetian courts, for instance, generated the *Roman de Fauvel* (see chapter 6), the verse chronicle of Geffroy de Paris, and the vast epic and romance compositions of Girart d'Amiens. See Dunbabin, "The Metrical Chronicle"; Girart d'Amiens, *Escanor,* ed. Trachsler, 1:8–10, 27–29.

(jongleurs, trade guilds, lawyers) were responsible for the majority of theatrical works. The works of Pierre Gringore, at the very end of our period, attest to his own multifunctionality and to a corresponding diversity of audience. Commissioned by the Duke of Lorraine and probably also by the royal court, associated with various branches of Parisian civic officialdom, he worked with numerous guilds in the production of royal entries and entertained popular audiences in Paris and the provinces.[13] Another instance of social adaptability were the authors and aspiring intellectuals who entered the Franciscan order in the thirteenth and fourteenth centuries because of the opportunities it offered, precisely for contact with a great diversity of potential audiences; indeed, John Fleming goes so far as to suggest that Franciscans were largely responsible for the institution of literature in medieval Europe.[14] In short, consumers of verse range from the most noble to the most popular.

While all these milieus have different interests, two features are common to a very large proportion of their verse production in the later Middle Ages. They all foster "live" performance of various kinds—public readings and enactments. And while these clearly retain affinities with older models of performance, such as that of a troubadour poet singing *cansos* before a court or a jongleur reciting *fabliaux* at a fair, they develop new frameworks and institutions of performance such as the ten-week-long public reading by Froissart of his romance *Meliador,* the lyric poetry competitions staged by the Puys of northern cities, the cycles of Passion plays that occupied whole urban populations for weeks at a time, or the political pageantry of royal "entries." The emergence of these institutions means that verse retains into the later Middle Ages an association with physical presence that it possessed in the twelfth century. The visibility of performance serves, at least potentially, as a correlate of veracity, while the communal dimension of performance can appear to guarantee the epistemic value of what is thus made present. At the same time, the competition from prose and the formal elaborateness of some of these new institutions make the claims of verse to be a vehicle of truth and knowledge more ambitious and self-aware than they had been in the early Middle Ages.

Public Reading

Reading aloud in the later Middle Ages is the object of Joyce Coleman's already mentioned *Public Reading and the Reading Public.* She calls it "prelection," a

---

13. See Brown's introduction to her edition of Gringore, *Œuvres polémiques,* especially 9; and her introduction to Gringore, *Les Entrées royales,* especially 22–23.

14. See Fleming, *Introduction,* 15.

calque on the Latin term *praelectio,* used by John of Salisbury to refer to the reading of a written text to one or more listeners, and distinguished from *lectio,* the reading of a work to oneself.[15] Among the French evidence cited by Coleman (111, 114) for the practice of vernacular prelection are the *dits* of Machaut and Froissart, which have also been scrutinized for evidence of modes of medieval reading by Deborah McGrady in her book *Controlling Readers.* The remarks that follow are indebted to both these scholars, our contribution being to differentiate the public reading of verse from that of prose, and to underline the potential epistemic dimension of such reading. We concentrate on the most ambitious of Machaut's *dits,* the *Voir dit* of 1363–1365, which describes the elderly narrator's rather pathetic courtship of a young girl, Toute-Belle. An aspiring poet, Toute-Belle places herself under the tutelage of the Machaut persona, who is an established writer, and the two exchange lyric verses and prose letters until eventually their relationship founders. The text of the *Voir dit* preserves these exchanges and insets them into the frame narrative, which, as befits a descendant of the *Rose,* is composed in octosyllabic rhyming couplets.

The mosaic of different kinds of writing that composes the text gives rise, as McGrady has shown, to a veritable survey of the different practices of reading that were available in Machaut's day: intimate, solitary consumption by the narrator or Toute-Belle of each other's letters and verses; reading aloud to another individual or a small informal group; court performances at the behest of a patron. As the *Voir dit* advances, texts that were intended to be kept private are divulged, and work as yet unpublished leaks prematurely into the public domain.[16]

Attentive primarily to the way the *dit* thus documents the author's lack of control over the reception of his work, McGrady does not linger over the different treatment accorded to the performance of verse and prose. Nevertheless, it is apparent from her analysis that prose is more closely associated with private reading and verse with reading, or singing, in public. Prose risks indiscretion; too late in the day, Toute-Belle recommends that the lovers exchange messages only in verse, the publication of which would do less harm (*Voir dit,* 782; *Controlling Readers,* 67). Although Toute-Belle is at fault in reciting the narrator's songs without his authorization, when she flaunts (*flajole*) his letters to her friends she commits an act of radical betrayal (*Voir dit,* 7366; *Controlling*

---

15. Coleman, *Public Reading,* 35.

16. Ibid., 92, shows that in the later Middle Ages, a first public reading of his own work by an author constituted a form of what we would call publishing, in which the work's reception could be gauged instantaneously.

Readers, 59–60). The premature performance of verse texts is undesirable because it presupposes a proper time for their public release, whereas for the prose letters no such publication is anticipated, at least within the fiction. Analogously, although the performance of verse can result in a humiliating reception for the poet, he is eager for it to be acclaimed by the right audience, whereas no general public is envisaged for the letters. It seems that readers should have forever been denied this aspect of the *dit* were it not for Toute-Belle's scandalous indiscretion and the narrator's bid to outdo her by attempting to control the public reception of the letters himself (cf. *Controlling Readers,* 67).

Froissart's *Prison amoureuse,* composed around 1372–73 in imitation of the *Voir dit,* echoes and confirms this distinction between verse and prose messages (*Controlling Readers,* 176–88). Wishing to communicate a *virelai* to his lady, the narrator of the *Prison* does not send it to her directly but instead encourages it to circulate freely, confident that it will eventually reach her ears. Even though public performance here, as in the *Voir dit,* is not necessarily gratifying to the poet (Froissart's lady publicly mocks his *virelai* with one of her own), general appreciation by an audience remains his goal where verse is concerned. When Froissart's prose letters are stolen by a group of ladies, however, the sense that this constitutes a violation of his privacy is conveyed by the sexual nature of the places occupied by the letters—whether the pouch hanging from his belt from which they are taken, or the ladies' bodices in which they are subsequently concealed. The episode concludes when the ladies return the letters on condition that they can keep the verses attached to them, a transaction that confirms the free circulation of verse as contrasted with the privacy reserved for prose. (The knowledge of poetry conveyed by the *Prison amoureuse* is explored in chapter 5.)

The poet Eustache Deschamps, one of Machaut's great admirers, offers another window onto reading in the *Voir dit.* His *Ballade* 127 describes his presenting a copy of the *dit* to Louis de Mâle, Count of Flanders, at Bruges, and being invited to read from it to the assembled court. Deschamps identifies the passage he selects as the one: "Ou Fortune parla si durement, / Comment l'un joint a ses biens, l'autre estrange" (Where he spoke so harshly to Fortune about how she unites some with the good things that she brings and holds others at a distance from them, 21–22). Coleman and McGrady both discuss the reasons why Deschamps lit on this passage, which would appear to begin at around line 8171 of the *Voir dit.* Placing the emphasis on the *fortuna* topos, Coleman proposes a political subtext;[17] McGrady focuses

---

17. Ibid., 115–17; "Text Recontextualized."

instead on the fact that the excerpt describes Machaut's own reading of Livy and suggests that Deschamps's choice seeks to "explore the important over-lap between public and private reading practices" (*Controlling Readers,* 162). The full import of the passage in surviving manuscripts of the *Voir dit,* she argues, requires unmediated access to the book as material artifact, in par-ticular to the rubrics, illustrations, and inscriptions that accompany the text describing Machaut's act of reading. By the very fact that he mediates this act, Deschamps denies any such contact to his audience, and instead monopolizes access to Machaut's text just as Machaut claims access to that of Livy. As a consequence, while Deschamps's enactment of Machaut's role is presented in the *ballade*'s refrain as a tribute ("en vostre louenge," in praise of you), it is also a usurpation.

Our contribution to this debate is simply to underline that Deschamps's choice fell on one of the most erudite passages of the *Voir dit.* We will see in chapter 3 how far-reaching were the implications of the *fortuna* topos for phil-osophical verse influenced by the *Roman de la rose* and by Boethius. Machaut's narrator presents himself as encountering it in Livy, as excerpted in the work of Fulgentius, the couplet conspiring to give the impression that this makes his source more rather than less learned, since it places both Latin names at the rhyme in the nominative form (Fulgentius: Tytus Livyus, 8185–86). The narrator performs an elaborate ekphrasis of the depiction of Fortune that includes Latin quotations; the original Latin appears in the illustrations in some of the manuscripts. The passage is generalizing rather than autobio-graphical, moralizing rather than affective, and that it is eminently excerpt-able is borne out by the fact that there are two manuscript copies that contain only this section of the *Voir dit.* It portrays Machaut as his various friends and protectors within the *Voir dit* wish him to appear: as a cleric occupied with the state of the world and with learned texts, rather than as a *faiseur* who fritters away his time on girls and love poems (see *Voir dit,* 7232–7557).[18] The refrain of the stanzas commenting on the various circles of Fortune makes explicit that he is now writing his book according to their preferences: "S'il est voirs ce qu'on m'en a dit, / Autrement ne di je en mon dit" (Thus it is true what they have said about her, and I don't say otherwise in my tale, 8269–70, repeated 8285–86 and so on). Deschamps's choice to highlight the Fortune passage is, from this perspective, at once a decision to direct a critical eye toward the amo-rous, lyrical aspects of the *Voir dit* and to promote Machaut as a learned poet. In short, however else Deschamps may have envisaged his performance, his

---

18. We thank Deborah McGrady for help with this section.

choice of this particular excerpt showcases an association between the institution of prelection, poetry, and *savoir.*

As Coleman has argued, public reading was a means not of compensating for illiteracy but of intensifying the impact of a written text (*Public Reading,* 85). This could be beneficial to bodily health, to emotional well-being, and to the mind. Performance, she proposes, facilitates learning and the transmission of knowledge more than private reading does. She quotes Radulphus Brito, for whom "we learn more by being taught than we find through our own efforts" (*Public Reading,* 90). When works of a political nature, such as treatises on government and mirrors for princes, were read to a group, audiences must have benefited from the seminar-style discussions that ensued (*Public Reading,* 97). Far from being a throwback to earlier modes of oral performance, the aural culture of prelection ushered in new forms of sophistication.

When we consider the *dits* of Machaut and Froissart, we at once see how this change is registered in the new form of the textual first person. In twelfth-century works, the textual *je* is usually that of a performer or narrator who is carefully distinguished from the author. In the works of Machaut and Froissart, by contrast, it invites confusion with the historical author, whose persona is that of a clerk: limited and even comic in some respects, perhaps, but undeniably well educated. When such works are read aloud by the poet himself, or by a fellow author, his physical presence endorses the reliability of whatever knowledge might be unfolded by the text. The institution of prelection in the later Middle Ages in France existed in tandem with changes in literary composition. Although verse could be performed at the wrong time by the wrong person, it could also confirm an association between public performance, verse, and knowledge that did not extend to all forms of prose—certainly not to prose letters.[19]

The Puys

These related qualities of later medieval poetry—the public nature of performance, the institutional infrastructure that frames it, and the epistemic value of verse—are particularly strikingly intertwined in the Puys. These competitions in devotional (usually Marian) poetry seem to have been initiated as early as the late twelfth century. From there, the impulse to institutionalize and professionalize the production of lyric poetry spread to other northern cities,

19. Bouchet, *Discours sur la lecture,* 98–109, 310, relates developments in late medieval prose to the increasing incidence of private rather than public reading.

and the Puys were at their most successful in the fourteenth and fifteenth
centuries. They are a distinctively urban and collective phenomenon, and also
a regional one, extending no farther west than Caen and no farther south
than Paris.[20] They were organized by *confréries*, mutual and/or professional
associations with a pronounced charitable and devotional character, whose
emergence has been regarded as reflecting the rise of corporatism in medieval
cities.[21] The oldest known *confrérie* is the Carité de Notre Dame des Ardents
of Arras, in which *jongleurs*—professional entertainers of all kinds—played
an important if sometimes contentious role. Though unusual in many respects
(not least the social diversity of its members), the Carité set the tone for subsequent associations in its interweaving of poetic ambitions and civic interest. Collectively controlling the city's means of communication, it was able to
mediate between conflicting interest groups.[22] The *confréries* that staged Puys
had all the necessary institutional apparatus of statutes and archives; surviving documents indicate that their membership was generally dominated by
social élites such as municipal officials, lawyers, clerics, and rich bourgeois.[23]
To belong to a *confrérie* was highly prestigious, and in some cases entailed
religious and secular privileges in return for a substantial subscription fee.[24]
The Puys themselves were normally held on an annual basis, as part of a day
of religious and secular celebration that also involved a mass and a banquet.[25]
In short, they formed part of a collective ritual not only of poetic devotion to
the Virgin but also of the *confrérie*'s self-definition and self-advertisement.
The Puy of the Immaculate Conception at Rouen, attested from 1486, was
even more socially involved: the presentation and judging of poems took place
before the general public rather than among the *confrérie* alone, binding the
association together with the wider urban population.

   In the Occitan-speaking area, the Consistori del Gai Saber of Toulouse
(founded ca. 1323) may have been established in emulation of the early French
Puys.[26] As in the Puys, candidates for the prizes offered by the Consistori were
required to compose and perform poems on religious subjects, primarily devotion to the Virgin, and the Consistori's ceremonies in her honor overlapped

20. This account draws on Hüe, *Poésie palinodique*, 223–357, and Gros, *Poète*, 30–106.
21. Gros, *Poète*, 30.
22. Symes, *A Common Stage*, 80–126, 206.
23. On the membership of *confréries* and the role of Arras, see Symes, *A Common Stage*, 115–18; Hüe, *Poésie palinodique*, 224, 229–36; Gros, *Poète*, 33–34, 39–40, 50.
24. E.g., Hüe, *Poésie palinodique*, 232–36; Gros, *Poète*, 40–44.
25. E.g., Symes, *A Common Stage*, 216–26; Hüe, *Poésie palinodique*, 281–89; Gros, *Poète*, 44, 51.
26. See Léglu, "Languages in Conflict."

with other forms of civic pageantry in Toulouse.[27] The situation of Toulouse differed from that of the northern cities, however, because of the aftermath of the Albigensian crusade, which submitted its Occitan culture to French influence, left it under a cloud of heresy, and established the Inquisition at Toulouse University. In this complex institutional context, staging annual poetry competitions in Occitan on religious themes was tantamount to an act of cultural resistance.[28] In order to reinforce the symbolic value of these competitions, the Consistori commissioned regulations—the *Leys d'Amors*—to be drawn up, which were for the most part compilations from Latin sources, and which set out formally to teach and examine poetry within a structure modeled on that of the university. In his second prose redaction of the *Leys* of 1356, Guilhem Molinier includes verse degree certificates as well as abundant information on judging standards and criteria. It seems that there was a gradual convergence between the competitions staged by the Puys and the Consistori in the fifteenth and sixteenth centuries.[29]

It is hardly surprising that all these competitions, so tightly woven into the intellectual life of their host cities, should exhibit a certain particularism: each had its preferred poetic genres and formal strictures, even if they were also influenced by one another.[30] The case of Rouen is examined by Denis Hüe in *La Poésie palinodique à Rouen*. On the one hand, many competing poets elaborate an imagery of Marian devotion that draws on site-specific metaphorical fields, important local activities such as navigation or the textile industry (714–26, 805–84). On the other, the Rouen Puy came to develop a prestige that stretched far beyond the city. After an initial period in which the winning poets tended to be local figures unknown to modern literary historians, poets of national standing began to compete there: André de La Vigne, Guillaume Cretin, Jean Marot (*Poésie palinodique,* 238–39). The value of prizes at Rouen was also considerable: the most exalted prize, for the winning *chant royal,* was worth one hundred sols tournois (290–91). This sum was four times the annual subscription to the *confrérie* in 1520 (232), and equivalent to over a week's wage for Jean Molinet in his capacity as Burgundian *indiciaire* (on which position see chapter 2).

Over and above their rootedness in specific urban societies, the Puys generate a form of poetry that insistently lays claim to conveying knowledge and

27. Léglu, "Performance and Civic Ritual."
28. Léglu, "Languages in Conflict."
29. Dauvois, "Évolution."
30. Gros, *Poète,* 31, 37, 98–99. Gros, *Poème,* 187–92, notes differences between the formal prescriptions of the Puy of the Immaculate Conception at Rouen and those of the Puy of Our Lady at Amiens.

truth. This is not simply because the Puy poets are heavily indebted to the authoritative discourse of theology.[31] It is partly because they articulate shared urban identities, common understandings of the world and of one's place in it; it is partly because their literary production is inseparable from practical acts of devotion, which hence ground the poetry both in everyday urban life and in an eschatological perspective. But it is also because the poetry of the Puys creates its own religious metaphors: it is apt to take ordinary objects and activities, not yet consecrated as figurative by preexisting religious usage, and transform them into tokens of a transcendental order. Hence in a number of poems the minting of coins, a privilege of Rouen, comes to stand for the redemption of humanity. Alloyed metal is first purified, then used to produce a coin of impeccable quality and value, whose traditional name also bears symbolic connotations: the *salut* (salutation), for instance, is a coin whose name evokes the Annunciation.[32]

Combining literary emulation, religious edification, and local urban solidarity, the activities of the Puys (in the north) and the Consistori (in the south) manifest, in the physical presence of performance, the potential for lyric poetry to shape and transmit knowledge in a way that far surpasses the courtly diversions of twelfth-century troubadours and *trouvères*.

Late Medieval Theater

Similar developments occur in late medieval theater, which, like lyric poetry, maintains continuity with the twelfth century while also renewing itself in many different institutional forms and embracing ever more ambitious subject matter. Among its manifestations, the great mystery cycles of the fourteenth and fifteenth centuries are not only the largest-scale poetic texts of the later Middle Ages in France but also among its most successful literary legacies, since they continued to be performed until late in the sixteenth century.[33] Intended for live performance, theatrical texts are difficult to interpret, and the theatrical experience to which they relate is difficult to reconstruct. Not all

31. This discourse was not itself monolithic. For the most important Puy in Rouen, for instance, privileging the doctrine of the Immaculate Conception was not ideologically neutral. Not only did the doctrine have political implications, but also the Puy's insistence on it seems to have dissuaded Jean Bouchet from taking part; Hüe, *Poésie palinodique,* 85–216, 362–71.

32. Ibid., 867–69. Other examples cited by Hüe include the Milky Way in a *chant royal* by Pierre Gaultier (628–30), and printing in a piece by Nicole Lescarre (695–700). On the role of analogy more generally in this period, see Randall, *Building Resemblance.*

33. Runnalls, "Mystères."

manuscript records are of complete texts; they include notes and prompts, and the roles of individual actors. More than the texts of any other genre they bear witness to constant revision, since the "same" play could be performed in different ways on different occasions; as Graham Runnalls puts it, "the history of French Passions could be said to be a virtually uninterrupted succession of reworkings of reworkings, of revisions of revisions."[34] Yet although their often provisional and fragmentary quality makes the transmission of theatrical texts somewhat marginal to the main literary tradition, at least until the advent of printing gave them a more stable form,[35] in other respects theatricality is central to the medieval concept of literature. Helen Solterer reiterates Paul Zumthor's salutary reminder that live performance and dramatic enactment "animated so many different forms of communication and expression that it is more telling to ask what was not characterized theatrically than to identify what was theatre."[36]

The later Middle Ages, far from marking a decline in theatricality, instead witnessed the migration of various previously narrative forms into theater. The most impressive examples of literary material following this path of *mise en scène,* as opposed to *mise en prose,* are in religious drama. Take, for example, the recasting of the miracle stories featuring the Virgin Mary that existed in octosyllabic rhyming couplets in the twelfth and early thirteenth centuries in the work of Adgar, Gautier de Coinci, and others. The *Miracle de Théophile* composed by the innovative Rutebeuf in 1264 is an experimental work that adapts one such miracle to the stage. The Virgin saves Theophile's soul by retrieving from the devil the contract the ambitious cleric had unwisely made with him, in which, in a precursor of the Faust story, he exchanged clerical preferment in this world for salvation in the next. Rutebeuf's isolated miracle play was followed in the fourteenth century by the *Miracles de Notre Dame par personnages,* a cycle of some forty plays that recast the earlier narrative poems wholesale. These *Miracles* were performed by the goldsmiths' guild on the right bank of the Seine between around 1339 to 1382: a successful run by any standards. Other popular saints' lives, which had previously existed only as narrative texts in verse, likewise made their way onto the stage. Jean Bodel's *Jeu de Saint Nicolas* of the turn of the thirteenth century, which has a verse narrative antecedent in Wace's *Vie de Saint Nicolas,* is an isolated early precursor of what was to prove a significant body of theatrical production in

34. Ibid., 470.
35. Ibid., 516.
36. Solterer, "Theatre and Theatricality," 181, citing Zumthor, *Essai de poétique médiévale,* 37–39.

the late Middle Ages.[37] Petit de Julleville records nine theatrical adaptations of the life of Saint Catherine, one from the fourteenth, seven from the fifteenth, and one from the sixteenth century.[38] There are also mystery plays dramatizing the lives of Saint Lawrence, Saint Martin, and Saint Denis, one version of the *Mystère de Saint Martin* being by André de la Vigne.[39]

The Bible is an even greater source of stories that get dramatized; it is unclear whether they are taken directly from the Vulgate or from existing vernacular translations. The story of Susanna and the Elders furnishes the material for at least two plays of which numerous performances are attested from the fifteenth and sixteenth centuries; the variations in composition and performance style between the various versions may reflect regional and/or local conditions.[40] The story of Judith and Holofernes attracts no less a virtuoso than the redoubtable *rhétoriqueur* Molinet.[41] Cycles of mystery plays covering the whole of salvation history are the largest-scale instances of adapting narrative to the stage. As with the Puys, the northern French cities were host to the most ambitious of these, Valenciennes, for instance, having two such cycles, one lasting twenty days and the other twenty-five.[42] The transition from narrative to theater often resulted in extremely elaborate verse forms, emphasizing the formal distinctness of dramatic texts from prose. The mystery plays of the later fifteenth century often exhibit particularly ambitious and varied versification.[43]

At the opposite end of the scale from the vast mystery cycles, the texts of royal entries condense into the form of short poems complex historical and political scenarios. Cynthia J. Brown describes pageantry devised by Pierre Gringore for the entry in honor of Mary Tudor in Paris in 1514. A *rondeau* was exhibited describing the Queen of Sheba's visit to King Solomon, and a seven-line decasyllabic stanza was recited to bring out the analogy between this and Mary's peace-bringing arrival at the court of Louis XII. When the dramatic events of the entry were subsequently committed to book form, prose makes

37. Symes, *A Common Stage*, 27–68.

38. See also Bouhaïk-Gironès, "Théâtre."

39. *Le mystere de Saint Laurent*, ed. Söderhjelm and Wallensköld; Runnalls, "Langage"; Runnalls, "Un Siècle." This play was performed in the first half of the sixteenth century. André de la Vigne's *Mystère de Saint Martin* (ed. Duplat) was performed in Seurre in Burgundy in 1496; see Runnalls, "Staging of André de la Vigne's *Mystere de Saint Martin*."

40. Knight, "Stage as Context."

41. Jean Molinet, *Le Mystère de Judith et Holofernés*, ed. Runnalls.

42. Runnalls, "Mystères," 497, 505.

43. E.g., Henri Chatelain, *Recherches sur le vers français*, 253–61; *Le Mystère de Judith et Holofernés*, 49–54.

its reappearance among the poems in order to transform back into a narrative the experience of performance.[44]

Claude Thiry has explored the ambiguous interface between narrative and theater with reference to another group of verse texts: didactic debates and morality plays. Citing numerous examples from the fifteenth century, Thiry demonstrates that many texts which adopt the form of a debate would have lent themselves to live performance even if they were not intended actually to be staged.[45] He observes of George Chastelain's *Paix de Péronne* (composed at the end of 1468), for instance, that it can be reckoned a "dramatic work" even though it is "not theatrical," qualifying as a "staged debate" rather than as a "debate on the stage."[46] Debate poems slide toward morality plays or vice versa, depending on the extent to which they exploit visual effect, variety of location, or the presence or absence of a narrator: a controlling *acteur-témoin* (author-witness) pulls a work in the direction of the debate poem with an overall narrative framework; in his absence a text drifts toward theater. Rather than seeing such features as criterial of generic difference, however, Thiry shows how important it is to recognize the *entre-deux* between narrative and drama. Many dialogue works seem to have been intended not for staging, nor yet for private reading, but for some kind of performance that was dramatized without being fully theatrical. The erasure of the boundary between narrative and theater is illustrated by Gauvain Candie's *Advisement de Memoire et d'Entendement* of 1504. Composed in a mixture of verse and prose, and with the role of *acteur* distributed among the characters who ensure the forward momentum of the action, it can be viewed as either a didactic *prosimetrum* or a play, or as both simultaneously.[47] (The *prosimetrum* is by definition a mixture of verse and prose on the model of Boethius's *Consolation,* exhibiting more or less variety in the metrical forms deployed. While the insertion of prose letters in verse *dits* such as the *Voir dit* and the *Prison amoureuse* makes them similar to *prosimetra,* we reserve the term for texts that observe, like Boethius, a more regular alternation of the two forms; see chapter 5.)

Morality plays and saints' lives are as didactic on stage as are their narrative equivalents,[48] while large-scale mystery plays and political pageants clearly manifest a concern for history that, as chapter 2 will show in more detail, remains consistently associated with verse throughout the late Middle Ages,

---

44. Brown, "From Stage to Page."
45. Thiry, "Débats."
46. Ibid., 208.
47. Ibid., 224–42.
48. Knight, *Aspects of Genre,* chaps. 3–4, discusses knowledge in morality plays.

despite authors of mainstream historiography adopting prose. In mystery cycles, the whole of salvation history is unfolded over weeks of performance time,[49] and plays may also include engagement with topical concerns.[50] Even farce, a form of late medieval theater widely regarded as simply entertaining, could advance knowledge in particular ways, typically through satire.[51] In the tableaux created for royal entries, and the somewhat similar pageantry adopted for festive events by the court of Burgundy, it is the sense of history being made in the here and now that is important. Such entries were at the same time cultural events and political acts, "a means of manifesting and dramatizing political concepts."[52] For example, many of Pierre Gringore's works have as their common purpose to "win French approval for [Louis XII's] political offensive in France during the period 1499–1513."[53] Entries represent a particularly novel and interesting form of "presence" for verse, given that their texts were characteristically not spoken but displayed, typically in an allegorical setting.[54] All these texts are thus involved in communicating what, in chapter 6, we term "ideological knowledge." Our objective here is not to analyze this knowledge but to stress that the public, physical performance of dramatic texts is in itself a means of manifesting their status as vehicles of such knowledge.

It is a commonplace of the criticism of late medieval theater to stress its communal nature. Actors and audiences were all drawn from the same community, and the action on stage thus represents the community back to itself. Such recursion in the legitimation of knowledge is described very exactly by Lyotard in *La Condition postmoderne* (42), except that he envisages narrative rather than theater: "A collective finds the substance of its social cohesion not in the meaning of tales but in the act of their recital. Narrative reference may appear to be to the past, but is in fact always contemporary with this act." For example, the fact that *sotties* are played before a large public means that, as Jean-Claude Aubailly says of them, each play "takes on, in some sense, the voice of public opinion."[55] Political drama makes public *to* the public the notion of what it might mean to *be* the public. In royal entries,

---

49. Ibid., chap. 2.

50. Longtin, "Chercher l'intrus."

51. Beam, *Laughing Matters;* and, more generally, Doudet, "Statut et figures." The *Farce de Maître Pathelin,* widely regarded as the masterpiece of the genre, has been read as an allegory of the deadly sins; *Maistre Pierre Pathelin,* ed. Smith.

52. Gringore, *Les Entrées royales,* ed. Brown, 20.

53. Ibid., 1; also Brown, "From Stage to Page"; and Hindley's introduction to his edition of Gringore's *Jeu du Prince des Sotz,* 32. On Burgundy, see Planche, "Du Tournoi au théâtre."

54. Blanchard, "Conception"; Brown, "From Stage to Page."

55. Aubailly, *Le Monologue,* 413.

the unfolding of the playlets and tableaux at different stations throughout
the city dramatizes the urban community's relation to its sovereign in such a
way as to constitute an evolving and embodied series of *miroirs des princes*.[56]
Alan Knight explains how the involvement of the whole population of Lille
in its annual procession, which ran for more than five centuries beginning in
1270, played out the tension between the wholeness of the community and
its diversity.[57] Robert L. A. Clark's study of the *Miracles de Notre Dame* is
perhaps the most sustained and sophisticated investigation of how enactment
as such, rather than the ostensible content of what is performed, serves as a
vehicle of social knowledge. These plays rehearse stories of individual fragility, the specific and labile configurations of sexuality and class of every erring
protagonist whom Mary saves, while at the same time stressing the existence
of an overarching community to which they can be restored. But whereas the
early miracle narratives on which the plays are based are about the salvific
role of the Virgin and the Church, Clark argues that the essential frame in
which to interpret the action in these plays is the goldsmiths' annual banquet
at which they were staged. A sense of group identity was not only reinforced
through the opulence of these occasions but actively policed as well, insofar as
attendance was mandatory and delinquent members were fined. For Clark,
however, the miracle plays are truly bourgeois not in highlighting the assets of
the community as a whole but in making the case for the individual's owner-
ship of his or her own sexuality and transgression.[58] Each individual member
of the audience thus witnesses, by enforced presence at the plays, the drama of
his own relation to the group and to its corporate concerns. In all these cases, it
is not the representation of ideology *within the text* that is significant as much
as the realization of that ideology *by means of its staging*.

The remarkable oeuvre of Pierre Gringore unites many of the features
we have observed in the latter part of this chapter. Composed in a range of
genres for many different kinds of audience, his works exhibit permeability
between verse drama and nondramatic verse since didactic material finds its
way into works such as the *Jeu du Prince des Sots et Mere Sotte*. The *tableaux
vivants* and *mistères* deployed in Gringore's various royal entries also show
how the category of the "staged" extends beyond the theater strictly speaking.
The Moralité in the *Jeu du Prince des Sots* illustrates the capacity of medieval
drama to embrace serious subject matter, the threat of divine punishment if
the political order is overtaken by abuses such as simony and hypocrisy. The

56. Gringore, *Les Entrées royales,* ed. Brown, 21, 23–25.
57. Knight, "Processional Theatre," 99.
58. Clark, "Community versus Subject."

fact that the whole French people is compromised by France's shortcomings is manifested by performances staged for the people's benefit. At the same time, Gringore's versification is extremely varied with regard to both line length and rhyme scheme. At the very end of the period covered in this book, the presence of verse is here emphatically persistent, both as performed text and as a transformed version of early medieval theatrical modes.

This chapter refutes the misconception that the "rise of prose" entails a decline in verse, any more than the "rise of literacy" results in a decline in orality. It demonstrates that, on the contrary, the association between verse and orality is reactivated and recontextualized throughout the later Middle Ages in France. While not all verse relies on oral performance, new institutions emerge with the specific purpose of enabling verse texts to be performed. There is next to no prose that is intended to be performed in this way. Indeed, it looks as though "prose" and "the stage" are cultural antonyms in this period; and while some verse texts are recast as prose, others are adapted to these new forms of staging. Most forms of late medieval staged verse engage with serious subject matter including classical learning, theology, history, or politics. In all cases, the fact of performance to an audience becomes a factor shaping the knowledge content of the texts concerned. The late French Middle Ages, in retaining the association between verse and presence, forge new connections between verse and knowledge that were not available prior to the establishment of prose.

CHAPTER TWO

Poetry and History

The last chapter showed that the public performance of verse which characterized the early medieval period continues throughout the later Middle Ages, and that new institutions and practices are invented that highlight the value of poetic texts as shared knowledge. In this chapter we address another determining characteristic of late medieval verse: its association with history. In the twelfth century, historiography explored various verse forms, often innovatively. Seemingly decisively severed in the early thirteenth century by promoters of prose historiography, the link between poetry and history was in fact reaffirmed in a number of ways in the later Middle Ages—so successfully, indeed, that multiple connections emerge between history writing (broadly conceived) and verse throughout the period. True, prose now enjoys undisputed ascendancy in the canonical historiographical genres; only a few writers continue older forms such as verse chronicle and *chanson de geste*. But most major authors of the late Middle Ages compose both lyric and historiography of some kind and also experiment with the late medieval lyrico-narrative forms of the *dit* and the *prosimetrum,* which tend to occupy an intermediary position between the two. With lyrico-narrative poetry as a bridge, tropes of *poetrie* such as personification, mythography, and allegory make their way into historiography, and the narration of history crosses back into lyric poetry.

These exchanges have important implications both for the kinds of knowledge that are transmitted in verse and for the status of verse itself as a mode of *knowing.* In the first place, they ground awareness that verse can transmit both knowledge *of* the past and the knowledge that can be acquired *from* the past: the recording of events engenders preoccupation with themes of chance, change, and destiny, which in turn provoke moral, philosophical, or satirical reflections. Second, the first-person orientation of many of these texts means that events as such tend to be subsumed into the experience of events, and the experience of events into the memory of that experience. Whereas in the last chapter we were able to identify an epistemic grounding of verse in physical performance, here we contend that verse becomes, even in the absence of bodily presence, a formal expression of the inevitable situation in time of subjectivity. Typically the subject concerned is the first person of the work's narrator/author/poet, but it can also be a fictional first person within the work, and potentially also its addressee, whose own experience is to be enlarged by an encounter with verse as an avatar of subjectivity. Finally, then, the dynamics of verse—both the inherent, formal properties of versification and its intertextual associations—come to connote the truth of the subject's experience of time, even if the precise content of that experience remains elusive. In exploring these ideas, we return later in the chapter to Agamben's insights into the capacity of poetry for truth which we outlined in our introduction. But we begin, as we did in chapter 1, with poets' own situation in the material institutions of their age.

Joint Patronage of Lyric and Chronicle

Just as new institutions developed to promote oral performance in the later Middle Ages, so the relation between history and poetry is reinvigorated by late medieval patronage, in which many writers are commissioned to write both prose chronicles *and* lyric (and/or lyrico-narrative) verse. Our earliest example of this connection is found not in a historical French court, however, but in a fictional ancient British one.

The *Roman de Perceforest* (ca. 1340–1344) claims to be the translation of a prose history from ancient Britain. In those days, its readers are informed, knights narrated their adventures every time they came to court so that the court historian could record them. The resulting chronicle survived the conquest of Britain by a Sicambrian-Viking invasion because it was hidden away and was only found over a thousand years later, in the early fourteenth century. The Count of Hainaut commissioned a French translation of this rediscovered text, thus producing the prose narrative of the *Perceforest* we now have. But in the ancient British past, significant events were also, we learn, commemorated in *lais:* narrative poems in strophic verse, which were performed at court for the edification of succeeding generations, and which are always described as being sung to a harp accompaniment. After the conquest, the Sicambrian king, wanting to wipe out all memory of Perceforest and his dynasty, suppressed them on pain of death, but fortunately they too had been recorded by the intrepid chronicler and were hidden, and then discovered and translated, along with his chronicle. The text of *Perceforest* retains the two historiographical modes, inserting the *lais* into its prose narrative at the points where they were composed or sung (though there is no music in any of the manuscripts).[1]

The ancient British chronicler imagined by an early-fourteenth-century author is oddly prophetic of the intimate bond that would develop between history and lyric poetry. Unlike their fictional precursor, however, historical poets were employed not merely to record lyrics in their chronicles but to compose actively in both genres. In the fourteenth century the most prominent example is Froissart, whose oeuvre comprises numerous lyrics, verse *dits,* and the verse romance of *Meliador* (which in turn contains inset lyrics) alongside the famous prose *Chronique* which he began in 1361, some twenty years after the *Perceforest* was written.[2] A century or so later, the link between poetry writing and history writing is institutionalized at the court of Burgundy in the post of official historian. Subsequently termed *indiciaire* (1473), this post is unique in employing writers to write history and lyric poetry as a full-time occupation, and is held successively by the distinguished chronicler-poets George Chastelain, Jean Molinet, and Jean Lemaire de Belges. Unprecedented in being full-time writers, *indiciaires* were also exceptionally well rewarded, making this the most coveted and enviable of patronage positions.[3] George Chastelain, the first to benefit from it, had an annual allowance of 657 livres tournois (l.t.), at least equivalent to that of a ducal counselor. Like the stipend of the French royal chronicler, it was paid in a single annual installment, indicating the permanence of the appointment and the ongoing nature of the duties. Chastelain also enjoyed a perpetual right of accommodation in a well-appointed ducal residence, practically a unique privilege for a courtier. Such rewards far exceeded those of other artists who had salaried court positions. Jean Castel's annual wage as the French royal chronicler, for example,

---

1. Lods, *Les Pièces lyriques;* more recently, Huot, "Sentences and Subtle Fictions," and "Chronicle, Lai, and Romance."

2. In the fifteenth century, Chartier likewise composed both prose and lyric works and had a double career as poet and administrator; Chartier, *Poetical Works,* ed. Laidlaw, 2–15.

3. This account of the post of *indiciaire* draws on Small, *George Chastelain,* 64–127; Dupire, *Jean Molinet,* 16–21; Jodogne, *Jean Lemaire de Belges,* 96–127; Thiry, "Rhétoriqueurs de Bourgogne," 106–8; Devaux, *Jean Molinet,* 25–139; Doudet, "Poétique."

was a mere 200 l.t. Molinet and Lemaire, whose tenure as *indiciaires* coincided with a much more difficult period for the dukes than did Chastelain's, were granted 240 l.t. annually in 1485 and 1507, respectively. (When Molinet's annual allowance was cut in 1496, he composed a poem, the *Gaiges retrenchiés,* which discreetly threatens strike action; he duly regained the lost sum the following year.)[4] In addition to material rewards, the *indiciaires* of Burgundy enjoyed (for writers) unparalleled political influence. No mere witnesses of events, Chastelain (in 1457) and Molinet (by 1497) became counselors to the duke, participating in court discussions, albeit not in the innermost decision-making circles.[5]

The fact that the term *indiciaire* is a neologism implies recognition that the post was without precedent. When he was first appointed in 1455, Chastelain did not have an official title; the position of *indiciaire* was inaugurated and ceremonially bestowed on him at the twelfth chapter of the Order of the Golden Fleece in 1473, together with a knighthood. Initially Chastelain's role was that of official historian, a position modeled on its counterpart in France. There Jean Chartier and Jean Castel, Christine de Pizan's grandson, had succeeded each other in the office of royal chronicler, thereby bringing into the orbit of the court a long tradition of monastic historiography based at the abbey of Saint-Denis. Characteristically, the Burgundian post was designed not just to mirror but to eclipse its French model in prestige and influence. It seems first to have been created as part of a wave of propaganda initiatives accompanying preparations that Duke Philip the Good was making for a crusade in 1454–55.[6] It reflects a preoccupation with historiography—especially their own place in it—which the Valois dukes promoted much more heavily than any previous patrons in French-speaking regions. But Chastelain's remit as chronicler was not restricted to Burgundy; it extended to the whole of Christendom, with particular reference to France and related territories,[7] and entailed not merely recording events but using his expertise to discern their significance and shape them accordingly, as this official description indicates:

---

4. Brown, *Poets, Patrons, and Printers,* 220–24.

5. Small, *George Chastelain,* 66, describes Chastelain as "a politically active and privileged insider," and notes that "the patronage model used in his appointment did not come from existing structures within the court" (114).

6. Ibid., 95–102.

7. Chastelain refers to his task in his *Exposicions sur Verité mal prise* as "la tresressongnable charge d'escripre tous les haulx et grans fais de la crestienté, souverainement de ce noble royaume et de ses dependances" (the most formidable task of writing about all the great and admirable events in Christendom, and especially those in this noble kingdom and surrounding areas, ed. Delclos, 43). Molinet's focus tends to be narrower; Devaux, *Jean Molinet,* 58–59.

Par consideration de ce qu'il est tenu de mettre par escript choses nouvelles et moralles, en quoy il [est] expert et congnoissant, aussi mettre en fourme par maniere de cronicque fais notables dignes de memoire advenus par chi devant et qui adviennent et puellent souvente fois advenir.

—(Lille, Archives départementales du Nord, B. 9880, fol. 29r)

(In view of his task being to record unusual and edifying events in writing, in which he is expert and discerning, and to shape in the manner of an official chronicle[8] notable deeds worthy of being remembered that have occurred hitherto, that are occurring, and that may occur on many a future occasion.)

Chastelain is charged not with investigating Burgundian ancestry or even with mapping the duchy's past, but with chronicling events on an ongoing basis, including those that have not yet taken place. His priorities are as much ethical and aesthetic as factual, his responsibilities above all to the future, where what is happening now will be remembered in the form in which he has cast it.

This understanding of the *indiciaires'* task may explain why, unlike royal chroniclers, they were employed to write poetry as well as prose; and why, as in the *Perceforest,* short occasional poems (*poésies de circonstances*) are often copied into manuscripts that are dominated by chronicles or historical documents, as if poems are as much part of the historical record as the other texts.[9] Indeed, Burgundian manuscripts are especially likely to transmit poems alongside or within chronicles and documentary pieces;[10] while the Burgundians also adopted the *Perceforest,* Duke Philip the Good commissioning a reworking of it, complete with *lais,* from David Aubert.[11] Though contrasting in scale, lyric verse and prose chronicle are parts of a single mission: to record notable events for the edification of their public and to the glory of their patrons, making sense of them in the light of the ethical frameworks with which one would expect a knowledgeable author to be familiar. Hence

8. Devaux, *Jean Molinet,* 33–46, notes of the use of *chronique/chroniqueur* in this period that they tend to designate officially commissioned histories/historians, particularly those relating to the French monarchy; hence the rendering "official chronicle."

9. Armstrong, "Avatars."

10. The practice is not peculiar to Burgundy, however. Jean Nicolai's *Kalendrier de la guerre de Tournay,* a strongly anti-Burgundian account of military actions in 1477–1479, is accompanied in the surviving manuscript by occasional poems, brief historical narratives, and documents; Armstrong, *Virtuoso Circle,* chap. 4. Short poems even appear in Jean Bouchet's *Annales d'Aquitaine,* a prose chronicle printed in several redactions from 1524 on, where they serve a primarily mnemonic function; Britnell, *Jean Bouchet,* 24, 53.

11. *Perceforest,* ed. Taylor, 11–14. Four manuscripts clearly identified as being by Aubert survive, all dating from the fifteenth century, of which at least two and possibly three can be linked to Burgundy.

the formal and linguistic elaborateness often associated with both the verse and the prose of the *indiciaires* and other *rhétoriqueurs.* These were the means by which an author could most effectively serve his patron and do best justice to the importance of the events he commemorated.[12] In no other period of French literature has lyric poetry been partnered in this remarkable way with history writing.

This does not mean, however, that verse and prose possess identical value as forms of historical discourse. Their relationship is illuminatingly encapsulated in a text from the end of our period, Jean Bouchet's *Anciennes et modernes genealogies des Roys de France.* Bouchet summarizes in prose the reign of each French king from Pharamond onward, then supplies a verse epitaph in the king's own voice. Characteristic of verse epitaphs from the mid-fifteenth century on, the first-person voice stands in for the dead ruler's "experience" as the reader is invited to imagine it. The juxtaposition of these verses with the prose narratives indicates the much more prominent imprint of the person, of the speaker or implied subject, on verse as compared with prose.[13]

The remainder of this chapter focuses more specifically on the association between history and poetry manifested in verse texts. In the next section we consider the late medieval renewal of history writing in verse, before, in the final section, reflecting on how late medieval lyric and lyrico-narrative poetry are concerned with registering temporality more generally. This separation between verse historiography and lyrico-narrative poetry will prove fragile, however. Both draw heavily on resources of *poetrie,* a compositional style not necessarily identified with verse but which nevertheless still sees in verse an additional, advantageous form of embellishment (see introduction).[14] And in both, objective narration of events is troubled by a preoccupation with subjectivity that remains in some degree incommunicable except as the *form* of the works concerned. The association between verse and history goes deeper than the commissioning of writers to compose *poésies de circonstances* as well as prose chronicles. As Bouchet's historiographical technique implies, if prose is best suited to recording the outer event, verse is more appropriate for capturing the inner, often mysterious nature of the lived event.

12. Devaux, *Jean Molinet,* 78–111; Small, *George Chastelain,* 116–27; Doudet, "Poétique," 235–49.
13. The *Genealogies* were first published in 1528; numerous later editions were printed; Britnell, *Jean Bouchet,* 114–15, 128–30; Rech, "La Culture historique." Armstrong, *Technique and Technology,* 191–205, notes that the editions of the *Genealogies* published in Bouchet's hometown of Poitiers position woodcut portraits of each king between the prose historical account and the epitaph, further highlighting the personal quality of the verse.
14. The point is eloquently made by Devaux, *Jean Molinet,* 111.

Verse Historiography in the Fourteenth and Fifteenth Centuries

Historiography is one of the most consistently innovative medieval genres, and although prose became established as the default form for late medieval history writing, it did not altogether put an end to experiments with writing history in verse. Nevertheless, by the fourteenth and fifteenth centuries, it is clear that to choose to write history in verse is to opt for marginality with respect to the canonical forms that prose historiography rapidly develops: prose chronicle, *mémoire,* or journal. These forms are moreover distinct,[15] whereas verse histories, by virtue of being marginal to them, inevitably find themselves on the margins of other verse genres too, and often seem generically somewhat hybrid in consequence. To describe them, scholars resort to catchall terms such as "verse historiography," "verse chronicle," or "poésie d'actualité."[16] Mention has already been made of the *poésie de circonstance,* or occasional poetry composed by the *indiciaires* and other *grands rhétoriqueurs,* but even this more familiar and more apparently precise term cannot be used to designate a single type of work as can, say, *mémoire* for prose writings.[17] Poetic texts play host to a range of historical themes and express them in a variety of forms; the examples we provide are necessarily selective and do no more than touch on universal history, which is discussed further in chapter 4.

Some authors revamp the octosyllabic rhyming couplet, which had become standard in verse chronicles of the twelfth century. Philippe Mouskés's *Chronique rimée* of the mid-thirteenth century, a 32,000-line history of the kings of France to 1241, uses this form to recast material from numerous *chansons de geste.* A later, 7,000-line *Chronique métrique* (1313–1317), often ascribed to Geffroy de Paris, borrows the racy style of thirteenth-century romance writers such as Gerbert de Montreuil.[18] Later again, Machaut's *Prise d'Alixandre* (1372?) uses octosyllabic couplets in ways that overlap with his many *dits,* while the cluster of features that loosely define the *dit* also lend themselves to the writing of historically oriented satires like the *Roman de Fauvel* (see chapters 5 and 6). The *Geste des ducs de Bourgogne* (after 1422), by contrast, is written in *laisses* of alexandrines, just like late medieval *chansons de geste* such as *Le Bâtard de Bouillon, Lion de Bourges, Florent et Octavien, Hugues Capet,* and

15. Thiry, "Historiographie et actualité." Thiry's otherwise fine account does not explicitly distinguish verse from prose texts.
16. Critics use the first two of these terms widely if ill-definedly; the third appears in Thiry, "Historiographie et actualité," 1030–31.
17. Thiry calls occasional writing a "polymorphous creation"; "La Poésie de circonstance," 111.
18. See Dunbabin, "Metrical Chronicle," 233–34, for the question of attribution, and 235–37 for discussion of the chronicle's style.

La Chanson de Bertrand du Guesclin de Cuvelier.[19] These long poems, which tread the borderline between epic and historiography, continue to be composed until at least the end of the fourteenth century, even though by this date the wholesale *mise en prose* of early medieval *chanson de geste* cycles is well under way.[20] Toward the end of the period, when poets opt for various stanzaic forms or for the alternating prose and verse of *prosimetrum,* the overlap between history and lyric poetry is at its most marked. A notable example is Christine de Pizan's *Ditié Jeanne d'Arc,* composed of 484 lines arranged in octosyllabic eight-line strophes. The first historical poem about Joan of Arc—it was completed July 31, 1429, before Joan's trial—the *Ditié* is a personal, pro-feminist celebration of a young woman's intervention in France's destiny, the author's last work, and her only return to verse after the seemingly definitive turn to prose from 1403 onward. The anonymous *Complainte de la Cité de Liège* of 1468[21] and Olivier de La Marche's 1483 *Chevalier délibéré* combine stanzaic forms with the armory of *rhétoriqueur* poetics: prosopopoeia in the former, heavy-handed allegory in the latter. The centrality of the first-person narrator in many of these forms, especially the lyrical ones, means that the recording of history merges with the narrator's experiencing and reacting to it. This favors the expression of personal commitment, political or moral, making some later medieval verse historiography a precocious form of *littérature engagée.*

Perhaps the most important example of verse historiography in our period is Machaut's *Prise d'Alixandre,* a nine thousand–line account in octosyllabic rhyming couplets of the capture of the city of Alexandria by Pierre I de Lusignan, king of Cyprus, in 1365. The poem contains so much historical detail that historians have often viewed it as a reliable source.[22] Machaut catalogues episodes in Pierre's campaign exhaustively, even mentioning the personnel involved by name (see, for example, *Prise d'Alixandre,* 4601–78). He repeatedly asserts his own reliability as an eyewitness or, failing that, the reliability of his sources.[23] Yet the *Prise* is curiously lacking in concrete historical anchorage.

---

19. On the relations between the *Geste des ducs de Bourgogne* and the *chansons de geste,* see Bennett, "Rhetoric, Poetics and History," 54–59.

20. Suard, "Y a-t-il un avenir?"; Roussel, "L'Automne de la chanson de geste." Suard notes the combining of different cycles in late medieval *chansons de geste.*

21. De Ram, *Documents relatifs aux troubles du pays de Liège,* 325–34.

22. Palmer's introduction to his edition of the *Prise d'Alixandre,* 18 (hereafter Palmer, *Prise d'Alixandre*), gives details of modern histories that use Machaut's poem as a source.

23. Ribémont, "Dire le vrai." Palmer, *Prise d'Alixandre,* 15, 27, mentions Machaut's having sought out eyewitnesses to events he did not himself witness; the only evidence, however, is from the poem itself. Machaut is also thought to have used Philippe de Mézières's *Vita* of Peter Thomas, described by Palmer as a panegyric to Pierre de Lusignan (*Prise d'Alixandre,* 17), but he does not explicitly acknowledge it as a source.

Nowhere, for instance, are the dates of the various sallies included, nor are their geographical locations particularly clearly indicated, so that anyone unfamiliar with the events of the campaign would be hard-pressed to gain a clear account of them from Machaut's text. Rather than attaching itself directly to an objective reality, the *Prise* seems always to filter it through poetic models. As Bernard Ribémont suggestively puts it, Machaut presents its narrative not as unquestionably historically accurate but rather as "a truth that can be conceived of as verifiable."[24] His account is one that might well be substantiated in external reality but can equally well be appreciated in abstraction from it.[25]

Machaut's choice of octosyllabic couplets for the *Prise* immediately associates it with his many *dits*, almost all of which share the same versification.[26] As the form par excellence of lyrico-narrative poetry in this period, this versification positions the *Prise* in a wider poetic and reflective universe where moral and political ideas predominate, rather than in a world of hard facts. This insertion is flamboyantly effected from the outset: a purportedly historical account opens with a resolutely literary 257-line prologue in which various gods come down from Mount Olympus and ask that a new Godefroi de Bouillon be bestowed upon the world, just at the moment when—by an amazing coincidence—Pierre de Lusignan is being born. Machaut's deployment of mythographic schemes in the service of his patron recalls his earlier *Fonteinne amoureuse,* where myths from book 11 of Ovid's *Metamorphoses* are likewise reworked for Jean, Duke of Berry (see chapter 3). The *Prise* seems to have been composed less to detail a military campaign than to glorify the life and person of Pierre I.[27] Ribémont may be overstating the case when he says that "chronicle is merely the support of hagiography";[28] as Deborah McGrady argues, however, Pierre certainly becomes an exemplum.[29] In this poetic environment even the seductively grounding lists of the Frenchmen sailing out to capture Alexandria have the ring of veracity-affirming fictions.

24. Ribémont, "Dire le vrai," 175.

25. Although Machaut himself does not name or qualify the genre of the work he is writing, Ribémont ("Dire le vrai," 173) suggests that the *Prise* "presents itself as a verse chronicle," and Palmer (*Prise d'Alixandre,* 24–25), calls the work an "aristocratic chronicle," by which he means it is more concerned to celebrate the deeds of the great than to analyze or explain them.

26. On this versification in later medieval narratives, see Chatelain, *Recherches sur les vers français;* on the links between Machaut's truth project in the *Prise* and the *Voir dit,* see Ribémont, "Dire le vrai," e.g., 174–75.

27. It would also be possible to think of the *Prise* as resembling a chivalric biography or *chanson de geste,* but the former is usually written in prose (Gaucher, *Biographie chevaleresque*), while the latter is composed in alexandrines (Palmer, *Prise d'Alixandre,* 28).

28. Ribémont, "Dire le vrai," 173.

29. McGrady, *Controlling Readers,* 273.

Were they not confirmed in Froissart's *Chronique,* there would be little reason to believe them.[30]

The historiographical writings of the *rhétoriqueurs* in the late fifteenth century likewise subordinate, and sometimes sacrifice, the communication of referential detail to other concerns. Witness the *Recollection des merveilleuses advenues,* begun by Chastelain and continued by Molinet, which recounts "merveilles / estranges a compter" (wonders strange to relate, vv. 1–2) from 1429 (events surrounding Joan of Arc) to 1495 (the death of Djem-Sultan, son of Mahomet II, at the French court).[31] Events are recorded more or less chronologically, in 148 hexasyllabic *huitains* with—for the most part—one *huitain* per event.[32] The two authors choose different types of *merveilles* to write about, but their methods of writing are broadly analogous. Like that of the *Prise,* the history contained in the *Recollection* is ultimately verifiable;[33] but again as with the *Prise,* its concrete anchorage is provokingly elusive. Thus both Chastelain and Molinet introduce their subject matter as a succession of experiences prefaced by variants of "j'ay veu," but neither ascribes dates to the historical moment being relayed, and often the recounting is willfully allusive and whimsically swept up in wordplay. The revolt and subsequent quashing of the townspeople of Ghent, for instance, are described by Chastelain in these terms:

J'ay veu Gand invaincue
Subjuguier a mes yeux
D'un prince soubz la nue
Le plus victorieux
Et d'espee mortoire
Vaincre les habitans.
Dont cas de telle gloire
Ne fut, passé mil ans. (*Recollection,* vv. 169–76)

(I've seen Ghent the Unvanquished subjugated—right before my eyes—by the most victorious prince under the sun, her inhabitants laid low by his lethal sword. There hasn't been such a glorious feat for a thousand years.)

30. Palmer, *Prise d'Alixandre,* 19.
31. George Chastelain/Jean Molinet, *La Recollection des merveilleuses advenues,* in Molinet, *Faictz et dictz,* 1:284–340.
32. Only four of Chastelain's and thirteen of Molinet's stanzas deviate from this pattern, as if the events in question are too portentous to be so narrowly contained.
33. Thiry, "Le vieux renard," 456, states that the events described have been culled from other historical sources, and that most if not all can be found in the chronicles of the respective authors, but that there is no systematic relationship between the *Recollection* and the chronicles. Such correspondences as can be adduced are detailed by Dupire in Molinet, *Faictz et dictz,* 3:989–1015.

Similarly, the episode of Adolphe de Gueldre's treatment of the Flemish in Tournai in June 1477 is given a typically virtuoso—and, for this poem, typically uninformative—treatment by Molinet:

> J'ay veu Tournay tournee
> En ung mauvais tournant
> Sans estre retournee
> Ses voisins bestournant
> Nos maisons, nos tourelles
> En cendre contourner
> Et Flamengs entour elles
> Durement attourner. (*Recollection*, vv. 577–84)[34]

> (I saw Tournai bowed but unbeaten by a dreadful event, her neighbors razing our houses to the ground, our towers being reduced to ashes, and the Flemings meeting a sorry fate among the debris.)

Whereas in other work by these authors the event is central even when allegorized (as, for example, in Molinet's epitaphs, *complaintes,* or *Trosne d'honneur*), here the short lines, brief stanzas, and intricate *annominatio* seem almost to obfuscate what actually happened. Even more than with the *Prise,* a reader of the *Recollection* could comprehend and benefit from these accounts only if he or she were already familiar with the episodes in question. Such lack of explicitness both presupposes and builds partisanship with Burgundian interest (see also chapter 6). More generally, what verse form and rhetoric enable the authors to do that the prose of their chronicles does not is to foreground the subjective *process* of memorialization over the *content* of memory. As its name implies, the *Recollection* both performs the act of remembering ("I saw...I saw...") and serves as an aide-mémoire for its readers. They are expected to "recollect" or bring to mind, with its help, things they might be presumed already to know, or else, if they are unfamiliar with the events concerned, to relate to them imaginatively as if they were memories of experiences they might have had.

Verse continues to be a medium for historiography to the end of the period. André de la Vigne's *Voyage de Naples* (1495–1498) has been called "an example of a purely historical treatment of political events by a Rhétoriqueur," in this instance Charles VIII's conquest of Naples.[35] The form adopted in his case, however, is that of a *prosimetrum,* alternating between prose and decasyllabic

---

34. The same wordplay is found over many more lines in Molinet's 1480s *Dictier sur Tournay* (*Faictz et Dictz,* 1:181–92), especially vv. 321–30.
35. See Brown, *Shaping of History,* 18.

lines arranged in stanzas of varying length, and while the prose is used to detail the events of the campaign, verse serves to praise and promote the king. Different forms again are also used to capture different subjective contemporary attitudes to the 1507 revolt of Genoa against the French and to Louis XII's campaigns in Venice in 1509 in Jean Marot's *Voyage de Gênes* and *Voyage de Venise,* respectively.[36] The former prefaces its account in a very unhistoriographical way with a series of disporting personifications and mythological figures. While Marot proceeds to describe the actions of the French victors in twelve-line stanzas, their Genoese adversaries are presented as allegorical caricatures in diverse dramatic settings in prose and various verse forms, thus drawing attention to them as unheroic and un-French. The *Voyage de Venise* quickly abandons the mythographic material used in its preface, but employs differing metrical forms—decasyllables for the military quotidian, groupings of three decasyllabic lines followed by one of four syllables to indicate the king's illustrious presence on the scene, and recapitulatory *rondeaux* which slow narration and sharpen focus on particular situations.[37] While the prose of the *rhétoriqueurs* also embraces mythical and allegorical schemes, the use of verse, by foregrounding linguistic artifice, draws attention to the ethical and aesthetic dimensions of these processes. Thus verse historiography could be seen as asserting that these too have significance as "history," however different they may be from the factual content of prose.

What emerges from these examples is that, while demonstrating that poetry *can* record history, they also imply that there is more to history, thus recorded, than meets the prose chronicler's eye. History writing in verse is equated not with the discovery and recording of available facts (which is not to say that in prose it always is, of course) but rather with gleaning and preserving knowledge from time; and this knowledge is to a greater or lesser extent inflected by the connotations of the particular verse forms that are chosen. Such quasi-allegorical exploitation of form accords with other features of the learned model of *poetrie,* such as personification, mythography, and other modes of allegory, which are also found in verse historiography (see introduction for the term *poetrie*). The presence of verse conjures an absent meaning, a "truth" about history that is not to be equated with factual detail because it is located not in external reality but in (not necessarily explicit or even conscious) subjective processes of reflection, sentiment, commitment, or memory. Whereas in *Stanzas* Agamben locates the capacity of poetry to know

36. Both poems were seemingly composed within a short period after the events they describe. See Marot, *Le Voyage de Gênes,* 59, and *Le Voyage de Venise,* ed. Trisolini, 7.

37. Brown, *Shaping of History,* 65–66.

in the strophic structure of thirteenth-century vernacular lyric, poets of the late Middle Ages discover it in versification more generally, since its forms lend themselves to representing a historically determined subjectivity.

Prime among these are the lyric or lyrico-narrative forms that late medieval historiography most often exploits. We now consider the way historical themes come to pervade these two traditions, and how they deal with the experience and recording of time.

Lyric, Lyrico-Narrative, and History

In *La Subjectivité littéraire,* Michel Zink charts a transformation from the twelfth to the thirteenth centuries in the situation in time of first-person poetry. Whereas early troubadours sing of their love as approximating to a preexisting eternal Idea, narrators of thirteenth-century *dits* are located in a particular here and now. Concluding with Rutebeuf, Zink's narrative ends where ours begins.

Exposure to the chill wind of temporality may be productive of comedy (as Zink shows is the case in Rutebeuf's personal poetry). But more profoundly, it gives rise to uncertainty about how to negotiate the onrush of instability and unpredictability, change and age, in which this experience of time consists. Poets from the late thirteenth century onward look for ways of limiting or counterbalancing mutability and contingency by recourse to some kind of order and form. For some poets, poetic reassurances of their mastery of time may correspond with an intellectual conviction that poetry can also convey a providential order, or a timeless world of forms. As we will see in chapter 3, however, the Boethian legacy of reflection on *fortuna* made late medieval poets more inclined to open up the dialectic between order and flux than to adjudicate between its terms. Philip Bennett's comparative reading of the *Prise d'Alixandre* and the *Geste des ducs de Bourgogne* shows how each negotiates differently the tension between envisaging history as an open-ended series of contingencies and discerning in it some overarching telos.[38] The development of the *formes fixes* can be seen as a response to similar uncertainties about our relation to temporality. Jacqueline Cerquiglini-Toulet suggests that forms marked by refrain, such as the *rondeau, ballade,* and *virelai,* are a poetic response to the uneasy, ephemeral quality of poets' experience of time. As the repetitions that make up a *rondeau,* for example, perform their rounds, their

---

38. Bennett, "Rhetoric, Poetics and History."

very reiteration, with the lines' meaning slightly altered by their new context, can be a way of conceding that time brings inevitable alteration while also contriving to measure, control, or slow its course.[39] Anxiety about the erosions of time and an outrageous bid to outmaneuver them shape the period's most enduring lyrico-narrative work, the *Testament* of François Villon.[40]

In support of our contention that poetry's permeation by the subjective awareness of temporality formed one of the bases for associating late medieval poetry with knowledge, we discuss the works of just two authors for whom this association seems especially productive: Eustache Deschamps, whose *ballades* explore all kinds of historical terrain that had not previously featured in lyric poetry, and Jean Froissart, whose authorship of lyric poetry and pseudo-autobiographical *dits amoureux* alongside his monumental *Chronique* illustrates the convergence between history and lyric in the theme of memory.

The prolific Eustache Deschamps (ca. 1340–1404) is the author of a record 1,175 surviving *ballades* as well as diverse other poems. He has often been portrayed as an observer and recorder of the minutiae of his time, and his poems are certainly tied into a particular historical here and now, whether they focus on the everyday and the banal or respond to events of a wider social and political importance.[41] The longest of them, the *Miroir de Mariage,* is a rather rebarbative didactic poem that straggles over some twelve thousand lines of octosyllabic rhyming couplets. Deschamps cites many historical exempla from antiquity and the Bible up to recent times in support of his critique of marriage and of women (portrayed as untrustworthy, unfaithful, and sensual).[42] A global historical vision is thereby broken up, dispersed, and reassembled, ostensibly for purposes merely of illustration. Yet the poem also comments on the exempla, using them to interpret the roles of husband and wife, which are thereby transformed into historical metaphors.[43] And Deschamps's interest in sound governance, justice, and the resolution of contemporary crises (such as the Great Schism) is as great as, or greater than, his apparent preoccupation with domestic relations within the home. Thus in the *Miroir* both universal history and conjugal satire are inflected in the direction of contemporary historical commentary.

But it is Deschamps's *ballades* that most fully reveal this sense of "being in time." They often treat topical themes, calling for a truce to the conflict

---

39. Cerquiglini-Toulet, "Écrire le temps."
40. E.g., Lacy, "The Flight of Time."
41. Sinnreich-Levi, *Eustache Deschamps.*
42. *Œuvres complètes,* vol. 9.
43. Minet-Mahy, *Esthétique et pouvoir,* 183–340, especially 224–25; also Stoneburner, "Le *Miroir de Mariage.*"

between the French and the English (*Ballade* 1148), or for the University of
Paris to intervene in the resolution of the papal schism (*Ballade* 1012), and in
this respect they infuse the *ballade* form with a new awareness of possessing a
political and social agenda. Nevertheless, Deschamps's *ballades* are not simply
focused on contemporary political events, nor are they a means of voicing
opinion through a popular literary form. His work is infused with tradition
as well as with current affairs. Deschamps recognizes and reflects the literary
influence of earlier poets, in particular Machaut, to whom he refers several
times; and as in the *Miroir de Mariage,* he also sets his poems within the flow
of history. This produces a sense of the *ballade* as a poetic space that looks both
backward to a social and literary golden age and forward to a political and
social future. Attachment to the contingent event does not, therefore, confine
the lyric form in a particular political moment but instead serves to historicize
it; thus, for example, Charles VI is "the new Charlemagne" who will bring
an era of peace to France (*Ballade* 1142). Yet the optimism produced by this
projection of a quasi-mythical past into a desired future is offset by the sense
of crisis and antithesis that haunts many of Deschamps's other *ballades.* The
century is aging and corrupt (*Ballade* 366), the body is prey to such worldly
pleasures that the soul is in peril of damnation (*Ballade* 274), the time of heroes
is past, and war is now waged by clerics and through the exchange of letters
(*Ballades* 253 and 846).

The contradictions and antitheses of Deschamps's body of poetic works
serve to root them in a temporality experienced as dynamic and conflictual.
The difficulty of reconciling new literary themes with the norms of literary
tradition interacts with the impossibility of maintaining the perceived social
and political stability of past eras. In its response to literary and social change,
Deschamps's poetry is the more conscious of itself as a site of flux and change
the more it searches its times for signs of permanence.

The sense of being caught in the passage of time, and being uncertain how to
negotiate it, impresses itself also on lyric and lyrico-narrative poetry. In chapter 3 we show how the motif of fortune is adopted from Boethius's *Consolation*
in such a way as to give a prominent role to the character Esperance (Hope),
who frequently takes a share of the role assigned by Boethius to Philosophy.
Whereas Philosophy exhorts the protagonist to rise above Fortune, medieval
poets are more inclined to surf it, trusting that—given time—circumstances
will change. While happenstance may be represented as hostile to them, its
potential always to reverse into its contrary is embraced as being the very
essence of a poetry that draws its life from duality and transformation; this
aspect of Hope is further developed in chapter 5. Hope, in one such duality,
is frequently counterbalanced by memory; alongside Esperance, Souvenir is

thematized and personified.[44] But whereas poets are generally optimistic with regard to the future, they are much more inclined to be pessimistic about retaining anything of value from the past. Froissart's poetic writings present especially complex reflections on the deficiencies of memory, which are the more relevant in view of his parallel career as a historian.[45]

In both his poetic compositions and the later books of the *Chronique,* Froissart's memories provide a vital link between the author and his work. In the *Prison amoureuse,* for example, his self-definition as lover and his capacity to identify with other lovers are based in personal experience: "Je le sçai especiaument / par moi" (I have particular knowledge of it through my own self, 68–69).[46] Froissart's poetic *dits* feature the author as narrator and lover, while book 3 of his *Chronique* sees an increasing resonance of his presence as author and protagonist within the frame of his journeying. At times the act of remembering and the act of writing seem even to merge into each other. In *Le Joli buisson de Jonece,* Froissart's memory of how he burned with desire when revisiting the bush of youth in a dream is what shapes his decision, at the end of the *dit,* henceforth to compose only religious poetry. And in the opening episode of the same *dit,* he represents himself in dialog with his thoughts personified as Philozophie, who prompts him to go in search of a portrait of his lady expertly made some ten years ago; the scene stages allegorically Aristotle's distinction between memory as a sensory trace and reminiscence as a mental activity:

> Tu dois par deviers toi avoir
> un coffret ens ou quel jadis—
> il y a des ans plus de dis,—
> tu mesis, et bien m'en souvient,
> (puis que dire le me couvient),
> un ymage bel et propisce,
> fait au semblant et en l'espisce
> que ta droite dame estoit lors.
> Se depuis tu ne l'as trait hors,
> encores le dois tu avoir.
> Je t'empri, or y va savoir:
> tu y sces moult bien le chemin,

---

44. Attwood, "Temps et lieux"; Cerquiglini-Toulet, "Un paradoxe mélancolique" and *La Couleur de la mélancolie.*

45. Zink, *Froissart et le temps.*

46. De Looze, *Pseudo-autobiography.*

et tu veras en parchemin
L'ymage que je te devis,
pourtraite de corps et de vis. (*Joli Buisson de Jonece,* 478–92)

(You must have somewhere close to you a strongbox in which long ago—more than ten years since—you placed, and I recall this well [since it's my job to talk to you about it], a beautiful and propitious image made in the likeness and the appearance of your true lady as she was then. Even if you have not since taken it out, you should still have it there. I beg you, go and find out: you know the way there well enough, and you will find the image that I am describing to you on parchment, portraying her figure and her face.)

All animate beings, according to Aristotle, are capable of memory; but only man possesses the intellectual power of reminiscence, which enables him to scour the storehouse of the mind in search of the particular memories that are retained there as if in pictorial form. In the *dit,* the personification of Philozophie represents reminiscence, and the portrait stored away in a distant treasure chest is the memory of which it goes in quest.

The subsequent developments of this scene, however, suggest that Froissart was also aware of the ways in which philosophers from the thirteenth century had critiqued and developed Aristotle's account. Their objection hinged on Aristotle's insistence on memory as a material imprint (or "sensible species") that could only be "intellected" (known to the mind) once it was abstracted in universal form. A consequence of this was that it would be impossible truly to remember singular things; a drawback of this, for Christian philosophers, was that it made contrition and retribution for singular events impossible to accommodate. Their response was to postulate that memory *could* involve intellectual knowledge of singular things, if by "memory" was meant the intellectual recall of the subject's own prior states of mind. To remember a thing would then be to recall experiencing it, and thus its existence as a singular thing, even if this did not involve intellectual knowledge of it as such. The object of memory would be lost to cognition, but the experience of remembering would be preserved. By revisiting its prior acts, the subject would be able to call to mind a previous encounter with a singular thing, even if the form in which it was recalled was a universal one, and thus the thing itself eclipsed. Duns Scotus's position, described in these terms by Janet Coleman, is exemplary: "When a man reminisces, he actively seeks to recall a mental image that corresponds with his continuously present universal understanding of something. He does not remember past *things* in themselves; he remembers past acts of knowing the formal aspects of things through sensible and intelligible species which represent those things in modes peculiar to active mind. He remembers only that which had and still has intelligible being for him."[47]

When in the *Joli buisson de Jonece* first Philozophie and then Froissart recall having the portrait painted and put away, this double reflection on prior mental acts seem to be alluding to scholastic revisions of Aristotle's account, whereby memory is not so much a content as a rehearsal of the mind's earlier acts. Throughout the episode we discover less about the portrait than about the subjective events associated with it: more precisely, the act of remembering the act of committing something to memory. In this way, memory becomes a history of consciousness; it becomes constitutive of identity, and this explains its appeal to Froissart as a topic of first-person poetry. As Michel Zink has put it, "[Froissart's] poems construct a representation of the self structured by the process of reminiscence, by the making present of memory to consciousness, where consciousness is nothing other than the reflection of memory."[48]

Not only does Froissart remember remembering his lady, but also the means whereby he does so is by remembering his own past writings. The identity recalled or reconstituted in the *dit* is that of himself as a poet. In a similar way, later in the *dit* the *content* of his love affair with this lady often remains curiously unavailable to Froissart; it is not so much called to mind as a set of events as the experiential residue is preserved and transmitted poetically, by what has been called "lyric memory." Repetitions of rhyme and phrasing link together narrative descriptions of his suffering, a love *ballade* composed while still in his dream about the bush, and his final *lai* to the virgin. Froissart's experience of the past survives primarily in these elements of poetic *form*.[49]

The scholastic account of memory reflected in Froissart's poetry posits, as one of its more paradoxical consequences, the possibility that the present can repeat a past that in some sense never was and certainly cannot be recalled to mind as such. This is a state of affairs that Jacqueline Cerquiglini-Toulet appropriately terms "melancholic." Analyzing Froissart's *Espinette amoureuse,* she shows how "everything happens as though for the poet experience was always the repetition or re-actualization of a past experience,"[50] and yet, at the same time, this past is always experienced as new or still to come. Froissart negotiates the dialectic of order and flux by means of a double movement in relation to time, one, ecstatic, "the suspended temporality of a lyricism of

---

47. Coleman, *Ancient and Medieval Memories,* 497; also Marenbon's account of memory in Scotus in *Later Medieval Philosophy,* 160–68; Kay, *The Place of Thought,* chap. 5.

48. Zink, *Froissart et le temps,* 168.

49. Kay, "Mémoire et imagination."

50. Cerquiglini-Toulet, "Un paradoxe mélancolique," 55.

communion," and a second, recuperative, "a movement of fixing in writing, characteristic, for the poet, of the melancholic gesture."[51] In a different approach to this same problematic, it has been suggested that the *Espinette amoureuse* and *Le Joli buisson de Jonece* manifest "the different ways in which poetic writing...transforms and replaces the lived experience with something which is more than itself, and yet essentially itself."[52] Giorgio Agamben supports reflection on how this surplus of poetic form alchemizes the particularity of the poet's experience so that it becomes universal. The poet's lived experience is de-subjectivized, as life and poetry are united in language to the extent that the figure of the poet becomes an "exemplary universal."[53] The knowledge that is enshrined in poetic form is never available as a direct, personal memory, but it is the means whereby individual experience of time can be changed into a more publicly expressed sense of history.

This private inaccessibility of his own past helps to explain Froissart's determination to record that of others.[54] In the *Prison amoureuse*, Froissart's personal love experience is doubled in that of his anonymous male correspondent and patron "Rose," who seeks Froissart's advice as he pines for a lady and dare not declare his love (letter 1). As we saw in chapter 1, the *Prison* is inspired by Machaut's *Voir dit*, whose narrative is shaped by the exchange of letters between the poet-protagonist and his lady. Froissart rewrites this to focus on two male writers; at once, experience and memory are extended away from the personal and autobiographical toward the social and collective. Significantly, also, the relationship with the patron creates a framework for the exchange of texts, where experience and memory become bound up with the creation, dissemination, and glossing of poetry. Author and text appear mutually interactive, as Froissart writes himself into his text, portraying his textual persona as preoccupied with composition, writing, and recording, to the extent that the text often falls into a *mise-en-abyme* of its own composition. His personal, individual memory functions as an integral aspect of the memory of a wider community that is created and perpetuated through the shared knowledge of texts, their diffusion, writing, and rewriting. The various letters and lyric poems that make up the text are described as being filed away by the narrator in a variety of boxes, pouches, and other hiding places, which

51. Ibid., 57.
52. Sinclair, "Poetic Creation." This view of poetry as fundamentally connected to life is paralleled by Machaut's conception of lyric poetry as having a particular "truth-value" through its origin in the rhythms of the body rather than in those of words; Cerquiglini, "*Un engin si soutil,*" especially 194–96.
53. Agamben, *End of the Poem,* 93–94.
54. Sinclair, "Froissart."

domesticate the refractory nature of experience by associating it with everyday objects and spaces.[55] At the end of the *Prison* they are all gathered together into one volume, to constitute the text we have as a record of what took place.

It is worth comparing these strategies of the *Prison* with Froissart's *Chronique.* Begun as a continuation of that of Jean le Bel, it gradually assumes the collaborative character of the *Prison amoureuse* as it relies increasingly on informants whose testimony the historian compiles. As in the *Prison,* too, memories are assigned to everyday objects and places. In book 3, many of the tales of battles, conflicts, deaths, and intrigue told to Froissart by his traveling companion Espan de Lyon are intrinsically linked to the places that both bring them to mind and commemorate them: castles recall sieges, towns evoke the memory of conflicts, and the deaths of two knights, Ernauton de Bisette and Montgaut de Sainte Basille, are memorialized by a stone cross raised at the spot at which they fell. This last tale is no sooner concluded than Froissart and Espan de Lyon arrive at the cross: "A ces motz cheismes nous droit sur la croix, et y deismes chascun pour les ames des mors une patenostre" (At these words we came immediately upon the cross, and we each said a *paternoster* for the souls of the dead).[56] When the dead are further remembered in prayer, this is a response to the physical cross as commemorating object rather than to the actual lived and recalled memory of the two men. The physical markers and memorials that punctuate Froissart's journey provoke an individual recollection based on a communal meaning and significance. The tales that Espan de Lyon tells are then entered into Froissart's written text, which in its turn acts as a means of memorialization. Both the physical and textual monuments are, however, inevitably partial, serving only as a provisional interpretation and representation of a particular historical discourse at a particular point in time.

Although Froissart has the dual role of writer and protagonist in both his poetic *dits* and his *Chronique,* the relation between writing and experience differs from one to the other in a way that it is tempting to attribute to the difference between verse and prose. In the *dits,* the Froissart persona is the repository of memories that are lacunary, evanescent, and subject to change, yet they are nonetheless indexed in the narrator-protagonist's mind as deriving from events in his own life. They may be supplemented by the memories of others, but it is the unreliable core of the personally experienced that is re-remembered and universalized in poetry as "lyric memory." This memory is associated with everyday objects and places—poems and letters located in

55. Froissart's eccentric filing system is studied by Cerquiglini-Toulet, "Fullness and Emptiness"; also McGrady, *Controlling Readers,* 184–85.
56. *Voyage en Béarn,* ed. Diverrès, 39.

pouches and boxes—but only once the first-person subject has become, as it were, objectified in layers of verse. The way Froissart assembles the fictional materials for his *dit* in his personal filing system will be paralleled later in the way Charles d'Orléans keeps a manuscript serving to record both his own lyric compositions and those of his guests, so that it doubles as a record of the visitors he has received.[57] Similarly, "coterie" anthologies of lyric poetry record the collective memory of the courts that produce them.[58]

In contrast, Froissart the chronicler-protagonist of the *Chronique* is less prone to problematize the experience of others. He is present at the recounting of the tales he later copies, but he is not their subjective site; instead he is the medium through which the memories of others are perpetuated as written text. By recording witnessed experience in association with features of the landscape, he fosters the illusion that universality inheres in past events and not solely in their textualization. The cyclicity, reexperience, and renewal that typify poetic experience and poetic form are replaced by the prose work's tying of memory to places and objects. Like the *dits,* the writing of the *Chronique* can be seen as a "geste mélancolique" which attempts to recuperate a lost past that perhaps never really was, and indeed this sense of loss permeates the *Chronique*'s later books. In the prose work, however, the sense of memory that inheres in poetic influence and intertextual tradition is lacking. This produces a different sense of time, one in which the impetus is backwards and melancholic, yet linked with the present (however tenuously) not just by writing but by aspects of objective reality.

Though in different ways, Froissart and Deschamps show how the involvement of lyric and lyrico-narrative in history both generates knowledge and helps to define its limits. *Faits divers* could be discussed in poetry and illumined by historical tradition. Poetry collections could constitute historical documents, and history could be written as collective "autobiography." Verse is caught up less in the event than in reflection, thought, and feeling, and this is what enables it to mediate between the personal and the public, whether by capturing time as memory and/or history, or by publicly performing belief. The failure of subjective memory intellectually to retain the content of objective reality can be recuperated as poetic form.

This chapter has shown, first, that there is an exceptional link between poetry and history in the late French Middle Ages; and second, that this link goes beyond the institutions of patronage to involve reflections on the first-person

---

57. Taylor, *Making of Poetry,* 83–145.
58. Ibid., 147–227.

subject's situation in time. Thus, although prose maintains the upper hand for the recording of historical events, verse remains significant as a means of evoking the way they are experienced. Different verse traditions put the weight more toward the other or more toward the self; if "public" poetry inscribes and renders the other, *dits amoureux* are more an investigation of self. Memories may be conjured in the minds of the readers of verse historiographers, even if they never experienced the events in question. In lyrics and lyrico-narrative *dits,* the first person's failure to remember may be what is most successfully communicated.

In all these cases, poetic form plays an essential role in the treatment of historical themes, a role quite unlike that of prose. It provides a means of staking a relationship to others (audiences and readers, antecedent and fellow poets, patrons, love objects) and to the poet's own past. Whether the emphasis is on the first person or the addressee, verse form acts as a form of personhood, by comparison with the impersonality of prose, a contrast that is particularly clear in the *Anciennes et modernes généalogies* of Jean Bouchet. Verse may not have the apparent transparency of prose, the sense that prose conveys of its own adequacy to record facts and events. But if in this sense it is less than prose, it can also evoke the truth of experience in a way that prose cannot. The quality *as* truth of the experience evoked by verse is only reinforced in cases, like that of Froissart, in which the content of that truth is seen as lying beyond representation. In all such cases, we might see poetry as providing a formal surplus that does not in itself have content but that stands in for a knowledge that is not, or cannot be, expressed.

CHAPTER THREE

Poetry and Thought

This chapter examines the sustained association between poetry and intellectual inquiry in late medieval French writing inspired by three crucial works: the *Roman de la rose* in the form continued by Jean de Meun; Ovid's *Metamorphoses,* especially by way of the *Ovide moralisé;* and Boethius's *Consolation of Philosophy.* The multiple overlaps among these three texts and their transmission make them influential conjointly as well as individually. Large swathes of Jean's continuation of the *Rose* consist of adaptations of arguments used by Boethius; Jean also mines Ovid extensively while at the same time sharing his preoccupation with love and sex.[1] The *Rose* and the *Consolation* are sustained first-person dialogs with personified abstractions, often invoking mythic exempla, while the *Ovide moralisé* combines the myths that make up the *Metamorphoses* with elaborate schemes of allegoresis. It is often impossible to tell, when one reads the *dits* or *prosimetra* of the later Middle Ages, which of the *Rose,* the *Moralisé,* or the *Consolation* is the shaping influence, so far have the three texts converged into a single poetico-reflective matrix. As time goes on, the more difficult it becomes not only to tease out its three constituents but also to distinguish its direct influence from its earlier mediations: the impact of the *Rose-Moralisé-Consolation* trio on Froissart is heavily mediated by Machaut; Machaut and Froissart then conjointly overdetermine its use by Christine de Pizan; and so on to the *grands rhétoriqueurs.*

1. See in particular Huot, *Dreams of Lovers.*

Although the combined imprint of these three texts on late medieval French literature is everywhere evident, the intimate relationship they collectively foster between poetry and thought has not previously been the focus of study. This chapter argues that the *Rose,* the *Moralisé,* and the French reception of the *Consolation of Philosophy* together consecrate verse as a means of both furthering and shaping philosophical reflection, stimulating especially those compositions conceived of as *poetrie* in which rhetorical complexity and intellectual challenge are combined (see introduction for an explanation of this concept). We argue that the use of verse *as such* interacts with the trajectories of thought generated within this textual matrix. All three texts, in their different ways, show the extent to which reason and understanding are conceived in relation to the body, so that any attempt to separate knowledge from the body inevitably reinscribes the body. As a result, they infuse philosophical inquiry with an erotic charge that leavens it with playfulness and humor. At the same time, they encourage poetic reflection on generation and the place of humanity in nature. Recognition of the body as grounding *both* verse *and* knowledge chimes with the continuing importance of physical performance and *mise en scène,* which we documented in chapter 1.

In addition, all three of these works are concerned with human exposure to chance and contingency, which they contrast with providence. They thus bring a philosophical perspective to bear on the association between poetry and history in the late Middle Ages. As chapter 2 showed, this association goes far beyond the fact that authors were commissioned to compose both lyrics and prose chronicle: once prose comes to denote the objective facticity of the event, verse connotes it more as subjective experience and is intensely preoccupied with temporality and memory. There was relatively little interest in the concept of fortune in the High Middle Ages;[2] it comes to prominence after the rise of prose, if not because of it. Two relatively recent books have drawn attention to the relation between late medieval French poetry *as* poetry and its intellectual preoccupation with fortune: Daniel Heller-Roazen's *Fortune's Faces* and Catherine Attwood's *Fortune la contrefaite.* For Heller-Roazen, the possibility that anything might be otherwise than it is (which is how he defines contingency) is manifested in the composition of the *Rose.* Instead of the traditional view of it as comprising a "text" and its subsequent "continuation," Heller-Roazen sees the mutation of the poem's first-person subject, and the two different guises assumed by the text, as performing this inherent contingency, which is rendered concrete in the text by the sequence on the double

2. Tilliette, "Éclipse."

nature of Fortune and her house (*Roman de la rose,* 5883–6144), and by Jean's adaptation (via Boethius) of Aristotle's thought on contingency. For Attwood, the figure of Fortune in late medieval French poetry is similarly synonymous with poetry by virtue of her doubleness/duplicity, although Attwood's readings tend to place more weight on the rhetorical nature of dualities than on strictly philosophical ones.

In this chapter we inscribe the preoccupation with fortune identified by these and other critics within the joint legacy of the *Rose,* the *Ovide moralisé,* and the *Consolation* to show how poetry in late medieval France promotes thought about embodied existence in a changeable world. By bringing into conjunction the themes of corporeal nature and inconstant fortune as sources and subjects of poetry *as such,* this textual matrix renders thinking in the medium of verse far-reaching and prestigious, yet also seductive and amusing, in ways that prove irresistible to later poets. As we argue at the chapter's close, some texts within this matrix, or some possible readings of parts of those texts, assert the mind's capacity to transcend fortune and the body and free itself by a process of sublimation from their limitations. Others, however, seem to revel in enjoyment of the body and/or the contingencies of embodied life—or at least they see no future in seeking to extricate themselves from them. In such cases, *connaissance* is shot through with *déconnaissance:* the recognition that knowledge has only a limited reach, remaining perpetually, humorously snagged on tomfoolery (see introduction for our presentation of Lacan's term *déconnaissance*).

The *Roman de la rose*

What did Jean de Meun think he was doing when he decided to take up and continue what he says was an unfinished poem and so create the *Roman de la rose* we now have? He is careful to distinguish his own contribution from this earlier *Rose.* We have only his word for the first author's name, Guillaume de Lorris, and the point in the text where he left off (line 4056). Jean's first significant episode, we know as a result, is the long speech by Raison, a fitting figure with whom to inaugurate the whirlwind tour of intellectual culture on which Jean takes us, and a seemingly unthreatening point of entry to the increasingly crazy assemblage that we meet there of Boethian thought, Ovidian seduction and innuendo, university politics, and anti-fraternal satire, all contained within a reworked version of Alan of Lille's dream-vision poem *De planctu naturae.* Although the influence of the *Roman de la rose* on the literature of the ensuing centuries has been abundantly documented,[3] focusing on the elements central to our study puts this legacy in a new light.

First, we stress that the success and prestige of the *Rose* ensure an association between intellectual adventure and *poetic* form. Most of the texts that imitate the *Roman de la rose,* however divergent from it in content (see chapter 1), observe the use of octosyllabic couplets. As David Hult has argued, Jean's "commitment to the letter is related...to the materiality of language itself and, in particular, to the ways in which that materiality can manipulate meaning in the space of vernacular expression....Jean proved to be a brilliant poetic master in the *Rose,* which...accounts both for his success, for the poetic imitators he spawned, and for the praise lavished upon him by even his fifteenth-century detractors."[4] As a result of this power of attraction, the *Rose* reroutes the emergent genre of the *dit,* which has hitherto been relatively small scale and primarily satiric or moral, into something much more intellectually ambitious. In Jean's hands it becomes a crazy double of scholastic genres such as the *disputatio* and the encyclopedia. And although the scale of his undertaking is rarely surpassed (Guillaume de Deguileville's expanded *Pèlerinage, Renart le contrefet,* and Christine de Pizan's *Mutacion de Fortune* can claim to do so; on the two last, see chapter 4), the *dits* that follow share with the *Rose* the basic character of a verse montage, often seriocomic, in which different kinds of discourse, orchestrated by a first-person voice, meet or clash.[5] The splicing together of divergent modes of writing is complicated, later in the tradition, by the practice of inserting various kinds of lyric and, still later, passages in prose (see chapter 5). This rich formal texture accommodates a willfully equivocal blend of philosophical speculation, political advice, moral considerations, and explorations of sentiment in which the first-person figure of the poet is both the source of the text and its protagonist.

One of the most interesting texts to explore this blend is the as yet understudied *Eschez amoureux* of about 1370–1380. This long poem, which at this writing has still not been edited in its entirety, replaces the key structuring images of the *Rose* such as the mirror and the garden, whose effect is to unite and interconnect the poem's various elements, with agonistic ones, notably that of the chess game, which instead demand the elimination or defeat of one element by others. The result, as Michèle Gally has shown,[6] is that the *Eschez*

---

3. The classic studies are those of Badel *(Roman)* and Huot *(Romance of the Rose);* see also Taylor, "Embodying the Rose."
4. "Poetry," 35–36.
5. Cerquiglini-Toulet, "Le Clerc et l'écriture."
6. Gally, *L'Intelligence de l'amour.*

is much more systematic than the *Rose* in the way it marshals personifications and their associated themes into complex schemes. But it also dramatizes its own failure to maintain their simultaneity other than in the mode of loss: knowledge and love appear mutually exclusive at the level of the plot; the two are held together only by virtue of one appearing negated. Thus the chess game is an image of seduction in which the lady, attentive to the rules of the game, maintains the upper hand, while the lover, lost in reverie, has no strategy but is fascinated by the erotics of the situation. Losing at chess marks him out as a love poet eager to win the lady; her success at the game, however, suggests that she will not be won (the unfinished state of the text leaves their relationship unresolved).[7] The Judgment of Paris, which frames the entire text, likewise opposes the choice of a life of love, an active life, or a contemplative one at the same time as it binds them together as simultaneously existing and interrelated options. The fundamental incompatibility between the sensual and intellectual life is conceded by the text itself:

Ainsy sont, en toutes saisons,
Sensualités et raisons
Communement en grant discorde;
Car raison a virtu s'accorde,
Et li sentemens corporeulx
N'entent qu'a delit savoureuz
Et a mondaines vanités. (*Échecs amoureux,* 809–15)

(Thus sensuality and reason are together in great disagreement, because reason is in harmony with virtue, whereas bodily sensation is concerned only with tasty delight and worldly vanities.)

The very lines of verse that stress the disharmony (*discorde*) between thought and the body hold them together in rhyme (*accorde*), while similarly, the tropes of the text succeed in holding love and knowledge together even though the plot drives them apart. The divorce between the two is fully achieved only with the prose commentary by Evrart de Conty, who demonstrates his admiration for his verse exemplar while at the same time resolving its fundamental aporia between *connaître* and *déconnaître* in favor of knowledge. If Evrart is actually the author of the verse text, this change of position would nicely illustrate the distinction between the treatment of knowledge in verse and prose.[8]

7. Mussou, "Apprendre à jouer?"
8. Ibid., 42–43, 55.

The *Rose*'s legacy of associating poetry and intellectual inquiry continues throughout the fifteenth century and beyond, for example, in Jean Meschinot's *Lunettes des princes* (1461–1465), a dream-vision poem that uses various verse forms and some prose as "spectacles" or lenses through which to "read" the exhortations of Raison and the teachings of the cardinal virtues. Also in the fifteenth century, practitioners of the *prosimetrum* combine, like authors of earlier *dits,* tropes from the *Rose* together with a mixture of forms, sometimes with far-reaching intellectual intent. This is perhaps most marked in Lemaire's *Concorde des deux langages,* in which the framework of a dream, the recycling of several of Jean de Meun's personifications, and the promotion of the temple of Minerva over that of Venus perform an allegory of the work's own ambition to enact a fusion of French poetry with philosophical enlightenment.[9] These sustained reflective works are not the only ones inflected by the philosophical poetics of the *Rose,* of course, and many of its features also percolate into shorter works, where they adopt a wide range of metrical forms, such as the *ballades* of Charles d'Orléans, which, if not strictly philosophical, nevertheless contain many reflections on fortune, consciousness, subjectivity, and desire.

It is also Jean de Meun who leads the way in recasting Boethius's *Consolation of Philosophy* as a (mock?) consolation to lovers, and thus humorously diverts the powers of philosophy from fathoming the nature of providence to addressing the torments of sexual desire. Jean was later to translate the *Consolation* into prose, but his translation is not nearly so influential on subsequent vernacular literature as his various reassignments, in the *Rose,* of Boethius's personification of Philosophy. In the *Consolation,* Philosophy is an austere figure who censures the imprisoned Boethius's laments and exhorts him to abstract himself from all bodily concerns so that his intelligence can unite him with the One supreme Good. In the *Rose,* she becomes three separate figures defined by their attitude to the lover's progress. Raison, whose speech recapitulates and indeed translates much of Philosophy's in Boethius's books 1, 2, and 3, predictably admonishes the dreamer against the goods of fortune and against carnal desires. Burlesquing Philosophy's hectoring style, La Vieille more practically offers tips on how to manipulate to one's best advantage some of the situations in which fortune places one.[10] Finally the figure of Nature, in whose mouth Jean scandalously places his version of Philosophy's discourse on providence, supports the dreamer's desire for the rose and sends Genius, her priest and phallic agency, to help him win it; with their help the *Rose* concludes

---

9. Armstrong, "Songe, vision, savoir," 62–65.
10. Huot, "Bodily Peril."

with an act of consummation. Controversy has reigned over interpretation of these episodes, but it is certain that Jean's provocative hijacking of Boethius as a support of erotic love is widely imitated, even if with different intent, by fourteenth-century authors of *dits amoureux* and by authors in various genres in the fifteenth century. This absorption of the *Consolation* into poetry that is at least partly about love and bodily reproduction cements the reciprocal relation between desire and knowledge that the *Rose*'s adaptation of the love quest framework to philosophical debate had already instituted. Some instances of how this influenced subsequent authors will be considered later, when the contributions to the matrix of Ovid and Boethius are addressed.

Although Jean's mind-boggling elevation of Nature to a seriocomic theological vade mecum was not itself reiterated, the inflection he gives to the treatment of nature is another respect in which the *Rose* exerted an influence on later poets. In the Middle Ages, as Michel Zink has phrased it, "the true meaning of nature is found not in gazing upon it, but in participating in it."[11] In chapter 4 we will see the different ways in which medieval encyclopedias explore this natural dynamic, but none of them theatricalizes human participation in nature's regenerative work in such a spectacular and unforgettable fashion as does Jean de Meun in his personifications of Nature and her priest Genius. This section of the *Rose* recasts and popularizes the representation of these two figures by Alan of Lille in his Latin allegory *De planctu naturae*, where they likewise rail against homosexuality and promote matrimony. But it also reflects changes in the intellectual climate in the one hundred years that separate the two poems. With the rise to prominence in the thirteenth century of Aristotle's natural philosophy in university curricula, the processes attributed to nature came to be understood as orderly and intelligible, and hence open to rational investigation, rather than as a miraculous revelation of divine power.[12] As we explore further in chapter 4, the philosophical implications of this understanding of nature should not be underestimated. Nature in this sense is not just a process in which we participate but the principle of order as a result of which the world is intelligible and amenable to study. As such, nature opens the door to other branches of philosophy, just as Aristotle's *Physics* serves in part as a preparation for his *Metaphysics*. Understanding the workings of natural phenomena becomes a preliminary to grappling with the nature of being as such.

Jean's representation of Nature jocularly registers this rational, Aristotelian turn with a salute to Aristotle's *Physics* (which would have been unknown

11. Zink, "Nature et sentiment," 44; also idem, *Nature et poésie.*
12. Murray, *Reason and Society;* Pairet, *Mutacions des fables,* 37.

to Alan) in which the comparison of Aristotle with Cain may not constitute an altogether ringing endorsement.[13]

> Et li convandroit prandre cure
> d'estre deciples Aristote,
> qui mieuz mist natures en note
> que nus hon puis le tans Caÿn. (*Roman de la rose,* 18000–18003)

> (And he should take care to learn from Aristotle, who observed Nature better than anyone else since the days of Cain.)

At the same time as reflecting the capacity for intelligibility of the universe, however, Nature herself is represented as a silly, hysterical woman. She invites her audience to understand natural processes as rational and to shun superstitions (such as the belief that we are controlled by the planets) as the condition of freedom; but more profound metaphysical questions, such as the Virgin birth, leave her nonplussed. She may be the true reflection in God's mirror (19869–70), but her own account of the properties of mirrors underlines their propensity to distort and foster illusion (18123–216).

The way Jean portrays Nature as an aspect of Boethius's Philosophy is thus both a reflection on contemporary intellectual developments and a comic interrogation of them. Later medieval poets follow his lead in representing their privileged involvement in nature's processes as a preparation for reflecting on other philosophical matters; at the same time, like him, they do not always treat this progression altogether seriously. Both Machaut (in his Prologue; see chapter 5) and Froissart (in the *Joli buisson de Jonece*) represent their identity as poets as stemming directly from nature, and both also work, in their texts, from corporeal nature to ethics and metaphysics.[14] Rational progression through poetry from physics to ethics is epitomized by Raison's words in Machaut's *Jugement dou roy de Navarre:*

> Voirs est que Nature norrit
> Par quoy li enfes vit et rit;
> Et Bonneürtez le demeinne
> Tout parmi l'eüreus demainne,

---

13. Polak, "Plato." Alan's figure of Nature has been reread from a queer theory perspective by Burgwinkle, *Sodomy,* chap. 5; Guynn, *Allegory,* 111–24.

14. Zink, *Nature et poésie,* 229–35.

Tant qu'il est temps qu'en lui appere
Que de Bonneürté se pere. (*Jugement dou roy de Navarre,* 3871–76)

(It is true that Nature is responsible for bringing a child up to live and smile, but
Felicity it is who leads him to the domain of well-being until such time comes
as it is fitting in him to be adorned by Felicity.)

Allegorically we can interpret this passage, and the wider context from which
it is taken, as saying that reason enables us to understand our corporeal nature
as the basis on which human beings prepare for the "supreme good." Christine de Pizan traces a similar trajectory from physics to other branches of
philosophy—ethics, politics, and metaphysics—in the *Chemin de long estude.*
In a passage reminiscent of both the *Rose* and the *De planctu,* the earth sends
a complaint to the court of Raison about the conflicts that assail it, and in the
course of debating possible political solutions, Raison's advisers, predominant
among them the personification of Sagece, offer their views on human nature,
government, and history but ultimately fail to find a solution to the earth's
problems.

Later in the fifteenth century, when the Aristotelian grip on the curricu-
lum slackens, the sense of progression from physics to metaphysics comes to
seem less automatic and the self-conception of the poet as nature's spokesman
less prominent. But the legacy of Jean de Meun's Nature is still palpable. For
example, in Martin Le Franc's allegorical defense of women, *Le Champion
des Dames* (1442), a debate on women's moral standing in society is briskly
widened when Nature intervenes and raises questions of human sin and free
will.[15] And in Lemaire's *Concorde des deux langages,* Nature is associated (in a
sermon by Genius) with cosmic plenitude and fecundity, and is later linked
with the personification Labeur Historien, who embodies didactic and historical writing (albeit not specifically poetry). As in the *Rose* there is considerable
doubt whether the preaching of Lemaire's Genius evokes a truly transcendental order—the parodic dimension of his sermon in the *Rose* is if anything
played up—but the *Concorde des deux langages* certainly shows the persistence
of the tradition of linking natural processes, poetry, and metaphysics, if not
altogether seriously.[16]

Finally, Jean de Meun's talent for creating vivid poetic depictions of intellectually influential concepts is manifested in the description Raison gives of

15. Ed. Deschaux, vol. 2, vv. 8873–9512.
16. Armstrong, "Yearning and Learning."

two-faced Fortune and her two-sided house (5883–6144). Attwood suggests
that Jean's model is book 8 of Alan of Lille's *Anticlaudianus,* which likewise
depicts her house as double and as the meeting point of contrasting rivers,
one calm and fresh, the other tumultuous and brackish. Similar depictions
are later used by Nicole de Margival in the *Dit de la panthère,* Michault Taillevent in *Le Régime de Fortune,* and Christine de Pizan in the *Mutacion de
Fortune.*[17] Given that the intellectual implications of this passage are dwelt on
by Boethius, we will return to it in the context of the *Consolation.*

The *Ovide moralisé*

The main Ovidian source of the *Rose* is the *Ars amatoria,* which is vigorously
mined for advice by both Ami and La Vieille in ways that continue the early
medieval emphasis on Ovid as a poet of love and seduction. But Jean's continuation also includes a wide range of classical myths that occupy a significant
place in the Ovidian corpus. And while much of its philosophical content is
openly displayed in the speeches of Raison and Nature, the poem also plays
on the expectation that readers familiar with medieval hermeneutics will experiment with reading these myths allegorically, that is, otherwise than *selonc
la lettre,* in what Raison already identifies as the craft of *poetes* (7132–38). By
way of encouragement, Jean offers examples of allegoresis, or parodic versions
of it, as when Genius scoffs at Guillaume de Lorris's Narcissus exemplum
for its failure to reflect divine truths (20, 249–637). Such passages may be indicative of a change of emphasis in the vernacular reception of Ovid. The
magister amoris never leaves the medieval literary scene, but he is nevertheless
upstaged by a more philosophical Ovid as medieval readers are increasingly
drawn to the *Metamorphoses* and its glosses.[18] This tendency is confirmed in
the early fourteenth century (probably between 1316 and 1325), when Jeanne
de Bourgogne commissions a poet whose identity we do not know, probably
a Franciscan, to translate the *Metamorphoses* into French.[19] The resulting text,
the *Ovide moralisé,* contains not only the first translation into French of Ovid's
entire poem but also translations of some of the existing glosses, as well as narrative expansions and new glosses contributed by the translator himself. The
Ovide moralisé was to provide subsequent generations of poets with an accessible version of the classical *Metamorphoses,* a storehouse of antique myths and

17. Attwood, *Fortune la contrefaite,* 156–57.
18. McGrady, "A Master," 98–99.
19. Possamaï-Perez, *L'"Ovide moralisé,"* 749–88.

history even more compendious than Ovid's original, and a model of different modes of allegorical reading—natural and historical, moral, and Christological. Above all, we would underline the importance of the translator's choice of verse for his project.

The *Ovide moralisé* is a vast poetic undertaking, virtually all in octosyllabic couplets. (Only the tale of Pyramus in book 4, 229–1169, is partly in tail-rhyme stanzas, while a few Alexandrine verses about the Apocalypse have been incorporated into book 14, 1689–1716.) Why did the translator opt for this verse form? Perhaps it made it easier for him to establish continuity with the Ovidian *contes* and *matière antique* of the twelfth century (he actually incorporates the *Philomela* attributed to Chrétien de Troyes and introduced a great deal of Troy material on the model of the *Eneas* and the *Roman de Troie,* all texts similarly in octosyllabic couplets); perhaps he also chose verse in direct tribute to Ovid's status as a poet. Medieval readers recognized the *Ars amatoria* as an art of love that is also an art of writing,[20] and the cosmic and political insinuations of the *Metamorphoses* are similarly inseparable from the elegant verse narratives in which they are couched. The association of the octosyllabic couplet with romance makes it an apt vernacular equivalent to Ovid's elegiac couplets, lighter than the hexameters of epic poetry to which the *Metamorphoses* oppose a graceful, subversive counterpoint. The *Ovide moralisé*'s poetic qualities are not often remarked on by modern critics, but they were clearly appreciated by medieval readers. The presence of turns of phrase and rhymes from the *Ovide moralisé* in the work of later French poets shows that they read the text as poetry and exploited it as a specifically poetic resource. For example, verbatim allusions to the moralist's rendering of the tale of Ceyx and Alcyone are found in Machaut's *Fonteinne amoureuse,*[21] and to the competition among the Muses in Christine de Pizan's *Chemin de long estude.*[22] Comparing the *Fonteinne amoureuse* with book 14 of the *Moralisé,* Richard Trachsler observes that almost all of Machaut's references to myths and legends not only can be traced back to specific passages of the moralized Ovid but also reiterate their "rhymes, isolated hemistichs, or ... whole blocks of lines."[23]

Self-consciousness about its own poetic qualities informs several episodes of Ovid's poem. A clear example is the competition between the true and false Muses on Mount Helicon in book 5, which hinges on their performing good

20. Allen, *Art of Love.*
21. Mühlethaler, "Entre amour et politique."
22. Kay, *Place of Thought,* chap. 6
23. Trachsler, "Cent Sénateurs," 190.

and bad examples of narratives of metamorphosis. When they fail to produce
good poetry, the false Muses are turned into the chattering magpies that, in
a sense, they already were. In book 10, the songs of Orpheus likewise effect
transformations in the landscape that seem to put into reverse those imagined
by the author of the *Metamorphoses:* the trees, many of which had previously
been human beings, come to life and gather round to hear him sing. We have
shown elsewhere how both of these scenes, already self-reflexive in Ovid, are
reworked in the *Ovide moralisé*. In the French version of the contest between
the true and false Muses, the true ones emerge as being in tune with divine
wisdom, while the false are identified as the muses of classical poetry; the
moralist not only aligns himself with the true Muses, as Ovid did, but also contrives to imply that Ovid's place is among the false ones.[24] Similarly, the story
of Orpheus becomes in the *Ovide moralisé,* among other interpretations, an
expression of the transforming power of the Church and thus of the resources
available to Christian poetry.[25] In both cases the French translator is able to
highlight his own contribution as a poet, thus adding a further frame of self-
consciousness to the episodes in question.

A third passage that reflects self-consciously on the *Metamorphoses* as philosophical poetry and deliberately emphasizes poetic form is the competition
between Athena and Arachne at the beginning of book 6, likewise reworked
in the *Ovide moralisé* in such a way as to reframe poetry as Christian and
French, and thus the ongoing successor to Ovid's pagan Latin.[26] The narrative picks up from the end of book 5, reminding us how Pallas learned of the
challenge posed to the nine Muses by the false ones (the future magpies). This
provokes Pallas's aside that she has faced similar competition from Arachne
(Araigne, *Ovide moralisé* 6.13), the most expert weaver in existence apart from
Pallas herself. Disguised as an old woman, the goddess goes to Araigne and
demands that she apologize to Pallas for presuming to surpass her as a weaver.
Disdainfully Araigne defies Pallas to put her superiority to the test. Pallas then
reveals her identity, and the contest begins. In her weaving Pallas performs
the foundation of Athens and Neptune's bid to name the city, refuted by herself before a council of gods. Its four corners contain exemplary depictions
of individuals who unsuccessfully defied the gods and were variously metamorphosed. The border of her tapestry is decorated with olives. Araigne's
weaving represents the shapes adopted by Jupiter in the course of his amours
with mortal women, all of whom had famous offspring by him, and also the

24. Kay, *Place of Thought,* chap. 6.
25. Ibid., chap. 4
26. Cf. Wolf-Bonvin, "L'Art de disparaître."

various transformations of Neptune, Phoebus, Bacchus, and Saturn. Her borders are ornamented with fronds of ivy and flowers of many colors. Araigne's portrayals are so vivid that Pallas tears up her tapestry and hits her on the head with her own shuttle. Outraged, Araigne hangs herself rather than submit to more indignities. Pallas's only concession is to allow her to remain hanging from her own noose as she sprinkles her with poison. We then witness the transformation of Araigne into a spider (6.308–18).

The parallel between this episode and the contest between the true and false Muses is obvious, the puzzling difference being that while the true Muses seem justified in their victory, it is unclear why Arachne/Araigne should be defeated when her weaving is so much more in harmony than Pallas's with Ovid's own technique in the *Metamorphoses*. In Pallas's handiwork the tales of transformation are relegated to the margins in order for the narrative of her own feats to take center stage; in the work of her rival, we revisit in pictorial form the events of *Metamorphoses* books 1–5, where the adventures of Jupiter, Phoebus, and Bacchus predominate. In the *Metamorphoses,* Ovid uses Pallas ironically as a figure of oppression, ridding the world of an alter ego. In the *Ovide moralisé,* by contrast, the French glosses adduce cast-iron reasons for Pallas's success. Pallas's grand narrative of the foundation of Athens is easily recuperated, by the moralist, as representing the divine plan. Her procedure of outdoing Ovidian-style metamorphoses forms an exact parallel to his own of segmenting and dwarfing Ovid's episodic text within the grand sweep of salvation history. The exemplary depictions in the four corners of Pallas's weaving are glossed by the French poet as images of the merits and eternal rewards of the contemplative life, thus confiming her as the goddess of wisdom. After his interpretation of Araigne's tapestry, which shows how it too can ultimately be understood in Christian terms, the moralist reads Araigne herself as a figure of False-seeming. She is like the person who assumes a life of simplicity in the eyes of the world so as to win worldly favor, but

> Ses oeuvres sont sans charité,
> plaines de fainte vanité.
> Teulz homs resamble bien l'iraigne,
> qui de soi trait la bele ouvraigne
> qu'ele tist assiduelment. (6.899–903)

(Her works are devoid of charity, full of assumed vanity. Such a person is indeed like the spider who draws her fine work from herself and weaves it assiduously.)

Arachne is like the devil who sets snares for us from which we can no more escape than a struggling fly from a spider's web (6.917–72). The depiction of her metamorphosis brings out the extent to which she is confined within her own corporeality. Even as it mutates, her body continues to weave, and there can be no doubting Arachne's fundamentally limited inspiration when her eight fingers become legs, her head shrinks away, and her belly swells (6.310–18). In sum, Pallas is identified with divine wisdom (*devine sapience*) and her work with revelation; hence it is infinitely superior to that of the devil (Araigne), or *fole outrecuidance* (foolish presumption), to whose death it inevitably leads. The whole episode, while following Ovid closely, is recast in such a way as to imply that if Ovid is sympathetic toward Arachne in the *Metamorphoses,* this only confirms that his aspirations are deceitful in character, and that his concept of poetry remains confined within a grotesque corporeality. Nevertheless, the moralist censures Ovid's thought, not his poetic medium. The fact that Pallas successfully challenges Araigne using the same textile form as her rival endorses the moralist's choice of the same poetic medium as Ovid to reweave the pagan *Metamorphoses* into a French Christian epic of revelation.

In fact the French poet's flowing couplets are highly successful at rendering the graceful sinuosity, narrative pace, and risqué eroticism of the Latin original; while he is mistrustful of pagan bodily pleasures, the moralist's poetic facility also betrays his fascination with them. This is well evidenced in an episode that the French poet supplied himself, the tale of Pasiphaë in book 8, which wittily flirts with the naughty acts he means to censure.[27] The outstanding beauty of Pasiphé, wife of King Minos of Crete, is detailed lasciviously with a sidelong glance at "tout l'autre surplus," which "trop y avroie à aviser" (the remainder [which] I would find it excessive to describe, 8.661–62). In another knowing *occupatio* the moralist denounces Pasiphé's wickedness, which he is reluctant to besmirch his mouth retailing, but manfully does so all the same. Her husband away, Pasiphé becomes mesmerized by a bull's *vit* (penis): something so dirty, says the poet, that he can't explain how it found its way into his mouth (8.767–73)! Pasiphé disguises herself as a cow in order to seduce the bull and conceives, giving birth to the minotaur ("demi home et demi toriau," half man and half bull, 8.933). As commonly happens in the *Ovide moralisé,* the allegoresis abruptly changes register. The marriage of Pasiphé with Minos is like the union of man with God, for man is modeled on God, made "à sa forme et à sa figure" (8.987); but then humanity left the bedroom of its spouse where it should have dwelt and thought only about the flesh, putting the soul

---

27. Blumenfeld-Kosinski, "Scandal"; Simpson, *Fantasy,* 154–58; Cerritto, "Histoires."

in peril and turning its love from God to the devil. In this episode the appeal of the flesh, and the capacity of poetry to place it in the poet's mouth despite himself, are strongly underlined.

It is difficult to do justice to either the poetic or the intellectual ambition of the *Ovide moralisé* on the basis of single episodes. If the *Rose* is a disorderly double of an encyclopedia, the *Moralisé* is an attempt to confer a single Christian meaning on Ovid's mythic meanderings and to discern a providential purpose in the incontinent flux of nature, justified by Ovid with reference to the pagan Pythagoras (*Metamorphoses,* book 15). The moralist pursues these aims with the aid of the notion of "form." In bodies that combine in grotesque couplings and hybrids that mutate before our very eyes, the poet can glimpse the potential for redemption and a return to conformity with the form they have in God's mind, in his divine wisdom, that is to say, in Christ. As a consequence of the fall, this conformity is always already lost and hence invisible, but the more bizarre and energetic an individual's mutation, the greater the hope of rendering discernible this once and future form.[28] The *Ovide moralisé* thus shares with the *Rose* a poetic vision of the physical world as a dynamic involving perpetual motion and change, forever obsessed with its own enjoyment, yet also a window onto metaphysical insights.[29]

Another feature common to these two great poems is their epistemephilia, in the sense both that they eroticize knowledge and that they conceive of the erotic as a means to knowledge. It is sex that drives both the plot and the intellectual machinery of the *Rose,* while the interpretations in the *Moralisé,* especially but not only in the early books, are addressed to stories of sexual encounter that are often violent or transgressive. Although the moralist invariably condemns sexual activity on the literal level, he never fails to find ways of investing it with religious meaning. Jupiter is the arch-seducer of the *Metamorphoses,* his philandering never far from bestiality whether he disguises himself as an animal or turns his victim into one. And yet, because he is the father of the gods, he is always read as a figure of God the Father. Both the *Rose* and the *Ovide moralisé* share a number of myths that are explicitly about sex and knowledge. Among the most prominent in the *Rose* are those of Narcissus and Pygmalion; Vulcan's snaring of Mars and Venus, which is told more than once, and involves knowledge of their adultery as something that Vulcan seeks to have, prove, and transmit; and the story of how Jupiter castrated Saturn and threw his genitals into the sea, from which Venus was

28. Kay, *Place of Thought,* chap 2.
29. Cf. Pairet, *"Formes,"* who overlooks the metaphysical import of *forme* to present the *Moralisé*'s metamorphoses as strictly superficial.

born. This last myth is narrated at the beginning of the *Moralisé* just as, at the start of Jean's continuation of the *Rose,* it casts doubt on Raison's capacity definitively to convey any meaning that is not in some degree contaminated with sexuality. Earning a rebuke from the lover for her unladylike choice of words, Jean's Raison ends up with Saturn's *couilles* in her mouth much as the author of the *Moralisé* finds a bull's *vit* in his; the glosses in both texts, however elevated, retain the taint of forbidden *savoir* or *jouissance.* Finally, of course, the *Ovide moralisé* shares with the *Rose* the assumption that one must read beyond the letter of the text, though (unlike the teasing reticence of both *Rose* authors) the *Moralisé* provides a superabundance of interpretations. It is easy to see how the two poems become harnessed to each other and conjointly influence the production of *poetrie*—of works, that is, that provoke intellectual reflection to unpack the latent import of their figures. And given that the *Rose* and the *Moralisé* share the same verse form, it is not surprising that their combined authority inclined their imitators likewise to write in verse.

When later French poets borrow mythographic material from the *Moralisé,* the significance they place on it is typically more courtly than theological but nonetheless manifestly indebted to the intellectual ambition of their source. Indeed, the interest of poets in relating myths to sexual love foregrounds the pressures of the body and its liability to change and thereby intensifies the ability of the stories to raise concerns of an ethical or metaphysical nature. We have highlighted the concept of form in the *Ovide moralisé* as a means of glimpsing an impulse toward unity in the very vicissitudes of transformation. The authors of subsequent *dits* open up a similar dialectic when they look to myth, and especially myths of metamorphosis, as a way of addressing questions of personal identity. Stories of mutation appear to provide limit cases through which to test a sense of personal continuity battered by circumstance, or rendered tenuous by human changefulness and age. The autobiographical tenor of the vernacular poems lends urgency to these questions: unlike in the *Ovide moralisé,* it is the identity of the first-person subject that is at stake. One form taken by this dialectical reversal of change into identity is the choice of a particular myth as a kind of personal emblem. Thus, for example, Froissart redeploys the myth of Actaeon in his *Espinette amoureuse,* in the *Joli buisson de Jonece,* and again in his *Chronique* ("Le Voyage en Béarn") to underline the vulnerability of a courtly author.

An example of how material borrowed from the *Moralisé* and inflected by the *Rose* builds an intellectual dimension in later medieval French poetry is provided by the myth of Ceyx and Alcyone, which forms part of the Greek background to the Trojan War recounted in book 11 of the *Metamorphoses,* shortly after the story of the Judgment of Paris. Ceyx is the king of a city in Thrace who departs on a sea voyage and then drowns when his ship is wrecked in a dreadful storm. His devoted wife, Alcyone, is counting on his return. To warn her of grief to come, Morpheus, one of the gods responsible for dreams, and whose name obviously evokes metamorphosis, adopts Ceyx's form and appears to Alcyone in a dream. Alerted to her husband's death and then seeing his corpse in the water, Alcyone commits suicide by throwing herself into the sea. But before she reaches the water, she is transformed into a bird, a halcyon (kingfisher). Ceyx is likewise transformed, and the two fly off together. Although the story is recounted touchingly, the moralist displays no sympathy with his protagonists on this occasion. Humankind (Ceyx) was invited to leave behind ignorance, pride, and attachment to worldly goods (Alcyone) in order to go on a pilgrimage "qui maine à la boneürté / de la souveraine clarté / ou touz biens, toute joie habonde" (that leads to the felicity of sovereign brightness where all good things and all joy abound, 3810–12). The ship that is wrecked is the mortal body and the sea is mortal life, with the wind as sin and waves as the world's fluctuating fortunes (3832–58). Alternatively the ship can be read as the Church, which leads to eternal life but is currently assailed by storms of corruption. A final "sentence…plus acordable / a l'entencion de la fable" (interpretation more in tune with the meaning of the fable, 4118–19) is that those too addicted to worldly pleasures are like birds gobbling up worldly goods (4143).

Jean-Claude Mühlethaler has traced the poetic reception of this section of the *Ovide moralisé* from Machaut to Christine de Pizan, charting the consequences of its changes of context. Unlike the moralist, he observes, Machaut in the *Fonteinne amoureuse* does not so much promulgate a meaning for the myth as enjoy its mystery. The story offers the opportunity both to explore the unreal world of dreams and to play on its poetic associations (notably with the dream in the *Roman de la rose* and the dream narratives in *Metamorphoses*, book 11). Machaut's writing is "born of reflection on the potential uses of the myth," the ultimate value of which is that it enables Machaut to reposition himself as the Ovid of his day.[30] Sylvia Huot continues the analysis, suggesting that poet and prince respond to the myth in different ways. The patron's interpretation is literal and partial: for the Duke of Berry on the brink of leaving his new wife on a dangerous embassy to England, Alcyone's dream offers a model of communication, and hence consolation, between separated lovers. This reading is undermined by other elements from the *Moralisé*, book 11, especially the Judgment of Paris. The poet's understanding is, by contrast,

---

30. Mühlethaler, "Entre amour et politique," 149.

complex and figural, preserving the hermeneutic boldness of the *Moralisé*. The skillful composition of the *Fonteinne amoureuse,* Huot concludes, celebrates poetry as "offering unlimited opportunities for contemplative or analytical reading."[31]

Characteristically, Christine de Pizan raises the stakes when she uses the same myth of Ceyx and Alcyone in the first part of *La Mutacion de Fortune* to explain her genesis as a writer. Like Alcyone she loses her husband in the storms of fortune, and like her is metamorphosed. But Christine's transformation is into a metaphorical man: this is the only way she can follow Machaut's project of becoming Ovid. As Christine underlines, her mutation is to be taken not literally but *par ficcion* (*Mutacion de Fortune,* 152) and *selon methafore* (1033). While metaphorically a man, she retains an identification with Alcyone as a woman and a prophet who benefits from exceptional knowledge. A few years earlier her *Epistre Othéa* exhorted its recipient, "Croy le conseil de Alchïone, / De Ceÿs te dira l'essoine" (Heed Alcyone's advice, she will tell you what befell Ceyx).[32] Though in some respects a man, Christine in the *Mutacion* retains Alcyone's visionary insight, which enables her to understand and comment on the whole of history in the remainder of the poem.[33]

These examples from Machaut and Christine show how the philosophical framework of the *Ovide moralisé* can be redirected toward an investigation of personal identity. Central to this identity, however, is the obligation of the vernacular poet to be a source of knowledge and enlightenment to others, especially the patron. The texts do not just echo the rhymes and vocabulary of the *Ovide moralisé* and exploit the resonances between its fables; they also preserve the intellectual bravura of their model even as they transpose it to other domains.

In the later fifteenth century, while the *Ovide moralisé* does have a long legacy, it is mainly in prose—both the prose redaction of the *Moralisé* itself, and in the pretentiously named *Bible des poetes,* a vernacular prose version of the *Metamorphoses* containing allegorical interpretations that derive partly from the *Ovide moralisé* and partly from Pierre Bersuire's Latin *Ovidius moralizatus.*[34] It is also an important source for book 1 of Jean Lemaire de Belges's prose *Les Illustrations de Gaule et singularités de Troie* (1511).[35]

31. "Reading the Lies of Poets," 48.
32. Ed. Parussa, 310, 79.4–5. See Parussa's note for the translation of *essoine* as "affaire" or "accident."
33. Mühlethaler, "Entre amour et politique," reviews the moral and political readings of the myth in Christine and Deschamps.
34. Six printed editions appeared between 1484 and 1531. See Moisan, "La Naissance du monde"; Moss, *Poetry and Fable,* 6–16.
35. Moss, *Poetry and Fable,* 24, 30.

The *Consolation of Philosophy*

If, in the *Fonteinne amoureuse,* the *Ovide moralisé* becomes linked with the *Rose* via the motif of dreaming, in Christine the will to make sense of life in the face of fortune just as clearly establishes a link with Boethius. The whole of our period bears the imprint of the *Consolation of Philosophy,* in which the author-protagonist, imprisoned and awaiting death, stages a dialog in alternating verse and prose with his capacity for philosophical thought, personified in the flashing-eyed figure of Philosophy. Medieval French poets seem to have been mesmerized by Boethius's overall visionary framework, in which a first-person subject, in the grip of melancholy, conjures a personification promising enlightenment.[36] Sometimes a vernacular Philosophie herself makes a consolatory appearance, as in Froissart's *Joli buisson de Jonece.* More commonly, from Jean de Meun's *Rose* to the *grands rhétoriqueurs,* Philosophy's role is taken at least some of the time by a figure designated as Raison. In the *dits amoureux,* personifications with a more affective value such as Esperance or Souvenir are more likely to play a part. Less frequently the narrator-poet himself adopts the structural position of the Philosophy figure, devoting the *dit* to consoling an aristocratic patron who, like Boethius, is in prison (as in Machaut's *Confort d'ami* or Froissart's *Prison amoureuse*) or runs the risk of being so (as in Machaut's *Fonteinne amoureuse*). In the fifteenth century, the schema takes on primarily Christian as opposed to secular value with Chartier's *Livre de l'Esperance,* on which more later.

These vernacular re-creations of the *Consolation* either are entirely in verse or else imitate the alternating verse-prose (*prosimetrum*) format of their model. They thereby uphold a link between poetry and philosophy that is often absent in the French Boethius translations. Prior to the prose translation by Jean de Meun that we have already briefly referred to, there were two French prose translations of this venerable philosophical dialog, and one French and one Occitan versification of its content (though the Occitan *Boecis* is too fragmentary to judge what its scope may have been).[37] The translations that were most dominant in the fourteenth century were entirely in prose,[38] although a glossed translation preserving the *prosimetrum* form of its original had the widest circulation in the fifteenth. Known by its title, *Livre de Boece de Consolation,* this version was accompanied by translations of glosses taken

---

36. Armstrong, "Yearning and Learning"; Kay, "Touching Singularity"; Huot, "Guillaume de Machaut," and "Re-fashioning Boethius."

37. Cropp, "Medieval French Tradition"; Courcelle, *Consolation,* part 5, especially 301–15.

38. The most influential fourteenth-century prose translation is that edited by Atkinson, *Boeces: De Consolacion.* Jean de Meun's translation is also in prose throughout.

from the twelfth-century Neoplatonist philosopher William of Conches.[39]
Why do literary reworkings of the *Consolation* overwhelmingly opt for poetic
form when the translations do not?

The predominance of verse in texts that, rather than translating the *Consolation,* situate themselves in its slipstream no doubt owes much to the influence of the *Rose.* As we have already seen, Jean's continuation not only adapts
large sections of Boethius's text but also inflects (or burlesques) Philosophy's
remedies so as to cure the sufferings caused by love specifically, thereby providing a mold into which subsequent authors of *dits amoureux* will gratefully
slip. The *Rose* also served as a vernacular model of intellectual inquiry cast
in the form of a dramatic dialog involving a range of personified abstractions and a single, first-person protagonist. The *Consolation* and the *Rose*
are more broadly connected through the practice of allegory, although neither indulges in the explicit allegoresis of the *Moralisé.* Then again, overlaps
between Boethius and the *Metamorphoses* may also have influenced (through
the *Ovide moralisé*) French poets' use of verse across the range of medieval
Consolation look-alikes. For instance, the myths found in Boethius's meters
also feature in the *Metamophoses;* and the theme of fortune in Boethius, as
well as being taken up explicitly by Jean de Meun, also overlaps with the treatment of nature (or Nature) as change in the *Rose* and in the *Moralisé* too. But
whereas the themes, tropes, and metrical forms of this tradition all become
melded together to form a single fertile mold, Boethius may have contributed
distinctively to its intellectual underpinnings. Although the immediate clue to
Boethian influence is a dialog between a protagonist and a figure who recalls
Lady Philosophy, the debt of medieval poets to the *Consolation* lies equally
(or maybe more) in the way they develop its verse passages. Whatever the
need for Philosophy's consolation—metaphysical, political, or personal—and
whatever its content, the *process* of consolation was widely reinterpreted in
the Middle Ages as deriving from poetry, while conversely, poetry was identified as the most appropriate medium for certain kinds of philosophical consolation. The various vernacular renderings of the *Consolation* center attention
on the first-person protagonist *as a poet* and rebalance the theme of consolation so as to accord prominence and sympathy to his or her mental acts, seen
as best expressed *through poetry.*

One means whereby this change of emphasis is produced is structural.
Boethius's text stages a dialog between the first-person protagonist and just one
personification, and concludes with the former being absorbed into the latter:

---

39. *Le Livre de Boece de Consolacion,* ed. Cropp.

being consoled by philosophy effectively means *becoming* it. For Boethius, this process of assimilation is also one of return to a primal state of illumination, a state of knowledge that the protagonist already possessed but had lost sight of because of the way his mind was darkened by his embodied state. *Anamnesis,* Plato's concept of how philosophy makes it possible to "unforget" this originary enlightenment, is celebrated by Philosophy in book 3, meter 9. French medieval treatments replace the one-on-one dialog with a more freewheeling structure whereby the first person encounters a series of different personifications all of which speak to different aspects of his or her singular ego, but none of which absorbs or overwhelms it. A burlesque instance of this structural change has already been noted in Jean de Meun's *Rose,* where Philosophy is divided into Raison, La Vieille, and Nature; in later texts it is generally treated with less levity, offering the protagonist opportunities to explore alternative paths. The first person, then, is the voice that persists while the personifications come and go. Often, additionally, the protagonist is explicitly identified as both the author of the entire text and a poet. This is achieved with marked insistence relatively early in the period in Machaut's *Remede de Fortune,* where the crisis that leads to the narrator's needing consolation stems from his shyness about admitting authorship of a lyric poem. This narrator is the author not only of the *dit* but also of the portfolio of *forme fixe* lyrics inserted into it in imitation of the formal variety of the *Consolation.*

In this way the medieval works answer a question that is left hanging by Boethius, namely, how, when, and by whom was the text of the *Consolation* written? A first reaction on reading the *Consolation* is to identify the author with the prisoner figure; he, however, dissolves into the figure of Philosophy before the work is over, and though he appears to give a blow-by-blow account of their exchanges, it is unclear how or when he might have written it down. A more sophisticated reading identifies Philosophy as the author, given that she is the protagonist's true self, the figure that the first person is always destined to become, and the only figure speaking when the text ends. Did she record it at some later stage, creating the first-person voice of the prisoner much as in book 1 she pretends to be Fortune? The author would then be an example of *Philosophie la contrefaite,* to adapt Attwood's title *Fortune la contrefaite.* A third possibility is signaled by John Marenbon, who notes that about two thirds of the meters do not in fact form a part of the dialog but rather stand apart from it and comment on it.[40] They must originate somewhere, and their author has to be identified above all as a poet. The medieval

---

40. Marenbon, *Boethius,* 147.

French tradition resolves these uncertainties by explicitly uniting in one person the equivalent of Boethius's prisoner (or, more rarely, of Philosophy) and the mysterious author of the meters. Although there may be an ironic distance between the textual first person and the extra-diegetic poet, the protagonist is nonetheless the same as him or her (perhaps at a different age). The French poems are thus usually more nakedly autobiographical than the *Consolation*. When the poet is identified with the Boethius figure, the ego in the grip of distress and the poet lamenting it are the same person, and ultimately the ego is consoled (or not) by the poetic work that, as poet, he or she creates. In the less common scenario in which the poet takes the role of Philosophy, it is the sage counselor who is simultaneously a poet, either addressing the ill-starred Boethius equivalent directly or explaining his situation to a general reader.

Another way in which medieval writers rebalance the *Consolation* toward poetry is through their manifest debt to the content of Boethius's verse, as much as to that of his prose. Rather than retaining the setting of the *Consolation*'s prose dialog, Boethius's prison cell, they usually opt for a natural locus of some kind. Among the factors that may have influenced this choice (which include the prevalence of natural settings in the *Rose* and the *Metamorphoses*) is the predominance of themes of nature and the cosmos in the *Consolation*'s verse passages.[41] The songs exhort the Boethius figure to see his imprisonment as something inessential and his true being as belonging in an ordered universe, regulated by love (book 1, meter 8) and natural law (e.g., book 2, meter 2).[42] The image of the caged bird whose true home is in the woodland glades (book 3, meter 2) is elaborated by La Vieille in the *Rose* in a mock-Boethian lecture on women's "natural" freedom. Subsequently the meters evoke Odysseus's wanderings (book 4, meter 3) or the steep torrents of rivers (book 5, meter 1). Following the meters into these open spaces makes it easier for the French poets to stage multiple encounters, rather than the head-to-head confrontation with Philosophy in the confined space of a prison that we find in the prose of the *Consolation*. In his experiments with different verse forms, Boethius also creates openings into different kinds of generic material just as the medieval poets do when they splice together different lyric forms. Among the material in these meters, as already indicated, are some of the myths and legends most frequently elaborated by late medieval poets, and also found in the *Ovide moralisé*: Orpheus, Hercules, Circe, Iphigenia, the Trojan War, and Ulysses. The meter that sings of Orpheus's luckless journey to the underworld

41. Ibid., 147–48.
42. This vision of cosmic harmony is especially in evidence in the *Chemin de long estude,* much of which reads like an extended Boethian hymn.

(book 3, meter 12) is an interesting passage in several ways. Initially proposing Orpheus as a negative exemplum, an instance of how *not* to follow your desire, as it develops it betrays sympathy for Orpheus's passion and admiration for his fabulous poetic talent. It thus exhibits a willingness to experience and explore distress which Philosophy's austere prescriptions would condemn. Though setting out to warn against seduction, the meter cannot fail to find Orpheus seductive and celebrates Orpheus's power to express his "powerless grief" (73). In this way, poetry is at once the pulse of distress and its consolation, resonating with the body and desire in ways quite foreign to the prose.

Boethius's meters, then, suggest that philosophy needs to be framed by poetry. Poetry provides a subtle framework in which to reflect on philosophical questions, and also alternative ways of relocating and experiencing those questions. Clear instances of medieval texts that respond to the *Consolation* as the framing of philosophy by poetry are Machaut's *Remede de Fortune* (ca. 1341) and Alain Chartier's *Livre de l'Esperance* (1428–1430). The *Remede de Fortune* is characteristic of mid-fourteenth-century poetry in registering intellectual distance from Boethius's Neoplatonism.[43] For Boethius's Philosophy, not only must the protagonist "unforget" his former enlightenment, but also doing so will reunite him with the One principle of Truth and Goodness (book 2, prose 9). For Machaut's generation, educated in favor of the Aristotelian conviction that only singular individuals exist and that the One of Platonism is Plato's biggest mistake, the Boethian solution is less appealing than what Boethius represents as the problem: the play of contingency on individuals. It is in individual affective states as they change with circumstance that the truth of human singularity can be sensed, and thus through poetic expression that it can be explored. Machaut concedes that knowledge of singular passion remains unknowable:

> Homs ne diroit sa maladie
> Jamais si proprement de bouche
> Com fait cil a qui elle touche
> Au cuer, si que dire ne peut
> Qu'il a, ne de quoi il se dueut. (*Remede de Fortune,* 1810–14)

(No one could so properly articulate his sickness by mouth as he whose heart is so touched by it that he cannot speak of what he has nor why he suffers.)

43. Kay, "Touching Singularity."

Such is the shortfall between the physical particular and the intellectual universal that the only true articulation of suffering is to admit the impossibility of articulating it. The "remedy" that the *Remede* proposes for fortune is not Philosophy but Esperance (hope), which consoles the lover-poet sufficiently to enable him to keep going (and thus keep him composing poetry), but not so much as to deprive him of his subject matter. The *dit* is interspersed with *forme fixe* lyrics which are its framework and *raison d'être* much as the meters are in the *Consolation.* Philosophically, they propound the reality of the singular one over the claims of a probably chimerical, Neoplatonic One. Philosophical endeavor that, in Boethius, is concentrated in the prose is located instead in verse.

Sylvia Huot's analysis of Chartier's *Livre de l'Esperance* shows that "the use of the poetic passages to gloss, nuance, or refute the arguments of the prose passages is even more explicit [in the *Esperance* than in the *Consolation*]," since "almost none of the poems are explicitly attributed to the characters within the narrative, and many are very clearly the commentary of the authorial persona," the gap between lyrics and prose narrative widening as the work advances. Just as Boethius's meters engage with human distress as well as consoling it, Chartier's religious lyrics constitute "a new poetic discourse that confronts the reality of human tribulations, and in so doing offers genuine moral and spiritual edification, and genuine consolation."[44] The medieval reception of Boethius, then, foregrounds the presence of the poet in reflective texts and emphasizes the value of poetry in the pursuit of reflection.

One final aspect of the interference between *Consolation* and late medieval poetry must be stressed. French poets were especially drawn to the passages in the earlier books of Boethius that describe the ravages of fortune; it was from the reworking of these passages, and notably that in the *Rose,* that the medieval *fortuna* topos is largely derived.[45] What has not been highlighted, however, is how this bias in their reception of the *Consolation* enables poets to divert philosophical dialog to whatever happenstance is of concern to them, and thus at once forges a link between consolation, philosophy, and lyric poetry. The commonest source of melancholy requiring consolation is the misfortunes of love; the Boethian frame permits them to recast this as an inquiry into the nature of love, and also of melancholy (Jean de Meun's *Rose* at once becomes an intertext to such inquiries).[46] Political circumstance is another common source of distress, and in making this a central theme, medieval writers amplify the *Consolation*'s relatively discreet political critique. In book

44. Huot, "Re-fashioning Boethius."
45. See Hunt, "Christianization"; Patch, *Goddess Fortuna.*
46. E.g., in Machaut's *Jugement dou roy de Navarre.* See Huot, *Madness,* 145–53.

1, Boethius's protagonist interprets his imprisonment as an act of injustice or tyranny; and medieval poets adapt the philosophical framework in order to offer consolation and advice to rulers, typically their patrons.

Invoking a political context in this way means that many reworkings of the *Consolation* are *poésies de circonstance* as well as poems about the pathos of circumstance. For example, Machaut's *Confort d'ami,* his most copied *dit,* was composed in 1357 purportedly to console Charles of Navarre during his imprisonment by the French king; and two important poetic consolations were composed by Lemaire in 1503 and 1505: *Le Temple d'Honneur et de Vertus,* in memory of Pierre, Duke of Bourbon, and *La Couronne Margaritique,* in praise of the recently widowed Margaret of Austria.[47] The circumstantial may sometimes be recuperated to a transcendental providential order, as Armstrong argues is the case in Lemaire; most reworkings of the *Consolation,* however, embrace the time-bound fluctuations of history, and Molinet, who recast it many times, rarely seeks any meaning exterior to historical events.[48] In general, then, the emphasis on fortune indicates that French poets opt for a world dominated by contingency rather than necessity, where the possibility is held open that things could have happened otherwise, an attitude often explicitly encouraged in the guise of a character named Esperance. The philosophical preferences examined in this chapter clearly contribute to, and even justify, the association between poetry and history examined in chapter 2. They further suggest that thought is sometimes celebrated in part because of the limits on what can be rationalized and what cannot.

A final example of the intersection between the *Rose,* Ovid, and Boethius highlights the way they associate temporality and the physical universe. When Philosophy (*Consolation* 5, prose 1) elaborates the theme of Fortune, she cites Aristotle's *Physics* (2.4–6), where Aristotle, in the course of a discussion of causality, decides to include consideration of the roles played by chance (*automaton*) and fortune (*tuché*). This may seem only a tangential moment in the *Consolation,* but it has major implications. What was to become the most influential treatment of *fortuna* for the Middle Ages is aligned here with its most authoritative discourse on *natura.* As we saw at the beginning of this chapter, Jean de Meun in the *Rose* responds to this same alignment by putting Raison, Fortune, and Nature all in play. But while Jean follows Boethius quite docilely in the part of Raison's speech that denounces Fortune, the *Rose* veers sharply away from the *Consolation* when Jean recasts Boethius's Philosophy as

---

47. Jodogne, *Jean Lemaire de Belges,* 170–203, 215–54. In his *Plainte du Désiré,* consolation is staged *within* the text rather than for an extratextual audience/recipient, as Paincture and Rhetorique attempt to console Nature for the death of Louis de Luxembourg.

48. Armstrong, "Songe, vision, savoir," especially 65.

Nature personified, at the very point at which she starts to talk about destiny. Jean's action in doing so was earlier described as "scandalous." The full significance of the scandal emerges more clearly now. Whereas Boethius's Philosophy directs the protagonist to transcend his limitations and contemplate the Supreme One, Jean's not committing these sentiments to Raison but entrusting them instead to Nature suggests that the answers to questions about human freedom, destiny, and providence might be available to us through natural philosophy, as a result of our reflections on the bodily universe.

Here this chapter's argument reaches its culmination. What is most significant about the intersection of the three texts we have examined here is their alignment of philosophy, nature, and fortune—in modern terms, of thought, the corporeal world, and contingency—as sources and subjects of poetry. Do we live in a world in which reason can discern "form," order, and intelligibility, or a world that it is reasonable to see as subject only to chance and flux? Are thought and language capable of making sense of the forces of nature, or are they hopelessly warped by their dictates? These dilemmas are formulated in, and addressed by, not only the *Roman de la rose* and Boethius but also Ovid's *Metamorphoses* and their medieval moralizations, which center, as we saw, on a dialectic between flux and consistency in which characters' very identity is constantly open to transformation by their bodily desires. And in the late medieval French reception of all three works, they are identified as topics specifically for investigation by poets, in the medium of verse.

Whereas the relationship between poetry and knowledge discussed in the two previous chapters was anchored in particular institutions, whether those of public performance or of patronage, there seems to be no such institutional basis to the influence of the three texts addressed here. The *Rose,* Ovid, and Boethius were read by clerical and secular poets, in both university and courtly contexts, and indeed outside France as well as within. But what seems an almost universal enthusiasm for this poetic triad provides an intellectual context in which better to comprehend the success of the institutions considered in chapters 1 and 2, since the impetus to reinforce poetry's connection to the body, and to measure it against the vicissitudes of history, is apparent in different ways in all three of its members.

We agree with Attwood and Heller-Roazen in seeing an inherent link between verse writing and fortune in this period. Human subjection to fortune shapes the experience of temporality and confronts human subjects with questions about contingency and necessity, order and flux. The dilemmas posed by these issues become fused with the nature of poetry itself, owing to the commitment to verse lodged by the *Rose-Moralisé-Consolation* triad. Further to these critics' commentaries, we underline the connections between fortune and nature. Human immersion in the "natural world"—sexual, material, and temporal—furnishes both a means to the knowledge that is sought in medieval philosophical poetry and a core of *déconnaissance* within it. Whether they eroticize learning or resist its inflection by the body, the *Rose,* the *Moralisé,* and the *Consolation of Philosophy* all admit that knowledge is subject to desire. The physical is always present by implication, even if the poems are deprived of the support of physical performance, and one of the means by which this presence is maintained is by the pulse of versification. The verse text is thus always situated with respect to the body, not just as a support for performance but as the unavoidable medium of the quest for enlightenment and the vehicle through which its meaning is apprehended—or distorted.

True, philosophy can be consoling, and the melancholy consequences of embodiment might be cured by an ascent through the faculties to the domain of pure reason where freedom lies. But does the Boethius figure escape from melancholy, or does melancholy linger on in his poetry, a counterbalancing of reason by the body? French poets, as we shall see in the final section of chapter 4, for the most part cling to the melancholic perspective. The *Roman de la rose,* by contrast, although it eroticizes the quest for knowledge, also offers moments of transcendence that seem more significant to some readers than to others. And the *Ovide moralisé* does not merely dwell on the very perversions of pagan imagination that it seeks to dispel but actually embroiders them, while at the same time demonstrating utter resourcefulness in ascending to the truths of revelation. How did medieval readers construe these equivocations? In our introduction we identified one of Lyotard's "language games" as citational, in the sense that knowledge, when quoted as such in another text, can appear to rely for its legitimacy on the fact of its having been cited, and thereby forfeit the very authority on which the process of citation is supposed to depend. When the authors of *dits amoureux* draw on Ovid and the *Rose* to frame moments of Boethian consolation, do they confirm its sublimating effect, or do they contaminate it with the potential *déconnaissance* of its frame? If the persistent use of allegory in these texts affirms the validity of the allegoresis over the original text, in line with what we called Lyotard's "exhortative model" (see introduction), how does it justify retaining the literal level at all, given that it is supposed to have been rendered obsolete by the gloss? (This problem is particularly acute in the *Ovide moralisé.*)

Whatever the answers to these questions, thought in these three foundational texts weaves its way sinuously around bodily nature and temporal contingency; it provokes subsequent writers to decide whether to live with their vicissitudes or rise above them; but it summons them to do so in verse.

PART II

TRANSMITTING AND SHAPING KNOWLEDGE

CHAPTER FOUR

Knowing the World
in Verse Encyclopedias and Encyclopedic Verse

The previous three chapters characterize late medieval French poetry as shaped by a vigorous reactivation of oral or aural culture, by an exceptional intimacy between poetry and history, and by the impetus to reflection of the conjoined influence of the *Rose,* the *Ovide moralisé,* and the *Consolation of Philosophy.* They show that poetry in this period both reflects and enacts the relation to the body of language and intellection, as well as human participation in temporality and the natural process. The next three chapters are structured somewhat differently. More comprehensive in their aims, each reviews the development throughout the period of the way poetry transmits and shapes a particular kind of knowledge: referential, textual, or ideological. Taking the first of these as its subject, the present chapter focuses on the development of encyclopedic writing in verse, since the encyclopedia is the genre par excellence for shaping and conveying knowledge of the world. It examines how the sometimes precarious processes of *savoir* interact with human subjectivity in such a way that this knowledge is inevitably to some extent compromised.

Medieval Encyclopedias

In the Middle Ages all vernacular encyclopedic writing takes place against the background of Latin. The composition of Latin compendia of knowledge flourished in western Europe, from the late eleventh through the thirteenth centuries particularly.[1] Most influential for vernacular verse encyclopedists in France were the *Elucidarium* and *Imago mundi,* both by Honorius of Autun, who wrote in the first third of the twelfth century.[2] Vincent of Beauvais's massive compilations in the second third of the thirteenth century also became landmarks for vernacular writers, particularly those who wrote in prose. Though collectively referred to by modern scholars as "encyclopedias," these compendia differ widely in organization, emphasis, and comprehensiveness, and it is not evident that their authors thought of themselves as contributing to a single, identifiable genre. The word *encyclopédie* does not appear in the vernacular until the end of our period (1522);[3] in French, texts are designated, if at all, as *traité* or *livre de clergie,* or even, in the case of the *Image du monde,* with the omnium gatherum term *roman.*[4]

In antiquity and the Renaissance, the word "encyclopedia" was understood as deriving from a conception of knowledge as a circle in which all the disciplines are interconnected.[5] Diverging from this model, the organizing trope of medieval compendia is more typically treelike, combining "branches" of knowledge in a hierarchical structure.[6] (The Occitan *Breviari d'amor* is an especially clear instance of organization in the form of a tree; see the illustration and discussion later in this chapter.) But like their classical and Renaissance counterparts, medieval encyclopedists set out to offer a systematic educational program for the young or, by extension, for the layman in need of instruction.[7] A performative character is explicit in those that adopt the time-honored format of a dialog between teacher and taught, the process of acquiring knowledge being modeled by the diegetic disciple in the

1. These paragraphs are based on Céard, "Encyclopédie"; Collison, *Encyclopaedias;* Kenny, *Palace;* Melczer, "Humanism"; Picone, *L'enciclopedismo medievale;* Ribémont, *Origines;* Segre, "Le forme et le tradizione didattichi," especially 134–41; Simone, "La notion d'Encyclopédie."

2. Other influential authors include Hugh of St. Victor, Bernard Silvester, William of Conches, Alexander Neckham, Alexander of Hales, Bartholomaeus Anglicus, and Gervaise of Tilbury.

3. Kenny, *Palace,* 15.

4. Ed. Connochie-Bourgne, 12–13; *Image du monde,* v. 11; Centili, "La seconda redazione," 173 (quoting v. 2). According to Shackleton, "Encyclopedic Spirit," 378–79, the title "encyclopedia" was conferred retrospectively on Alan of Lille's *Anticlaudianus* in a printing of 1536, and on Ramón Llull in one of 1565.

5. *Encyclopédie* is coined from the Greek encuclopaidei, found just once in Quintilian, *Institutiones oratoriae* 1.10.1.

6. Indeed, the Renaissance image of the circle is a figure of interconnection rather than a template for organization. Reversion to a treelike disposition is found in Descartes; Levi, "Ethics," 172.

7. Françon, "Humanisme," 525. Françon documents slippage by the time of Cicero from the notional addressee as child to citizen.

manner of Honorius's *Elucidarium,* a text that was repeatedly translated into both French and Occitan.[8] Even though the alphabetically ordered encyclopedia makes its first appearance in the Middle Ages,[9] most medieval examples are intended to be read through from start to finish, as is made clear, for instance, by the prologue to the first redaction of the *Image du monde:*

Si lise tout premierement
et adés ordeneement
si qu'il ne lise riens avant
s'il n'entent ce qui est devant. (5–9)

(He should read the very beginning and then in order, so he doesn't read on unless he has understood what precedes.)[10]

While it is helpful to distinguish between encyclopedias as works that systematically organize many disciplines and summas as treatises offering comprehensive coverage of just one, the medieval view that theology encapsulated all the other sciences means that, in practice, summas of religious knowledge overlap extensively with encyclopedias. This is especially the case when, as ordinarily happens, encyclopedias begin with God and then work down to the created world. Overshadowed by divinity, the human knowledge they outline includes awareness of its own limitations: it cannot possibly measure up to the divine. Adam's sin, the master says discouragingly to his student in the *Lumere as lais,* means that however hard we labor, we cannot know all there is to know.[11] Preferred Latin titles such as *imago* or *speculum,* or the vernacular *image* or *mappe,* situate both encyclopedias and religious summas as an image or reflection of the world, and may imply acknowledgment of their works' imperfect mimesis of totality.[12] Among the works this chapter discusses are some that, like the *Lumere as lais,* can be considered religious summas, as well as more secular encyclopedias.

8. Lefèvre, *L'Elucidarium.*
9. Collison, *Encyclopaedias,* 46; for alphabetical ordering in other forms of compilation, see Goyet, "Encyclopédie."
10. Cf. *Placides et Timéo,* a late-thirteenth-century French prose dialog between a philosopher and a royal prince, which warns readers not to skip so much as a word lest they miss a vital step; ed. Thomasset, 2.4. Continuous reading is also demanded by antique encyclopedias; Collison, *Encyclopaedias,* 21.
11. Ed. Hesketh, vv. 2540–51.
12. Connochie-Bourgne, "*Miroir* ou *image.*"

From Vernacular Verse Encyclopedias to Verse Encyclopedic Texts

As the development of vernacular encyclopedism in France is not widely known, we begin with a brief outline. First, in verse, from the twelfth century onward are found works devoted to a particular field of knowledge such as bestiaries, lapidaries, *computs* (texts enabling the calculation of calendars), and geography (notably Pierre de Beauvais's pre-1218 *Mappemonde*).[13] Then, in the second third of the thirteenth century, there comes the brief age of the vernacular verse encyclopedia. The text usually hailed as the first French example is the *Image du monde,* of which a first version, extending over 6,586 lines of octosyllabic couplets in the edition by Chantal Connochie-Bourgne, was composed in 1245.[14] It was preceded, however, in Anglo-Norman by the anonymous *Petite Philosophie* (ca. 1230), which, like the French *Image* and the *Mappemonde,* freely adapts Honorius of Autun's *Imago mundi.* The 1245 *Image du monde* was rapidly followed by at least one other verse redaction and a *mise en prose.* While the prose version, dated 1247 by its editor, is closely modeled on the first verse redaction, the second rhymed version, thought to date from 1248, completely overhauls and restructures the original, expanding it to a length of nearly eleven thousand octosyllabic lines.[15] This later rhymed *Image* was either preceded or followed by an intermediate redaction that amplifies the original verse text without revising it to the same extent.[16] Some but not all scholars think that all the versions of the *Image du monde,* verse and prose, are by the same author, probably named Gossuin de Metz. The *Image du monde* proved a medieval best-seller: if we take all its versions together, more than two hundred manuscripts survive.[17] Ironically, in view of all the energy that must have been expended on revising it, the original verse redaction remained the most widely circulated.[18]

This brief window in the second third of the thirteenth century also saw the production in Occitania of the much shorter *Thezaur* of Peire Corbian (sometime between 1230 and 1250), which reads more like a recapitulation of fields of knowledge than a guide to their content.[19] In a similar time frame,

---

13. Pierre de Beauvais, *La Mappemonde.*
14. See also Connochie-Bourgne, "L'Œuvre exemplaire."
15. Centili, "La seconda redazione," and her edition "La seconda redazione"; also Connochie-Bourgne, "Pourquoi et comment?"
16. See Prior's introduction to his edition, 5–7; Centili refers to this as "Redaction *H*" because it is transmitted by MS BL Harley 4333.
17. Connochie-Bourgne, *L'Image du monde,* 6.
18. Ibid., 39–40, lists seventy, and describes all those the whereabouts of which are still known.
19. Léglu, "Memory, Teaching, and Performance."

vernacular verse devotional summas also appear, like the *Manuel des pechiez* of William of Waddington (ca. 1260) and the similarly Anglo-Norman but rather more encyclopedic *Lumere as lais* by Peter of Fetcham (ca. 1267, just under fourteen thousand lines long).[20] We are aware of only one verse encyclopedia being composed in the last third of the thirteenth century, and that not in France but in Occitania, a region that (like Anglo-Norman England; see chapter 1) tends to conserve verse longer than northern France. The work in question is, however, the most ambitious of them all: the *Breviari d'amor* by Matfre Ermengaud of Béziers, composed from 1288 to around 1292, and remaining unfinished at approximately 35,000 lines. Both it and the *Lumere as lais* are discussed later in this chapter.

As this outline makes clear, no sooner is the verse encyclopedia launched than it faces stiff competition from prose. The first French prose work generally recognized as an encyclopedia is none other than the *mise en prose* of the verse *Image du monde*. It was conspicuously less successful than the verse versions, surviving in only eight manuscripts, although it did serve as the base for subsequent translations into Hebrew (1280) and later, by Caxton, into English (1480). Brunetto Latini's famous *Tresor* of the mid-1260s marks his own turning away from the verse encyclopedism of his earlier *Tesoretto* and establishes the primacy of the prose medium. It is followed before the end of the century by the *Livre de Sydrac*[21] and *Placides et Timeo*. A number of religious treatises with a broadly homiletic remit are likewise composed from the middle years of the thirteenth century onward. The best known are the *Miroir du monde* (possibly 1270s), a French prose treatise on vices and virtues, and its even more influential close relative, *Le Somme le roi,* written in 1278–79 by the Dominican Friar Laurent of Orléans for Philip the Bold; the two works were often confused or transmitted together.[22]

Before the end of the thirteenth century, barely half a century after it has begun, the composition of vernacular verse encyclopedias and religious summas comes to an abrupt halt—although, significantly, manuscript production of the existing works does not, the verse *Image du monde,* for example, being copied well into the sixteenth century,[23] and having significantly more

20. On date and authorship, see Hesketh's edition, 3.1–5, where Fetcham is identified as a town in Surrey, England. On other Anglo-Norman devotional works, see 3.5–11.

21. Connochie-Bourgne, "La Tour de Boctus." The text, which at this writing had not yet been edited in full, stages a dialog between a pagan king, Bochus, and a Christian *astronomien,* Sydrac; the scholar avoids being executed for refusing to acknowledge the pagan gods by answering the king's questions about the Christian religion.

22. *The Mirroure of the Worlde,* ed. Raymo et al., 6–11.

23. Kenny, *Palace,* 18.

manuscript witnesses than Brunetto Latini's *Tresor.*[24] By the fourteenth century, then, prose is the standard form in which to compose both of these encyclopedic genres. Here is a case in which the rise of prose seems indeed to have precipitated a decline in verse. This decline, however, corresponds with a new birth: that of the verse encyclopedic text. From the late thirteenth century on, rather than aspiring to know the world in a unified way, verse authors instead record how our experiences of knowing it tend toward fragmentation and distortion. They take pieces from the encyclopedist's map of knowledge and insert and variously frame them within other texts that are not themselves verse encyclopedias, but that, by virtue of these insertions, merit the designation "encyclopedic verse." This development from verse encyclopedias to encyclopedic verse transforms the way French poetry transmits knowledge of the world.

From the last third of the thirteenth century, Jean de Meun's continuation of the *Roman de la rose* provides an influential model for combining passages of scientific interest alongside moral, theological, and historical content. So too does the *Ovide moralisé,* the allegoreses of which collectively contain not only a summa of religious doctrine but also a universal history and vast amounts of information about geography and cosmography.[25] The insertion of encyclopedic passages within broadly didactic texts becomes a literary vogue contemporary with, and analogous to, the technique of so-called lyric insertion (see chapter 5); the two practices are sometimes found in the same texts, as, for example, in Froissart's *Joli buisson de Jonece,* to which we return in the last section of this chapter. In encyclopedic texts the emphasis on process and participation typical of the medieval encyclopedia remains, but the experience that is thereby being shaped is no longer that of a student in need of education (a role often heartily derided, as in the *Rose*). Rather it is that of a reader or addressee with wide-ranging cultural tastes and distinctly adult preoccupations such as erotic love and government.

Whereas verse encyclopedias embrace unity rather than totality, the unsystematic treatment of kinds of knowledge in encyclopedic texts openly admits that totality is impossible. In attempting to explain this shift from verse encyclopedias to encyclopedic verse, we need first to understand how thirteenth-century vernacular encyclopedias are structured, and then how that structure was undone from within by one of their own tropes: that of the tree of knowledge.

---

24. Brunetto Latini's *Tresor* survives in seventy-seven copies, *Sydrach* in sixty-three, and *Placides et Timeo* in eight.

25. Ribémont, "L'*Ovide moralisé*"; Possamaï-Perez, *L'Ovide moralisé,* 730–48.

Verse and Prose: Organizing Knowledge in Vernacular Encyclopedias

An interesting overview of possible schemes of knowledge is given by Guil-hem Molinier in the 1356 redaction of his prose treatise, the *Leys d'amors* (1:71–82). Initially, he explains, philosophy was conceived as comprising the seven liberal arts—grammar, rhetoric, and dialectic in the *trivium,* geometry, arithmetic, music, and astronomy in the *quadrivium*—but this conception has since been overtaken. One scheme, which he attributes to Augustine, adduces as its three principal subdivisions the rational or logical, the moral, and the natural; the logical sciences comprise grammar, mathematics, dialectic, and rhetoric (in that order); the natural sciences comprise physics, alchemy, as-tronomy, and medicine; the moral science is undivided. Another scheme, says Molinier, supplements the liberal arts with the mechanical and the magical arts. Yet another has its basis in universal history: before Law, with Law, with Grace (in our time).[26] The distribution for which he ultimately opts (1:76–77) distinguishes between the theoretical, the practical, and the logical sciences, and is adapted from Brunetto Latini, whose *Tresor* is organized as a hierar-chical arrangement of branches of knowledge (see figure 1). Theology is the privileged discipline, as it was in medieval universities; other disciplines are slotted in as seems appropriate.[27]

Despite their variety, all Molinier's schemes presuppose a classification of the sciences. His conception of the encyclopedia is taxonomic and prosthetic: it is a means whereby the reader can acquire a set of tools corresponding to a set of disciplines. This is also the conception that determines the arrangement of Brunetto's *Tresor.* Perhaps the clearer *ordinatio* of prose treatises lends them to categorizing fields of knowledge in this way. Vernacular verse encyclopedias, by contrast, appear less to work through a taxonomy than to attempt a single, sequential understanding of the world. Starting with God and creation, they proceed, following their authors' preferences, to place emphasis either on the natural world (the *Image du monde*) or on human morality and spirituality (*Lumere as lais, Breviari d'amor*). The difference between prose and verse is not absolute, of course: putting theology first is not very different from putting God first. Verse encyclopedias, however, seem concerned above all to inquire into the nature of the world and to disclose the means by which we can grasp it. Consistent with what we have seen of other late medieval verse texts, they assume or insinuate subjectivity. As a result, they pose both metaphysical and

26. Isidore, *Etymologies* 8.9.
27. Connochie-Bourgne, "'Theorike' et 'théologie,'" argues that Brunetto makes rhetoric the most valued of the practical arts and theology the most valued of the theoretical ones.

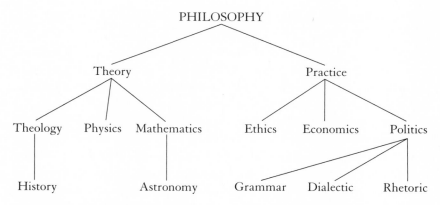

Figure 1   Diagram of how the disciplines relate to one another in Brunetto Latini's *Livres dou Tresor.*

hermeneutic challenges: What do we know of the world's nature, and how do we interpret it?

This interplay of metaphysical and hermeneutic implications emerges when one compares the first and second redactions of the verse *Image du monde.* Immediately following the opening with God and creation, the first redaction addresses human nature as made in the image of God yet liable to sin. At this point it inserts a chapter on the seven liberal arts, after which it moves on to the world of nature. Here are the rubrics of the opening book in London, BL Arundel 52:

> Le premiers chapitres est de la puisance de deu
> Li seconz pur quei deu fist le mond
> Li tierz por quei fist deu home a sa samblance
> Li quartz por quei deus ne fist home quil ne peust pecher
> Li quint por quei et coment les vii ars furent trouuez et lor ordre
> Li vi des iii. manieres de genz que li philophe [*sic*] poserent al monde et comment clergie vint auant en france
> Li vii de la maniere des vii ars
> Li viii de nature coment ele oure et que co est. (fol. 74v)

> (The first chapter is about God's power
> The second, why God made the world
> The third, why God made man in his likeness
> The fourth, why God did not make man in such a way that he could not sin
> The fifth, why and how the seven liberal arts were discovered, and their order

The sixth, of the three orders that philosophers distinguish in the world, and how
the order of *clergie* came to the fore in France
The eighth, of nature, how it operates, and what it is.)

Discussion of the natural world is framed first by our understanding of God's
purpose, and second by our own capacity to know. The religious opening reminds the reader of humanity's dependence on God and its inherent propensity to sin. As Connochie-Bourgne has shown, the liberal arts are the means by
which human reason is guided not only toward knowledge of the world as it is
now but also to an understanding of man's own original nature and his position in the divine plan.[28] Learning about the world is, at the same time, learning about oneself; knowledge that is presented as scientific is, at the same time,
moral knowledge. After thus calling attention to the way all understanding
is molded by our position in creation, book 1 continues its examination of
our earth and its elements; book 2 is dominated by geography and book 3 by
cosmography and astronomy.

The hermeneutic cast of this version of the *Image du monde* reflects the
influence of Isidore's *Etymologies,* pervasive in the early Middle Ages, and
summarized thus by Bernart Ribémont: "There is, in Isidore, a unitary vision
of Creation which is revealed through language as an intuited continuity
between man and the origins of the natural world and which is decipher-
able by means of an analysis of signifiers." As a result, "Isidore's etymological
method functions as the effort to create meaning in the context of a theory of
knowledge that relies upon a return to origins in the most traditional sense of
the word."[29] Although poetry as such is not at issue for Isidore (the *Etymologies*
is a prose work and does not envisage verse as a category), Isidore's emphasis on how the world needs to be grasped in its historicity through language
nonetheless clearly influences verse encyclopedists.

Barely two years later, the second verse redaction experiments with a different order whereby knowledge is presented less as a moral and spiritual
relationship, via language, to our divine origins than as a rational, intellectual
relationship with our situation in God's creation.[30] The difference emerges
clearly in the opening book, in which, instead of the exposition of human

28. Connoichie-Bourgne, "L'Œuvre exemplaire," 72. On Augustinian influence in the
Image, see Prior's introduction to the prose version, 32.

29. Ribémont, *Origines,* 17, 49.

30. Centili, "La seconda redazione," 177–84, makes the point in slightly different terms.
Connochie-Bourgne, "Pourquoi et comment?" 150, sees the difference between the versions primarily as one of audience, the second redaction being intended specifically for wealthy bourgeois
and merchants.

understanding being intercalated between God and nature, it follows them. Here are the opening rubrics of the second redaction as given in Centili's edition (based on Paris, BnF, ms. fr. 25353):

> Li premier chapitre est de Dieu e de sa grant bonté
> Loenge de la grant bonté de Dieu
> Li segont chapitre est de le nature que Diex cria premierement
> La description de nature: cen que li ancient en distrent
> Li tierz chapitre por quoi Dex fist le monde
> Por quoi Dex fist l'onme a sa semblance
> Por quoi Dex dona a honme poeir de fere bien ou mal
> Li quart chapitres est en quell maniere les ars furents trouvees
> Conment les clergies furent salvees par le deluge
> Conment les clergies furent retrouvees après le deluge
> Comme les VII ars liberaux sunt ordenees...etc.[31]

> (The first chapter is about God and his goodness
> Praise of God's great goodness
> The second chapter is about nature, which God created first
> Description of nature and what the Ancients said about it
> The third chapter, why God created the world
> Why God made man in his likeness
> Why God gave man the power to do good or evil
> The fourth chapter is about how the arts were invented
> How learning was saved by the flood
> How it was rediscovered after the flood
> The order of the seven liberal arts...etc.)

Instead of the natural world being the mysterious object that man strives to penetrate, with the benefit of a privileged relationship to God and the help of the liberal arts, now nature mediates between God and such knowledge as man is able to command. Though an object of his knowledge, it is also an aid to understanding. As part of the natural world, divinely ordained even if fallen, we can aspire to comprehend it. The second redaction of the *Image du monde* thus signals a more truly ontological strand in medieval encyclopedism that to some extent reverses the assumptions of the Isidorean hermeneutic. Jean de Meun's equivocal depiction of Nature in the *Roman de la rose*—is she a

---

31. Centili, "La seconda redazione," 203.

source of knowledge or merely one of its objects?—may be a reflection, within a single work, of these strangely twinned yet divergent epistemologies.

In the next section we explore how these two approaches to knowledge are compounded in a figure found in both the Anglo-Norman *Lumere as lais* and the Occitan *Breviari d'amor:* the tree of knowing good and evil. Both texts fall at the intersection of encyclopedism with the religious summa and treat questions of knowledge and interpretation from a more theologically informed perspective than the *Image du monde.* In the *Breviari* these epistemic paradoxes are explored in relation to poetry explicitly, as that of the troubadours is quoted and glossed.

Ontology and Hermeneutics in the "Tree of Knowing"

Both the *Lumere as lais* and the *Breviari d'amor* attribute a determining significance to the tree that God planted in paradise but whose fruit he forbade Adam and Eve to eat. In both texts the knowledge associated with the tree is represented as a process rather than an accomplished content. In the *Lumere,* Peter renders the Vulgate *lignum scientiae boni et mali* of Genesis 2:9 with an infinitive phrase that transforms the tree from one of *the knowledge* of good and evil to one of *knowing* them: "l'autre fust de mal et bien / saver ot sur tute rien / vertu" (the other, the tree of knowing good and evil, had more power than any, 63–65). In the *Breviari,* Matfre similarly designates the tree with an infinitive: "l'albre de saber lo ben e lo mal" (the tree of knowing good and evil, passim). And in both texts the tree supports important reflections on how these processes of knowledge are impaired. First, the tree exposes the extent to which our understanding of the world is always imperfect because it is always contaminated by desire; second, it shows the history of knowledge to be impossible to trace, since it is not clear if it originates in desire or if desire originates in it. The problematic of the tree, in other words, corresponds to the epistemological dilemma framed by the two versions of the *Image du monde.* Perception that is corrupted by the natural desires of our fallen state limits our capacity to apprehend the nature of things; and the uncertain origins of knowledge impact our ability to interpret it. The irresolution between ontology and hermeneutics, comic in the *Rose* here, strikes a somber chord.

For the most part, the *Lumere* is a dialog between a master and a student compiled using Peter Lombard's *Sentences* and Honorius of Autun's *Elucidarium,* but it begins with a preface authored by Peter himself (1–694), in which the themes of the tree of knowledge and the original sin that resulted from it are developed at length (63–178). Although eating the fruit of the tree brings knowledge of good and evil, Adam in fact already possessed this knowledge before eating the fruit (67–68); what it brought him was the *experience* of evil (69–70). With the origins of human knowledge problematized at the outset, the *Lumere* proper begins in the traditional way with an account of God, creation, the angels, and man, thereby quickly looping back to the topic of the forbidden fruit and the consequences of eating it (2383–2756). Eve and Adam sinned through the disobedience of the flesh; Eve more than Adam was guilty of carnal desires. The disobedience of the flesh, however, was also the *result* of eating the apple. In a similar paradox, it seems that knowledge was both acquired and lost in the fall. Without the fall, man would have had knowledge (*conisance,* 2496) of God, of himself, and of the world; he would have had knowledge (*science,* 2509) of everything without needing to learn; and he would have enjoyed a self-transparent knowledge (*science,* 2521) of his own soul in which there would have been only pure desires. But now that man has been undermined by sin, "ignorance est mis pour science / Et pur bien voler concupiscence, / Malice pur deboneireté" (ignorance is set in place of knowledge and base desire instead of pure will, evil intentions instead of original nobility, 2527–32). Although knowledge now is lacking to us, in another sense eating the apple has brought us knowledge of that lack.

Part religious summa and part encyclopedia, the *Breviari d'amor* similarly envisages desire both as responsible for the knowledge we acquired in the fall and as the result of the fall; and it sees the fruit of the tree of knowledge (or rather, of *knowing*) both as the means whereby knowledge was lost and as a source of knowledge—in this case, of a far greater and more positive kind than in the *Lumere*. In the Occitan treatise, the tree of knowing is grafted onto another tree, the *albre d'amor,* or "tree of love," that is described at the beginning of the *Breviari*. For Matfre, the *albre d'amor* is at once the organizing principle of his book and his means of mapping the world. It is depicted in a magnificent full-page illustration in the majority of manuscripts, and Matfre's vast text, composed "per declarar las figuras / del albre d'amors obscuras," (so as to clarify the obscure figures of the tree of love, 21–22), posits itself as a gloss on this image (see figure 2).

We noted earlier that a treelike structure tends to be the organizing trope of medieval encyclopedias. It often harks back to the "Porphyrian tree," a familiar image deriving from the way Porphyry, in his *Isagoge,* represents Aristotle's category of substance (*essentia* in scholastic Latin, or what philosophers today call "Being") as a set of branches forking downward from the genus to its species and subspecies and thence to individuals.[32] The tree of love

---

32. Collison, *Encyclopaedias,* 32, 47.

Figure 2   Image of the "tree of love" in the *Breviari d'amor* of Matfre Ermengaud. From London, BL Harley MS 4940, fol. 9r. Love descends from the top of the tree via the genus Love represented by the "Lady of the tree" and flows downward into the branches of "human law" (on the left) and "natural law" (on the right). The tree of knowledge of good and evil is the grafted tree that grows upward from this left-sloping branch; on the opposite side, the tree that is grafted is the tree of life. The leaves on these two grafted trees represent the virtues that they bear, but they have not been labeled with their names in this particular manuscript; the other two smaller grafts have not been depicted in it either. © The British Library Board.

in the *Breviari* clearly shares this ontological function. Starting with God and descending through creation, it charts the flow of God's Being-as-Love as it is realized throughout the universe.[33] Matfre's tree has two main branches, corresponding to the classical distinction between natural law, which governs all the natural world, and human law, which governs the behavior specifically of human beings.[34] The legal framework is integrated into the tree of love by the fact that, for Matfre, human law covers the specific capacity of human beings to recognize God's love for them, to love him in return, and to love their neighbor (this part of the encyclopedia is essentially about religious life); whereas natural law governs the sexual and reproductive love that human beings share with other animals (and is Matfre's opportunity to talk about secular life). In depicting these two forms of law as deriving from God as Love, Matfre points to what he sees as their origin as the means to understand them properly. The *albre d'amor* thus serves an ontological purpose (showing the interrelation of all Being in God, on the model of the Porphyrian tree), and a hermeneutical one (interpreting the principles regulating human behavior in the light of our origin in God's love).

As long as God's creatures are faithful to their divine nature and obedient to the laws to which they are subject, they are virtuous and fruitful. In order to represent and encourage this capacity for good, Matfre posits four growths additional to the *albre d'amor,* two of which are grafted onto each of its two main branches. The main graft on the side of human beings and human law is the tree of life, planted in Eden according to Genesis 2:9; its leaves are the cardinal and theological virtues, and its fruit is eternal life. The main branch of the *albre d'amor* constituted by all animate creatures also supports two grafts. The small one has, as its fruit and leaves, children and the qualities of parenting; it designates a section of the encyclopedia that deals with love of one's offspring, which was intended to follow the section on sexual love but was never completed. The most important graft on the side of animate beings, and the counterpart of the tree of life on the other side, is grafted onto the branch of sexual love: the *albre de saber.*

If a treelike structure such as the *albre d'amor* lends itself to conceptualizing relations between beings and the tracing of significance back to its point of origin, both of these features are thrown into disarray by the existence of these grafts. Having other, different trees grafted onto its stock unsettles its capacity to represent the One-ness of all Being.[35] And grafting also insinuates

33. Kay, *Place of Thought,* chap. 1.
34. This was first pointed out by Meyer, "Matfre Ermengaud," 20.
35. Kay, *Place of Thought,* chap. 1.

uncertainty about priority and the path that interpretation should follow.[36] On the one hand, the grafts implanted onto the tree of love are in some sense secondary to it; on the other hand, it is obviously possible for an older tree to be grafted onto a younger stock. When the tree of knowing good and evil is grafted onto the branch of sexual love, it is clear that Matfre is positing an intimate association between knowledge and carnal desire. But it is not plain which, if either, of the two is prior to and thus determines the other. (We rediscover this indeterminacy from a different perspective in chapter 5 in our discussion of the reversibility of lyric insertion.)

Let us now look specifically at Matfre's account of the *albre de saber*. Although his fullest discussion of it is reserved for the section on sexual love (27252–34539), the tree of knowing is first presented much earlier. Like the *Lumere* though at more length, the *Breviari* begins with God, the creation, and the fall. Matfre follows the Bible closely as he retells how Adam and Eve were forbidden to taste the fruit of the tree; when they disobeyed, the outcome was guilt, exile, and death (7978–8205). But when he returns to the *albre de saber* in the context of sexual love, it has become a tree of the virtues that can be acquired in the course of a secular life. Its leaves, as detailed by Matfre, are the qualities possessed by those with a truly courtly understanding of sexual love: largesse, courage, courtliness, humility, and so on. These worldly virtues and vices are now the good and the evil whose knowledge is transmitted by the tree. *Fin' amor* properly understood, Matfre claims equally unexpectedly, promotes matrimony as the most desirable of all the worldly virtues: the fruit of the tree of knowledge of good and evil is a married couple's capacity to produce children.

Matfre explicitly raises the question why the *albre de saber* should be presented in such a contradictory fashion. How can a fruit that was hitherto forbidden, and whose consequences were so disastrous, also be so virtuous (27541–47)? His answer is that everything depends on intention (*entencio*, 27549). Lovers who wish to acquire the knowledge of the tree must learn to control their will by avoiding excessive contact with women and by keeping their language as pure as possible. Control of meaning is the same as control of intention, because speech gives form to thought, and thought corrupts desire. The tree is a source of virtue for those who are pure of spirit, and the rarefied discourse of the troubadours can guide us to achieve this purity in earthly desire. Matfre prepares the ground here for his interpretation and commentary of approximately 260 extracts from troubadour poetry that are interspersed in his discussion of sexual love.

36. Kay, "L'Arbre et la greffe."

Thus it becomes apparent that for Matfre, understanding human nature in relation to divine love, and knowing the human capacity for virtue, can both be achieved by a correct reading of vernacular love poetry; but the stakes are high. On the one hand, such poetry poses a terrible danger to readers, equivalent to the temptations undergone by Adam and Eve in the garden. Just as God forbade Adam and Eve to eat the fruit of the tree, Matfre prohibits his readers from reading the "treatises" (*tractatz*) that follow. The only exceptions are the *tractat* providing remedies against love (33882–35439), and "the one about the branch" ("aquell del ram," 27621), the section dealing with the *albre de saber,* which lists the virtues of the tree and the vices that threaten to destroy them (31934–33462). Matfre prohibits the other *tractatz* as being liable to lead readers into mortal sin: "for one can scarcely read the treatise without eating the forbidden fruit and succumbing to carnal delight" (quar a greu lieg hom lo tractat / que no mange del frug vedat, / al delieg carnal cosenten, 27643–45). Yet if readers are successful in maintaining good love as the human reflex of divine love, the tree of knowledge of good and evil, from having been the death-bearing tree, can become the foundation of an ethical life. Readers must therefore read according to a hermeneutic of charity, which not only will enable them to benefit from Matfre's text (27659–62) but also will be the *only* means whereby they can apprehend their true nature as loving beings within the totality of Being as Love.

In the *Breviari,* then, the process of knowing good and evil requires a complex negotiation with the contradictory structure of the grafted tree. Because the *albre de saber* is a graft, it is both secondary to and prior to the experience of sexual love represented by the branch onto which it is grafted. Repeating the action that constituted the fall—that of eating its fruit—is perilous, but it is also the sole means of returning to the time before it and of restoring our unity with God's Being. The fractured hermeneutic and ontology of the graft are Matfre's way of imagining how the consequences of sin can succeed in effacing their own cause. Central to this process is the proper understanding of love poetry.

Grafted Trees and Grafted Flowers (*Florilegium*)

The excerpts of troubadour song that stud the last seven thousand or so lines of the *Breviari* make up an abundant *florilegium.* Like the *albre de saber,* the quotations can be conceived as grafts from earlier texts, from which Matfre wrestles "sound doctrine, sound arguments, and sound judgments, sound qualities and sound behaviors" (bonas doctrinas, / e bonas razos, e bos sens, / bos aibs e bells captenemens, 27786–88) on behalf of his readers. He does so through a paradoxical leap back, via the graft, so as to read the quotations as expressions of love as it was or should have been were it not for the fall. Valerie Fasseur has already shown how troubadour songs are resignified by Matfre in harmony with his theological tenets.[37] Here we examine just two examples of how he recuperates originary meaning from the excerpts that he quotes, one from the "perilous treatise" and one from the "treatise of the tree."

The first is a stanza from Folquet de Marselha's "Per Dieu, amors, ben sabetz veramen" that features as part of the debate between Matfre and love's detractors (*maldizen*) which opens the *perilhos tractat*. The *maldizen* are the first to quote Folquet, claiming him for their cause by quoting another song in which Folquet appears to renounce love (28281–88). Matfre counters with a second quotation from the same song, contending that the *maldizen's* understanding is faulty: Folquet's complaint was not against love but against false love (28195–202). Matfre observes that in "Per Dieu, amors, ben sabetz veramen," Folquet upholds true love but is aware of its exalted demands, and thus of the risk of falling short of them:

Mas de ver'amor ell mezeis
digs que falhimen non pot far,
e que mais s'en fera blasmar,
si fezes lunh'error o mal,
quez un autr', aitan quan mais val,
don digs az est' amor mout gen:
Mas vos no·m par puscatz far failimen,
pero, quan failh cell qu'es pros ni prezatz,
tan quan val mais, tan n'es plus encolpatz
qu'en la valor puega·l colp' e dichen. (28211–20)

(But of true love, he himself said that it could not err, and that the worthier a man is, the likelier it is that he would be criticized more than someone else if he committed some fault or wrong. And therefore he spoke nobly to this love: "But it does not seem to me that you could possibly err, and yet, when a man errs who is worthy or esteemed, then the greater his reputation, the more he is blamed, because just like worth, reproach rises and then descends.")

Matfre's reading of this stanza opposes not only that of love's fictional detractors but also that of an actual, roughly contemporary gloss transmitted

37. Galent-Fasseur, "Mort et salut."

by one of the troubadour songbooks known to Occitanists as *chansonnier H.*[38] The *H* commentator incorporates this stanza into his diatribe against women's high-handed behavior. He begins with customary prescriptiveness: "aqestas coblas mostran qe las grans autas dompnas no creson poder faillir" (these *coblas* show that great ladies of high rank believe they can do no wrong). He then interprets the stanza as meaning that the greater women's rank (*ricor*), the lower their fall; although they may be forgiven the specific fault they have committed, once they have erred, they will never be free from shame and suspicion. The stanza is reduced to its incipit, which differs from Matfre's text in that it reads, "Mas vos non par poscatz far faillimen" (but it does not seem to you that you could commit a fault).[39] For the *H* glossator, Folquet's text is an aggressive and justifiable denunciation of haughty women; for Matfre, by distinguishing between the supreme value of love and the disgrace that may engulf those who practice it unworthily, Folquet is conveying, in a nutshell, the lesson of the whole *perilhos tractat:* that lovers must both embrace *ver' amor* (true love) and recognize the perilous consequences of betraying it. By this bold reading, Matfre makes the troubadour the vehicle of his own encyclopedic purpose.

Each of the quotations in the section on the tree of knowledge of good and evil is chosen in order to promote a particular virtue borne by the tree. The introduction to our second example, an excerpt from Arnaut Daniel's "En breu brisara.l temps braus," is characteristic in the way it highlights the virtue in question, here *proeza* (excellence):

> Encaras han li aimador
> proeza gran per est'amor
> lo qual non lur toll vens ni gels,
> per sso digs N'Arnautz Daniels,
> a cui Dieus do verai repaus:
>> Amors es de pretz la claus
>> e de proeza estancs
>> don naicho tug li bo frug,
>> ab qu'om lialmen los cuelha;
>> qu'un non deligs gels ni muelha
>> mentre·s noirigs el bon tronc;
>> mas si·l rom trefas ni·l cuelh
>> vertz mor tro lials lo s'agre. (*Breviari,* 32568–80)[40]

---

38. Vatican Library Lat 3207.

39. Poe, *Compilatio,* 211.

40. We adapt Ricketts's edition of lines 32579–80 in order to preserve the line division of the *Breviari* manuscripts (also retained by Richter in *Die Troubadourzitate*). In Ricketts's text, *vertz*

(In addition, lovers have great excellence through this love, which wind or ice does not strip them of, and for this reason Arnaut Daniel [to whom God grant eternal rest] said: "Love is the key of merit and the post of excellence from which grow all good fruits, provided they are picked lawfully; for ice nor damp does not destroy a single one as long as it is nourished by the good trunk; but if an evil man plucks or picks it, it [the fruit?] dies green until a loyal person takes delight in it.")

This translation is rather unsatisfactory, but it confirms the insight of other critics that Arnaut Daniel's tree image appealed to Matfre as a *mise en abyme* of his own *albre d'amor*.[41] We go further, however, in seeing in this stanza an allusion to the practice of grafting. How can love and excellence both be produced from the same plant? If *estanc* is understood as "stock," so that love is the stock on which other virtues are grafted, the text becomes much clearer. The opening lines of the quotation would then mean "love is . . . the stock that makes it possible to cultivate *proeza,* the source of all good fruit." Arnaut's image would then be encapsulating the whole of the *Breviari* not just as a tree, but as a tree of love onto which trees of virtues are grafted. The line following, moreover, specifically evokes the danger of taking its fruit in a manner contrary to law. The quotation, then, more precisely mirrors its immediate context in the *Breviari:* that of the *albre de saber* and its forbidden fruit.

Unfortunately it is difficult to say precisely how this image is developed because the excerpt's final lines are somewhat opaque. Gianluigi Toja edits the song in a form different from the one it takes in the *Breviari* in both word and line division:

q'un non delis gel ni niula
mentre qe·s noiris el bon tronc;
mas si·l romp trefas ni culvertz
peris tro lials lo sagre.[42]

(For neither ice nor fog destroys a single one of these fruit as long as it is nourished from the good trunk; but if an evil man or a rascal plucks it, it perishes until an upright man sanctifies it.)

---

falls at the end of the penultimate line of the stanza, as it does in all editions of Arnaut's song. Note also that in Ricketts's 1976 edition, the last rhyme word was given as *sagre,* revised in the forthcoming edition to *s'agre.*

41. See Nicholson, "Branches of Knowledge," 380–81; and Galent-Fasseur, "Mort et salut," 437.

42. Ed. Toja, 11:13–16.

By reading *culvert,* "rascal," in the penultimate line, Toja stresses the malice of any person who picks the fruit illicitly, before then invoking, not altogether clearly, some kind of sacred context that could efface the wrong thus committed. In *Breviari* manuscripts, however, the world *vertz* opens the final line instead of ending the penultimate one. We translated, "but if an evil man plucks or picks it, it [the fruit?] dies green until a loyal person takes delight in it." But if we adopt Toja's gloss on *sagre* as "sanctify," we can understand instead, "but if a wicked person breaks off the fruit or picks it contrary to the law, that person dies cut off in his youth, unless he is sanctified by someone who observes the law." Or more freely, "the one who picks the fruit of the forbidden tree is struck down unless he is redeemed by the One who upholds law." In short, Arnaut's brief lyric stanza, as quoted by Matfre, comes to convey the essentials of the Christian faith from the fall to redemption—a far cry from its meaning in the *chansonnier* tradition, where it is probably no more than an ingenious eulogy of *fin' amor.* Matfre barely alters its wording, but he manages to recode, or resignify, it in such a way as to endow it with the originary sense that it *should* have had.

We see how Matfre's act of quotation intensifies the temporal paradox of the graft. He includes the extract from Folquet de Marselha in such a way as to make it appear—contrary to its treatment elsewhere—to uphold a lofty ideal of pure love easily corrupted; now he has added the Arnaut excerpt in what similarly appears to be a revised or at least reinterpreted form. In this respect the quotations are certainly *later* than the *Breviari.* At the same time, not only do they derive from *earlier* poems, but also they transmit an *ententio* that belongs to a time long before their supposed authors, Folquet and Arnaut, composed them, the time of God's *ententio* for redemption. The *mise en abyme* that these quotations effect extends, beyond the topology of the tree and the graft, to our originary place in the love of God forfeited by the forbidden fruit and its consequences.

Like other medieval encyclopedias, the *Breviari* plots knowledge as a process in which the reader must participate. And more than any other, it pushes against the ontological and hermeneutical challenges that verse encyclopedias and religious summas all to some degree confront. If the *Divine Comedy* can be reckoned a vernacular verse encyclopedia, it is the only one to have gone further than the *Breviari* in its program of rereading poetry, since Dante adds classical authors to the hermeneutic mix. We would question, however, whether Dante's poem is ontologically as ambitious as Matfre's, since the *albre d'amor* and its constituent grafts present a uniquely complex model for representing Being as Love in God.

Whatever Dante's achievements, in France vernacular verse encyclopedists seem to concede the enormous challenges raised by the *Image du monde,* the *Lumere,* and the *Breviari.* Finding both the path of ontology and that of hermeneutics to be equally problematic, by the end of the thirteenth century they abandon the aspiration to encyclopedic unity as being too much for a single subjectivity to apprehend. Encyclopedia writing becomes exclusively the domain of prose, perhaps because prose, more objective and less situated, lends itself better to enumerating the contents covered by the various disciplines. The emphasis proper to verse, that of disclosing knowledge and understanding, instead finds expression in what we call encyclopedic texts.

In the two final sections of this chapter, we consider how universal history and cosmology are treated in encyclopedic texts. These two topics have been singled out for discussion because universal history, which marshals events from creation to the end of the world, corresponds with the hermeneutic strand in medieval encyclopedism (understood in the Isidorean sense of tracing meaning back to its origins), while cosmology, which seeks to grasp the workings of the natural universe, corresponds with its ontological strand. If a full command of either is impossible, then at least the processes of *savoir* can be used to disclose their partiality.

Universal History in Encyclopedic Texts

Partiality is flaunted in encyclopedic texts that fragment, dwarf, or otherwise radically reframe universal history. While their authors are not necessarily as pessimistic as those of the *Breviari* and the *Lumere,* the theme of a paradoxical "tree of knowing," by means of which knowledge of man's place in time is both gained and lost, seems to have helped to promote interest in universal history as a way of making sense of everything yet simultaneously as that whose overall sense escapes us. Because of our exclusion from eternity, the total meaning of time is inevitably elusive, and the processes of *savoir* are the closest we can get to overall *science.* Another, related reason for the interest of encyclopedic texts in universal history is that the place encyclopedias accord to history is variable and sometimes nonexistent. In the *Breviari,* just before the account of creation there is a short account (6757–902) of how world history is divided into six ages; it is illustrated with a circle representing the ages of a universal history (see figure 3). Though not extensive, in a sense this passage determines the whole of the rest of the text, from before human existence to redemption through love; a similar conception of salvation history motivates the *Lumere as lais,* but it is nowhere made explicit, and the work accords no place at all to secular history as such. In verse versions of the *Image du monde,* history shrinks to the short chapter on the development and transmission of *clergie.* In Brunetto's *Tresor,* history is classified under theology, that is, among the "theoretical" as opposed to the "practical" sciences. Thus history is either a unifying principle of knowledge that is hard to grasp, or else a part of knowledge that is difficult to place.

The perfect circle described in figure 3 is never realized; instead it is dismantled in the ways universal histories appear in late medieval encyclopedic verse. The *Ovide moralisé* weaves a fragmented version of salvation history into the glosses surrounding Ovid's juicy tales; as we saw in chapter 2, Eustache Deschamps intersperses his critique of marriage and women in the *Miroir de Mariage* with gobbets of global history, with the result that the battle of the sexes and political events come to serve as weirdly distorting mirrors one of the other. We have chosen to focus on two texts that do not fragment universal history like these do but instead frame it in unlooked-for ways, and that further offset verse against prose: the anonymous *Renart le contrefet* and the *Mutacion de Fortune* of Christine de Pizan.

Renart le contrefet casts doubt on the capacity of encyclopedic verse to comprehend universal history by setting it within the frame of the beast epic—for beasts, after all, have no understanding of history. This vast rambling text, in octosyllabic couplets like the *Roman de Renart,* which serves as its point of departure, survives in two redactions, one of about 32,000 lines and the other about 41,000 lines long. The eponymous fox has a more specifically political role than in the *Roman de Renart,* one seemingly influenced by Fausemblant in Jean de Meun's continuation of the *Roman de la rose.*[43] Renart's use and abuse of history occurs primarily in branch 2 of *Renart le contrefet* (*Renart le Contrefait,* 1:35–297, vv. 3199–22214). When Tibert the cat invites Renart into his tent, there is an extended ekphrasis of the paintings that decorate its interior, ranging in a disorderly fashion from the conquest of Troy (3759–3850) to the story of Jason and Medea (4119–38), to Caradoc (4325–4422), the battles of Lancelot and Meleagan (4423–36), and the plagues of Egypt (4437–90). Summoned before the lion king to account for his misdeeds (5977–82), Renart responds that his "arts" predate the creation of the world (5985–88), and proceeds to recount a universal history of their efficacy through such episodes as the fall of the angels, the creation and fall of man, the Tower of Babel, the story of David, and the rule of Caesar (this brings us to line 9230). Prompted by the king, Renart further exemplifies his activities in the exploits of Alexander and the rise and fall of the ancient empires of Babylon, Greece, Carthage, and Rome. As Nancy Freeman Regalado observes, "the historical materials

---

43. Badel, *Le Roman de la rose,* chap. 5, though Badel's reading of *Renart le contrefait* does not give enough credit to the poem's energy and originality.

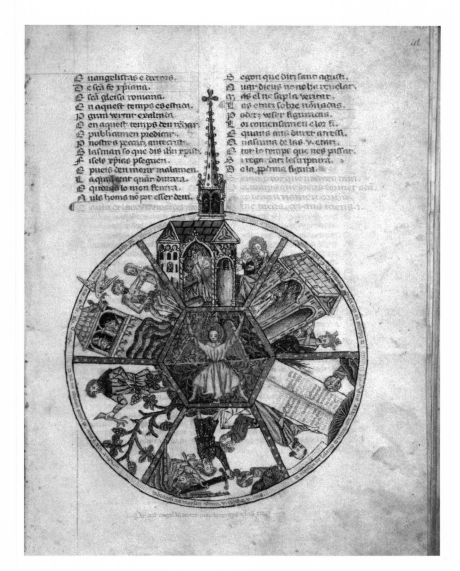

Figure 3   Image of universal history from the *Breviari d'amor* of Matfre Ermengaud. From Lyon, BM MS 1351, fol. 42r. Starting with the Fall and ending with the Church, the intervening images depict Noah, Abraham, the sacrifice of Isaac, Moses with the tablets of the law, and Solomon building the temple, perhaps illustrating the gamut of different possible relations to the law. Reproduced with permission of the Bibliothèque Municipale, Lyon.

in *Renart le contrefet* are folded *inside* the satire, thereby transforming the whole history of the world into a monstrous exemplum of deceitful *renardie.*"[44] History is both a totalizing narrative and one that is suborned by individual desire—in this case, one that is malicious and diabolical in nature.

Soon after this point, the king asks Renart to use prose instead of verse:

> Mais je te charge par exprez
> Que de rymer tu te deportes,
> Et qu'en prose tu le m'aportes,
> Car y porras myeulx exprimer
> Leurs vyes et leurs fais compter
> Que en rymant tu ne feroyes,
> Car du langage y perderoyes. (22198–204)

(But I charge you expressly to desist from rhyme and tell it to me in prose, because you will better express their lives and deeds than you would in verse, which wastes words.)

The lion seemingly favors prose as more concise and more suited to expressing sacred history. Since "se deporter" (22199) also means "take pleasure in," perhaps he also seeks to quash the malicious delight Renart takes in his own slewed historiography. The dialog structure whereby the king elicits information fades into the background as Renart narrates in prose the history of Christian empire and its saints. His exposition adopts a more impersonal mode, less tainted by his own character, as though his fallen, animal account of universal history were temporarily "voiced over" by the narrator's intuition of the divine. The branch ends with a pious verse prayer that we be spared Renart's deviant ways (22405–14). In this text, then, universal history is framed on the outside by foxy evil but hollowed out from within by the promise of redemption that is rendered in a form seemingly external to fallen subjectivity by the medium of prose.

Although it is not perverse like *Renart le contrefet,* Christine de Pizan's *Mutacion de Fortune* treats universal history in a manner that is just as provocative and eloquent a testimony to the way authors of encyclopedic verse experienced its totality as compromised; again, prose irrupts as a reminder of this. Christine begins this text with an account of her personal misfortune when, losing her husband to death soon after their marriage, she metaphorically

---

44. See Regalado, *"Chronique métrique,"* 275.

became a man (see chapter 3). She then describes the citadel of Fortune to which she is taken, its gates, their guardians, and the paths that lead to it (1461–2472). This is followed by a section on the institutions and estates of the world that live in Fortune's house (2473–7052). Nearly the whole of the rest of the text consists in her account of universal history as it is depicted in the paintings that decorate the interior of Fortune's great hall. Barely has she begun, however, than Christine interrupts her account with a thousand-line ekphrasis of a depiction of the sciences "par bel ordre ordenees" (ordered in a fine and orderly manner, 7186), presided over on high by the figure of Philosophy (7173–8068). In essence, Christine here presents us with the outline of an encyclopedia, which is structured according to the two branches of theoretical and practical knowledge (the division depicted on Philosophy's robe in the *Consolation*), and which thereafter follows the same subdivisions as Brunetto Latini's *Tresor* (see figure 1). Theoretical knowledge comprises theology, physics, and mathematics (including arithmetic, music, geometry, and astronomy); the practical sciences are ethics, economics, and politics, with grammar and rhetoric being ranged under politics. Admitting that this outline has been something of a digression (8069–70), Christine then resumes her historical survey for about twenty thousand lines, concluding somewhat hastily with the problems of contemporary Europe and her own unhappy experiences.

The bizarre ways in which universal history is framed in the *Mutacion* are especially reminiscent of the paradoxical temporality of the biblical knowledge trees in religious encyclopedias. At the outermost limit, the whole of secular time is inserted into Christine's personal history, making autobiography appear the frame through which the history of the world has to be read (just as, in the encyclopedias, the fall into temporality is both precipitated and followed by human desire). It is also structured by the four walls of Fortune's hall; as Christine's own life comes to make sense in terms of the overall fluctuations of history, or at least to be relativized by them, she experiences a kind of "consolation of Fortune" rather than a consolation of Philosophy. This casting of Fortune in Philosophy's role is perhaps the boldest instance of the "transformation of Fortune" of the work's title: in the *Consolation* it is Philosophy that mimics and plays the role of Fortune, the better to denounce her inherent falsity; but in the *Mutacion* the priority is reversed, and Philosophy occupies a seemingly incidental role *within* the works of Fortune/history.

Although Philosophy is described within the unfolding of historical time, she is located above it, and independent of it. The outline encyclopedia that Christine presents at this point is a digression, and history has no place among its disciplines. Moreover, if history is part of Fortune and Fortune is the antithesis of Philosophy, there *should* be no room for history in Philosophy;

yet our lives are part of history and vice versa, as the structure of the *Mutacion* makes plain. In her digression on Philosophy, therefore, Christine questions the aspirations of medieval encyclopedism as it had become under Brunetto Latini's influence in her own day. Posited as a process of disciplinary learning, the medieval encyclopedia appears to her to be disconnected from the way we experience our lives, namely, as subjective and historical. When approaching it from the perspective of her own experience, Christine can only include "philosophy" as a digression beyond her comprehension. For example, she says of the assembled sciences, "Car je ne compris pas, sanz faute, / Au cler la grant soubtilité d'elles" (For unquestionably I did not clearly understand their great subtlety, 7190–91). Posited as a unity, the medieval encyclopedia also poses questions about the relation of the parts to the whole, and Christine draws attention to this in the bizarre way she inserts the whole of history into what is only part of the history of only one individual; she then drops the whole of Philosophy into the *science* of history, which apparently has no place in it. The question of whether "theoretical" science constitutes a whole is nicely brought out in these lines:

> [La theorique] nous enseigne la premiere
> Question: de savoir entiere-
> Ment cognoistre les choses belles
> Des natures celestieles
> Et des terriennes aussi. (7275–79)

> (The theoretical science teaches us the initial question: that of knowing in their entirety the beauteous things of the celestial realms, and of the terrestrial ones too.)

The fracturing of the word "entierement" so as to create a rhyme with "premiere" suggests that even the first question posed by the theoretical sciences may not be capable of being answered with any completeness.[45]

As with Renart's in *Renart le contrefet,* part of Christine's history is in prose; but whereas the diabolical fox adopts prose for Christian history, Christine chooses it in order to hasten her way through the history of the Jews:

> Si ne soit tenu a faute,
> Pour ce qu'ay de santé deffaute,

---

45. Cerquiglini-Toulet, "Des Emplois seconds."

> Dont troublé mon entendement
> Est a present aucunement;
> Et qui de bien rimer se charge,
> Ce n'est mie petite charge,
> Et par especial histoires
> Abriger en parolles voires! (8741–48)

(Don't hold it against me, for my mind is currently somewhat disturbed by my poor health; and it is onerous to undertake to rhyme well, and in particular to render these stories concisely and accurately.)

If prose detaches the more Christian elements in Renart's narrative from his *renardie,* in Christine's case it equates to a reluctance to expend her diminished personal energy on Jewish history. To write in verse is an effort of personal engagement, and of all the material she has before her, this seems to her the least worthy of that effort. The momentary puncturing of both texts by prose implies that in both, verse is what makes history most compellingly expressive of personal conviction. The contrast in the choice of which parts of history are cast in prose in the two texts confirms the opposing character of Renart and Christine as narrators and their complementary capacity to "own" through verse certain kinds of subject matter. It does not mark any divergence in the value attaching to verse or prose.

In both texts, too, though in different ways, the hermeneutic process has become more fully internalized. Encyclopedic knowledge trees had already implied that universal history was framed and twisted by the history of individual desiring subjects. The abandonment of the encyclopedia in favor of the verse encyclopedic text, whether satirical (as in the *Renart*) or confessional (as in the *Mutacion*), makes it possible for this framing to become explicit.

Melancholy and Cosmology in Encyclopedic Texts

If history in encyclopedic verse is twisted and reframed by individual experience, we can discern a similar process of distortion occurring in the knowledge of nature. Encyclopedias set out to describe nature as a totality; encyclopedic texts fragment it in response to the author's own position within it. This frequently occurs when he or she is afflicted with melancholy.

Thanks to the dissemination of antique scientific knowledge, notably by encyclopedias, late medieval authors and readers saw melancholy as more than a state of mind.[46] It was a complexion that resulted from the predominance of the melancholic humor, or black bile, which in turn reflected an imbalance in the four elements toward cold and dryness, and away from warmth and damp. Melancholy was exacerbated by winter and by old age, in which cold and dryness likewise predominate; correspondences between the elements, humors, bodily functions, and illnesses, seasons of the year, ages of man, and planetary bodies, were commonplace (see, for example, figure 4). When Machaut begins the *Jugement dou roy de Navarre* by representing himself as melancholy in a winter setting, he is knowingly invoking this familiar encyclopedic trope. It is also found in a recognizable if condensed form in lyric poetry, as in Charles d'Orléans's famous *ballade* "En la forest d'ennuyeuse tristesse."[47]

Melancholy holds a privileged position among the complexions; it is the one to which philosophers, physicians, and theologians paid the greatest attention.[48] The widely read *Problemata,* attributed through the Middle Ages to Aristotle, reflects on both the medical implications of melancholy and its association with genius. There was a widespread belief, propagated by, among others, Constantinus Africanus in his *Viaticum,* an extremely widely circulated medical vade mecum, that lovesickness—and even the absence of sexual activity—provoked melancholic and delusional states.[49] Theologians pondered the relation between melancholy and the sins, especially sloth and *accidie.*[50] As we saw in chapter 3, one of the effects of the *Consolation of Philosophy* was to license a cult of melancholy, especially for the reflective poet. As a result, melancholy is embraced by medieval authors both as a part within a unified and coherent conception of our nature and as the position within it that generates an altogether exceptional perspective on the rest. This melancholic perspective might be represented as delusional, but it might also be singularly inspired and profound, beyond the capacities of an ordinary person. (This view of melancholia as a pathology that dares to confront truths from which saner minds are shielded persists in Freud's "Mourning and Melancholia.") Thus the circle of the humors depicted in figure 4, like that of universal history in figure 3, is commonly realized in a fractured or distorted way.

In the preceding chapter we considered texts in which, seemingly under the influence of the *Roman de la rose,* poetry was identified as allied with nature

46. See, for example, reflections on the theory of the humors in relation to the elements in the *Ovide moralisé* 15.3312–5767, and the *Tresor* 63–89.
47. Ed. Mühlethaler, 180–82, *Ballade* 63; Planche, *Charles d'Orléans ou la recherche d'un langage,* 598–612.
48. See Radden, *Nature of Melancholy.*
49. Wack, *Lovesickness in the Middle Ages;* the edited text is on 186–93; also Huot, *Madness.*
50. Delumeau, *Péché,* 189–208.

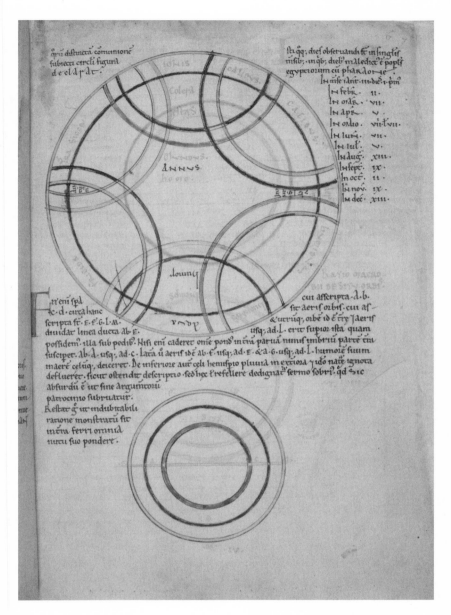

Figure 4　Diagram representing the interrelation of the elements and their properties, the humors, and the seasons, both within the world as a whole, and within man the microcosm. The outer ring reads (clockwise from the top): fire, hot (repeated), air, damp, water, cold, dry earth. Choler and summer are ranged under fire, blood and spring under air, winter and humor (for phlegm?) under water, and autumn under dry earth (not enough room was left for melancholy); in the center we find world, year, and man. From a twelfth-century Latin scientific textbook preserved in BL MS Cotton Tiberius C I, fol. 7r. © The British Library Board.

in understanding the world and in leading poets from physical to metaphysical understanding. In some, nature is further understood in the light of the scientific encyclopedist tradition. Froissart's *Joli buisson de Jonece* develops the theme of melancholy to provide an unusually clear illustration of how it is both a part of cosmology and the part that exercises the greatest distorting influence on how we perceive the whole. At the start of the poem the protagonist's plight as a melancholic is illumined when he is told, in his dream, about the ages of man and their connection with the planets, a passage that would not be out of place in an encyclopedia.[51] Attempting to relive his youth and past love, he approaches his lady in the "bush of youth" of the title, but his brush with desire proves just too fiery for someone as cold and dry as he has become. The poem ends on a religious note, as Froissart abandons love poetry in favor of writing to honor the Virgin. The value of this conclusion, however, is relativized by its appropriateness to his aged humor. Is the poet exceptionally inspired, or is he merely succumbing to his melancholy complexion?

Similarly, Christine de Pizan's *Chemin de long estude* draws extensively on the encyclopedic tradition while at the same time repudiating it in favor of a deliberately partial, incomplete *savoir*.[52] The text begins with Christine plunged in melancholy as a result of her husband's death. The imbalance of her own humors leads her to see the whole universe as composed of warring elements. The dream journey she undertakes with the Sybil is a miniaturized encyclopedia comprising a *mappemonde* and a cosmology; it makes Christine aware that the upper reaches of the cosmos, while breathtaking in their beauty, will not solve the earth's problems. After staging a series of poetic debates about knowledge, power, and loss (which contain, by way of exempla, fragments of universal history), the text ends with a failure of agreement as to the way forward that is consonant with the author's melancholy state.

The use of encyclopedic materials by Froissart and Christine de Pizan is well known, but our emphasis on melancholy as the privileged part within the whole opens a new perspective on their works. By responding to the partial and imperfect *savoir* of medieval encyclopedias, these encyclopedic texts emphasize partiality and incoherence, thereby gaining a specifically poetic purchase on the world that seems the more compellingly authentic, more subjectively true, for its failure to measure up to the unified knowledge of encyclopedias.[53]

51. Burrow, *Ages of Man,* 36–54.
52. Ribémont, "Christine de Pizan."
53. Akbari, "Movement," shows that in Christine's works that begin in melancholy, sublimation intervenes more quickly and with more intellectual ambition in the prose than in the verse texts.

A final illustration of how melancholy can challenge understanding of the cosmos is one that, to our knowledge, has not been identified by other critics. Two of the poems composed in the course of the *querelle* surrounding Alain Chartier's *Belle Dame sans mercy* contain cosmological passages that are inspired by the encyclopedic tradition, and offer an opening into encyclopedic knowledge, while at the same time negotiating the melancholia to which these poems' narrators are subject.[54] The opening poem by Chartier himself establishes the melancholic mindset of the rest of the cycle. Chartier's narrator, absorbed in gloomy thoughts at the death of his lady (1, 49), finds a double in another morose knight (83), whom he subsequently overhears vainly begging his lady to reciprocate his love. The lady diagnoses the knight's melancholy as a passing folly of which he can be cured (377–80). Reprising her rhyme "folie": "merencolie," the God of Love takes Chartier to task in a subsequent poem, the *Excusation de Maistre Alain,* for inflicting the delusions of his own lovesickness on unsuspecting readers:

> Si tu as ta mirencolie
> Prise de non amer jamés,
> Doibvent acheter ta folie
> Les autres qui n'en peuent mes? (*Excusation* 33–36)

> (If you are afflicted with melancholy as a result of never loving, is it right that others who can't help it should pay the price?)

The question is thereby posed whether what is at stake in the original poem is essentially a moral question (how ought the knight and the lady to behave?), or an epistemic one (are the knight and the poet delusional?). As the cycle develops, contributors engage more readily with the moral alternative. The lady's lines are quoted in one of the early responses to the *Belle Dame,* the *Accusation contre la Belle Dame sans mercy* of Baudet Herenc (397–99), as evidence of her turpitude. Although at the end of Chartier's poem the knight's eventual death is only a matter of hearsay, in the rest of the *querelle* his death is generally accepted as a fact, and his "homicide" raises the stakes of the lady's lack of "mercy." The frame narrator throughout the cycle is consistently melancholic, and the question whether this stance is one of delusion or privileged insight is rarely raised.

---

54. *Le Cycle de "La Belle Dame sans mercy,"* ed. and trans. Hult and McRae. Our translations were checked against those in Alain Chartier, *The Quarrel of the "Belle dame sans mercy,"* ed. and trans. McCrae. See also Armstrong, *Virtuosos Circle,* chap. 1.

Two of the later poems, however, the anonymous *Dame loyale en amour* and Achille Caulier's *Cruelle femme en amour,*[55] incorporate material deriving from the treatment of cosmology in the encyclopedic tradition, and thereby address the implicit epistemic challenge of the original poem. *La Dame loyale en amour* continues the moral concern of its predecessors, exceptionally exculpating the lady on the grounds of her exemplary fidelity to a prior lover. Imitating Chartier's summons before the God of Love in the *Excusation,* the narrator presents himself and the lady undertaking a celestial journey to Love's court which is reminiscent of Christine's with the Sybil in the *Chemin de long estude.* As they climb upwards through the heavens, the first thing that happens to them is that they lose their material bodies and assume an incorporeal substance like that of the angels.

> Apprés ces mos fusmes ravis
> Et en l'air bien hault eslevés,
> Et nos corps materïaulx vifs
> Angeliquement ordonnés. (*La Dame loyale,* 185–89)

> (After these words we were snatched up and elevated high in the air, and our living, material bodies became composed like those of the angels.)

Thus rendered transparent like crystal (192), they are no longer made up of elements and therefore no longer liable to melancholy. By implication, everything that happens in these higher spheres is cognized directly, in the manner of the angels, without language or the senses. As the narrator and the lady continue their ascent, encyclopedic cosmological tropes accumulate. They journey east toward the rising sun, through heavens of different colors, to a sphere that is completely clear and bright (233–40), and is illuminated by the planet Venus (268). Here they are set down before Love's throne. An advocate named Verité (Truth) takes up the lady's defense, which occupies most of the rest of the poem. Truth's revelations seemingly confirm that the delusions of melancholy have been left behind. The narrator's words in the penultimate stanza of the poem commit him to relinquish melancholy and heed his lady "and preserve [him]self from delusion" (et [s]oy garder de decepvoir, 880). For, he says in the closing stanza, Truth demands that a man should avoid persisting in a love service that will drive him to his death (881–88).

---

55. Both poems are quoted from *Le Cycle de "La Belle Dame sans mercy,"* ed. and trans. Hult and McRae, respectively 169–243 and 245–437.

When Achille Caulier undertakes his riposte to *La Dame loyale,* his main aim seems to be to discredit the earlier poem's apparent escape from delusion into Truth. At the beginning, his narrator, reiterating the standard trope of the cycle, is represented as beside himself with melancholy ("sans memore, sens, ou advis" [with no memory, sense, or right judgment], *La Cruelle femme en amour,* 76) and falling prey to hallucinations (77–80). The place to which his imaginings transport him contains, in reminiscence of the *Mutacion de Fortune,* murals depicting everything that there is, has been, will be, or might come to pass (97–104). In a gesture toward encyclopedist representations of the Trinity, the place is of no known geometry, and its crystalline floor is so slippery that the narrator can barely keep his footing. Lettering informs him that this domain is the combined work of Imagination and Melancholic Care (Fantasie and Soussy, 136). Theological reminiscences thereby converge with the depressing implication that a melancholic view is the only possible one.

The narrator of *La Cruelle femme* then repeats the heavenly ascent of his predecessor in *La Dame loyale,* except that the cosmological details are omitted, and he is simply taken up in a cloud (139) to the bejeweled citadel of the God of Love, where he enjoys a rewarding stroll through a cemetery of famous dead lovers. This episode dismantles the encyclopedic pretensions of *La Dame loyale.* Caulier, by making it clear that his narrator's ascent is to a melancholy heaven (a lovers' cemetery no less), draws attention to the way the supposed cosmological spheres in *La Dame loyale* remain essentially trapped within preoccupations of love: its anonymous narrator's claim to have left the elemental world behind is unfounded. Caulier's final thrust against *La Dame loyale* comes when his narrator too appears before Love's court, and a second figure of Verité steps forward, dramatically claiming that he is the true Truth and denouncing the Verité of the earlier poem as none other than a Fiction (Fictïon, 331) constructed by Poëtrie. This true Truth proceeds to demolish the arguments of his "fictional" counterpart in *La Dame loyale.* Given the insistence of the melancholic frame, we are led to understand that there can be no engagement with the truth outside of melancholy, which exposes as a fiction the anonymous poem's defense of women's virtue.

Caulier's contribution to the *querelle* of *La Belle Dame sans mercy,* then, is to reinforce the stance of other encyclopedic texts: melancholy is not merely an inevitable part of cosmology; it is also the distorting part that governs how we view the whole. Whether inspired or delusional, it is our only possible perspective, determining what will pass for Truth and what for Fiction.

The success of early medieval Latin encyclopedias led, in the thirteenth century, to the production of vernacular verse encyclopedias. Though composed within a narrow time frame from around 1230 to around 1292, these works were copied and diffused through the centuries that followed, and were undoubtedly hugely influential. They express lofty, perhaps impossible ambitions: both to know the nature of reality and to understand its origins. It may be that they gave way to prose encyclopedias because, modeled on prose books in Latin, they lent themselves more readily to encyclopedism as a survey of disciplines, as promoted by Brunetto. For whatever reason, only two verse encyclopedias, the *Lumere as lais* and the *Breviari d'amor,* were actually composed during our period of study, and both tend more toward the related genre of the religious summa. Situating knowledge in an eternal perspective, both attest to the difficulty of construing it in a unified way. We have seen this difficulty encapsulated in the "tree of knowing," where knowledge finds itself bound in a complex and maybe irresolvable relation to temporality, desire, and loss. Though confident that the world can be known and mapped up to a point, medieval verse encyclopedists also concede that knowledge of the world is inherently imperfect and paradoxical.

We have followed two of the fault lines that give rise to this recognition: that of universal history, which corresponds to the hermeneutic demand to know and understand our origins; and that of cosmology, which answers to the drive to comprehend the makeup of the world. Both universal history and cosmology recur as "encyclopedic insertions" in the vast production of encyclopedic verse that followed in the wake of the shift of encyclopedias proper from verse to prose. They are relativized and rendered partial in a variety of ways, including satire and comedy. This comic-pathetic strain in encyclopedic texts owes much to the success of the *Rose*-Ovid-Boethius matrix discussed in chapter 3, and indeed their conjoint influence is one of the factors that seem to have ensured the proliferation of such works, since the *Rose* and the *Ovide moralisé* are themselves prominent examples of encyclopedic texts, while the *Consolation of Philosophy* offers itself to medieval readers as a model for pondering the relation of cosmology to melancholy. Although verse encyclopedias are few in number, the scope for multiplying examples of encyclopedic texts is inexhaustible, and there are many other topics—such as optics or ophthalmology—that we could have examined in them.

In our next chapter we shall see how poetry itself is an especially privileged site of knowledge, since, like history and nature, it is both the object that is known and the means through which it is grasped.

CHAPTER FIVE

Knowledge and the Practice of Poetry

Chapter 4 examined how poetry transmits "referential knowledge" as defined in our introduction: knowledge of the domains that underpin our grasp of the cosmos, such as theology, history, and nature. Yet poetry is also an object of knowledge in ways more specific to itself, and it is on these that this chapter focuses. Our concern is to show the *reflexivity* of verse, its simultaneous role as both a means to knowledge and an object of knowledge. We begin by considering the properties of poems that poets claim to be praiseworthy. Our discussion then turns to intertextual allusion, which reveals the capacities of poetry. Through it poets may construct horizons of audience expectation and endow formal features with new meanings, exhibit their grasp of their literary heritage, and reshape knowledge by transforming ideas inherited from previous poems. We devote particular attention to two closely related practices: quotation and lyric insertion. Through quotation, poems present other poems as already encapsulating certain forms of knowledge; the technique provokes reflection through selectivity or distortion and is apt to problematize ideological assumptions or genre boundaries. Lyric insertion raises questions about the relationship between framing and framed texts, each of which offers knowledge about the other. Similar processes are apparent in *prosimetrum,* a complex and prestigious form whose use in this period extends from Chartier to Lemaire de Belges and which is foreshadowed in the work of various earlier poets. By their very complementarity, prose and verse effectively comment on each other; the tasks performed by verse indicate the ways in which authors and audiences perceived it. Common to all these phenomena is the conviction

that poetry belongs in the world and mediates how we view it. The same conviction is evident in the material transmission of poetry in manuscript or print,
which we consider throughout: paratextual and contextual features encourage specific modes of reception and suggest relationships between the texts
juxtaposed in anthologies.

Poetic Quality in Theory and Practice

A well-known and relatively early comment on poetic quality appears in
Machaut's *Fonteinne amoureuse* (1360–61), in which a first-person narrator overhears a princely lover lamenting his lady's absence. The lament is
formally distinct from the octosyllabic couplets of the surrounding narrative: it consists of fifty stanzas, each of sixteen lines with the chiastic scheme
aaabaaabbbbabbba; every fourth line has four syllables, and the rest are decasyllabic. While the stanzaic form is itself technically challenging, the true extent
of Machaut's formal achievement lies in his use of rhyme. As the doleful prince
himself observes, every stanza in his lament introduces a new set of rhymes:
"Cent rimes ay mis dedens ceste rime, / Qui bien les conte" (I have put a hundred rhymes into this poem, if they are properly counted up, 1021–22).[1] The
narrator has transcribed the lament, and on reviewing the text he confirms
the prince's claim (1050–52). Hence Machaut signals the technical rigor of
the lament's composition not once but twice. Indeed, the first-person verb in the
prince's claim enables the poet's own voice to show through: this is not only
a sorrowful lover who speaks but also a proud verbal artist.[2] Machaut's outstanding variety of rhymes prompts emulation by Froissart, who incorporates
a lament with almost identical versification into his *Espinette amoureuse* (ca.
1369) and similarly draws attention to his hundred different rhymes.[3]

Formal sophistication, then, is seen as a desideratum in poetry, part of the
knowledge that a competent poet, and indeed a competent audience, should
exhibit. The value ascribed to an understanding of compositional technique
is widely attested. Jean de Le Mote's *Parfait du Paon* (mid-fourteenth century)
and the anonymous *Pastoralet* (ca. 1422) contain fictional accounts of poetic
contests in which well-informed audiences reward poets' ingenuity and note

---

1. Text from Machaut, *Fountain of Love,* 89–239.

2. On the play of poetic and princely voices, and on further manifestations of virtuosity in the
Fonteinne, see Huot, "Reading the Lies of Poets," 29–34; Brownlee, *Poetic Identity,* 188–91, 195.

3. Poirion, *Poète et le prince,* 407, 433, sets Machaut's feat in its wider context. See also Froissart, *Espinette amoureuse,* 2340–42.

technical faults such as hypermetry.[4] Competitive exchanges between real poets similarly manifest a drive toward innovation and increasing sophistication.[5] In the devotional verse competitions known as Puys, the formal parameters to which competing poets must adhere are often precisely circumscribed.[6] Even the Puy d'Escole de rhétorique of Tournai, a small-scale monthly gathering of enthusiasts where conviviality and entertainment counted for more than edification, pays close attention to detail. The Escole's statutes stipulate that each month's submissions must be copied into a manuscript by one of its members "qui notera en marge les faultes de chescune ligne, se aucunes en y a" (who will note in the margin the errors in each line, if any exist).[7] Manuscript anthologies devoted to Puy poetry vary widely in their compilatory principles, but in all cases the juxtaposition of competitive poems encourages readers to compare and evaluate them.[8] It is hardly surprising that when the Parisian printer Pierre Vidoue published a collection of poems from Rouen's Puy of the Immaculate Conception in 1525, his title page should describe the Puy poets as "scientifiques personnaiges" (experts).[9]

In French, this kind of knowledge is systematized to a greater or lesser extent in the *arts de seconde rhétorique*. From Deschamps's *Art de dictier* to Pierre Fabri's *Grand et vray art de pleine rhétorique,* published posthumously in 1521, the *arts* vary widely in the detail and precision with which they outline and evaluate aspects of versification. They are formally diverse: most comprise alternating prose explanations and verse examples, though the chapter "Des rimes et comment se doivent faire" (On Rhymes and How They Should Be Constructed) of Jacques Legrand's *Archiloge Sophie* contains no examples and Evrart de Conty's discussion of verse just one.[10] Two surviving *arts* are solely in verse; significantly, they are much more closely bound up with voice, presence, and performance than the prose *arts*. One is unique in devoting attention to theater, and has been described as presenting poetry as "a staging of voice."[11] The other insists on presence through the verse examples themselves, either

4. Taylor, *Making of Poetry,* 23–33.
5. Armstrong, *Virtuoso Circle.*
6. Gros, *Poème,* 187–92; Hüe, *Poésie palinodique,* 270–72, 915–35.
7. *Ritmes et refrains tournésiens,* [ed. Hennebert], xx.
8. Gros, *Poème,* 218–42, and Hüe, *Poésie palinodique,* 431–85, examine the manuscript corpus.
9. *Palinodz,* title page. Hüe, *Poésie palinodique,* 486–539, examines Vidoue's anthology.
10. Legrand, *Archiloge Sophie,* 141–44; Evrart de Conty, *Livre des eschez amoureux moralisés,* 166–73.
11. *Instructif de seconde rhétorique,* in *Jardin de Plaisance,* ed. Droz and Piaget, vol. 1, fols. a_{ii}v–c_{iii}r. See Kovacs, "Staging Lyric Performances," 13–14 (quotation 14); Tilliette, Cerquiglini-Toulet; and Mühlethaler, "Poétiques en transition."

by deixis (for instance, "Vecy ung rondel / Que je forge et double" [Here is a *rondeau* that I am fashioning and copying out], 263) or by personifying the examples (for instance, "Je suis rethoricque enchainée" [I am linked verse], 255).[12] The *arts*' authors are not equally expert: some are poets of great talent and experience, such as Deschamps and Molinet; others are less illustrious figures affiliated with particular local poetic cultures, such as Fabri (Rouen) and Baudet Herenc (Lille); still others, such as Legrand and Evrart, are essentially encyclopedists whose technical understanding of poetry is not always highly developed.[13] Audiences are similarly diverse: that of Deschamps seems relatively knowledgeable, that of several others less so, while the printed *arts* doubtless reached a much more heterogeneous public than did those transmitted only in manuscript.[14] Terminology varies over time, and from one author to another.[15] Yet despite their diversity, the *arts* share a set of important principles. Their very existence indicates that the systematization of versifying practice was regarded as both possible and desirable; their development indicates an increasing awareness of vernacular poetry.[16] Versification is perhaps not the most exciting topic for treatises on poetry—many modern commentators have been disappointed in the *arts*' apparently modest ambitions—but it is a body of knowledge considered worth transmitting and acquiring.[17]

Closely bound up with this attitude is the *arts*' normative character. Deschamps sets the tone: "Et se doit on tousiours garder en faisant balade, qui puet, que les vers ne soient pas de mesmes piez…car la balade n'en est pas si plaisant ne de si bonne facon" (One must always take care in writing a *ballade*, if possible, that the lines not be of the same number of feet [i.e., syllables]…for such a *ballade* is neither very pleasing nor of such good form).[18] Subsequent authors do not all share Deschamps's views. Fabri is much more restrictive on *ballade* form, claiming that "s'il excede huyt lignes et huyt syllabes, ce n'est plus ballade" (if it has more than eight lines per stanza and eight syllables per line, it is no longer a *ballade*).[19] But a common principle emerges: to know

---

12. All references are to *Recueil,* ed. Langlois, 253–64. In "linked verse" the first syllable of each line repeats the rhyme of the previous line.

13. These distinctions derive from Gros, *Poème,* 97–98. Legrand's and Evrart's reflections on number and proportion in verse are, however, notably sophisticated in comparison with those of other *arts*. See Roy, *Cy nous dient,* 37–40; Hüe, "Le Vers et le nombre," 32–39.

14. Taylor, *Making of Poetry,* 40–46, discusses the *arts*' functions and likely audiences. On manuscript and print reception, see also Armstrong, "Versification," 121–39.

15. On varying understandings of technical terms and forms, see *Recueil,* ed. Langlois, 427–73; Thiry, "Prospections et prospectives," 556; Gros, *Poème,* 98–121, 129–49.

16. Gally, "Archéologie."

17. Taylor, *Making of Poetry,* 41, notes Glending Olson's dismissive verdict on Deschamps.

18. Text and translation from Deschamps, *Art de dictier,* 72–73.

19. Fabri, *Grand et vrai art,* 2:88.

versification means to be able to distinguish good forms from bad. This distinction tends to lie in the relative complexity and difficulty of the forms. The easier option for a poet is ipso facto the less impressive one. Molinet's *Art de Rhétorique* (ca. 1492), for example, warns against "plattes redittes" (outright repetition) and "redittes en sens" (the use of synonyms) at the rhyme.[20] Yet practice is much more diverse than the *arts* suggest. The *ballade* remained highly flexible: even the Rouen Puy permitted more leeway than Fabri.[21] Rather than recording what poets actually did, the *arts* offer formal definitions that are essentially prescriptive.

Various *arts* adopt a more descriptive approach when indicating associations between particular forms and types of subject matter. An anonymous treatise explains how a heterometric stanza is typically used:

Complainctes, lamentations,
Regretz par tribulations
En ce point que nous les faisons
Se font souvent.[22]

(Laments, elegies, and expressions of painful sorrow are often composed in the manner adopted here.)

The statement's modality is typical: rather than explicitly recommending form-content relationships, the *arts* tend to identify prevalent tendencies without passing overt judgment. In this and other respects they provide valuable evidence of the assumptions and expectations that a knowledgeable audience might share. The *arts'* precepts, indeed, become increasingly apparent in poetry. Poets of the late fifteenth and early sixteenth centuries often use forms that can be fruitfully interpreted in the light of the *arts'* pronouncements, while several *arts* appear in manuscript or printed poetry anthologies, encouraging comparisons—however invidious—between theory and practice.[23]

20. *Recueil,* ed. Langlois, 251. Molinet identifies the rhyme *aler/ambuler* (go/walk) as an example of *redite en sens;* ibid., 250.

21. On Fabri and Puy practice, see Gros, *Poème,* 146–47; Mantovani, "Pierre Fabri"; Rouget, "Une forme reine." On *ballade* form, see Jung, "Naissance," "Les plus anciennes ballades," and "Ballade."

22. *Recueil,* ed. Langlois, 262. Evrart de Conty even reflects on the thematic resonances of different line lengths in *Livre des eschez amoureux moralisés,* 168–70.

23. Studies relating the *arts* to contemporary poetry include Thiry, "Rhétorique"; Cornilliat, *"Or ne mens";* Armstrong, *Virtuoso Circle.* Deschamps's *Art de dictier,* four of the *arts* edited by Langlois, and L'Infortuné's *Instructif de seconde rhétorique* all appear in poetry anthologies. On their manuscript and printed contexts, see Deschamps, *Art de dictier,* 6–7; *Recueil,* ed. Langlois,

Ultimately, whether or not the *arts* influenced poetic composition, they testify to the values expressed by Machaut, Jean de Le Mote, and the Puy juries. The knowledge of forms, how to respect them and how best to deploy them, is a major criterion of aesthetic success.

In some important instances the knowledge of poetry is conceived more broadly. As noted previously, the Occitan poetic treatises both predate the *arts de seconde rhétorique* and make more ambitious claims for the ethical and philosophical value of poetry. Not that formal expertise is neglected; it occupies an important place, for instance, in Guilhem Molinier's *Leys d'amors.* Book 2 of the 1356 prose version seems to provide the first vernacular instance of poetry being identified as "second rhetoric"; it outlines the criteria for judging poetry in the Consistori's annual competition and provides a comprehensive account of versification, moving from the most specific elements (phonemes) to the most general (genres) via rhyme, line length, and stanzaic form.[24] Similarly to the judging criteria of the northern French Puys, those of the Consistori reward ambition and precision. If two poems are equally correct in formal terms, the piece with the loftier *sentensa* (import) should win: praise of God or the Virgin Mary trumps all other themes. Conversely, if two poems have equally elevated themes, the winner should be the composition that entails the greater technical difficulty. Thus *coblas unissonans,* in which every stanza in a poem has the same rhyme scheme and sounds at the rhyme, prevail over *coblas doblas,* in which the sounds change every two stanzas; and *rimas caras* (rare or precious rhymes) are preferred to *rimas communas* (ordinary rhymes).[25] Not for nothing is the prize known as a *joya* (joy), a term that recalls the *joy* with which a lady rewards a courtly lover. In poetry as in love, suffering, work, and dedication deserve recompense. Hence in the *Leys,* poetry has its own prestige in the context of the Consistori's activities. But it is also a prestigious object of knowledge because it accompanies and connects other such objects: the Occitan

---

xix–xx, xlii–lvi, lxviii–lxxi; Armstrong, "Versification"; Kovacs, "Staging Lyric Performances," 13–14, 16; Taylor, *Making of Poetry,* 251–60.

24. Book 2 begins with the rubric "Comensa lo segons libres de la seconda maniera de rethorica, laquals procezish am rims" (Begins the second book of the second manner of rhetoric, which proceeds with rhyme, 2:13). The "first rhetoric" is identified with prose. Molinier's formulation seems to derive from an implicit distinction in Brunetto Latini's *Livres dou Tresor,* 3.10. Brunetto values rhetoric and theology most highly among the practical and theoretical arts respectively, though his interest throughout is in government. See Connochie-Bourgne, "'Theorike' et 'théologie.'" For further discussion of the notion of "second rhetoric," see Lubienski-Bodenham, "Origins"; Cornilliat, Mühlethaler, and Duhl, "La Poésie parmi les arts."

25. *Leys d'Amors,* 2:15–29; the examples appear at 25–26. For the sense of *rimas caras,* see Paterson, *Troubadours and Eloquence,* 182. The Consistori follows different principles than the narrator of Machaut's *Fonteinne amoureuse:* the former rewards consistency of rhyme (in *coblas unissonans*), the latter values its variety.

language, promoted as an authoritative medium in book 3, which outlines its grammar and usage; and in particular the various branches of philosophy, which dominate book 1. For Molinier, to know poetry is not just a matter of technical skill; it presupposes a certain ethical awareness, and at the same time enables practitioners to refine that awareness.

The knowledge of poetry also has larger implications in Machaut's *Prologue* (ca. 1371), which introduces the most comprehensive manuscript anthologies of his work.[26] The poet is visited by two personifications, who charge him with creating "Nouveaux dis amoureux plaisans" (new, pleasing poems of love, 5), and each presents him with three allegorical children to help him write them. Nature appears first, with her offspring "Sens, Retorique, et Musique" (Sense, Rhetoric, and Music, 9); Amours follows, with her children "Doulz Penser, Plaisance, et Esperance" (Sweet Thought, Pleasure, and Hope, 64). Nature's significance is twofold. First, her appearance before Amours implies that form and composition take precedence over subject matter. Nature is identified with corporeal form, in the ways we have noted in Jean de Meun's *Rose* and elsewhere (see chapters 3 and 4), while her children all evoke aspects of poetic technique. Sens denotes the ability to endow content with form, while Retorique is associated specifically with versification (261–64), and Musique with Boethian and Augustinian musical theories.[27] Not that poetry is solely a matter of versifying. It is also informed by inspiration, for Nature has created the poet "à part" (separate, 4).[28] Nature's responsibility for the poet's distinct vocation reflects her second crucial quality: her metaphysical dimension as a principle that renders the world intelligible. Poetry expresses that intelligibility: Sens, Retorique, and Musique all embody relationships between the poet and the cosmos, founded on principles of order, coherence, and proportion. A quality peculiar to verse is indicated here, which Deschamps's *Art de dictier* would later formulate more explicitly. This is its association with what has been termed "therapeutic order," the capacity of proper poetic form to provoke aesthetic and/or ethical satisfaction in both its author and its audience.[29] Hence in the *Prologue* as in the *Leys d'amors,* an understanding of poetry rests

---

26. Text from Machaut, *Fountain of Love,* 1–19. On the manuscript tradition, see Roccati, "Guillaume de Machaut, 'Prologue' aux œuvres."

27. Cerquiglini-Toulet, *"Un engin si soutil,"* 15–21; Brownlee, *Poetic Identity,* 16–19; Lukitsch, "Poetics of the *Prologue,*" 259, 264–68.

28. Inspiration also has a role in L'Infortuné's *Instructif,* which associates poetry with Apollo and "Sophie" (Divine Wisdom). See Tilliette, Cerquiglini-Toulet, and Mühlethaler, "Poétiques en transition," 18–20.

29. Dixon, "Conclusion," 223–24, coins the expression "therapeutic order" and discusses its manifestations.

on a grasp of philosophical concerns, which a talented poet may convey and enhance through form as well as content.

 Intertextual Allusion

Many works that deal explicitly with poetry and its qualities allocate considerable space to examples of verse forms, often extracts of preexisting compositions. These examples indicate a crucial, if obvious, principle: the knowledge of poetic technique rests on the knowledge of particular poems. We might regard this as an instance of the mental operation known in medieval philosophy as abstraction, through which humans attain knowledge of universals by progressively abstracting immaterial forms from the objects perceived by their senses, or from the productions of their imagination.[30] Skilled poets must be skilled readers; the poets of late medieval France frequently advertise their skills by alluding to specific poems, either explicitly or through intertextual parallels that a knowledgeable audience could identify.[31] So pervasive is the process of allusion, and so varied its effects, that a comprehensive treatment is impossible. In what follows we consider a small selection of examples that illustrate its most important epistemic values.

Formal features of poetry tend to function by appealing to, and sometimes swerving away from, expectations established on the basis of their previous use. They thereby constitute objects of knowledge, which poets may use with or against the grain of the associations they have acquired. During the late thirteenth century, for instance, various courtly lyrics employ hendecasyllables to end their stanzas, apparently responding to developing public tastes by exploiting the established popularizing flavor of the line.[32] Simultaneously, Arras's highly experimental literary culture saw the flourishing of three distinctive verse genres—the *jeu-parti, resverie,* and *fatrasie*—that de- and recompose the forms and language of the courtly love lyric, juxtaposing them with other registers and discourses and thereby critiquing inherited poetic structures.[33] Other intertextual connections are manifested as implicit or explicit competition. Poets may display their skill by ostentatiously matching

---

30. Ancient and medieval philosophers propose various accounts of abstraction: see de Libera, *Querelle des universaux,* 98–99, 266, 342–43, 384–89.

31. Manuscripts sometimes signal authors' expertise in reading poetry and even require similar expertise of readers. The most important anthology of Machaut's work, BnF, ms. fr. 1584, provides a striking example. An illustration of the *Prologue* depicts Machaut himself as a reader, while the volume's organization and layout are aimed at readers accustomed to scholarly books. See McGrady, *Controlling Readers,* 37–38, 81–83, 104.

32. Floquet, "Considérations," 134–35.

33. Gally, "Poésie en jeu."

the formal achievements of others, as when Froissart's *Espinette* echoes the *complainte* in Machaut's *Fonteinne*. They may indeed seek to surpass those achievements: the continuations of Chartier's *Belle Dame sans mercy* (1424), which we considered in chapter 4, develop increasingly elaborate narrative settings.[34] In all cases poets treat their craft as a body of knowledge, which can be acquired and mastered by reading and writing verse. The overall effect is to encourage increasing compositional sophistication.

Froissart's major *dits* indicate some of the ways in which allusion can reveal the capacities of poetry. Scholars have widely acknowledged these poems' profoundly intertextual character: the ways in which the *Espinette amoureuse* and *Prison amoureuse* recast Machaut's *Fonteinne amoureuse* and *Voir dit;* the reworking and critique of the *Espinette* in the *Joli buisson de Jonece;* the use in all three poems of mythological material, including pseudo-Ovidian tales that recombine motifs from existing myths.[35] These transformations of earlier poetry testify to Froissart's ingenuity but also make an important epistemic claim for poetry. In chapter 2 we argued that Froissart's works problematize access to experience. Any experience is always already mediated, for example, through reminiscence, imagination, or the perspectives of others. Very often this mediation takes place through poetry, and in this sense it can be claimed that textuality shapes experience in Froissart's *dits.*[36] Poetry, including *poetrie,* constitutes the horizon of expectation against which humans understand themselves and others, and provides the language through which they voice that understanding. This is most obvious in love relationships, which consistently bear out the principle of Machaut's *Prologue:* as Nature precedes Amours, so form precedes content and eloquence precedes sentiment.[37] Pre-existing poetry generates amorous inclinations and sustains and develops relationships—if not always successfully. It is through a joint reading of the romance *Cléomadès* that the *Espinette*'s protagonist falls in love with his lady (696–787). In the *Prison,* Flos's love is first expressed through a *virelai,* of which his lady hears only later, eventually learning it by heart (273–342), while Rose

---

34. Armstrong, *Virtuoso Circle,* discusses this and other examples of competitive virtuosity.

35. On the *Espinette* and *Fonteinne,* see chapter 1; Huot, "Reading the Lies of Poets"; McGrady, "Guillaume de Machaut," 112–13. On the *Prison* and *Voir dit,* see chapter 2; Nouvet, "Pour une Économie"; McGrady, *Controlling Readers,* 170–89. On the *Joli buisson,* see Kibler, "*Le joli buisson*"; Kay, *Place of Thought,* 123–49; Sinclair, "Poetic Creation." On Froissart's retelling and confection of mythological narratives, see Huot, *From Song to Book,* 305–23; Kelly, "Imitation," 108–12; De Looze, *Pseudo-autobiography,* 120–24; Lechat, "*Dire par fiction,*" 253–343.

36. De Looze, *Pseudo-autobiography,* 102; Sinclair, "Poetic Creation." Studies of other aspects of mediation in Froissart, notably memory, include Zink, "Amour en fuite"; Kay, *Place of Thought,* 123–49; Sinclair, "Froissart."

37. Content and sentiment are nevertheless indispensable. Lechat, "Place du *sentement,*" notes that *sentement* (experience) is both an affective state for poets and a source of poetic content.

believes his dream (2252–3420) to have been inspired by the pseudo-Ovidian story of Pynoteus that Flos has composed for him:

> "Flos, chiers compains et grans amis..., je me tins environ demi heure sus mon lit, pensans et ymaginans sus mon songe et considerans pluiseurs coses, ne dont ceste vision pooit venir; mais, tout consideret et ymaginet, je n'en svoie qui encouper, fors la matere de vostre livret de Pynoteüs et de Neptisphelé." (letter 8, 1.4–9)

> (Flos, my dear companion and great friend..., I stayed in bed for around half an hour, thinking about my dream and analyzing it, and considering numerous possible causes of this vision; but when I had considered and analyzed everything, I didn't know what to blame, other than the content of your little book about Pynoteus and Neptisphelé.)[38]

The very pseudonyms "Flos" and "Rose" are of course literary themselves, while on different occasions the ethics of love are explained through reference to illustrious lovers from poetry and myth: Tristan and Iseut, Pygmalion, Narcissus, and others (*Prison* 213–22; *Joli buisson* 3154–3365).[39] More generally, characters frequently respond to situations by composing poems and communicate by sending poems to each other. All these practices confirm both the social nature of experience in Froissart and its close relationship with poetic composition and exchange. This relationship is not exclusive to lovers and poets: Froissart's first-person protagonists may be either or both of these, but also have general and sometimes universal traits.[40] Froissart demonstrates that to know poetry is a necessary condition for being not only a competent poet or reader but also a properly functional social being.

Nevertheless, if poetry is an essential intermediary to experience, it is an unreliable one. Froissart constantly suggests the limitations of poetry's interventions into the world and its vulnerability to divergent or simply erroneous interpretation. The *Espinette*'s protagonist slips a *ballade* into a book that he lends to his lady, only to find it returned apparently unread (864–972). The subsequent compositions that he addresses to her are scarcely more successful,

---

38. On these episodes, see respectively Nouvet, "Pour une Économie," 343–44; McGrady, *Controlling Readers,* 172.

39. Nouvet, "Pour une Économie," 347–49, discusses pseudonyms in the *Prison.*

40. Attwood, *Dynamic Dichotomy,* 110–29; Sinclair, "Poetic Creation." Experience is also socially and textually grounded in other poets' work. The literariness of love is apparent in Machaut (Cerquiglini-Toulet, "*Un engin si soutil,*" 141–42), while the *ballade* constitutes a social practice for Deschamps; Boudet and Millet, *Eustache Deschamps,* 29–30.

and the relationship remains unresolved, the poem closing with an expression of hope for "confort" (consolation, 4195) from the lady. The *Espinette* ends happily only as the narrative of a young poet's apprenticeship: his final composition is a *lai* (3915–4146), widely regarded as a particularly difficult and prestigious form.[41] In the *Prison,* Flos's initial *virelai* is well received at a feast, but his lady sings another, much to his dismay (419–69); he interprets the lady's song in various ways, coming to no clear conclusion (497–570); he proposes partial and distorting explanations of the Pynoteus myth to Rose and Rose's lady (letter 9, 121–55; letter 12, 52–157), and of Rose's own dream (letter 9, 14–98).[42] The *Joli buisson* mentions the *Espinette* in an enumeration of Froissart's previous works (443–52), but the earlier piece is apparently of no documentary value to the poet-protagonist, whose recollections of his past love do not tally with the *Espinette*'s account.[43]

The fallibility of poetry as a means of understanding oneself and engaging with others is intimately connected to the importance of allusion and reworking in Froissart. Both are symptoms of poetry's openness to appropriation by others, to be learned, glossed, misread, rewritten, stolen (as befalls a set of letters and poems from Rose to Flos; *Prison* 1082–1198), or—worst of all—ignored. Such openness lies at the heart of poetic composition, in two ways. On the one hand, preexisting poems admit of adaptations and responses; later poets cannot escape their literary heritage, but neither are they enslaved by it.[44] The point is best illustrated by a false allusion: the *Espinette*'s tale of Papirus and Ydoree, which the protagonist claims to recount "Ensi qu'Ovides le devise" (as Ovid tells it, 2672), but which is an original creation apparently derived from various literary motifs.[45] Froissart has rewritten Ovid in a radically new way, by exporting rather than importing; not by retelling or glossing his work, but by fashioning a narrative that recalls the *Metamorphoses,* whose specious attribution—however briefly—reshapes the Ovidian corpus in the reader's mind. On the other hand, the composition of new works is an open and collaborative process, decisively influenced by a poet's audience. This is made abundantly clear in the *Prison,* which enjoys a certain programmatic status in Froissart's poetic production: appearing at the midpoint of the two

41. Froissart himself comments on the difficulty of the *lai* in the *Prison* (2199–2203). See also Poirion, *Poète et le prince,* 399–426.

42. Nouvet, "Pour une Économie," 345–47, examines Flos's unsatisfying interpretations. Huot, *From Song to Book,* 321–22, and Kelly, "Imitation," 111–12, discuss other myths that lend themselves to divergent readings.

43. See chapter 2; Kay, *Place of Thought,* 138–39; Sinclair, "Poetic Creation."

44. Nouvet, "Pour une Économie"; Sinclair, "Poetic Creation"; Cerquiglini-Toulet, *Couleur de la mélancolie,* 57–80.

45. Froissart, *Espinette amoureuse,* 38.

extant manuscript anthologies of Froissart's *dits* and lyric poems, it expresses "the principles that serve to unite the collection as a whole."[46] Flos's poetry is increasingly influenced by the reactions of his readers, initially those of his lady, and more importantly those of Rose and Rose's lady. The poet negotiates his work with these readers, making it clear in his final letter to Rose that further amendments may be envisaged (letter 12, 50–52).[47] For Froissart, then, poetry shapes and is shaped by human interaction. His intertextual practice, and the apparent unreliability of poetry in his narratives, indicate that a poem is never complete, always reactualized by each new act of reception.[48] To know poetry is to have a knowledge that constantly evolves, for both the means and the object of knowledge remain in flux.

Esperance and Allusion

Allusion may also convey and reshape knowledge and truth, as the ideas transmitted in poetic texts are transformed in later poems that derive from or respond to them. The notion of hope, for instance, undergoes various changes across the period as poets deploy the personification Espoir or Esperance in different ways. Important in the courtly love lyric, this figure has a very minor role in the *Rose,* though the fleeting references provide a germ for development in later texts.[49] Amours grants Esperance to the lover, describing her as a source of "confort" (consolation, 2601) who enables lovers to endure suffering in the expectation of future happiness, and accompanies them steadfastly in the face of tribulation (2604–28). She is accompanied by three other figures: Douz Pensers, Douz Palers, and Douz Regart (Sweet Thought, Sweet Speech, Sweet Glance, 2629–2748). Yet as Jean de Meun's portion begins, the lover casts doubt on Esperance's reliability, gloomily musing after Bel Acueil is imprisoned:

> Mains en deceit par sa promesse,
> qu'el promest tel chose souvent
> dom el ne tendra ja couvent. (4044–46)

(She deceives many people with her promise, for she often makes promises she will never keep.)

46. Huot, *From Song to Book,* 312.
47. McGrady, *Controlling Readers,* 170–89, discusses the collaborative nature of poetic activity in the *Prison.*
48. Bouchet, *Discours sur la lecture,* 211–38, notes the constitutive role ascribed to readers in much late medieval writing.
49. On Espoir/Esperance in the courtly lyric, see Poirion, *Poète et le prince,* 534–35.

Subsequent poetic treatments of Espoir/Esperance (the two terms are often interchangeable in a given text) are allusive, in that the personification inevitably recalls previous texts in which she (or he) appears, and thereby encourages an intertextual mode of reading. Many poets paint the figure in most or all of the colors set down in the *Rose*. She appears in squarely amatory contexts, usually as part of a group; she consoles lovers but is easily lost and can therefore be deceptive.[50] Nicole de Margival's allegorical dream narrative *Le Dit de la panthère,* composed between 1290 and 1328, exemplifies this tendency. Amours sends Esperance to the lover's aid, along with Dous Penser and Souvenir (Memory); she encourages the lover, helping him achieve a happy outcome in his dream. On waking, however, the lover realizes that he has not won his lady's favor after all, and has no hope of doing so.[51] Yet Esperance and her companions have an additional quality, absent from the *Rose:* they explicitly encourage the production of poetry. The lover recites a *dit* (823–964), the first of many lyric insertions, in response to their request that he speak his mind.

This association of hope with composition later becomes prominent in Machaut's *Remede de Fortune,* the most thorough treatment of hope in an amatory setting. Esperance effectively kick-starts the *Remede*'s sequence of fixed-form lyrics. Appearing in response to the lover-poet's non-lyric *complainte* (lament, 905–1480), she lulls him to sleep with a *chant royal* (1985–2032); when he awakes, he produces lyrics of his own. As noted in chapter 3, Machaut's Esperance is in part a recasting of Boethius's Philosophy. Consequently, in striking contrast with earlier poetic treatments, she is a counterpart not to amatory threats such as Dangier or Male Bouche but to the vagaries of Fortune. Not that she is straightforwardly opposed to Fortune: she permits the lover-poet to engage with contingency, submitting to Fortune rather than rising above it. Hope enables him to avoid dangerous extremes of feeling, and thereby to retain both the eloquence and the heightened emotional states that provide his compositions with form and content.[52] Machaut's *Voir dit* restages the Esperance-poetry relationship: the personification berates the poet's persona for his ingratitude (4224–51) and requires him to compose a song to make amends, a task he duly accomplishes (4342–4597). What she demands, moreover, is not one of the briefer and more common forms, a "Rondel, balade ou virelai" as suggested by her companion Confort d'Ami (Friend's Consolation, 4294), but a *lai,* the only instance of this form among the *Voir dit*'s very

50. On the tendency of late medieval personifications to form groups, see Strubel, *"Grant senefiance a,"* 179–82.

51. Ed. Ribémont, 784–822, 2114–20, 2193–2221.

52. Kay, "Touching Singularity," 31–35; Brownlee, *Poetic Identity,* 37–63.

numerous lyric insertions. Hope, it appears, not only sustains poetry but also enables it to reach the heights of virtuosity.[53]

Froissart's *dits* present Espoir/Esperance in terms very similar to those of Machaut and the amatory tradition. In Rose's dream in the *Prison*, Esperance is accompanied by personifications that might be expected to foreground the place of hope within cognition: she is the daughter of Atemprance (Temperance), sent with her siblings Avis (Prudence), Souvenir, and Congnissance (Knowledge) to console Rose, imprisoned after the allegorical army of Orgoel (Pride) has defeated his own (2907–41).[54] But the significance of these figures is purely amatory: in glossing the dream, Flos interprets the prison as the suffering that Rose undergoes because of his lady's unresponsiveness or his own jealousy, and the children of Atemprance as the thoughts of his lady's goodness and beauty that console him at such moments (letter 9, 61–98). What is particularly apparent here is the literariness of Flos's interpretation, its dependence on the horizons of expectation established by preexisting allegories such as the *Rose* and *Remede*. Christine de Pizan's *Mutacion* (1400–1403) takes a more interventionist approach to the poetic heritage. Superficially, the reassuring demeanor of Esperance recalls her description in Machaut's *Remede* (1501–58):

> de cuer est franche et entiere,
> Doulce, piteuse et sanz orgueil...;
> Sa regardeure oste d'esmay. (*Mutacion,* 2412–13, 2434)[55]

(she is noble and constant in heart, gentle, compassionate, and devoid of pride; her face dispels fear.)

Yet her relationship to Fortune, and her sphere of activity, differ significantly. The uneasy coexistence between Esperance and Fortune in the *Remede* gives way to outright subordination: Esperance is one of the gatekeepers of Fortune's allegorical castle, along with Richece, Povreté, and Atropos (Wealth, Poverty, Death, 1617–2876). This setting indicates how far hope's significance has expanded. Christine's Esperance has the familiar double-edged quality, essential yet unreliable, but is no longer restricted to an amatory role. Rather,

---

53. Brownlee, *Poetic Identity,* 123–28.

54. Some of these figures accompany Espoir/Esperance in various other poems. Souvenir is a regular companion (for example, in Machaut, *Dit dou Vergier,* in *Fountain of Love,* 21–87, vv. 749–68), while in the *Voir dit,* Esperance's entourage includes Attemprance and Bon Avis (4259–60). Their concentration in the *Prison,* however, is unusual.

55. Ed. Solente.

she influences human activity in general, combining Hope as a theological virtue with more worldly manifestations of the concept. She permits life to continue; nobody can reach paradise without her; she promises wealth and honor, favoring the bold but detesting cowards; she lies and deceives (2448–2508).

The theological sense of hope is little explored in fourteenth-century vernacular allegorical poetry, with the exception of Deguileville's *Pèlerinage de vie humaine,* in which Esperance takes the form of an object: the staff that Grace Dieu presents to the pilgrim and whose significance she explains.[56] Theology takes center stage in Chartier's *Livre de l'Esperance,* however. The Boethian schema of consolation and didactic dialogue, adapted to courtly ends in Machaut's *Remede,* regains its religious orientation. Esperance even takes on a new appearance. While previous works describe her in ways that highlight her beauty and/or grandeur, Chartier's description focuses on two symbolic attributes: a box of unguents made from the prophets' ancient promises and a golden anchor whose fluke is attached to the heavens in the certainty of divine mercy (prose 10.98–106).[57] An even more striking contrast with Chartier's predecessors emerges as Esperance teaches the *acteur.* She distinguishes herself from various forms of false hope: "presumptive," not backed by action on the part of those who hope; "defective," sustained by an illusory faith in transient worldly goods; "opinative," based on misguided confidence in human reason; and "frustrative," placed in the vagaries of fortune, which has led to heresies (presumptuous, defective, opinionated, futile; prose 12.16, 58, 90; prose 13.3).[58] This typology encourages knowledgeable readers to reflect on the unreliable amatory personifications of Machaut, Froissart, and other poets, to identify which particular delusion they might represent. Chartier, in short, contests previous conceptions of Esperance and equips his readers to reassess literary history.[59] At the same time, he establishes a theological tradition of personified hope that competes with the amatory tradition in later poetry.

56. For the first redaction, see ed. Stürzinger, 3673–3808.

57. All references are to Chartier, *Livre de l'Espérance.* On these attributes, see Rouy, *Esthétique,* 22–24.

58. On Esperance's teaching, see Huot, "Re-fashioning Boethius"; Minet-Mahy, *Esthétique et pouvoir,* 404–97.

59. Indeed, Molinet draws on Chartier when glossing the Esperance of Guillaume de Lorris. The *Livre de l'Esperance* characterizes hope as "certaine attente de la beneureté future par grace de Dieu et par prevention de ses saintz merites" (the certain expectation of future happiness through God's grace and thanks to his divine goodness, pr. 10.54–56). Molinet's *Roman de la Rose moralisé* notes that hope sustains humans in all their endeavors, not only love, and that in particular it offers a consoling perspective on heavenly rewards. He amends Chartier's formulation to "certaine expectacion de beatitude a venir venant de grace et des merites precedents" (the certain expectation of future heavenly reward deriving from grace and previous meritorious acts, fol. e1v).

In Martin Le Franc's *Champion des Dames* (1441–1442), the two notions coexist in distinct personifications: Espoir is associated with Venus or carnal love (1145, 1608, 1617), while Esperance is aligned with the divine principle of Amour (2061, 2108) and the redemptive role of the Virgin (23461).[60] Charles d'Orléans similarly characterizes Espoir as ambivalent and increasingly deceptive, while Esperance is generally more healthy and reliable.[61] René d'Anjou mobilizes the traditions in different works.[62] In *Le Mortifiement de Vaine Plaisance* (1455), Esperance helps purge the heart of its earthly vices. By contrast, in *Le Livre du Cœur d'amour épris* (1457), she proves an increasingly unreliable guide during the knightly heart's amatory quest. Early in the narrative René wittily capitalizes on the familiarity of Esperance in the courtly love tradition, describing her as "ung pou ancienne par semblance" (rather old-looking, 4.5–6), as if the attractive figure of Machaut's *Remede* had aged over the intervening years.[63] She soon demonstrates an unnerving propensity to disappear almost instantaneously after speaking, much to the bemusement of onlookers (27.1–5, 52.1–8). Esperance is later unmasked as an amatory delusion: she appears on a tapestry alongside Foul Cuider (Foolish Presumption, 2279–83).[64] Finally, the *Séjour d'Honneur* of Octovien de Saint-Gelais (1489–1494) stages the two traditions within a single narrative charting the *acteur*'s enjoyment and ultimate rejection of worldly pleasures. Vaine Esperance rules over an island on which the *acteur* succumbs to the vanities of court life (2.xvi–2.4); Bonne Esperance helps him repent (4.xviii).[65] Hence as poetic treatments of hope multiply, its potential meanings accumulate. Successive personifications selectively actualize these meanings, shifting and enriching them in ways that become apparent through poets' active engagement with their predecessors.

Quotation and Knowledge in Poetry

In considering intertextual relationships, we distinguish between the terms "quotation" and "citation." Quotation reproduces a preexisting text, whereas citation invokes an author's name or the title of a work, for instance, as an authority, without reproducing what that author or work says. Superficially,

60. Ed. Deschaux.
61. Planche, *Charles d'Orléans,* 497–508.
62. Strubel, *"Grant senefiance a,"* 284–91.
63. Ed. Bouchet.
64. Ibid., 457 n. 1.
65. Ed. Duval.

outright quotation is the most straightforward of intertextual phenomena, as the quoted portion of a preexisting text may be unambiguously identified. From an epistemic viewpoint, however, quotation has diverse and often surprising effects. As Lyotard's reflections on legitimation indicate (see introduction), the relationship between the quoting and the quoted poem is at least double-edged: Does the authority of the quoter rest on that of the quoted, or vice versa? The process is inevitably imbued with the suspicion, on behalf of both authors and audiences, that knowledge resides elsewhere: in the quoted author, the quoting author, a knowledgeable audience, or a portion of it.[66] Hence the selectivity inherent in quotation is provocative. It stimulates audiences to reflect on why one particular formulation, rather than another, should have been extracted and reproduced.[67]

Matfre Ermengaud's *Breviari d'amor* arrestingly indicates some of the ambivalences that quotation may involve, particularly in the Occitan tradition, in which poetry is considered an important source of knowledge. We have shown in chapter 4 how troubadour quotations are reinterpreted to underpin Matfre's theological argument. On the one hand, then, ethical and theological value is ascribed to poetry; on the other, poetry cannot be unproblematically aligned with ethical or theological discourse. Moreover, the very boundaries of Matfre's quotations are blurred. While the beginning of a quoted passage is normally signaled, its end is indicated only rarely, as if the quoted poet remains virtually present after his words have been adduced. Indeed the text surrounding the quoted passage typically echoes its lexis, in a process akin to the overlay of voices in free indirect discourse. The *Breviari*'s manuscript presentation replicates this pattern: features of layout and decoration tend to signal the beginnings but not the ends of quotations, while the extent of verbatim reproduction is not consistently identified.[68] Quoting and quoted voices, then, are not presented as distinct subjects and objects respectively. Rather, they enter into a kind of symbiosis that reflects the paradoxical temporality of Matfre's theology, in which consequences can be made to obliterate their causes.

While the use of quotation has an exceptional intellectual density in the *Breviari*, it has varied and far-reaching effects in northern French poetry. In particular, it is through quotation that poets in the late thirteenth and early

---

66. Kay, "Knowledge and Truth." This epistemic instability makes it difficult to sustain taxonomic distinctions between types of quotation of the kind proposed in Tucci, "Modes de la citation," beyond the level of individual poems.

67. Antoine Compagnon calls this process "solicitation" in *Seconde main*, 23–25.

68. Kay, "How Long Is a Quotation?"

fourteenth centuries stage a delicate relationship between the familiar and the unfamiliar, challenging established genres and developing new forms. Adam de la Halle's *Jeu de Robin et Marion,* widely acknowledged as a theatrical transposition of characters and settings from the *pastourelle* genre, quotes a number of refrains from existing songs.[69] Besides their theatrical functions, the quoted refrains draw attention to *pastourelle* conventions and hence to Adam's innovative play upon them, notably the transformation of the knight's role from a mediating narrative perspective to a relatively impotent onstage character. Yet Adam also seems to draw at least some refrains from previous Arras poets, and thereby to continue a practice of locally sourced quotation in Arrageois poetry.[70] His quotational techniques, indeed, enact various forms of displacement—of genres, of familiar textual fragments, of the *pastourelle*'s established sociosexual roles—that may be pregnant with political significance. The *Jeu* is often thought to have been first performed at the court of Charles I of Anjou (1227–1285) in Naples, shortly after the Sicilian Vespers revolt and an invasion by Peter III of Aragon had ended Angevin rule over Sicily. While the play's precise resonances cannot be reliably identified, it has rich allusive potential in a post-Vespers context.[71] Besides consoling expatriate French aristocrats by offering rustic nostalgia, it dramatizes the fragility of knightly authority, and of French courtly culture's claims to hegemony.[72]

Adam himself becomes a privileged source of quotations in the *Dit de la panthère,* which reproduces nine extracts from his love lyrics, including two complete songs (1589–1628, 2556–2600).[73] Most extracts appear in conversations between the timid lover and Venus, who unsuccessfully exhorts him to declare himself to his lady. It is the lover who first quotes Adam, reproducing three stanzas that encourage discretion and reticence in love, and characterizing the poet as an amatory authority: "nostre clerc Adams, / Qui fu d'amis ja moult aidans" (our learned Adam, who has been a great help to lovers, 1067–68).[74] But Adam's authority can easily be mobilized on both sides of an argument: Venus later quotes three extracts, including three stanzas of the very song from which the lover had first quoted. Both parties dismantle the

---

69. Brownlee, "Transformations"; Huot, "Transformations," 158–60.

70. Saltzstein, "Refrains"; Menegaldo, "Théâtre et musique." On the play's relationship with Arrageois culture in more general terms, see Symes, *A Common Stage,* 232–76.

71. Symes, *A Common Stage,* 258–66.

72. The vibrancy of Sicily's earlier court culture exerts further pressure on Angevin self-perceptions. See Mallette, *The Kingdom of Sicily;* and Butterfield, "Historicizing Performance," on the post-Vespers significance of the *Jeu.*

73. Berthelot, "Nicole de Margival," 9–12, identifies the lyrics quoted.

74. This reception reflects the exemplary quality of the voice in Adam's songs, identified in Huot, "Transformations," 149–53.

carefully developed arguments of Adam's songs, selecting the motifs that best suit their own positions in ways that an informed audience could doubtless recognize.[75] Committed to love service, the lover then reproduces an entire song "por mon estat descrire" (to describe my state of mind, 1588); yet he remains unwilling to communicate with his lady, as Amours and Venus advise. After waking from his allegorical dream, he expresses his continuing acceptance of love's pleasure and pain by quoting Adam twice more; but the last quotation, a complete song that is also the final lyric piece in the *Panthère,* is the only one of which Adam's authorship is not mentioned. Hence Adam's ostensible authority evaporates as the narrative unfolds: his elaborate statements on amatory ethics disintegrate into sententious claims that only cancel one another out; his language may express the lover's thoughts, but it does not enable the lover to meet the expectations of Amours or Venus; ultimately his very name disappears. Margival's use of Adam signals not dependence on a canonical poet but a shift from old to new lyric forms. While Adam's songs are traditional *cansos,* the latter part of the *Panthère* is dominated by songs that the lover composes after awaking; these adopt newer forms such as the *ballade* (2295–2315) and *chant royal* (2384–2428).[76] It is with these forms, as the fate of Adam's songs indicates, that the lyric's future lies. On a much more general level, the quotations reflect the way in which the *Panthère* recasts, juxtaposes, relativizes, and hence renews inherited texts and narrative schemata, including the *Rose,* the allegorical dream, and the love quest.[77] Quotation thus contributes to a highly self-conscious narrative that exemplifies the protean qualities of the *dit,* in contrast with the more clear-cut traits of established genres such as the love lyric and courtly romance.[78]

Quotation lies at the heart of an entire late medieval lyric form, the *serventois,* first attested in the late thirteenth century as a composition in honor of the Virgin Mary that adopted the incipit and versification of a preexisting love lyric. Over the fourteenth and fifteenth centuries, quotation assumed greater significance: each stanza came to begin and end with a line from a love poem. Closely associated with the Puys, and thus with the formal ingenuity and rigor that they encouraged, the *serventois* drew much of its interest from its conversion of profane to sacred discourse.[79] But it is far from alone in ideologically distorting the texts that it quotes. The same tendency is apparent in the literary

---

75. Berthelot, "Nicole de Margival," 7–8, notes this selectivity.
76. Hoepffner, "Poésies lyriques," 214–27, examines these contrasts.
77. Ed. Ribémont, 25–39.
78. On the *dit* in relation to other forms, see Ribémont, "Avant-propos"; Léonard, *Le "dit,"* 343–54.
79. Gros, *Poème du Puy marial,* 19–123.

debates of the early fifteenth century: the *Querelle de la Rose* (1401–1403), an exchange in which Jean de Montreuil and Gontier and Pierre Col defend Jean de Meun's ethics and aesthetics against Christine de Pizan and Jean Gerson; and the *Querelle de la Belle Dame sans mercy,* in which Alain Chartier's poem is subjected to various responses and continuations.[80] Participants in the *Querelle de la Rose* use quotations polemically, quoting Jean de Meun in support of their standpoint and reproducing their opponents' terminology when refuting their arguments; in one letter Gerson even misrepresents his addressee, Pierre Col, the more effectively to counter his views.[81] Selective quotation also takes place at the level of manuscript copying. Most notably, Christine edits the correspondence for inclusion in anthologies of her own work, excluding Jean de Montreuil's letters and presenting the debate as essentially public rather than private, a very different conception from that of Jean de Meun's defenders.[82] A generation later, continuators of the *Belle Dame sans mercy* quote Chartier, and one another, with great attention to detail. Words and events from the earlier poems are carefully examined in allegorical courtroom scenes; the poets contest attitudes that have previously been adopted, demonstrating their competence in close reading and argument.[83]

As Christine's editing of the *Querelle* indicates, quotation may distort not simply the values of the quoted text but its very linguistic integrity. This phenomenon is particularly striking in Villon's *Testament,* which refers frequently and explicitly to a range of intertexts, poetic and otherwise. Villon's allusiveness tends to destabilize meaning, and his distortion of quotations contributes to this effect. Some passages are quoted so selectively as to be misleading, while other references are plainly erroneous: many scholars have noted that when Villon's persona mentions "le noble *Rommant / de la Roze*" (the noble *Roman de la rose,* 113–14), the context reveals that he should be citing *Le Testament de Jean de Meun.*[84] Such practices are symptomatic of crucial interrelated themes in the *Testament,* the fragility of human memory and of written documents.

---

80. Edited in *Débat,* ed. Hicks; *Débat,* ed. and trans. Greene; Chartier, *Le Cycle de "La Belle Dame sans mercy,"* ed. and trans. Hult and McRae<ED: altered for consistency with final notes in Chap 4); Chartier, *Quarrel.* Although the *Querelle de la Rose* was conducted exclusively in prose and partly in Latin, its preoccupation with vernacular poetry makes it highly relevant for our purposes. Key studies include Desmond, *"Querelle"*; Solterer, "Fiction versus Defamation."
81. Hill, *Medieval Debate,* 179, 189–90, 225–26, 228–29; *Débat,* ed. and trans. Greene, 117.
82. See *Débat,* ed. and trans. Greene, 45–48 and 113–14, for an example of pro-*Rose* editing; Cayley, *Debate and Dialogue,* 81–86.
83. See Cayley, *Debate and Dialogue,* 141–43; Poirion, "Lectures," 698–700; Calin, "Intertextual Play," 36–37; and the commentaries in Chartier, *Quarrel,* and *Le Cycle de "La Belle Dame sans mercy,"* ed. and trans. Hult and McRae.
84. All references are to Villon, *Poésies complètes,* 89–253. On Villon's misquotation and its implications, see Regalado, "Villon's Legacy"; Armstrong, *"Testament,"* 68–70.

Hence Villon's use of quotation (and citation), like the other examples we have noted, shows how poets can deploy knowledge of previous poetry to support compositional innovation, formal virtuosity, or thematic enrichment. The poetic heritage directly sustains the ongoing development of poetry.

Lyric Insertion

Lyric insertion is closely related to quotation: early examples of insertion are dominated by the reproduction of preexisting lyrics.[85] Scholars have tended to adopt taxonomic approaches to the technique, surveying its various functions or categorizing individual insertions or entire texts.[86] In practice these approaches tend to demonstrate that any given text partakes of different categories. This is hardly surprising: lyric insertion is not only extremely diverse but also intimately bound up with formal instability, the interrogation of genre, and the problematization of binary distinctions such as lyric/narrative, song/speech, and oral/written.[87] Hence in the case of insertion, from an audience's perspective, poetry's reflexivity might be more aptly characterized as *reversibility*. We can always regard each element, the insertions and the narrative, as in some sense framing the other and hence presenting us with knowledge about it. The locus of knowledge, in short, cannot be fixed. This reversibility is apparent in the *Dit de la panthère*. The narrative offers us two forms of knowledge of the lyrics, corresponding to the two types of song we encounter. Adam's songs are framed as exemplary statements of love ethics, though their exemplarity is undercut as the narrative unfolds. By contrast, the songs that the lover composes after waking are presented as symptoms of his love, and as his only real source of satisfaction in the absence of his lady's favor. Conversely, these two kinds of insertion each propose a certain perspective on the narrative. The quotations from Adam ironically gloss the failed love quest: neither the lover nor Amours and Venus can do justice to the ethics that Adam promotes. Rather, as the protagonist's songs reveal, the narrative charts not so much the education of a lover as the development of a poet—and indeed, in the protagonist's use of newer forms, the development of poetry itself.[88]

85. Boulton, *Song in the Story,* surveys the roles of lyric insertion.
86. Cerquiglini-Toulet, "*Un engin si soutil,*" 23–28; Taylor, "Lyric Insertion."
87. Butterfield, "*Aucassin et Nicolette,*" 81–89. We employ the terms "lyric" and "narrative" throughout for the sake of convenience, though their connotations are not always appropriate.
88. On the insertions, see also Berthelot, "Nicole de Margival"; Huot, *From Song to Book,* 203–8; Butterfield, *Poetry and Music,* 259–63; Cerquiglini-Toulet, "*Un engin si soutil,*" 29–30.

Though its reversibility is constant, the use of lyric insertion develops significantly across this period. There is a broad shift from reused lyrics in the thirteenth century to original compositions in the fourteenth; after Nicole de Margival, the only author to use others' lyrics extensively is Froissart, who reworked his verse romance *Meliador* to incorporate the compositions of his late patron Wenceslas de Brabant.[89] The forms of the insertions also change, with courtly song giving way to fixed-form pieces and music gradually disappearing. When Chaillou de Pesstain expands the *Roman de Fauvel* (1316–1317), he inserts numerous examples of what Nancy Regalado has termed "the most forward-looking vernacular genres," including *ballades, rondeaux,* and motets, all with musical notation.[90] In Machaut's *Voir dit* a relatively small proportion of the lyrics are identified as having musical settings, and notation is often absent from manuscripts, while the surviving anthologies of Froissart's *dits* and lyrics contain no notation.[91] The epistemic interplay between insertions and their surrounding narratives also evolves, in ways that we shall track across some of the major works already discussed in this chapter.

In Machaut's *Remede de Fortune* the lyric insertions encompass the range of contemporary forms from *rondeau* to *complainte,* each represented by a single piece. Scholars have noted that the lyrics seem to generate the characters and events in the narrative, in particular the appearance of Esperance to the lover-poet.[92] The lyrics, then, present the narrative as an exercise in discursive expansion. At the same time, the narrative explores the relationship between contingency and writing in ways that offer insight into the lyrics.[93] Poetic composition, as we have seen in chapter 3, is fostered by the experience of changing fortune and facilitated by avoiding extreme states of mind. Manuscripts may reflect and modify these perspectives. Illustrations in the earliest surviving Machaut anthology testify to the lyrics' dual nature as written texts that are destined to be sung; they thereby foreground the poet's compositional investment in his work as well as the strong emotion that generates creativity.[94] The former dimension is privileged in the most comprehensive Machaut anthology, where a table of contents devotes a separate section to the insertions and identifies their genres, implying that the *Remede* is essentially a showcase for

89. Cerquiglini-Toulet, *"Un engin si soutil,"* 25, 30–32; Boulton, *Song in the Story,* 275; Taylor, "Lyric Insertion"; Menegaldo, "Amateurs et professionels."

90. Regalado, "Songs of Jehannot de Lescurel," 158.

91. On the *Voir dit,* see McGrady, *Controlling Readers,* 129–45. On the Froissart anthologies, BnF, mss. fr. 830 and 831, see Froissart, *Espinette,* 9–14.

92. Kay, "Touching Singularity," 34.

93. Ibid., 33–35.

94. On the *Remede*'s illustration in this manuscript (BnF, ms. fr. 1586), see Huot, *From Song to Book,* 249–59.

the full range of Machaut's lyric artistry.[95] Yet the lyrics' layout has further implications. They are radically distinguished from the narrative, which is presented in conventional two-column verse with occasional decorative initials. They are all musically notated, normally for their opening stanza alone; the first insertion, a *lai* (fols. 52r–54r), is notated throughout. The resulting visual contrast between lyrics and narrative is accentuated by the use of red ink for the staves, and by a greater density of decoration in the insertions, where initials mark individual stanzas in all pieces except the *lai* and *rondeau* (fol. 78v). Hence the lyrics constitute zones of high decorative intensity. A different mode of reception is promoted, more meditative and less linear than for the narrative, attentive to the lyrics' formal complexity and affective qualities. At the same time, the lyrics' presentation differs from that of the notated lyrics grouped later in the manuscript. Non-notated verses in the insertions are each transcribed on a separate line, like the surrounding narrative verse; the independent *ballades, rondeaux,* and *virelais* (fols. 454r–494v) adopt the traditional *chansonnier* layout, with notation for the first stanza and subsequent stanzas transcribed continuously like paragraphs of prose.[96] The discreetly contrasting layout suggests that the *Remede* lyrics have been, in a sense, transformed by virtue of their narrative setting.

This transformation is more obvious in the *Voir dit* in the same manuscript, where all the lyrics are transcribed in the same way as the narrative verse: one verse per line, without notation, albeit with a greater frequency of decorative initials.[97] The *Voir dit* has been seen as the classic case of what Jacqueline Cerquiglini-Toulet calls *montage,* in which lyrics seem to generate the surrounding narrative. The visual assimilation of the insertions to their context, however, reminds us that this is not a one-way relationship: the narrative performs the work of staging the lyrics.[98] In epistemic terms, too, each element acts on the other. The narrative communicates, evaluates, and (mis)interprets the lyrics: love poems do not simply reflect events and emotional states but intervene to shape them. Conversely, the different voices in the lyrics—the poetic persona and his lady/protégée, Toute-Belle—draw attention to the

95. BnF, ms. fr. 1584, fol. Bv; see Huot, *From Song to Book,* 277; McGrady, *Controlling Readers,* 98–101.

96. On *chansonnier* layouts, see Le Vot, "Notation musicale," 157.

97. The layouts of the *Remede* and *Voir dit* in another Machaut anthology, BnF, ms. fr. 22545–46, are very similar. Earp, *Guillaume de Machaut,* 87–92, describes this manuscript and BnF, ms. fr. 1584. McGrady, *Controlling Readers,* 138, describes the presentation of the *Voir dit's* notated insertions in BnF, ms. fr. 9221.

98. On *montage* in the *Voir dit,* see Cerquiglini-Toulet, "*Un engin si soutil,*" 32–33. Formal and functional distinctions between the lyrics and the surrounding verse are not absolute; Boulton, "Guillaume de Machaut's *Voir Dit,*" 41–42.

ways in which the surrounding verse and letters multiply voices and perspectives, and hence diffuse narrative authority.[99] Poetry, it is implied, is a resource for working through the complexities of intersubjective understanding.

Froissart's use of lyric insertions in his major *dits* is heavily influenced by Machaut, though reflection and critique become increasingly evident. In the *Espinette* the insertions are exclusively composed by the first-person lover-poet; the one apparent exception, a consolation pronounced by his lady (2757–2996), figures within his own dream. The lyric forms exhibit increasing formal sophistication as the narrative proceeds, while their insistent engagement with Machaut's work is most clearly demonstrated by Froissart's emulation of the lament in the *Fonteinne amoureuse*.[100] The insertions, then, reveal that the narrative charts a poet's development in relation to an illustrious predecessor. Conversely, the narrative draws attention to the creative activity that shapes the lyrics. The poet apologetically comments that one of his *virelais* is too short (2453–63), and often refers to his composing by verbs that connote craftsmanship: *ordonner* (compose, 1495, 1554, and so on), *maçonner* (fashion, 1254). Metadiscourse of this kind plays a greater role in the *Prison*. As in Froissart's principal intertext, the *Voir dit*, lyrics are delivered by different voices and subjected to varying receptions. Their narrative contexts are less dominated by immediate amatory concerns than in the *Espinette:* it is Flos's relationship with Rose that permits him to complete a *lai* that he had left unfinished (3482–3514), while descriptions of composition often mention the necessary time or materials, or the technical issues involved.[101]

In the *Joli buisson de Jonece,* the narrative's sustained reassessment of the *Espinette* reveals the lyric insertions to be dominated by unreality and sterility. They almost all appear within the dream in which the poet revisits his youthful love experience; the sole exceptions are the closing *lai* addressed to the Virgin (5198–5442), effectively a rejection of love poetry, and the first *virelai* (563–91), in which the poet remembers his lady and thereby enters a mental state conducive to his dream, as he acknowledges after waking (5082–5135). Some of the lyrics, addressed by a lover to his lady, seem incongruous in their narrative context. The poet recites one of these (1768–99) to please Jonece, whose teaching he has just failed to understand, so distracted has he been by the *locus amoenus* around him; others are delivered by amatory personifications, whose voices cannot coincide with those of the insertions

---

99. Boulton, "Guillaume de Machaut's *Voir Dit*"; Cerquiglini-Toulet, "*Un engin si soutil,*" 159–200; Butterfield, *Poetry and Music,* 267.
    100. On the versification of the insertions, see ed. Fourrier, 42–46.
    101. Huot, *From Song to Book,* 311–16.

(e.g., 2491–2519, 2746–74). Within the dream, the most substantial lyrics are eight *souhaits* expressing wishes for ideal conditions for love, an unattainable idyll conveyed in subjunctive and conditional constructions.[102] Moreover, the love lyrics are dominated by circular forms that privilege recurrence and reversal over linear progression. Refrains play a crucial role in the *virelais, rondeaux,* and *ballades;* the *souhaits* adopt a symmetrical form, whose second half reverses the rhyme scheme of the first.[103] Consequently, a suspension of temporality exacerbates the love lyrics' shaky ontology. Illusory expressions of inner states, they remain resolutely outside the passage of time on which the narrative reflects so sensitively.[104] These insertions contrast sharply with the closing *lai,* whose very form lends itself better to discursive development, and which recasts amatory images from the preceding narrative in devotional terms.[105] The narrative implies that although poetry is well suited to expressing human love, it is better employed to didactic ends.

Chartier's *Livre de l'Esperance* evinces an attitude very similar to that of the *Joli buisson,* though lyrics are used quite differently and, in accordance with the model of Boethius's *Consolation,* inserted into prose rather than verse.[106] As noted in chapter 3, most insertions are voiced by the implied author, who has already benefited from the teaching of Foy and Esperance within the narrative, and who echoes the arguments of these virtues or resists those of the demonic personifications who threaten to make Entendement despair. While prose is aligned with the contingent, verse thereby takes on a transcendent character.[107] Equally, the formal features of the insertions highlight important themes in Chartier's prose and, conversely, lend themselves to interpretation in light of those themes. The mimetic qualities of the lyrics' rhyme schemes have often been noted: symmetrical forms connote divine order; patterns of successive rhymes echo the teleology of salvation history.[108] Significantly, the lyrics do not adopt the fixed forms characteristic of courtly poetry. As the narrative context confirms, poetry is placed in the service of spiritual renewal. Villon's practice, a generation later, is very different: the *Testament*'s lyrics insist on contingency rather than transcendence. Villon sets established *ballade* and *rondeau* forms against a background of octosyllabic *huitains;* but the insertions are not wholly distinct from their context in respect of versification,

102. Sinclair, "Poetic Creation."
103. Ed. Fourrier, 40–45.
104. Kay, *Place of Thought,* 123–49.
105. Sinclair, "Poetic Creation."
106. The discussion that follows is heavily indebted to Huot, "Re-fashioning Boethius."
107. Minet-Mahy, *Esthétique et pouvoir,* 500–503.
108. Ibid., 507–8; Huot, "Re-fashioning Boethius"; Rouy, *Esthétique,* 337–49.

function, or voice.[109] They cannot, therefore, be straightforwardly aligned with the *montage* technique that had typified lyric insertion for over a century; neither element, the lyrics or the *huitains,* appears logically or ontologically prior to the other. At one level this represents an expert poet's knowing play on inherited techniques, through which he asserts himself against his predecessors. But this play takes on another value when considered alongside other features of the *Testament:* its use of incomplete allusion and misquotation, the thematic importance of transience.[110] In this light poetry appears subject to constant change. Not only do poets develop new techniques, but also the passage of time renders poetry's very language elusive to posterity.

Prosimetrum

Chartier and Villon, then, offer contrasting epistemic routes for lyric insertion. Later poets respond to these possibilities in different ways when, following the example of the *Esperance,* they compose *prosimetrum* works on moral or political subjects. Scholars have found *prosimetrum* difficult to define; in chapter 1, for instance, we noted the limitations of Godzich and Kittay's contention that prose and verse sections "must self-consciously differ."[111] It is not commonly considered to include works in which prose and verse operate at distinct ontological levels, and therefore excludes verse narratives that contain prose letters—the *Voir dit,* the *Prison amoureuse,* Christine de Pizan's *Livre du Duc des vrais amans*—and verse texts accompanied by glosses or paratext in prose, for instance, Molinet's *Voiage de Napples*[112] or Destrées' hagiographic poems. Nor is the term applied to verse compositions in which prose features for essentially contingent reasons, such as the *Mutacion de Fortune,* where Christine alleges that she must write in prose while she is unwell (8731–48). Claude Thiry usefully encapsulates the features normally ascribed to *prosimetrum:* "Prose and verse alternate within a narrative scenario that invites allegorical interpretation, and an organic link is established between the two types of rhetoric."[113] The principles according to which prose and verse are employed, however, vary widely; the range and instability of *prosimetrum* compositions cannot be overemphasized.

109. Armstrong, *"Testament,"* 70–73.
110. Regalado, *"Effet de réel, Effet du reel"*; idem, *"'En l'an de mon trentiesme aage.'"*
111. Godzich and Kittay, *Emergence of Prose,* 46.
112. Molinet, *Faictz et dictz,* 1:277–83.
113. Thiry, *"La Fantasie subit ymaginée,"* 83.

If Chartier's *Esperance* provides the principal formal model for the *rhétori-queurs' prosimetrum,* it is his prose *Quadrilogue invectif* that most influences their use of political discourse. This discourse, and its use of poetry, are much less transcendent than in the *Esperance:* as part of their public role, the *rhéto-riqueurs* engage tendentiously with current and recent events. In this sense the use of verse alongside prose indicates two key aspects of these works. In the first place, poets and audiences regard them as prestigious. As a formal choice, *prosimetrum* indicates its author's compositional ambition; once again, complexity is valued. This prestige also has an ideological underpinning, however, for a *prosimetrum* work has a microcosmic quality: it combines two forms that tend to complement each other in these writers' overall output, as noted in chapter 2. While partaking of the chronicle through its use of prose, it also has the more public character of verse, apparent in its dominance in theater, Puys, and other communal literary phenomena. Yet various im-portant *prosimetrum* works cannot be assimilated to this sociocultural model. Some are overwhelmingly moral or theological, with no significant politi-cal or occasional dimension: Jean Meschinot's *Lunettes des princes* (1461–65), Octovien de Saint-Gelais's *Séjour d'Honneur,* René d'Anjou's *Mortifiement de Vaine Plaisance,* the output of Pierre Michault.[114] René's *Livre du Cœur d'amour épris,* based on the schema of the romance quest, has even less in common with political *prosimetrum.*

These problems of categorization strongly suggest that *prosimetrum,* like lyric insertion, calls generic boundaries and binary distinctions into question.[115] The relationship between prose and verse in many texts cannot be character-ized in terms of clear formal or functional oppositions such as narrative/lyric, discursive/emotive, or narrator/characters. Contrasts between different verse forms are often as important as those between verse and prose, while both prose and verse may employ different types of rhetoric within a single text.[116] Even Molinet's *prosimetrum,* relatively consistent in its complementary use of prose and verse, resists generalization. While prose normally conveys moral and political arguments and verse plays a more affective role, their narrative organization varies, and their effects depend heavily on ideological contexts.[117] Chastelain's *Epitaphes d'Hector* (1454) is still more distinctive: it was writ-ten for the stage, and indeed represents the only attested use of prose in the

114. Michault's *Dance aux Aveugles* appears in *Œuvres poétiques,* ed. Folkart, 69–139.
115. Singer, "Clockwork Genres," 241, identifies this quality in formally diverse texts of different kinds.
116. Cornilliat, "Prosimètre et persuasion"; Schoysman, "Prosimètre et *varietas.*"
117. Thiry, "Au Carrefour"; Cornilliat, "Prosimètre et persuasion"; Armstrong, "Pros-imètre et savoir," 131.

theater of our period.[118] The range of verse-prose interactions seems to reflect an experimental approach by poets who seek to refine or depart from previous *prosimetrum* compositions—not least, in many cases, their own.

Nevertheless, meaningful distinctions between prose and verse can often be identified. While neither form is epistemically privileged, each may implicitly offer knowledge about the other and reveal its own value in the eyes of poets and their audiences. In the case of verse, this value may be as a vehicle for wisdom and authority, particularly toward the end of a long narrative. In the final section of the *Lunettes des princes,* the *acteur* reads a book in which each of the four cardinal virtues delivers a moral lesson in a different verse form; similarly, verse is exclusively used for the closing sections of the *Séjour d'Honneur,* where the *acteur* is upbraided for his past life, and subsequently repents and is absolved (4.xviii–xxvi). Not that this obtains throughout: verse also expresses the *acteur*'s near-suicidal despair earlier in the *Lunettes* and the seductive rhetoric of various worldly personifications in the *Séjour.*[119] Varied versification often characterizes individual speakers, by contrast with other voices or through the established connotations of specific forms. In the *Epitaphes d'Hector,* Hector's verse is more varied and sophisticated than that of his killer Achilles, who is unambiguously presented as morally inferior.[120] Neither prose nor verse has a monopoly on discursive argument, but prose is the exclusive medium for the latter part of the action, where Alexander the Great facilitates a reconciliation between Achilles and Hector. While verse expresses distinctions between the characters, prose seems to constitute a common ground on which they can meet. Verse is thereby aligned with particularity and subjectivity, and prose with negotiation and understanding, no small issues in a play conceived and performed to accompany delicate political negotiations between French and Burgundian ambassadors.[121]

The distribution of forms in the *Livre du Cœur d'amour épris* is relatively unadventurous: prose is used for the *acteur*'s narrative discourse in his allegorical dream, and verse for direct speech by the characters within that dream, as well as for written documents such as the epitaphs of notable historical figures.[122] In other words, verse expresses the allegorical world when it is not mediated by the *acteur*'s language. It is thus associated with higher levels of being and understanding, with personified abstractions and posthumous

---

118. Doudet, "Aux frontières du prosimètre."
119. Ménager, "Vers et prose."
120. Doudet, "Aux frontières du prosimètre," 39.
121. Ibid., 30–32, outlines the context of the *Epitaphes'* performance.
122. Exceptions to this distinction are minimal; ed. Bouchet, 200, 492.

renown, whereas prose is the register of ordinary mortals. Similarly, in the dream in André de la Vigne's *Ressource de la Chrestienté* (1494), moral and political personifications express themselves in verse while the narrator is restricted to prose.[123] In both cases verse is again the province of subjectivity, of first-person as opposed to third-person discourse. In many other *prosimetrum* works, however, personifications speak in both prose and verse. This is true of Molinet's political allegories, though the complementary functions of prose and verse are rich in implications. Typically the first verse section is a lament, elicited by a crisis such as war or the death of a prince. Far from proving therapeutic, these laments leave their speakers more sorrowful than ever; a consolatory address in prose then partly restores their morale.[124] Verse seems to wield a dangerous power, which prose seeks to "tame" but cannot wholly overcome. The "wildness" of these verse laments is, indeed, attested in manuscripts, where they are often transcribed as independent poems.[125] *Prosimetrum* thus accentuates the diversity of verse's forms and their roles. In so doing it reminds us that when a *prosimetrum* author writes in prose, he is not choosing prose against verse; he is choosing prose against octosyllabic couplets, or decasyllabic *huitains,* or *ballades.* Hence prose can be seen as another kind of verse, one that simply happens to lack meter and rhyme.[126] From this perspective, *prosimetrum* effectively annexes prose to verse, regardless of their relative quantitative or thematic importance in any given text. It seems to mark poetry's revenge on the "rise of prose," and even the genesis of the prose poem.

This chapter has explored increasingly complex and problematic ways in which poetry legitimizes the knowledge of itself, to employ Lyotard's terminology (see introduction). Metadiscursive comments on poetry are the most obvious instance of reflexivity: here poetry explicitly presents the knowledge of itself *as* knowledge. More widespread and typical are the various forms of intertextual association by which a poem appeals to our knowledge of other poems, and thereby offers knowledge about itself and/or poetry in general. In these cases the alluding text constitutes the means to knowledge of other texts, which are objects of that knowledge but are simultaneously the means to knowledge of the alluding text. This feedback loop may produce remarkable

123. Ed. Brown, 43.
124. Cornilliat, "Prosimètre et persuasion."
125. Armstrong, "Manuscript Reception," 322.
126. Though in some cases prose even contains rhyming and metrical elements; see, "Practice," 272. Jacques Legrand theorizes this possibility, noting that rhyme may exist in prose as well as verse; Legrand, *Archiloge Sophie,* 141.

effects. The knowledge of an accumulating and diversifying poetic tradition, for instance, transforms the concept of hope through Espoir/Esperance's personified avatars. Yet as Lyotard suggests, to legitimize knowledge is ultimately to destabilize it. Quotation is a case in point: its characteristic reversibility creates not just a back-and-forth of knowledge between the quoting and the quoted poem but an uncertainty as to where knowledge lies. The complications of reflexivity are also apparent in lyric insertion, where graft and host each serve as both the framing and the framed element, and in *prosimetrum,* where clear formal distinctions collapse as prose is absorbed into verse.

Whatever "textual knowledge" may be at stake, a poem cannot produce this knowledge in isolation; it relies on an audience's shared understanding. The ability to identify formal features and appreciate their value is a necessary condition for this understanding but not a sufficient one. The *Leys d'amors* and Machaut's *Prologue* set out much more ambitious requirements: to understand poetry is to understand its role in the universe, to share a set of metaphysical assumptions. Other audiences need other forms of knowledge. To follow Froissart's ongoing investigation into poetry's cognitive role entails familiarity with Machaut's work, the wider tradition of courtly love poetry, and Froissart's own evolving output.[127] As the example of Espoir/Esperance shows, concepts are apt to acquire meanings in relation to previous poetic depictions. Practices of poetic competition and quotation presuppose that poets and their public are aware of precise intertexts—or, at least, aware that a precise intertext exists somewhere. Lyric insertion and *prosimetrum* are subject to development and experimentation in ways predicated on knowing audiences. The knowledge of poetry, in short, is produced by appealing to a preexisting community, or by founding a community where none had existed before. When this knowledge is bound up with ideological concerns, as in didactic or political *prosimetrum* works, the interpellation of communities is all the more important. It is to this issue that we turn in our final chapter.

---

127. In turn, knowledge of all these fields underpins an appreciation of the intertextual and cross-cultural negotiations at work in Chaucer's *Book of the Duchess;* Butterfield, *Familiar Enemy,* 269–91.

CHAPTER SIX

Textual Communities

Poetry and the Social Construction of Knowledge

In our introduction we described "ideological knowledge" as embracing political, social, and religious assumptions. A deliberately broad notion, it enables us to address a wider range of poetic texts than terms such as "didactic" or "ethical" would permit. Crucially, "ideological knowledge" is not confined to explicit moralizing discourses; it also embraces what is not said, indeed what cannot be formulated. These different forms of knowledge coexist uneasily, as the *Breviari d'amor* tellingly illustrates. Matfre presents both explicit and implicit forms of ideological knowledge: the former concerns religious doctrine, in which sexual love assumes an unfamiliar place in a divinely ordered cosmos; the latter emerges from his interventionist reinterpretations of the troubadour corpus to support his contentions in the *perilhos tractat*. Matfre invests troubadour song with authority, but in unexpected ways that produce a provocative tension between two kinds of established knowledge: religious orthodoxy and the courtly love tradition. Neither is straightforwardly reproduced; rather, each is transformed as a new form of knowledge is generated.[1] Knowledge production of this kind has tended to escape scholarly analysis, which has concentrated on overt ethico-political didacticism.[2] We concentrate

---

1. Bolduc, *Medieval Poetics of Contraries,* 89–128, notes the mutually defining relationship of the sacred and profane in the *Breviari* (96–98) and the positioning of author and audience in respect of the knowledge that Matfre conveys. See also chapter 4.

2. Kelly, *Christine de Pizan's Changing Opinion,* is a valuable study of the changes and challenges that opinion undergoes in Christine's prolific output, albeit not specifically her poetry.

instead on the unspoken, unspeakable forms of thought that constitute "ideology" for modern theorists,[3] and their interplay with more explicit poetic
themes. This interplay characteristically takes one of the various forms of legitimation identified by Lyotard (see introduction), the processes of reduplication through which poets attempt to secure the knowledge they present *as*
knowledge—and, in so doing, risk destabilizing that knowledge. Hence, far
from reproducing commonly accepted *doxa,* legitimation may expose fault
lines in established patterns of thought, for instance, as the persuasive force
of rhetoric is compromised by the disjunction between a poem's semantic
and pragmatic dimensions, between what it says and what it does to its audience.[4] Our examples, treated in broadly chronological order, present a range
of ideological challenges: to conventional binary distinctions, to the cultural
valence of commonplaces, to the transcendental validity of moral concepts,
and to the relationship between the authority of poets and the authority of
their messages.

It is through a poem's audience, in particular its sense of community, that
ideological knowledge manifests itself. Whether poems reproduce or challenge
widely held beliefs, the knowledge their audiences find in them is socially constructed. Hence communities, and means of interpellating them, are important to our analysis. Their centrality to constructions of ideological knowledge
has been acknowledged in the case of propaganda, characterized as "a political
grammar of the conscious and unconscious . . . which reaches out for unanim-
ity within a group it often helps to define."[5] Some communities are materially
actualized, for example, urban literary cultures such as in thirteenth-century
Arras or the intellectual circles in and around the University of Paris, and
princely courts such as that of Charles d'Orléans at Blois.[6] Physical realization,
however, is not essential. Various communities are "virtual," constructed by
the ways in which poems position their audiences. The *Breviari* again provides
a useful example. Matfre interpellates his readers as "fin aimador" (true lovers, 169), united with God in love and knowledge.[7] Hence, wherever they may
be located and whatever they may individually think of Matfre's arguments,
the *Breviari*'s readers are constituted as having a common relationship to a

---

3. On Slavoj Žižek's influential approach to ideology, for example, see Kay, *Žižek,* 104–7,
132–39.
4. The relationship between rhetoric and speech acts is important in modern political
thought; see notably Palonen, *Quentin Skinner,* 133–72.
5. Taithe and Thornton, "Propaganda," 3–4.
6. On these milieux, see especially Symes, *A Common Stage;* Corbellari, *Voix des clercs;* Taylor, *Making of Poetry.*
7. Kay, "Grafting the Knowledge Community," 368–70.

particular socio-symbolic order. In this sense, Matfre's poem *performs* a textual community. It thereby indicates a crucial feature of communities, to which some recent thinking in ethics has drawn attention: what holds them together is not necessarily what their members have in common but their relationship to something *else*. A community coheres as a result of absences; its gaps and noncohesion are central to its constitution.[8] Hence the *Cour amoureuse* of Charles VI and the Puy of the Immaculate Conception at Rouen are communities not through any commonality that their members might exhibit, but through their members' relationships to women and to the Virgin Mary respectively, relationships posited in the poetry they produce.[9] A corollary of poetry's relationship to audiences is that ideological knowledge is subject to change: as a play is staged at different times and places, or a poem transmitted in varying physical contexts, new publics can construct its significance in new ways. Even when it pretends to transcendence, in other words, ideological knowledge is contingent; this contingency will be a recurrent motif in our analysis.

Arras in the Late Thirteenth Century

The case of Arras is an instructive starting point for reflection on audiences as communities, for the city was characterized by multiple divisions. Most obvious was that between the *cité,* the seat of the bishopric, and the *ville,* dominated by the abbey of Saint-Vaast, by royal and comital representatives, and by the city's *échevins* (aldermen).[10] The city's literary community, constituted as the Carité, could apparently mediate in local disputes.[11] This mediating function is also visible on a symbolic level, in the Carité's poetic production. While most of its output adopted familiar courtly forms that owe little to local conditions,[12] its ludic genres point toward an inchoate urban poetics. As noted in chapter 5, members of the Carité composed and exchanged *jeux-partis, resveries,* and *fatrasies.* In challenging the principles of courtly love, or of logical and linguistic coherence, these forms evoke familiar discourses only to question them. A new kind of knowledge thus emerges, a knowledge to which verse is central because of the various incongruous contrasts in which it plays

8. Agamben, *Coming Community;* Dinshaw, *Getting Medieval,* 22.

9. On the *Cour amoureuse,* see *La Cour amoureuse,* ed. Bozzolo and Loyau.

10. Berger, *Littérature et société,* 25–116; Symes, *A Common Stage,* 30–32, 44–63, 239–40.

11. Symes, *A Common Stage,* 206.

12. Berger, *Littérature et société,* 19–258, edits a number of Arrageois poems of more explicit local interest.

a part. The ludic forms undermine some fundamental cultural distinctions—courtly/noncourtly, lyric language/ordinary language, sense/nonsense—and thereby stage an implicit plurality and discontinuity. These modes of being are distinctly *urban;* they correspond both to lived experience in medieval cities, characterized by socioeconomic and political diversity and instability, and to literary images of that experience, in which the city is typically a deceptive locus that promotes social intermingling.[13] Hence the *jeux-partis, resveries,* and *fatrasies* of Arras present a sociology of city life, an ethos that is nonexclusionary (albeit not anarchic, for poets observe strict formal principles).[14] The conditions of these poems' composition and performance reflect this ethos: they were exchanged on a relatively open and egalitarian basis rather than through closed competitions.[15] In this sense the Carité's poetry seems to help form the distinctive "public sphere" of open exchange that Carol Symes has persuasively shown to function in Arras.[16]

A better-known Arras cultural production, the *Jeu de la Feuillée* of Adam de la Halle (1276), positions its audience and characters to very similar effect. The play is deeply rooted in Arrageois public life, though the circumstances of its performance are uncertain. While this makes it impossible to grasp the precise nuances of the *Feuillée*'s social comment, Symes observes that its broad significance rests on the eponymous *feuillée* (bower), a real public object that housed a reliquary, erected in the city's Petit Marché each summer for a period of public viewing, and often embroiled in institutions' competing claims to urban space. The *Feuillée* was quite possibly performed in this context, and is likely to have contributed to expressing and even resolving the social tensions that often arose around public displays.[17]

More broadly, when considered alongside the ludic poetry practiced in Arras at the same time (and to which Adam contributed in eighteen *jeux-partis*), the *Feuillée*'s subversive humor acts as a solvent. Adam's (self-)mocking techniques dissolve the barriers between different kinds of experience. The social roles of individuals are opened up to transformation from the outset: the play opens with the figure of Adam proclaiming that he has changed his clothes ("mon abit cangiet," 1) with a view to resuming his studies after a period of married life. Diverse social groups mingle, notably in the tavern, a frequent

13. On intraurban conflict, see Heers, *La Ville,* 203–97. On literary images of the city, see Cerquiglini-Toulet, *"Un engin si soutil,"* 130–31; Zumthor, *Mesure du monde,* 111–41.
14. Gally, "Poésie en jeu," 74–75.
15. Symes, *A Common Stage,* 223–26.
16. Ibid., especially 2–3, 127–30.
17. Ibid., 183–231. All references to the *Feuillée* are to Adam de la Halle, *Œuvres complètes,* ed. Badel, 286–375.

literary synecdoche for urban life and a reflection of the shifting, contested, easily transgressed nature of space in the city.[18] These processes are reinforced in two further ways. First, the *Feuillée* is formally heterogeneous, with diverse and overlapping plotlines and echoes of numerous existing genres.[19] Its octosyllabic meter, widely used in narrative and other verse, makes these echoes all the more perceptible. Second, various lines suggest that barriers between cast and audience occasionally break down in performance, as characters move into and out of the space occupied by spectators (for instance, 340, 363). On one level the *Feuillée* may indeed contribute to negotiations between social groups, or promote the Carité's own sense of comradeship;[20] on another it conveys implications congruent with the nonexclusionary urban ethos expressed in ludic poetry. Social interaction in cities, it is suggested, involves negotiating the unexpected, moving between milieux and spaces, reinforcing or adjusting one's public persona as necessary.[21] For the city dweller, identity is not permanently fixed; it is constantly reactualized through performance in changing public contexts. The difficulty of interpreting the *Feuillée,* in the absence of clear evidence about its performance, only reinforces this principle.

The *Roman de Fauvel*

Both in the original two-book redaction by Gervès du Bus (1310, 1314) and in Chaillou de Pesstain's interpolated version, which incorporates numerous lyrics, *Fauvel* transmits much more overt forms of sociopolitical knowledge than the poetry and verse drama of Arras.[22] A satirical tale of the eponymous horse, which embodies falsehood and other vices, *Fauvel* employs a range of well-established discourses such as sermon, allegory, and beast epic. It comments both on general social trends, notably the way in which the world has been "berstorné" (turned upside down, 335), and on specific episodes such as the career of the royal favorite Enguerran de Marigny and the trial of the Templars.[23] Gervès and Chaillou exploit highly familiar didactic motifs: the symbolic connotations of animals, the threats posed to rulers by flatterers. These

---

18. Symes, *A Common Stage,* 135–59, comments on space in Arras. Cerquiglini-Toulet, "*Un engin si soutil,*" 130–31, adduces examples of the tavern as urban microcosm.

19. McGregor, *Broken Pot Restored,* 41–95.

20. Lütgemeier, *Beiträge,* 133–41, proposes the latter view.

21. Symes, *A Common Stage,* 70–71. On the public persona in medieval society more generally, see Fenster and Smail, *Fama.*

22. All references are to Gervais du Bus, *Roman de Fauvel,* ed. Långfors.

23. Bent and Wathey, Introduction, 9–10; Mühlethaler, *Fauvel au pouvoir.*

complement each other, hence overdetermining the clarity with which *Fauvel* denounces corruption at court (though Chaillou's text includes disruptive elements, to which we return later in this chapter).[24] Verse plays a significant role in establishing the text's moral tenor. The narrative is in octosyllabic couplets, reinforcing its affiliations with the *Roman de Renart* and its satirical perspective on society, while the lyric elements in Chaillou's version draw attention to Fauvel's hypocritical use of courtly language.[25] Both versions seem to originate in the royal chancery, a highly educated and well-informed milieu, close to the institutional power to which they are addressed. In particular, the single witness of Chaillou's interpolated *Fauvel* (BnF, ms. fr. 146) is an exceptionally complex anthology, clearly conceived as a coherent initiative and possibly sponsored by a court faction led by Charles de Valois, the uncle of Philip V (1317–1322), who has often been identified as the volume's likely addressee.[26] *Fauvel*'s first-person narrator, and its interpellation of readers, reflect the context in which it circulated. The narrator tends to assume a highly authoritative position in cognitive terms; by adopting an explicitly pedagogical stance toward his audience, occasionally explaining terms and images, he presents himself as a knowledgeable speaker of uncomfortable truths. Nevertheless, particularly in the second book, his subordinate social status is reflected in his marginal position: he is a disempowered witness of events that he cannot influence. The effect is uncomfortable, for the satirist and his target, the flatterer, seem to be doubles of each other. Both seek to influence a courtly audience through eloquence, albeit to different ends and with differing degrees of success. In this sense the satirist is a virtuous but ineffectual flatterer. Consequently, Gervès's narrator compromises his critique of court flattery even as he voices it. Chaillou's *remaniement* offers a more complicated but more authoritative narratorial voice which, through a set of self-assertive comments, draws attention to his role in appropriating and continuing the work of Gervès, knowingly engaging with Jean de Meun's handling of similar issues in the *Rose*.[27] In conjunction

24. Mühlethaler, *Fauvel au pouvoir,* 35–142, notes the familiarity of *Fauvel*'s imagery and lessons.

25. On the relationship between Fauvel and Renart, see ibid., 38–52; on the effects of inserted lyrics, see Regalado, "Songs of Jehannot de Lescurel," 164–65.

26. On the chancery and court circles in which *Fauvel* was produced and received, see Mühlethaler, *Fauvel au pouvoir,* 387–400; Lalou, "Chancellerie royale"; Vale, "World of the Courts"; Wathey, "Gervès du Bus." On BnF, ms. fr. 146, see especially Morin, "Jehannot de Lescurel's Chansons"; Bent and Wathey, Introduction, 4–8.

27. On the narrator's voice, see Mühlethaler, *Fauvel au pouvoir,* 168–88; idem, "Discours du narrateur, discours de Fortune"; Brownlee, "Authorial Self-representation." Bolduc, *Medieval Poetics of Contraries,* 141–65, examines the ways in which BnF, ms. fr. 146 draws attention to Chaillou's compositional activity and to the authority (specifically the religious authority) of his message.

with the manuscript's material value and semiotic density, this voice positions the "implied reader" of fr. 146 as both aesthetically well informed and politically powerful. This is a reader who knows a literary allusion when he sees one, knows what damage evil counselors can wreak, and knows how to respond to admonitions by selecting which examples to follow and which to avoid.[28] Hence fr. 146 constructs a community by establishing common ground between Philip V, the chancery, and a court faction.

But readers able to recognize familiar motifs can also recognize unfamiliar ones. This is crucial to the effect of both Gervès' and Chaillou's second books, where the personification of Fortune is transformed. In the first book, as in Jean de Meun's *Rose* and so many poems influenced by it, Fortune is a figure of contingency; her influence enables Fauvel to gain power.[29] Yet in the second book, when Fauvel seeks her hand in marriage so as to rule the world, Fortune refuses him. During a long speech she reveals that her highest manifestation is as divine providence: enjoying a transcendent overview of the cosmos, she mediates between God and terrestrial events (2251–2354).[30] Fauvel, then, has misinterpreted his prospective bride in assuming that she represents contingency alone, in keeping with literary tradition. The community of *Fauvel*'s readers stands united in its failure to predict Fortune's unpredictable reversal into its opposite.

The defamiliarized portrait of Fortune is linked to her important role in developing an eschatological perspective.[31] She identifies Fauvel as a harbinger of Antichrist (3109–10), whose coming coincides with the triumph of evil in the world prior to the Last Judgment. Does this perspective tame Fauvel, reassuring us against the vices he embodies through the promise of salvation? Not quite. Fauvel proceeds to marry Vaine Gloire (Vainglory), whereupon Chaillou's version introduces a set of associated rituals and festivities. The implications of this narrative sequence are twofold, and doubly unsettling. On the one hand, Chaillou disrupts *Fauvel*'s satirical discourse by introducing a charivari: as Fauvel prepares to join Vaine Gloire in bed, a masked procession in the street outside objects to the ill-sorted marriage. The episode may be read as an expression of political protest, and hence assimilated to the critique

---

28. Bolduc, *Medieval Poetics of Contraries,* 138–40, notes the expertise required to make optimal sense of BnF, ms. fr. 146. On the manuscript's admonitory function, see Dillon, "Profile of Philip V," 227. The notion of the implied reader derives from Iser, *Implied Reader.*

29. On Fortune and contingency, see chapter 3, and Heller-Roazen, *Fortune's Faces,* 63–99. On the first book of *Fauvel,* see Mühlethaler, *Fauvel au pouvoir,* 42–45.

30. Mühlethaler, *Fauvel au pouvoir,* 46–52; idem, "Discours du narrateur"; Badel, *Roman de la Rose au XIVᵉ siècle,* 212–20; Hunt, "Christianization of Fortune," 106–12; Attwood, *Fortune la contrefaite,* 14–15, 32, 121, 124.

31. On eschatological motifs in Fortune's speech, see especially Palmer, "Cosmic Quaternities."

of court flattery,[32] but it also undermines the narrator's moral exhortations. Although the charivari is a traditional channel of social condemnation, it also has its own anarchic energy, and thus partly resists the very moral order and discipline that *Fauvel* implicitly promulgates to ward off corruption. On the other hand, Fauvel's dangerous resilience becomes evident after a tournament held at the wedding feast, where personified virtues and vices engage in single combat.[33] The virtues triumph, but Fauvel is undaunted. Hérésie takes him to the fountain of Jouvence (Youth), where his powers are renewed; the narrative ends with the narrator praying for France to be delivered from Fauvel and his kind. Hence Fortune's metamorphosis into providence underlines not Fauvel's ultimate destruction but his threat to the world. Her role makes very particular demands on the implied reader, on whom it intensifies the interpolated *Fauvel*'s admonitory effect. The narrative does not comfort readers with the promise that falsehood, and the other evils that Fauvel represents, can be overcome. Rather, it fosters the anxiety that these evils can appear anywhere and are difficult to extirpate, not least in themselves.[34] In these crucial respects Chaillou's interpolated text reveals how *remaniement* can both enrich and subvert poetry's ethico-political thrust.

First-Person Narrators and the Status of the Poet

In the work of many subsequent poets, the role of first-person narrators is at least as central, and as vexed, as in *Fauvel*. Watriquet de Couvin, a near-contemporary of Chaillou, takes an uncharacteristically straightforward approach, securing the authority of his first-person voices in various ways.[35] His moral themes, such as estates satire and the role of the cardinal virtues, are highly conventional; they carry the weight of a lengthy tradition, which also reflects on the voices that express them.[36] More strikingly, Watriquet's voices frequently assert the seriousness and value of his work, proudly advertising his patronage relationships and his role as an adviser to courtly society, and often thematizing the composition and reception of his poetry.[37]

32. Mühlethaler, *Fauvel au pouvoir,* 130–38.

33. The episode partly derives from Huon de Méry's *Tournoiement Antéchrist;* ibid., 67–68.

34. This reading is indebted to Guynn, *Allegory and Sexual Ethics.*

35. Watriquet's dated or datable poems span the period 1319–1329; Cojan-Negulescu, "Watriquet de Couvin," 125–28.

36. Ibid., 177–84, 279–88, 363–64, notes the conventional character of Watriquet's moralizing. Corbellari, *La Voix des clercs,* outlines his predecessors' didactic poetics.

37. Huot, "Writer's Mirror," 38–42; Cojan-Negulescu, "Watriquet de Couvin," 211–20, 237–65.

Manuscript illustrations contribute to presenting the poet's relationship with his public as empowered participation within a courtly environment. On an intratextual level, the narrator's advisory function is implied in images that accompany allegorical narratives in the two most important Watriquet manuscripts, Paris, Arsenal, ms. 3525 and BnF, ms. fr. 14968.[38] The miniatures tend to depict the first-person narrator at the edge of the scene he witnesses, thereby underlining a key technique of Watriquet: the gradual unfolding of didactic allegories, whereby an initially enigmatic motif or event is described before the narrator and/or an accompanying personification interprets its moral significance.[39] This process positions Watriquet (if not always his narratorial surrogates) as the "subject supposed to know": to believe that an enigma will be elucidated, the audience must believe that there is a subject who has the knowledge they currently lack, in other words, the poet.[40] Equally, on an extratextual level, certain key illustrations draw attention to patrons and audiences. In fr. 14968 an initial miniature represents the poet twice, both speaking and presenting a book to his patron; the image that introduces the *Dit du connestable de France* shows the Duke of Bourbon commissioning the poem from Watriquet; the parodic *Fastrasie* is illustrated by a scene of the author performing before Philip VI with his fellow poet Raimondin.[41] It is significant that the illustrations depict different audiences. The poet is not bound to one court or patron; the community that he addresses is joined together by shared ethical and aesthetic values, not physical contiguity or socioeconomic interdependence. Watriquet is visually distinguished from the other figures in these images by a parti-colored tunic, usually yellow and green, which he and his various personas are depicted as wearing throughout both fr. 14968 and Arsenal 3525.[42] Parti-colored clothing commonly indicated the wearer's subordinate status, and was often worn by entertainers; yellow usually had negative connotations; green connoted energy both *in bono* (youth, vigor) and *in malo* (inconstancy, disorder).[43] In conjunction these sartorial traits position the poet as subservient to his courtly public yet thereby also confirm and advertise his relationship with that public. Both miniatures and poems assert

38. Cojan-Negulescu, "Watriquet de Couvin," 28–35, describes these volumes. Huot, *From Song to Book,* 224–25, suggests Watriquet's involvement in the preparation of fr. 14968.

39. Cojan-Negulescu, "Watriquet de Couvin," 466 n. 619, comments on these illustrations. On accompanying personifications, see ibid., 438–42; on allegorical interpretation, see Huot, "Writer's Mirror," 42–43.

40. Kay, "Poésie, vérité, et le sujet supposé savoir."

41. Huot, "Writer's Mirror," 37–38; idem, *From Song to Book,* 225–30.

42. Huot, *From Song to Book,* 225; Cojan-Negulescu, "Watriquet de Couvin," 31.

43. Mertens, *Mi-parti als Zeichen,* 10–15, 54–58; Pastoureau, *Figures et couleurs,* 40–42.

the poet's integration into the community whose values he articulates, a social class rather than a particular court.

The poet's predicament is more complex in many later pieces. From Machaut to Lemaire de Belges, whether in amatory or in political or didactic poetry, first-person narrators are often marked by inadequacy of some sort, and hence by incomplete assimilation to their audience. When they first appear, they are not merely impotent or incompetent; they always wield a certain authority, for instance, as poetic technicians. Yet other traits seem to undercut that authority: they are gauche lovers, socially subservient, or physically deformed. The protagonist of Machaut's *Fonteinne amoureuse* alludes self-deprecatingly to his cowardice (85–155); those of Froissart's major *dits* are not notably successful in pressing their amatory suits through poetry; that of Lemaire's *Concorde des deux langages* is ejected from the Temple of Venus for the paucity of his offering to the goddess.[44] Jacqueline Cerquiglini-Toulet has compellingly argued that such traits reflect the position that the court poet assigns himself, subordinate and disempowered but able to look sideways at his surroundings and renew his audience's perceptions of the world.[45] This has much more to do with imaginary self-representation than with poets' real cultural status. Machaut and Froissart often allude to being sought after by patrons; Chartier manifested his eloquence as a public servant as well as a poet; the Burgundian *indiciaires,* as noted in chapter 2, enjoyed high esteem and exerted an influence far beyond the aesthetic. Yet the pose of marginal servant does characterize many literary images of the poet-public relationship. It takes on a very particular character in respect of the social or moral knowledge that a poem conveys and the communities through which that knowledge is manifested. By contrast with Watriquet's protagonists, his successors' squinting, cringing, shambling, derisory narrators are not profoundly assimilated to their public. Audiences are not invited to emulate the protagonists of the *Fonteinne, Espinette,* or *Concorde;* a poet's lifestyle is emphatically not presented in aspirational terms. On the contrary, poets offer good examples of how *not* to love, to cope with personal setbacks, to win friends and influence people. Their audiences cohere as communities through processes that anthropological and psychoanalytic discourses have made familiar: by disowning poets, the better to define themselves collectively. We might usefully think of these hapless protagonists as abject, essential yet intolerable to the social body's sense of itself.[46] It is derision and suspicion toward courtly

44. On the *Concorde,* see Armstrong, "Yearning and Learning."
45. Cerquiglini-Toulet, *"Un engin si soutil,"* 112–15; idem, "Écriture louche."
46. On the abject, see Kristeva, *Powers of Horror,* 1–31.

poets that cause their public to cohere as a community. Indeed the audience is tacitly encouraged to practice a self-policing analogous to that promulgated in *Fauvel*. There is potentially a poet in all of us, is the implication, and we must wipe him out.

Yet this process of disavowal is not clear-cut. Poets are not rejected outright; nor does their rejection simply promote the public's solidarity. Rather, as a narrative unfolds, attention is often displaced onto other matters. A protagonist may be ill equipped to pursue his ostensible preoccupation—fulfillment in love, say, or social advancement—but this failure does not define a poet completely. Other lessons emerge from the wreckage, for instance, on how to govern well or deal with fluctuating fortune. Some of these are conveyed through the protagonist himself, who has acquired appropriate authority through a gradual learning process; others are conveyed through the textual structure, around a protagonist whose voice remains unsatisfactory. In either instance the extratextual poet is invested with authority: he is not to be emulated, but he is also the subject supposed to know. If his art is disavowed as insignificant or nonserious, this ultimately makes it all the more effective as a vehicle of ideology because it operates covertly.

The *Fonteinne, Espinette,* and *Concorde* exemplify these tendencies in various ways. In the *Fonteinne* the clerkly narrator and princely lover are caught in a play of similarities and contrasts: the prince is also a poet, the narrator is also in love, and the two share a dream containing an account of the Judgment of Paris. Crucially, as we noted in chapter 3, the prince and narrator interpret the dream's mythological motifs differently. The prince's more superficial understanding is undercut by the narrator's explicit comments on the social responsibility of princes (1161–1204), and by the well-known and catastrophic implications of Paris's preference for Venus and the life of pleasure she embodies. A parallel is implied between Paris's choice and the prince's preoccupation with his lady in the face of difficult social realities, notably his imminent departure into exile. The prince's attitude is tacitly questioned even as the narrator lends him a supportive ear. The two figures' differing approaches to *reading* poetry, in the form of myth, draw attention to their contrasting ways of *producing* poetry. An amateur lyric poet, the prince spontaneously expresses his emotion in verse. Though appropriately shaped, his verse is not accompanied by reflection nor invested in as an artistic product. It takes the narrator, a full-time professional poet, to transcribe the prince's lament and recognize its formal qualities. As in Froissart's *Prison amoureuse,* the professional poet can set the amateur's verse in a narrative context and explain what it means; he thereby helps define an ideology for his courtly audience. In the *Espinette* the protagonist's paradoxical status is

related to a key theme in Froissart's major *dits,* the impossibility of negotiating social interactions otherwise than through the provisional mediations
of memory and textuality. In particular, this impossibility colors relations
between the sexes. As the protagonist stumbles from one encounter to the
next, his misadventures warn the courtly public that life and love aren't like
they are in books: an apparent *locus amoenus* may prove uncomfortable, as
Froissart's narrator discovers when, kissing violets at his lady's request, he
is pricked by thorns (3513–31). The narrator of Lemaire's *Concorde* learns
rather more than his earlier counterparts. After leaving the Temple of Venus,
he comes to find out about the Temple of Minerva, where moral and historical writing—and the dead authors who practice it—flourish eternally,
and where French and Tuscan culture may be reconciled. The perspective
of a transcendent republic of letters sits in an uneasy tension with contemporary realities: Franco-Italian military and cultural conflict loomed large in
Lemaire's occasional poetry of the period, which accompanied the *Concorde*
in early printed anthologies. Hence the text's sociopolitical thrust is twofold.
Ethical and historical truths are not contingent upon national borders and
dynastic interests; but those truths can never be attained in a pure state in
this world, and we must acknowledge that our perceptions are situated and
contaminated.

The contrasts between the *Fonteinne* and the *Concorde* should not lead us
to assume that, in narrative poetry produced over the intervening century
and a half, poet-narrators increasingly learn from their experience. Protagonists manifest their equivocal status and relationship with their audience in diverse ways, though ideological knowledge is constantly prone to
change. Villon's *Testament* is a case in point. Its first-person voice, which
specialists often term "the testator," is positioned with respect to readers in
two ways. First, his self-representation is allusive and incomplete, tempting
readers to fill the gaps with biographical constructs but denying any possibility of confirming them.[47] Second, his exploitation of familiar forms and
dense intertextual reference presupposes a highly knowing audience. Even
if this audience constituted only a minuscule proportion of Villon's actual
readership, the *Testament* contains so many of what Michael Riffaterre terms
"ungrammaticalities"—incoherencies of expression, suggesting that a poem
is producing meaning through intertextual play—that such knowingness
comes across as the condition to which readers should aspire.[48] Both these
techniques lock the testator and his language into a particular time and place,

47. Regalado, *"Effet de réel, Effet du reel"*; idem, *"En l'an de mon trentiesme aage."*
48. On readers' assumed expertise, see Taylor, *Poetry of François Villon.* On Riffaterre's
model of intertextuality, see Riffaterre, *Semiotics of Poetry;* Allen, *Intertextuality,* 115–32.

as Clément Marot acknowledged when editing Villon's poetry only two generations later:

> Quant à l'industrie des lays qu'il feit en ses testaments, pour suffisamment la congnoistre & entendre, il faudroit avoir esté de son temps à Paris, & avoir congneu les lieux, les choses, & les hommes dont il parle.[49]

> (To recognize and properly understand the ingenuity of the bequests he made in his testaments [i.e., the *Lais* and *Testament*], a reader would have to have lived in Paris in his day, and known the places, things, and people of which he speaks.)

Both the marginal social groups and the high literary culture of Paris in the early 1460s seem crucial to the audience's understanding yet are always already lost to the audience. The effects on the knowledge conveyed in the *Testament* are significant. It has long been recognized that the poem's overtly didactic or pseudo-didactic elements, the testator's reflections on death and poverty, are familiar in fifteenth-century poetry, albeit expressed in memorably distinctive form.[50] Yet the testator's location, in a highly specific yet irrecuperable world, conveys further implications. Explicitly, and in ways that often undercut conventional moralizing discourses, human life and institutions are characterized as transient.[51] Implicitly, however, Villon indicates the limitations not only of humanity's physical resources but also of its intellectual capacities. In interpreting other people's behavior as well as their poetry, in assessing the present as well as the past, we must acknowledge the fallibility of our memory and understanding. This knowledge, which is "ideological" because it concerns the reliability with which social and moral attitudes can be formed, is predicated on the changes that time will inevitably bring about. Denied full comprehension of the *Testament* by these changes, Villon's readers form a "textual community" of the kind described by Brian Stock: they are bound together by their relationship to a text they do not understand.[52]

Christine de Pizan

The instability of both reception and legitimation is crucial to the ways in which Christine de Pizan's verse conveys ethical, social, and political knowledge.

---

49. "Prologue," in Marot, *Œuvres poétiques complètes,* ed. Defaux, 2:775–78 (quotation 777). Marot's edition was first published in September 1533; ibid., 1361.

50. An important early thematic study is Siciliano, *François Villon.*

51. Armstrong, *"Testament,"* 64.

52. See introduction; Stock, *Implications of Literacy.*

Discussion of Christine's didacticism has tended either to disregard distinctions between prose and verse or to privilege the substantial prose works that dominate her later production: the *Advision Cristine, Cité des Dames, Livre des Trois Vertus* (all 1405–6), *Livre de la Paix* (1412–1414), and others.[53] Certainly there are important elements that subtend her whole output. One of these, the responsibility that readers must actively assume in drawing lessons from her work, is a central theme in what follows.[54] It would be unjust, however, to claim that "she does not attribute different signifying practices to prose and meter."[55] From the beginning of her career, poetic form plays an important role in shaping knowledge and in grounding the relationship between author and public.

In sequences of short lyrics, an implicit critique of courtly *doxa* initially emerges through form before its status as knowledge is made clearer. The *Cent balades* (ca. 1394–1399) obliges audiences constantly to revise their expectations through two interrelated techniques. On the one hand, Christine pushes at the limits of *ballade* form by producing an impressively wide range of stanzaic structures.[56] On the other, particular themes and formal features are frequently established through a short sequence of *ballades* only to be varied thereafter. While the opening poems adopt a first-person voice that readers are likely to identify with Christine, the twelfth *ballade* introduces a male voice; grief is a unifying topic for the first twenty pieces, yet the twenty-first expresses the excitement of a lady in love.[57] The overwhelming impression is that courtly commonplaces are being treated with suspicion. This stance comes into sharper focus at the end of the sequence: while amatory subjects have hitherto dominated, a final group of *ballades* (91–99) exhorts readers to repent so that social ills may be remedied. To make sense of this group within the sequence, readers must both reassess the earlier poems and interpret the closing *ballades* against them. The didactic pieces do not simply supersede the love lyrics; rather, they acquire their full meaning only through what has come before, and in light of the variations played out across the *Cent balades*.

---

53. Studies include Kelly, *Christine de Pizan's Changing Opinion;* Forhan, *Political Theory;* Krueger, "Christine's Anxious Lessons"; Blanchard and Mühlethaler, *Écriture et pouvoir,* 21–26, 42–58. For approaches to Christine's didactic verse and its relationship with prose, see Richards, "Poems of Water"; Kay, *Place of Thought,* 150–76; Cerquiglini-Toulet, "Introduction"; Akbari, "Movement from Verse to Prose."

54. On the reader's role, see Kelly, *Christine de Pizan's Changing Opinion,* 71–74; Krueger, "Christine's Anxious Lessons."

55. Richards, "Poems of Water," 225.

56. Christine de Pizan, *Œuvres poétiques,* ed. Roy, 1:1–100. See Paden, "Christine de Pizan"; Laidlaw, "The *Cent balades*," 64–66.

57. Laidlaw, "The *Cent balades*," 67–70.

Christine's audience come to construct a moral and social argument for them-selves: in the face of earthly transience and vice, courtly *savoir-vivre* is no sub-stitute for genuine virtue.[58]

Similar precepts are implied in the *Cent balades d'amant et de dame* (1410–11), which traces the development and eventual failure of an aristocratic love relationship through the two protagonists' alternating voices, and which again displays an experimental approach to *ballade* form.[59] Scholars have often noted that the sequence points toward the inadequacy of courtly values and, more generally, the fragility of human endeavors permanently threatened by arbitrary powers such as love and fortune.[60] These issues become much more explicit in a *lay de dame* (*lai* in a lady's voice) which follows the *ballades* in the sole extant witness: British Library MS Harley 4431, a comprehensive anthol-ogy of Christine's poetry and prose completed in 1410 or 1411, commonly termed the Queen's Manuscript, as it was dedicated to Isabeau de Bavière and probably commissioned by her.[61] In the *lay* a lady castigates unreliable lovers and the destructiveness of love itself. The poem effectively glosses the *ballade* sequence, deploying learned exempla to illustrate the harm that love causes; it also undermines the attitudes to love expressed in *lais* and *complaintes* tran-scribed earlier in the manuscript.[62] Both these sequences, then, cause their audiences to generate arguments by responding to formal innovation and the juxtaposition of voices and attitudes, then legitimize those arguments through more overt moralizing discourse. Yet this "exhortative" model of legitima-tion, as Lyotard suggests (see introduction), is potentially disruptive. An audi-ence appreciative of compositional technique may consider the interest of these poems to lie primarily in formal virtuosity; hence *Cent balades* 91–99 and the *lay de dame* would seem to load a gratuitous didactic weight onto the sequences. Equally, the *lay de dame* lends itself all too easily to interpretation in the context of the *Cité des dames,* which precedes the *Cent balades d'amant et de dame* in the Queen's Manuscript. From this perspective the *lay*'s suffering lady takes on the status of a latterday Dido or Medea (*Cité* 2.55–56), embody-ing female constancy in love, so that readers are likely to reassess the *ballades* with this theme uppermost in mind.

Between the two *ballade* cycles, Christine produced verse works whose forms have quite different epistemic implications. The demands they make

58. Ibid., 64, 77; Adams, "Love as Metaphor," 153, 161.
59. Ed. Cerquiglini-Toulet. On the sequence's prosody, see Paradis, "Une polyphonie narrative."
60. Adams, "Love as Metaphor," 157–59.
61. "The Making of the Queen's Manuscript," http://www.pizan.lib.ed.ac.uk/.
62. On the *lay de dame* and its effects, see Altmann, "Last Words."

upon readers, however, and the problems of legitimation that they attest, are broadly similar. The *Epistre Othea* (1400) consists of multiple interrelated elements among which verse has a central function. Its kernel is a verse epistle from the eponymous Othea, a pseudo-antique goddess of wisdom invented by Christine, which outlines chivalric values to the Trojan hero Hector. This is divided into one hundred short texts, mostly octosyllabic quatrains, each accompanied by two prose interpretations: a *glose* (gloss) explains the verse's historical or mythographic allusions and develops lessons in knightly behavior, then an *allegorie* (allegory) offers a tropological or anagogical interpretation of the verse. Fifty manuscript witnesses are recorded, indicating that the *Epistre* had a significant impact; several contain illustrations of some or all of the verse texts. The textual structure stimulates a contemplative mode of reading that makes meaningful connections between the verse and prose texts, and in some cases also between visual and verbal media.[63] Most important, the prose expositions highlight the allusive character of the verse and position it as *requiring* interpretation. The *Epistre*'s composition might seem to encapsulate the assumption, challenged by Agamben (see introduction), that philosophy is needed to reveal the truth that poetry unknowingly produces. Inevitably, though, the revelation—what Lyotard would term the legitimation of knowledge—is problematic. The very presence of plural commentaries, in the *glose* and the *allegorie,* is potentially destabilizing. What is more, Christine's readings of myth are often innovative and risk incurring the suspicion of readers familiar with more established interpretations.[64] In this light the most reliable epistemic quality of the verse is not so much the lessons in good government or virtuous conduct to which it alludes as the mnemonic value lent by its pithiness and formal patterning.

Christine's two long verse narratives from 1403, the *Chemin de long estude* and *Mutacion de Fortune,* both open up a moral issue to readers' judgment, though the role of verse and the degree of explicit didacticism vary. In the *Chemin* Christine's persona witnesses a debate among the four influences that rule the world—Noblece, Chevalerie, Richece, and Sagece (Nobility, Chivalry, Wealth, and Wisdom)—who must each explain to Raison their responsibility for the earth's suffering (2811–3008). The influences believe that a single figure should rule the world but cannot agree on who this should be. Each

63. Ed. Parussa. See also Mombello, *Tradizione manoscritta;* Hindman, *Christine de Pizan's "Epistre Othéa";* Desmond and Sheingorn, *Myth, Montage, and Visuality;* Noakes, *Timely Reading,* 110–34; Krueger, "Christine's Anxious Lessons," 20–21; Akbari, "Movement from Verse to Prose," 136–38.

64. On Christine's interpretations, see Dulac, "Travail allégorique"; Jeanneret, "Texte et enluminures." Christine de Pizan, *Epistre Othea,* ed. Parussa, 31–70, outlines the *Epistre*'s sources.

argues that the quality she embodies is the most important for a ruler and proposes a different unnamed candidate to govern the world. Raison's council cannot decide in favor of any one influence; Christine must submit the matter to the court of France for judgment (6279–6383), and the poem promptly ends as she wakes from her dream. It is entirely apt that the claims of the four influences be referred to Christine's audience: resolution cannot be achieved within the narrative because no speaker makes an unanswerable case. Sagece is structurally privileged—she is the last to speak, and her arguments (4083–6078) occupy much more space than those of the other three combined—so that readers are likely to take the most account of her arguments. Yet they cannot neglect the other influences, which all make persuasive claims for their relevance to world government.[65]

The *Chemin*'s use of verse might appear almost incidental, especially because its form is not particularly distinctive. It adopts the standard narrative meter of octosyllabic couplets, with occasional localized exceptions: decasyllables for a prologue addressing Charles VI (1–60); heptasyllables for the opening narrative passage, where the poet's persona reflects on her misfortunes before she is consoled by reading Boethius (61–252); and *rimes croisées* (*abab-cdcd...*) for a letter in which the earth appeals to Raison to alleviate her torment (2599–2706). But verse acquires a particular significance in light of the debate that takes up over half the *Chemin,* and of Christine's own recent poetic output. The combination of an unresolved debate with nonstanzaic verse is common to the *Chemin* and to three love debates composed in or shortly after 1400: the *Debat de deux amans, Livre des trois jugemens,* and *Dit de Poissy,* which precede the *Chemin* in a number of manuscript anthologies.[66] Each debate adopts the *vers coupés* (truncated lines) used in one of their major sources, Machaut's *Jugement dou roy de Behaigne:* a continuous sequence of decasyllables, interrupted at every fourth line by a tetrasyllable that introduces a new rhyme.[67] The formal contrast between the *Chemin* and the love debates encourages readers to reflect on other ways in which the poems diverge, in particular the reasons why each debate lacks a final verdict. Like the *ballade* sequences, the love debates imply that courtly conventions are unsatisfactory: the questions

65. Kay, *Place of Thought,* 157.
66. All these texts are edited in *Love Debate Poems,* ed. Altmann (for dating, see 6). Five manuscripts contain all three debates; four also transmit the *Chemin,* though this never follows the debates immediately. These are BnF, mss. fr. 835 and 836 (which most scholars think formed a coherent sequence with two or three other manuscripts); BnF, ms. fr. 604; Chantilly, Musée Condé, mss. 492–493; and MS Harley 4431. *Love Debate Poems,* 36–43; Christine de Pizan, *Chemin,* ed. Tarnowski, 59–61; Laidlaw, "Christine de Pizan—A Publisher's Progress."
67. On the relationship between these poems and Machaut's *jugement* pieces, see Altmann, "Reopening the Case."

raised cannot be answered because courtly love relationships cannot end happily.[68] It is for a very different reason, as we have seen, that none of the claimants in the *Chemin* can plead her case successfully: the question cannot be adequately answered within the multiple-choice format available. Just as the closing sequence of the *Cent balades* compels a reassessment of the preceding lyrics, the *Chemin* throws into sharp relief the limited horizons of amatory discourse in the debate poems. Yet the *Chemin*'s audience is no more able to weigh the speakers' cases than is the council of Raison. We may be stimulated to reflect on the competing claims of the various influences, but this reflection cannot be translated into decisive moral and political action.

The incongruous relationship between history and philosophy in the *Mutacion,* discussed in chapter 4, is partly manifested by an oscillation between two techniques of legitimation. Prior to the account of universal history, the account of Fortune's house and its inhabitants is exhortative. Different social groups elicit overt moral comment: noblemen are all too often self-indulgent and corrupt (5131–5504); some financiers are helpful, but most should be treated with suspicion (6167–6320). The historical narrative, by contrast, adopts a primarily "incarnational" approach to legitimizing ethical and social knowledge. Events very largely speak for themselves; only at the very edges of her account does Christine indicate its purport, as a demonstration that mutable Fortune makes all things transient (7110–67, 23595–636). Christine explicitly articulates her own response to the world's instability as a private ethical choice: she has opted for a "vie astracte [et] solitaire" (withdrawn and solitary life, 23636). At the same time, a more public and political conclusion is implied. By deploying the themes of *translatio imperii* and *translatio studii,* Christine suggests that it has been France's destiny to assume the political and cultural supremacy previously held by Rome, but that France is also bound to be surpassed in turn, and all the more quickly if its estates fall into vice.[69] Both forms of legitimation are bound up with the use of verse. As we observed in chapter 4, the temporary shift to prose paradoxically reminds us that the *Mutacion* is essentially a verse work, that history is being personalized and aestheticized. We are reminded of the situated nature of verse: world history is being presented *from* a particular standpoint *to* a particular audience, namely the "princes de la haulte tour" (princes in the high tower, 23610), whom Christine addresses at the end of the *Mutacion.* It is these earthly rulers who must make something of the history she tells; who, faced with her rhetorical question "Sont ses mutacïons petites?" (are her [i.e., Fortune's]

68. Ibid., 150.
69. Walters, "*Translatio Studii*"; Brownlee, "Image of History."

transformations small? 23616), must find not only an answer but also a means of coping with change. This may not be as difficult as the judgment that Christine refers to the *Chemin*'s audience, but the moralization of history brings its own discontents. There is a curious discrepancy between the historiographical sledgehammer that the *Mutacion* hands us and the moral nut that we are invited to crack with it. The very nature of exemplification is at stake. To argue that sublunary affairs are contingent, must one demonstrate the contingency of *all* earthly endeavors, or only *some* of them? If the former, the enterprise is doomed to failure: the *Mutacion* makes patent the impossibility of universal history. If the latter, why invest in such a comprehensive account?

Christine returns to the dangers of courtly love with the *Livre du Duc des vrais amans* (1403–1405), which recounts the waxing and waning of a relationship. As a brief prologue in the poet's voice makes clear (1–40), the tale is told in the voice of the male partner, the eponymous Duke.[70] The distinction between poet and protagonist facilitates a telling critique of courtly love, as many scholars note.[71] As the narrative proceeds, the commonplaces of amatory literature prove increasingly incompatible with social realities. A long prose letter to the lady from her former governess, the Dame de la Tour, outlines the social harm that courtly love is apt to wreak, particularly on women: one's reputation, and that of one's family, may be irrevocably damaged (letter 5). She does not decisively turn the lady away from the Duke, but lasting happiness proves unattainable for both. Criticized for neglecting proper military commitments in favor of local tournaments, the Duke leaves to spend a year campaigning in Spain (3368–3431); the relationship is thereafter marked by more sorrow than joy, not least because the lady is dishonored in public opinion (3538–48). Following the narrative are lyrics ostensibly exchanged between the Duke and his lady during their separation; the narrative itself contains nineteen lyrics, mainly *ballades,* almost all in the Duke's voice.[72]

It is in prose, in the Dame de la Tour's letter, that Christine explicitly develops a moral and social argument. Aristocratic living, she suggests, involves complex negotiations attentive to multiple claims: family, household, clients. Once the uncompromisingly single claim of courtly love pulls this web out of shape, it can unravel horribly. In this sense the *Duc* echoes the more explicit

70. All references are to ed. Fenster.

71. Ibid., 23–27; Krueger, *Women Readers,* 217–46; Kelly, *Christine de Pizan's Changing Opinion,* 129–38; Kelly, "Christine de Pizan and Antoine de la Sale," 176; Laird and Richards, "*Tous parlent par une mesmes bouche.*"

72. On the lyrics, see ed. Fenster, 14–16, 34–38.

messages of Christine's near-contemporary prose work the *Livre des trois vertus,* which indeed incorporates the Dame de la Tour's letter.[73] Yet the suspicion of courtly amatory values is also apparent in the surrounding verse, both the narrative and the inserted lyrics. The narrative verse employs heptasyllabic rather than octosyllabic couplets, an unusual formal choice, associated with lack and wrongness by the beginning of the *Chemin,* which appears in both extant manuscripts containing the *Duc.*[74] Christine's epilogue draws attention to the virtuoso rhyming in the heptasyllables, which are all in *rimes léonines* (in each rhyming line the final tonic vowel is preceded by the same consonant; that consonant is preceded by the same vowel). The prologue has already explained that the *Duc* is a commissioned work, which the poet would rather not have had to write (1–13); in this light the *rimes léonines* assert Christine's aesthetic control over, and ethical distance from, her imposed subject matter.[75] Equally, as a poet the Duke can neither reflect on his own work nor direct much of it at any audience other than himself until the narrative is over. His lyrics within the narrative are mostly spontaneous outpourings of sentiment. Rather than facilitating communication, as so often in Froissart's amatory *dits,* they are associated with *lack* of communication, solitude, silence. The Duke speaks or thinks his earlier compositions while alone; not until halfway through the poem does he deliver a lyric to a human listener, his cousin, to whom he has been revealing his feelings (1859–87). The group of lyrics that follows the narrative ends with a *complainte,* in which the lady laments her suffering and sense of betrayal; this has been interpreted as "a lyric counterpart and an unfortunate fulfilment" of the Dame de la Tour's letter.[76] Hence the *Duc*'s verse components convey a largely implicit moral and social discourse. The Dame de la Tour's letter plays an important role in legitimizing this discourse, enabling audiences to *know* that they know that courtly language and values are dangerously incompatible with social life. Yet the Dame imposes her view only temporarily. The lady decides to end her relationship with the Duke but then gives way to his protestations. Once again, legitimation proves questionable: prose glosses verse, only to be promptly contested and resisted within the narrative. It is for the reader, further guided by the closing poems, to assess the merits of the Dame de la Tour's arguments.

73. Ibid., 25.

74. One of these is the Queen's Manuscript; the other is BnF, ms. fr. 836, owned by Jean, Duke of Berry, and perhaps originally prepared for Louis, Duke of Orléans. Ibid., 38–42; Laidlaw, "Christine and the Manuscript Tradition," 238, 244.

75. Krueger, *Women Readers,* 239–40.

76. Ibid., 241–42 (quotation 241). This assessment of the *complainte* is widely shared; see Laird and Richards, "*Tous parlent par une mesmes bouche,*" 123; Margolis, "Clerkliness and Courtliness," 146–48.

In all these works, reception and legitimation are both central and problematic. This is apparent in Christine's prose as well as her verse. In the *Advision,* for instance, an introductory gloss invites readers to interpret the *poetrie*
of the first part on three levels: as applicable to the world, the individual,
and France.[77] Common to Christine's didactic writing is an optimistic attitude
toward her audiences. Interpellating them as willing learners, she encourages them to form their own opinions, albeit by using the tools and techniques
that she provides. Readers must use their discernment (a crucial element of
Christine's epistemology), weighing conflicting attitudes or making connections between what is spoken and what isn't.[78] It is consistently through this
process of reflection and discernment that Christine's audience and its knowledge are constructed, as a virtual community of readers invited to develop
the correct view on a moral issue. There are nevertheless clear differences
between verse and prose. First, as we have shown, specific properties of verse
actively contribute to shaping knowledge. This remains true of Christine's
final work, the *Ditié Jeanne d'Arc* (see chapter 2), the stanzas of which are
grouped according to numerological principles that give a religious significance to contemporary history.[79] Indeed, various lapses in the *Ditié*'s versification suggest it was composed rapidly in response to events: poetic form reveals
the impact of history by its very flaws.[80] Second, the legitimation of knowledge
is more clearly limited or faulty than in Christine's prose. The *Advision* and
Cité provide considerable explicit guidance for the audience, notably through
Christine's authorial persona, who enacts the kind of reasoning process that
readers are expected to follow.[81] Exhortation is often more implicit in verse;
audiences are more prone to distraction by the fascination of formal ingenuity,
the plurality or incongruity of moralizations, the impossibility of judgment.
Christine's verse positions her readers in specific and meaningful ways, but it
is not necessarily from there that they look back at her.

Rhétoriqueur Political Poetry

In the topical verse and *prosimetrum* of the late fifteenth and early sixteenth
centuries, implicit ethical, social, and political knowledge is again manifested

77. *Livre de l'advision,* ed. Reno and Dulac, 5–10; Kelly, *Christine de Pizan's Changing Opinion,* 71–74.

78. Discernment, or the making of moral distinctions, is represented in Christine's thought
by terms such as *discrecion* (discretion) and *esplucher* (to sift); Kelly, *Christine de Pizan's Changing
Opinion,* 22–23, 27.

79. Kosta-Théfaine, "Le *Ditié.*"

80. *Ditié de Jehanne d'Arc,* ed. Kennedy and Varty, 17.

81. Kelly, *Christine de Pizan's Changing Opinion,* 169–78.

through the poet-audience relationship. The fundamental contingency of that relationship, however, is repeatedly revealed. *Rhétoriqueur* political poetry is dominated by the rhetoric of praise and blame; its formal features, often highly sophisticated, contribute significantly to its sense both by alluding to preexisting poems and by producing particular emotive effects.[82] It also relies on notions that had become heavily codified through academic philosophy and vernacular didactic writing. Poets might disagree on how far a particular ruler embodied principles of justice or good government, but there was a strong consensus on what those principles entailed in themselves.[83] But this poetry also assumes that the audience has a certain set of political loyalties, and that historical circumstances can be mapped onto a given moral framework. When these assumptions come to the surface, their legitimacy—and potentially that of the explicit knowledge a poem conveys—may become vulnerable. This may happen, for instance, when a poem's reception reveals possibilities for recontextualizing its political argument. At such points, tensions appear between ideological precepts and the political contingencies that poets have fitted to them—or, conversely, between political contingencies and the ideological weight they are made to bear.

An exchange between Chastelain and Meschinot exemplifies this process particularly well, for the poets' moral reflections gain historic specificity solely through their reception. Chastelain composed a series of twenty-five decasyllabic *sixains,* titled *Les Princes,* criticizing an unnamed ruler's inappropriate actions. Meschinot developed the theme in a series of *ballades,* each of which uses one of Chastelain's stanzas as its envoi. These pieces have often been seen as thinly veiled attacks on Louis XI but do not indicate this explicitly; their moral discourse is couched in general terms.[84] An audience is not obliged to read them as topical polemics, though it may apply their arguments to real rulers if appropriate parallels suggest themselves. Such parallels are intermittently visible in the textual tradition of Chastelain's stanzas. One manuscript (KBR, ms. 11020–33) presents the *Princes* alongside four similar stanzaic sequences, each surveying the vices of a particular social group. In this context Chastelain's *sixains* belong to a tradition of didactic verse; there is no suggestion of topical relevance. By contrast, in the most important anthology of his work (Florence, Biblioteca Medicea-Laurenziana, MS mediceo-palatino 120),

82. Thiry, "Rhétorique et genres littéraires"; idem, "La Poétique des grands rhétoriqueurs"; Cornilliat, *"Or ne mens."*
83. On vernacular political didacticism, see especially Devaux, *Jean Molinet,* 173–200; Blanchard and Mühlethaler, *Écriture et pouvoir,* 7–58.
84. Hüe, "Prince chez Meschinot," 188–93.

the *Princes* immediately follow two substantial prose works that are clearly linked to Louis XI. The *Traité par forme allégorique sur l'entrée du roy Loys en nouveau règne* (1461) expresses the Burgundian author's optimism at the new French king's accession, but its title indicates Chastelain's subsequent disappointment: "le fruit n'en ensievy point tel à l'acteur come il eust bien cuidié et esperé" (the outcome did not prove to be what the author had believed and hoped for, fol. 175v). Louis is criticized more explicitly in the *Déprécation pour messire Pierre de Brézé* (1461–62), a protest against the king's imprisonment of the seneschal of Normandy. In this context the *Princes* seem directed specifically against Louis.[85] Audiences evidently could and did read political poetry in light of their own values and understanding of current events, whether or not the poetry explicitly authorized them to do so.

The reception of Molinet's *prosimetrum* allegories exhibits a similar tendency. Unlike the *Princes* and Meschinot's *Ballades des Princes,* these works clearly indicate the historical circumstances that provoke moral reflection and exhortation; yet those circumstances may be effaced or changed in the process of transmission. Molinet's earliest datable composition, the *Complainte de Grece* (1464), urges Christians to liberate Greece from Turkish rule and praises Philip the Good as ideally suited to lead a crusade. Various abridgments and reworkings transform these themes and make quite different requirements of readers.[86] Many witnesses transmit the verse sections alone, which emphasize Greece's suffering—exploiting the affective connotations of their stanzaic forms— and make no explicit reference to Philip.[87] In some instances the *Complainte* is updated to present Maximilian of Austria or Charles V as Christendom's champion, while the victim of the Turks is occasionally changed to Constantinople or the Holy Land. Hence a basic schema lends itself to a range of situations: the roles of victim and potential rescuer may be filled by different actors or left vacant for readers to complete. Yet these de- and recontextualized *Complaintes* often distort Molinet's rhetoric. Aspects of political symbolism, such as astrological or heraldic imagery, lose their relevance or coherence as the actors' identity changes. Hence a double gap opens up between general moral schemata and particular events. On the one hand, the *Complainte*'s varied reception shows that the schemata can be mobilized for other events. On the other, and more pertinently for the audience of any specific witness, the events might

---

85. On these manuscripts, see ibid., 190–91; Bliggenstorfer, "*Castellani Georgii Opera Poetica Gallice.*" Doudet, *Poétique de George Chastelain,* discusses the *Traité* (626–38) and *Déprécation* (352–53, 531).
86. Armstrong, "Dead Man Walking."
87. Ibid., 83, notes the implications of the verse forms used.

be conceived in different terms. The *remaniements'* absences and incongruities suggest that familiar schemata and symbols are of limited use in drawing out the significance of concrete political realities. These effects are also apparent when verse laments from Molinet's *prosimetrum* works are transcribed as separate poems (see chapter 5). Since these pieces typically lack historical detail, they become reusable; accompanying texts in anthologies may suggest new situations and referents. One major anthology contained two separate versions of the lament from the *Ressource du petit peuple* (1481) as well as the complete text.[88] Their coexistence, apparent to an attentive reader, powerfully reveals the extent to which ethical discourse and historical circumstance can be separated.

The reception of political poetry is addressed explicitly in Chastelain's *Exposicions sur Verité mal prise,* an allegorical narrative in prose that systematically glosses his own *Dit de Verité.*[89] Both pieces date from 1459–1461, a tense period in Franco-Burgundian relations. Philip the Good and Charles VII were in dispute over claims to the duchy of Luxembourg, while Philip had granted asylum to Charles's son Louis (the future Louis XI), whose relations with his father had become highly acrimonious.[90] Chastelain's *Dit* apparently responded to French poems attacking Philip (441–44); in decasyllabic *huitains* it vigorously defends the duke and castigates French attitudes. According to the *Exposicions,* the *Dit* provoked such violent criticism in French quarters that Chastelain sought to defend and explicate it. The *Exposicions* effectively stages an anti-French reading of the poem only to sweep it away by an interpretation that justifies Chastelain's work, defends Philip, and promotes conciliation and respect between France and Burgundy. Scrutinizing the *Dit* from beginning to end, the personification Ymagination Françoise (French Imagination) identifies thematic and stylistic elements that in her view reflect a treacherous and ungrateful attitude to France. Entendement (Understanding) responds by reinterpreting, contextualizing, or qualifying expressions in the poem.[91] He often reveals oblique allusions in the *Dit* to refer to unexpectedly specific events and issues: a comment on French disdain for Philip's embassies (397) proves to be based on the trial of Jean II, Duke of Alençon, in 1458, at which the views conveyed by a Burgundian embassy had been disregarded (147–48).[92] Such comments lend a much more precise quality to

88. Tournai, Bibliothèque communale, ms. 105 (destroyed in 1940). See Armstrong, "Practice of Textual Transmission," 274.

89. Thiry, "Stylistique et auto-critique."

90. Vaughan, *Philip the Good,* 346–54.

91. Ed. Delclos, 10–12, summarizes the political arguments of both texts.

92. Thiry, "Stylistique et auto-critique," 107–8, comments on this gloss. On the treatment of Philip's embassy, see Delclos, *Témoignage,* 227.

the ethical and political knowledge conveyed by the *Dit;* yet they also characterize the poem's implied audience. Two qualities are essential to reading the
Dit properly without the help of the *Exposicions*—which, to judge by surviving witnesses, may have been the lot of many readers.[93] One needs not only a
good grasp of recent history but also a particular appreciation of what lessons
that history teaches. In other words, the best way to read the *Dit*—and, by
extension, Chastelain's other political work—is to have agreed already with
its author. The same conclusion is suggested by the *Exposicions'* apparently
contradictory indications concerning literal and figurative reading: Entendement reproves Ymagination Françoise both for understanding the *Dit* literally (137) and for disregarding its literal sense (82).[94] How can readers tell what
is literal and what isn't at any given point, other than by knowing in advance?
The *Dit*'s ideal readers, then, are those who give Chastelain the benefit of the
doubt and are already aware of the poem's standpoint. A kind of anamorphosis is achieved: the *Dit*'s meanings cohere only when it is approached from a
particular angle.[95] The community of readers is interpellated on the basis of
political affiliations that the poet takes for granted, indicating with outstanding clarity that such communities are exclusive as well as inclusive. The readers excluded from that community, moreover, are none other than the *Dit*'s
explicit addressees. Chastelain apostrophizes the French ("François," 97), but
it is not for Charles VII's supporters that his ideological discourse makes sense.
In light of this red herring, it is perhaps unsurprising that Chastelain's poem
caused him to be "durement mesvolu" (the object of great ill-will, 26), as he
claims in the *Exposicions'* prologue.

A similar process is at work, albeit in a very different context, in André
de la Vigne's *prosimetrum* allegory *La Ressource de la Chrestienté*. Composed
shortly before Charles VIII's Neapolitan campaign of 1494–95, the *Ressource*
encourages support for the expedition by ignoring Naples almost completely.
La Vigne focuses instead on the prospect of a crusade against the Turks, for
which Naples was widely regarded as a potential base, though more secular
factors undoubtedly motivated Charles's venture.[96] Various personifications
discuss the matter in decasyllabic stanzas of varying forms: Dame Chrestienté

93. The *Exposicions* accompany one of the two complete texts of the *Dit* that survive in manuscripts of the period. See ed. Delclos, 19–20; Doudet, *Poétique de George Chastelain,* 714–15.

94. Doudet, *Poétique de George Chastelain,* 786–87, notes this contradiction and suggests that
Chastelain is encouraging active, dynamic interpretation.

95. We use "anamorphosis" in its art-historical rather than its psychoanalytic sense. On the
latter, and its manifestation in medieval poetry, see Kay, *Place of Thought,* 50–51, 67–69; Simpson, *Fantasy, Identity and Misrecognition,* 255–56.

96. Ed. Brown, 17–23.

(Lady Christianity), Dame Noblesse (Lady Nobility), and Bon Conseil (Good Counsel) collectively persuade Magesté Royalle (Royal Majesty) to lead French forces against the Turks, despite the objections of Je-ne-sçay-qui (Someone-or-Other). Naples is mentioned just once in the earliest version of the *Ressource,* a manuscript owned by Charles himself (BnF, ms. fr. 1687).[97] What is more, it is Je-ne-sçay-qui who makes this single allusion (1162–63). Naples seems to constitute an uncomfortable truth that must be disavowed; it is voiced only at the margins, by a figure who prefers worldly pleasures to defending Christendom, whose opinions are not well received, and whose very name deprives him of a stable identity.[98] Hence La Vigne requires his audience already to share two beliefs. First, they must be convinced that crusading is worthy and viable. If not, the allegorical narrative shows that no amount of persuasion will win them over: La Vigne's personifications convince only those who already agree. Magesté Royalle is inevitably receptive to Dame Chrestienté and her supporters, as befits the Most Christian King, but Je-ne-sçay-qui remains unmoved.[99] Second, the audience must believe that a campaign in Italy is simply a prelude to the real business of crusading. Within La Vigne's narrative, even Je-ne-sçay-qui believes this: he objects to the perils of crusading, not to the expedition against Naples (944–1183). Once more, the relationship between political verse and its audience reveals the importance—and the fallibility—of the covert ideological work that poetry performs.

Theater in the Late Middle Ages

The production of ideological knowledge in theater reflects the difficulty of controlling reception. At first glance, plays confirm common knowledge in many obvious ways. Mysteries reinforce or enrich awareness of sacred history; farces play out established cultural representations of relationships between the sexes and between different social groups; *moralités* and *sotties* mobilize familiar didactic and satirical discourses.[100] Yet theater conveys and legitimizes more implicit, less familiar forms of social or religious knowledge through

97. Other versions devote very little more attention to Naples; ibid., 22.

98. Brown, *Shaping of History,* 12, notes that Je-ne-sçay-qui represents general opposition to Charles, not a particular social group. Two miniatures in fr. 1687 depict the figure with attributes of all three estates.

99. Beaune, *Naissance,* 207–29, discusses the development of the notion *très-chrétien* in relation to the French king and nation.

100. On the ideological familiarity of these genres, see Knight, *Aspects of Genre,* 23–25, 48–49, 68–88; Aubailly, *Monologue, le dialogue et la sottie,* 413–42.

the very fact of performance. Chapter 1 has shown how the *Miracles de Notre Dame* and the annual Marian procession of Lille dramatize social tensions and thereby enable them to be temporarily negotiated. Moreover, such forms of knowledge may be received and actualized in different ways: no two spectators watch exactly the same play.[101] The risk of uncontrollably varied reception, and the strategies adopted to minimize that risk, are often central to an understanding of ideology in theatrical texts.

In some cases the risk is all too apparent. Some forms of Parisian theater were subject to outright censorship.[102] Political tableaux in ceremonial entries, and the accompanying verse compositions, were typically produced by different groups whose interests might not coincide. Careful planning of the overall event was essential to ensure coherence, while actors or written texts were usually employed to explain individual tableaux for spectators.[103] Similar strategies accompanied the performance of many *moralités,* with prologues indicating the plays' message.[104] The potential for divergent interpretation increases in Gringore's *Jeu du Prince des Sotz et de Mere Sotte* (1512), part of a wave of poetic propaganda supporting Louis XII's military campaigns against Pope Julius II and his allies.[105] Gringore's play comprises a *sottie, moralité,* and *farce,* each of which uses various octosyllabic and decasyllabic stanzas; the whole is introduced by a *cry,* an announcement that often prefaced *sotties,* inviting fools to watch the performance.[106] The *sottie* stages the opposition between the benign Prince des Sotz (Prince of Fools), representing Louis, and the aggressive Mère Sotte (Mother Folly), standing for Julius; the *moralité* represents the gradual reconciliation of the personifications Peuple François (The French) and Peuple Ytalique (The Italians); the *farce* takes place in a domestic setting and turns on a typically bawdy conjugal plot. Gringore's political argument is clear in the *sottie,* and more obvious still in the *moralité,* where characters'

101. Clark, "Community versus Subject," 45. Courtly audiences were much more socially homogeneous than urban ones (for an instance of court-based performance, see Devaux, "Molinet dramaturge"), but spectatorship remains plural in that context.

102. Bouhaïk-Gironès, "*La Sottie de l'Astrologue,*" 69–70.

103. Gringore, *Entrées royales,* ed. Brown, 20–29; Brown, "From Stage to Page"; Small, "When Indiciaires Meet Rederijkers," 136. Small (134–38) notes a striking instance, albeit in a Dutch-language context, in which an inappropriate message slipped into an entry. When the future Emperor Charles V entered Bruges in 1515 as the new Count of Flanders, resident Hanseatic merchants organized a tableau that implicitly promoted the Hanse rather than Bruges.

104. Knight, *Aspects of Genre,* 25–27.

105. On Louis's campaigns and the literature that supported them, see especially Brown, *Shaping of History,* 91–146; Baumgartner, *Louis XII,* 209–27; Scheller, "Ung fil tres delicat"; Hochner, *Louis XII,* 156–75; Britnell, "Aspects."

106. On Gringore's versification, see ed. Hindley, 40–44; on the *cri* in the *sottie* tradition, see Aubailly, *Monologue, le dialogue et la sottie,* 294–95.

names transparently indicate their significance.[107] So unambiguous are these
elements that the *Jeu* has sometimes been regarded as a royal commission.[108]
Yet the *sottie* and *moralité* are followed by the *farce,* which offers a familiar but
quite different kind of social knowledge—about the tensions between sexual
desires and social structures.[109] This juxtaposition may be assessed in at least
three ways; there is no reason to assume that Gringore's audience would adopt
one stance rather than another (or indeed that they would adopt any). From
one perspective, the traditional "anthropological" knowledge of the *farce*—
assumptions about what men and women do, to and with each other, inside and
outside marriage—makes the tendentious *sottie* and *moralité* more acceptable
by associating their antipapal arguments with deeply rooted cultural stereo-
types that are difficult to contest. From another, the *farce* defuses the political
content of the *sottie* and *moralité,* coupling them with a familiar comic form
that does not threaten an audience's worldview in the same way as a critique
of papal authority and integrity. From yet another, the contrast between the
farce and the preceding elements highlights Gringore's political discourse by
contrast and sensitizes an audience all the more to its urgently topical character. While the *Jeu*'s individual elements offer little room for misinterpretation,
their combination may produce interference. Ambiguity could be reduced by
performing only one or two elements: the *sottie, moralité,* and *farce* lend themselves to separate performance.[110] Hence the *Jeu* may produce a wide variety of
effects before different audiences and in different sociopolitical contexts.

The interplay between topical relevance and familiar structures, which so
decisively shapes the sense of Gringore's *Jeu,* is evident in many theatrical
forms. Entries stage history in the making, as noted in chapter 1, but also rely
heavily on typological parallels. When Louis XII's new bride, Mary Tudor,
entered Paris in 1514, one of the tableaux represented the Queen of Sheba
visiting Solomon. Accompanying verses, both displayed and declaimed, made
clear the analogy between the biblical episode and Mary's gift of peace to Louis.[111] Current events and actors are fitted into transhistorical patterns that give
them meaning, in ways aptly described by Lawrence Bryant: "Particulars, in
the metaphysics of the occasion, were transformed into universals."[112] Perhaps

---

107. This significance is reinforced on stage by traditional costumes and attributes, whose
connotations could readily be recognized; ed. Hindley, 50–52.

108. Ibid., 47, considers that Louis probably commissioned the *Jeu;* Gringore, *Œuvres
polémiques,* ed. Brown, 240, and Britnell, "Aspects," 106–8, are more circumspect.

109. Knight, *Aspects of Genre,* 141–70, analyzes the conjugal farce.

110. Ed. Hindley, 47; Mazouer, *Théâtre français du Moyen Âge,* 275.

111. Brown, "From Stage to Page," 53–56.

112. Bryant, *King and the City,* 15.

more surprisingly, mystery plays could convey knowledge specific to local conditions. Their broadly familiar basic narratives, grounded in the Bible or hagiography, could be realized in ways appropriate to their receiving contexts.[113] Comparing two plays that present the biblical tale of Susanna and the Elders, Alan Knight has shown that their composition and staging produce differing social and religious meanings.[114] One, incorporated into the vast *Mistère du Viel Testament,* which was apparently performed in Paris in the early sixteenth century, highlights the patriarch's role within the nuclear family and the cosmic context in which the story unfolds. Another, performed in the late fifteenth century as part of Lille's annual procession, foregrounds a domestic setting as the context within which individual virtue is exercised. Another component of the *Mistère du Viel Testament,* a *Mystère de Judith et Holofernés* probably composed by Jean Molinet, closely follows the biblical narrative but introduces an important antiwar theme.[115] Mysteries, then, are not just ritual enactments of collective memory; precisely because their plots are well known, poets can insert more particular elements. The *sottie* evinces a quite different relationship between specificity and familiarity. Its satire is essentially topical, though broad social trends are a more common target than particular current events. The figure of the fool, however, is a universalizing device. Some fools are condemned for deliberate wickedness, others celebrated because their folly serves a moral authority, but nobody in the *sottie* is not a fool. Folly is not peculiar to a given social group, time, or place; it underlies all human activities, constituting a permanent framework within which to make sense, if sense there be, of contemporary life.[116]

In all theatrical forms, verse is crucial to the very possibility of performance. Poets generally maintain "mnemonic rhyme," a technique of providing cues for actors whereby successive speakers share the lines of a couplet.[117] Even the simplest versification, then, facilitates contact between performers and public. Contact, but also distance, a vital consideration, since the onstage action did not necessarily take place in a discrete space that set the actors apart from their audience. Verse immediately differentiates the performers' language from that used around them; it helps signal that what the audience is seeing is a cultural product that requires a particular form of attention.[118] With these issues in mind, we would be justified in claiming that the interpellation of

113. On the essential familiarity of historically based theater, see Knight, *Aspects of Genre,* 19.
114. Knight, "Stage as Context."
115. Molinet(?), *Mystère de Judith et Holofernés,* ed. Runnalls, 20–30.
116. Dull, *Folie et rhétorique,* 69–100.
117. Burgoyne, "Rime mnémonique"; Di Stefano, "Structure métrique."
118. Symes, *A Common Stage,* 131, notes this link between verse and theatricality.

theater audiences in late medieval France depends heavily on verse. In addition, particular formal features can be fundamentally related to conditions of performance, whether practical or ideological. As Darwin Smith notes, the interplay between versification and syntax in the *Farce de maître Pathelin* enables performers to expand and vary the text according to their needs in specific situations.[119] On a larger scale, the traffic of mystery plays across communities, the persistent reworking, expansion, and hybridization that are so fundamental to the genre's development and diffusion, is often accompanied by formal elaboration.[120] The clearest instance is that of Jean Michel's *Mystère de la Passion,* which expands on the middle two days of Arnoul Gréban's four-day play (ca. 1450), and was performed over four days in Angers in 1486.[121] In its 34,429 lines, Gréban's *Passion* includes seventy-four different stanzaic forms, thirty-five distinct varieties of fixed-form lyrics, and six different line lengths; Michel's play of 29,926 lines boasts 124 stanzaic forms, twenty-five fixed-form varieties, and seven different line lengths.[122] This prosodic extravaganza contributes to the glory not only of human redemption but also of Angers as a site for large-scale devotional theater. But size isn't everything: verse can have a precise relationship to a mystery's explicit doctrinal message. In Gréban's *Creacion du Monde,* which introduces his *Passion,* stanzaic forms acquire clear connotative values that recur throughout the play: thus the *sixain* is associated with the perfection of creation, or with diabolical challenges to that perfection.[123] Hence "theological demonstration rests on the text's prosodic architecture."[124] Though doubtless imperceptible in performance, Gréban's versification attests to the ways in which poetic form can convey religious knowledge.

A number of common tendencies and historical shifts have emerged across our survey. Most obviously, the ideological knowledge conveyed by verse is characteristically plural, not monological. *Fauvel*'s satirical discourses, general and specific, accompany the production of ethical anxiety and self-policing; ambivalent poetic personas both repel their audiences and lead them to unexpected kinds of knowledge. The interplay between spoken and unspoken

---

119. *Maistre Pierre Pathelin,* ed. Smith, 89, 97–98.
120. Runnalls, "Mystères de la Passion," outlines practices of *remaniement* in Passion plays.
121. Ibid., 488–92.
122. Details are from Gréban, *Mystère,* ed. Jodogne, 2:132–39; Michel, *Mystère,* ed. Jodogne, cii–cxii; Smith, "Question du Prologue."
123. Smith, "Question du Prologue," 151–64. The *Creacion* occupies vv. 1–1510 of Gréban, *Mystère,* ed. Jodogne.
124. Smith, "Question du Prologue," 141.

knowledge, and the ways in which this is exhibited in textual performance and reception, reveal the contingency of the ideological knowledge that verse conveys. Much of the implicit ideology in theater, from the *Feuillée* to Gringore, is selectively shaped through performance. *Fauvel* and *rhétoriqueur* poetry both show that rewriting and recontextualization can take political poetry in new directions. The role of textual personas in binding together a poet's audience is characteristically shaped by manuscript contexts (Watriquet, Christine), or the thematization of poetry's transmission (Villon).

While contingency pervades the production of ideological knowledge throughout our period, two broad developments are apparent. First, the communities through which that knowledge is manifested seem to become more specific, or at least more explicitly specific, over time. The *Feuillée* is a rare early example of verse overtly geared to reception within a determinate sociohistorical setting. *Fauvel* was produced and circulated in an even more precise milieu but does not inscribe the royal chancery within its lines. Christine de Pizan typically solicits a very general readership, *all* princes or *all* women; it is through manuscript production and presentation that particular audiences are constructed.[125] By contrast, *rhétoriqueurs* not only are more openly propagandist and factional but also effectively preach only to the converted, while Villon's *Testament* paradoxically engages readers on the basis that they are *not* the Parisian contemporaries who can make sense of it. Second, as religious and political subject matter takes on increasing importance—a development apparent in the role of the *indiciaires* and their counterparts, and in the sheer scale of mystery plays—so it is more explicitly legitimized as knowledge. Arrageois poets do not clearly indicate to their audience that they convey an urban ethos; nor do the protagonists of many earlier *dits* articulate the lessons encapsulated in their misadventures. Later poets are apt to take a more exhortative approach. Even in her *ballade* sequences, Christine incorporates elements that gloss the knowledge she offers; the *rhétoriqueurs* do not conceal the ideological lens through which they view historical circumstances; in theater, prologues and the like typically underline the implications of the onstage action. Inevitably, however, legitimation generates instability. Christine's glosses can be contested and the *rhétoriqueurs'* assessments dissociated from the events that ostensibly provoke them.

Underpinning all these phenomena are two fundamental qualities of late medieval verse. First, poetry positively invites interpretation. In contrast with the transparency claimed by prose, it encourages audiences to seek additional

---

125. On Christine's concurrent production of manuscripts for different patrons, see McGrady, "What Is a Patron?" 198; Laidlaw, "Christine and the Manuscript Tradition."

meanings.[126] Second, as we noted in chapter 1, the choice of poetry is a mark both of subjectivity and of public orientation. Poetry always implies a subject, and often makes it explicit in some way: the use of first-person narrators, the physical presence of actors declaiming lines. But that subject is never isolated; it constantly interpellates its audience, obliging them to engage with the poem and with the socio-symbolic order that it invokes. The public quality of verse, and the diversity of ideological knowledge that it transmits, suggest that the poetry of late medieval France teaches its audience a common and very important lesson. Whatever else a poem may say about social beliefs, structures, and practices, it says that they always have a place for poetry.

126. Dixon, "Conclusion," 219–21.

Conclusion

This book records a collective investigation into the role of poetry in transmitting and shaping knowledge in France from about 1270 to approximately 1530. Our aim throughout has been to highlight the distinction between prose and verse, often overlooked by scholars, and to show how, contrary to expectation, verse not only continues—despite the rise of prose—to have a positive association with knowledge, but also develops—in the face of prose—new and privileged means of engaging with it.

Our core conclusions are these. Many forms of knowledge—historical, philosophical, referential, poetic, ideological—are transmitted in works that are poetic in form, or at least composed to a significant extent in verse. What is more, once prose is established so that verse is no longer the default medium of composition but what linguists call a "marked" form, poetry creates the expectation of having supplementary meaning, which in late medieval France is perceived as pertaining to knowledge, even if it cannot always be formulated as *connaissance* or *science*. Consequently, late medieval verse, far from being secondary to prose in epistemic value, develops a distinctive relation with knowledge as an art, or process, of *savoir*, which enables it to transmit and shape knowledge in ways that prose does not. While the claims of prose to legitimize knowledge rely on its content appearing to be exhaustive and self-explanatory, the truth of verse comes to be upheld by its form, which eludes recuperation as content. It is worth returning to the parallel we drew in our introduction with the status of black and white photography after the advent of color: in both cases the ostensibly superseded medium benefits from its apparent disadvantage to assume a position of privilege.

One reason why modern critics have underestimated the epistemic value of late medieval verse is that we are attuned by contemporary culture, where most literary genres seem set on a line of convergence with the novel, to attribute a disproportionate importance to narrative. Beyond the domain of literature, narrative has become an influential paradigm in the social sciences and related disciplines.[1] Yet if narrative is not specific to literature, it cannot constitute a sufficient condition for "literariness." Herein lie our study's wider implications for literary historiography: it seeks to rehabilitate verse as distinctive from other kinds of writing and as deserving specific reflection.[2]

In the late Middle Ages, notwithstanding occasional instances of verse narrative, verse is indeed no longer primarily a narrative medium; that role has largely been assumed by prose. Verse, however, is the preferred vehicle of many constantly evolving lyric and dramatic forms, and most of all of that ramifying and varied body of writing that comes under the heading of the *dit,* including *prosimetrum* works, which are not always conventionally considered *dits* but exhibit similar compositional principles. As we have also shown, the kinds of reflection pursued by authors of *dits* in this extended sense, or indeed of other late medieval verse genres, are not primarily moralistic or Christian-didactic. Only a minor proportion of what we call "ideological" knowledge can be considered in these terms, and even then the poetic governing its expression is arguably more epistemic than ethical. Lyrico-narrative, philosophical, learned, encyclopedic, historical, political: the *dit* in its widest definition gathers together many different kinds of texts in a kind of "archi-genre" in which knowledge is always at stake.[3]

Distinctive to our project has been the inclusion of *all* of France in our coverage. Occitan poetry is typically studied only in association with early French medieval literature. Its impact on fourteenth- and fifteenth-century writers in the *langue d'oïl* is usually overlooked entirely, or else seen as mediated by the Old French *trouvères.* In this respect, critics of Middle French appear to attribute a finality to the Albigensian Crusade that historically it did not have. While the crusade and its aftermath undoubtedly altered the course of

1. Somers and Gibson, "Reclaiming."

2. In this sense we echo Agamben's ongoing reflection on the relationship between poetry and philosophy; see his *Stanzas* and *End of the Poem.*

3. Léonard, *Le "dit,"* 344, defines the form in broad terms but notes that exceptions are numerous.

Occitan poetry from the mid-thirteenth century onward, many of the developments we find in post-Albigensian Occitan literature—the investigation of the spiritual value of *fin' amor,* the practice of lyric insertion, the development of lyrico-didactic forms—are parallel to those found elsewhere in Europe. If anything, the post-Albigensian erosion of southern courts and the Inquisition's scrutiny of orthodoxy precipitated a greater epistemic turn in Occitan literature than occurred in northern France, or at least an earlier one. The late-thirteenth- and early-fourteenth-century Occitan texts on which we concentrate, the *Breviari d'amor* and *Leys d'amors,* are among the most precocious and effective in France in articulating and theorizing a privileged relationship between poetry and knowledge.

Poetry's relationship with knowledge arises from a number of features that together constitute the "situatedness" of poetry. Literary form is inevitably a means of "situation," and versification is so specifically because of its correlations with voice and the body in time. But we have avoided the traps of abstract formalism by stressing that, in late medieval France, the characteristics of verse are sustained and reinforced in particular ways. Chapters 1–3 lay the groundwork for the analysis of verse's situatedness; the subsequent chapters develop its implications.

Poetry is usually orchestrated by the grammatical first person, which may be materialized as the work's performer—the reciter in the case of *praelectio,* a cast of actors in theater—but which is more commonly identified as the subjectivity that is the source and agent of writing. Given the preference for nonnarrative genres, the first person is not typically a narrator but a discursive interlocutor presenting his (or, as Christine de Pizan's work powerfully exemplifies, her) contributions to reflection, learning, or ideology. In this way verse emerges as a formal correlative of subjectivity, absent or present, and as the ground on which to stake a relationship to others (audiences and readers, antecedent and fellow poets, patrons, love objects). Different verse traditions emphasize self and other to differing degrees: "public" poetry inscribes the other to a greater extent, while the *dit amoureux* is more an investigation of self. Ideologically charged poetry renders community in the way it insists on the situatedness of readers or audience and interpellates them to assume a relationship to it. The form of the verse text, whether public or private, acts as a form of personhood by comparison with the impersonality of prose. This is why poetry, far from being confined to recording private experience (the usual modern conception of poetry), is the privileged interface with sociality in the Middle Ages. It is hardly surprising that verse epistles, in which a first-person voice located in a determinate time and space directly addresses an individual or group, flourished in the second half of our period.[4] Poetry's situatedness may involve a strong sense of place (as in the poetry of Arras, Toulouse, Rouen, or Burgundy), but it does not of itself imply restriction; medieval poetry could reach large audiences, and some situations, such as that of the learned community receptive to the *Rose*-Ovid-Boethius nexus of textual production, are not identified with any one place.

Late medieval poetry is also situated with respect to the flow of time. We have reiterated the centrality of different kinds of historical content, from verse chronicle to Deschamps's poetry, from biblical drama to the disjointed histories of encyclopedic texts. Poets become historians and historians poets, a development that, as we have seen, takes various forms including institutional commissions and rewards. Intellectually, the preoccupation with history is associated with reflection on fortune; subjectively, it translates into meditation on memory and experience. We spoke in the introduction of this period as one confident in the value of its own mediation; the temporal situatedness of its poetry illuminates the character of this mediation. Medieval writers generally position themselves in relation to a model, even if that relation is conflictual. If their model is in verse, they will tend to write in verse; and an author's choice to write in verse is far more likely to evoke a traditional situation than prose, by its very nature, is prone to do. Despite the many poetic innovations of the late Middle Ages, the relation between poetry and knowledge can thus be described as "conservative," or at least "preservative," in the sense that it maintains contact with past models, or positions itself in relation to a preexisting network of ideas, or valorizes past experiences or events. Even when poetry is more responsive to the *hic et nunc* than to universal history, this very feature quickly becomes traditional.

We note, however, that the models concerned are always intrinsic to the Middle Ages, or at least rendered continuous with it, so that while verse authors rely on and exploit antique thought (Aristotle, Ovid, Boethius), they typically know it in a form already reworked and transformed by their own immediate predecessors. Medieval tradition is thus one that owns its own origin. The very way in which poets link medieval culture to that of antiquity affirms the gap between them. Medieval poets are humanists in a mode unlike that of earlier or later renaissances. For those cultural movements and their most powerful late medieval avatar, Petrarch, access to the remote past—whether or not it is conceived as a totality, and however unattainable it may prove in practice—is

---

4. LeBlanc, *Va Lettre Va*. LeBlanc identifies more specifically personalized elements in prose than in verse epistles (33–44), but the fact remains that verse is inherently situated and personalized in ways that prose is not.

an ideal.[5] For the poets of medieval France, by contrast, access to antiquity is typically achieved only by passing along a chain of intermediary figures, a metonymic sequence of cultural transmission that cannot be short-circuited, as Renaissance poets hoped, by metaphorical affinities between the classical past and the present. Hence, although cultural historians often differentiate the Middle Ages from early modernity in respect of historical consciousness— absent in the former, present in the latter—a more accurate contrast seems to lie in medieval *mediation* of the past as opposed to early modern *dislocation* from it.[6] Historical consciousness emphatically exists in the late Middle Ages: the past is neither in continuous synchrony with the present nor isolated from it, but is accessible through processes of mediation perceived as conscious and fallible. Indeed, in the works we have read, anxiety about the human capacity to know the past is much more prevalent than confidence in it. In this sense too, poetry, by virtue of its formal features, can infer its own situatedness in time without the need to consolidate it by explicit temporal content.

Perhaps surprisingly, given the widespread tendency to identify it with Christian didacticism, the temporality in which late medieval poetry situates itself is predominantly secular. Verse writers readily ground philosophy in worldly themes such as love, politics, or history; they do not hesitate to recontextualize religious history and doctrine in corporate and commercial settings or to expose them, embodied in rival guilds or individual contestants, to secular competition. Our study of encyclopedism suggests that, when faced with the options of totality and partiality, verse opts for partiality; and that, rather than pursue a theologically grounded concept of history, as the early encyclopedias do, the encyclopedic texts of the fourteenth and fifteenth centuries eschew theologically informed universal history in favor of experimenting with willfully fragmented or slewed versions of the history of the world. Equally, in political poetry, theological schemata are the servants rather than the masters of tendentious argument. Poetry inclines for the most part to anchor abstract thought in experience, or at least in the image of experience that poetry seems especially apt, in this period, to provide.

It is the capacity of poetry to connote its own situatedness in this way that makes it susceptible to endless recontextualization. As our study of poetry's

---

5. Panofsky, *Renaissance and Renascences,* 42–113, distinguishes the early modern Renaissance aspiration, to view antiquity as a totality, from the *bricolage* of antiquity that characterizes the twelfth-century Renaissance and Carolingian *renovatio.* Greene, *Light in Troy,* 171–96, notes early modern Renaissance poets' sense of tragic isolation from the past. On Petrarch's conception of antiquity, see Greene, *Light in Troy,* 81–103.

6. On the periodization of "medieval" and "modern" and its implications, see De Grazia, "Modern Divide," 455–58.

knowledge of itself has shown, poetry is—like nature in the encyclopedic tradition—both an object of knowledge and the means whereby one can know. This doubleness or duplicity is manifest in the various procedures of self-commentary, quotation, and allusion detailed in chapter 5. Here we see at work the kind of replication of knowledge to which Lyotard has drawn attention. Knowledge is never securely knowledge unless it is at the same time knowledge about knowledge, and a validation of knowledge *as* knowledge. Such doubling is inherent to medieval poetic practice. The explicit enactment of a community's shared myths constitutes the most basic form of reduplication that Lyotard discerns, and this is what gives value to much medieval performed poetry (see chapter 1). Reflecting another of Lyotard's models, which we have termed "exhortative," texts are insistently moralized or glossed, and antique poetry is reinterpreted in line with present interest. The recording of history, especially in verse, is valued in itself but sometimes also for something other than itself: the insights into ethics or government that "moralization" furnishes. The allegorical transposition of historical events, in texts such as the *Voyage de Gênes*, continues this reduplicative structure. Works that combine elements from a number of sources, like Nicole de Margival's *Dit de la panthère*, Machaut's *Remede de Fortune*, or Froissart's *Prison amoureuse*, operate in ways closer to Lyotard's "speculative" model, in which knowledge is validated by being subsumed into ever larger, more comprehensive frameworks on the model of the scholastic genre of the summa.

Nevertheless, while undoubtedly echoing Lyotard's categories of the pre-postmodern grand narrative, medieval poetry's reduplicative structures are so unstable as to reveal themselves as "language games" *avant la lettre*. The *poetic* first person, for example, is often to be construed ironically, and thus does not straightforwardly guarantee the philosophy (chapter 3) or sense of community (chapter 6) that it appears to convey. Elsewhere it may be caught up in a play of doubling (chapter 6), or be a victim of melancholy delusion (chapter 4), in ways that undermine its pretensions to know. In many texts that rely on glossing, allegoresis, or other explicit didactic techniques, these practices of legitimation may fall short through failure of cohesion (chapter 3) or self-evident tautologies (chapter 6). The *Ovide moralisé* unfailingly furnishes interpretations of the *Metamorphoses* that transpose its meaning utterly and thereby create a double text in which the reader is assured that both parts belong together yet is often at a loss to see *how*. The citational mode is especially liable to being destabilized, since it can be unclear what is being cited in what (see the discussion of the evolution of the *Rose*-Ovidian-Boethian matrix in chapter 3), and since quotation and context are apt to relativize each other (chapter 5).

Late medieval poetry is committed, then, to preserving and validating knowledge, but these processes reveal their own shortcomings. This means, to refer to our introduction, that this poetry is ultimately less concerned with *science* or *connaissance* than with *savoir*—less concerned, that is, with mental contents than with mental acts, processes, and expertise (*savoir faire*). Of course there are abundant *connaissances* on display in verse writing of all kinds, and one of our concerns has been to separate out the many fields of knowledge with which poetry engages (see especially chapters 4–6). Yet the common strands between these chapters also identify consistencies in the processes of *savoir* that they involve. Thematic insistence on change and mutability, on gleaning knowledge from time, on learning as an individual activity whose results are at best a partial achievement; and a concept of the practice of poetry as always involving interference between potentially changing contexts—all these are features of late medieval poetry that favor viewing it as caught up in process.

A corollary of this privileging of *savoir* is that while late medieval poetry preserves, transmits, and validates knowledge, these processes need not be present to the mind. They are, however, metaphorically implied by the very aspects of poetic texts that highlight the incompleteness of their *connaissances,* such as the various fault lines that we have identified traversing medieval texts, from encyclopedias to the didactic verse narratives of Christine de Pizan. It is for this reason that we have consistently suggested that the *savoir* of medieval verse texts is upheld by certain absences that hold the place of unspecifiable truth. For example, in chapter 2 we found that in verse historiography such as the *Prise d'Alixandre,* the reader is relieved of the need to check Machaut's "facts" against the historical record by virtue of the way his poem resonates with other political, moral, and reflective works in the same poetic form. More broadly, we suggest that a subjectivity divorced from any physical person provides a vestige of truth on which knowledge may be sensed to depend. This non-knowledge within knowledge can take the form of *déconnaisance,* as in cases where intention may be foiled by sexuality, memory may play false or be frankly unattainable, or experience can provokingly retain a core of inaccessibility.

In all such cases we might see poetry as providing a formal surplus, which does not in itself have content but stands in for a truth that is unavailable to knowledge. Given the role of verse as what both supplements and challenges knowledge, we could propose adding the category of "poetic legitimation" to the list begun by Lyotard, in which the wide formal variety of medieval poetry would play its part. If so, however, it would only be in the sense that verse shows up the truth of the failure of legitimation—which is why it can assume the form either of truth or of *déconnaissance*. The direction of our thinking here converges with Agamben's contention that medieval poetry, by virtue of its form, has access to both knowledge and enjoyment, though our concept of enjoyment for this period embraces practical engagement, relaxation, and imbecilic desire as well as the more exalting manifestations of "joy" that Agamben discerns in the troubadours and Dante.

The situatedness of the relationship between poetry and knowledge thus belongs also in the historical context of the rise of prose. With this in mind, let us return to the issue of periodization broached in the introduction. There we defined the beginning of our period in relation to scholasticism, the age of the university, the availability of books, and belief in the value of mediation. To this we can now add that it also coincides with the development of new institutions that guaranteed the production and appreciation of a wide range of verse genres, many of them also new. In sheer range and quantity of production, the most striking outcome of these changes is the proliferation of different forms of theater. But the development of new lyric forms, in particular the disinvestment from the *grand chant courtois* in favor of the *formes fixes,* is also decisive. Reinforced by the development of a patronage system in which poets were commissioned to compose lyric poetry alongside historical works, the new lyric forms lend themselves to combination with every other existing genre: they are inserted into *dits,* romances, and dramatic works, and interact with prose in the various experiments with *prosimetrum.* Another factor that decisively marks the onset of our period is the extraordinary success of the threefold generative matrix constituted by the *Rose,* the *Ovide moralisé,* and the medieval reworkings of Boethius's *Consolation.* Interest in these texts coincides with the burnout that afflicts the vernacular verse encyclopedia and results in the widespread composition, in its place, of encyclopedic verse. Alongside new forms of dramatic and lyric poetry, then, our period is defined by the gradual unfurling of various forms of reflective *dit.* A further consequence of the explosion of learning in the late thirteenth century is the professionalization of poetry itself; and among the institutions of performance, the Puys are major contributors to this poetic self-disciplining. Whether in Arras or in Toulouse, the founding of communities to foster the production and study of poetry is a hallmark of the onset of our period, and characteristic of its course. Thus, while we hesitate to pinpoint a single moment as determining, there is significant convergence on the 1260s and 1270s as marking the start of the associations that we have charted between verse and knowledge.

An even greater hesitation accompanies attempts to situate the end of our period. It is important to avoid reifying precisely those distinctions between "Middle Ages" and "Renaissance" that recent reflection has shown to be difficult to sustain; nor should we hypostatize a cultural movement, the early modern Renaissance, as a historical epoch.[7] A number of important cultural shifts, however, do take place around 1530, even if their historical roots go back much further. The development of a new mode of humanistic learning that seeks to eschew a mediating tradition in favor of what Thomas M. Greene has called "subreading," a dynamic interaction between readers and ancient texts whose alterity is acknowledged, is only the most familiar of these.[8] As we point out in our introduction, this led to other shifts in poetry, of which elements already existed in our period but which became much more prominent thereafter, particularly with the Pléiade. Alongside the adoption of classically derived forms and the privileging of immediacy more generally, claims were made for poets and poetry as vehicles for higher forms of knowledge. In some instances this knowledge was conceived as *connaissance,* in that poetry was considered to offer higher forms of epistemic content than other genres. In others it was conceived as *savoir,* and associated with more exalted mental processes than are accessible to non-poets; Neoplatonically derived notions of poetry's divine origins and inspirations, which sporadically appear in works from the late fifteenth century, often assume prominence in Pléiade poetry.[9] It is in the 1530s that major new vernacular poets, whose work begins to point toward these changes even if it does not fully assimilate them, begin to be published in significant volume: Clément Marot, Marguerite de Navarre, Maurice Scève.[10] Print culture itself takes on a new form: while early printing owed a great deal to manuscriptural practices, new technological, commercial, and aesthetic trends emerge around 1530.[11] One symptom of these is a turn away from late medieval poets whose work had been frequently printed in the early sixteenth century, such as Meschinot, Chartier, Molinet,

---

7. Tucker, *Forms of the "Medieval."*

8. Greene, *Light in Troy,* 93–94.

9. Castor, *Pléiade Poetics,* 24–36, 195–99, charts the theme of "divine fury" in the Pléiade's output. Earlier instances appear in the poetry of Jean Robertet and the *Instructif de seconde rhétorique* (see chapter 5). See Zsuppán, "An Early Example"; Tilliette, Cerquiglini-Toulet, and Mühlethaler, "Poétiques en transition," 18–20.

10. Two hundred seventy-eight sixteenth-century editions of Marot's work have been identified, ranging in date from 1521 to 1597; only three were printed before 1530, while ninety-six appeared in the period 1531–1539. Marguerite's poetry was first printed in 1531; seventy-seven sixteenth-century editions of her work in verse and prose are attested. The earliest known edition of Scève's poetry dates from 1536. See Pettegree, Walsby, and Wilkinson, *French Vernacular Books.* On the affinities between poets of this generation and the Pléiade, see Nash, "Literary Legacy." Thiry, "Jeunesse littéraire," outlines the complex and gradual nature of Marot's early development, in which *rhétoriqueur* elements are never entirely jettisoned.

11. Smith, "Medieval Roots"; Labarre, "Incunables."

and Lemaire.[12] Equally, the influential matrix described in chapter 3 loses its prominence. Printing of the *Rose* ceases after the late 1530s; few French translations of Boethius appear after 1520; allegorizing versions of Ovid's *Metamorphoses* are superseded from the 1530s by plain text editions in Latin, and by French translations that relegate moralization to prefaces or omit it entirely.[13] Finally, cultural activity is more markedly centralized, dominated to a much greater extent by Paris and the royal court; in other cultural circles, notably Lyon, court structures are less significant.[14]

The contrasting roles of poetry during and after our period are neatly encapsulated in the differences between two lyric forms: the *rondeau,* extremely widely practiced from the early fourteenth to the early sixteenth centuries; and the sonnet, which, adopted from medieval Italy rather than antiquity, emerges in French only after the 1530s.[15] The *rondeau*'s form and typical modes of transmission indicate its situated character. Its dominant formal feature is a refrain, which tends to inhibit the possibility of narrative development and to position the lyric voice as speaking from a particular moment, unrepeatable and irrecuperable. This impression is reinforced by the ways in which *rondeaux* frequently constitute a form of social interaction, a medium through which members of poetic coteries construct their relationships with one another. Manuscript and printed anthologies of *rondeaux* do not normally present fixed sequences; the dominant model is the multiauthor miscellany, in which, if any organizing principle is visible, it is likely to be the process of exchange between poets.[16] By comparison, the coordinates of *hic et nunc* are

---

12. Meschinot's *Lunettes des Princes* went through twenty-eight editions, of which the earliest is datable to 1492; only three datable editions are attested after 1534. The earliest datable edition of Chartier's verse was produced in 1484; very few editions postdate 1535. Three editions of Molinet's collected poetry appeared in Paris between 1531 and 1540, after which datable editions are very rare. The verse and prose work of Jean Lemaire de Belges was frequently published, but only three editions of his collected works and three of particular poems appear after 1535. See Pettegree, Walsby, and Wilkinson, *French Vernacular Books.*

13. Forty-five editions of the *Rose* were printed in the fifteenth and sixteenth centuries: twenty-eight appeared up to 1530, the remainder in the period 1531–1538. Six editions of French translations of Boethius appeared by 1520, and only two in the remainder of the sixteenth century. See Pettegree, Walsby, and Wilkinson, *French Vernacular Books.* No extant manuscript witnesses of the *Livre de Boece de Consolation* (see chapter 3) postdate 1500; ed. Cropp, 22–28. On developments in the publication of the *Metamorphoses,* see Moss, *Ovid,* 37–39.

14. Knecht, *Renaissance Warrior and Patron,* 425–77, outlines Francis I's cultural patronage (in evidence from the beginning of his reign in 1515). On Lyon, see Ford and Jondorf, *Intellectual Life in Renaissance Lyon.*

15. On the sonnet's early development, see McClelland, "Sonnet ou quatorzain?"; Rigolot, "Qu'est-ce qu'un sonnet?"; Gendre, *Évolution,* 31–107.

16. On the form and uses of the *rondeau,* see Poirion, *Poète et le prince,* 317–26, 333–43, 348–60; Taylor, *Making of Poetry.*

not inscribed into the sonnet with anything like the same force. Not only does it lack a refrain, but also it contains more rhymes, and has a linear rather than circular structure. While the typical *rondeau* constantly returns to two rhymes, the sonnet normally follows a fixed two-rhyme scheme in its quatrains with a more flexible set of three different rhymes in its tercets.[17] More important still, the sonnet does not partake of the *rondeau*'s interpersonal, disposable character; rather, it aspires to monumentality. Taking their lead from Petrarch's *Conzoniere,* French practitioners of the sonnet typically integrate it into carefully orchestrated, single-authored cycles; they may subsequently revise the poems and sequences, but the basic principle of anthologization remains the same.[18] This practice transforms the relationship between the individual lyric and those transmitted alongside it. A *rondeau* is a transaction in an ongoing commerce; a sonnet is a building block in a completed edifice. The voice located in time gives way to a voice that claims permanence. In conjunction with other traits of post-1530 poetry—the value placed on imaginative genius, the aspiration to transcend the distance separating the poet from both antiquity and posterity—the use of the sonnet indicates a different practice of legitimizing knowledge. Lyotard's "exhortative" and "speculative" models collapse into his "incarnational" model. The relationship of poetry to classical intertexts, the absorption of poems into cycles, themselves derive their value as knowledge from the authority ascribed to the poet's mind, an authority that the poet's productions recursively demonstrate.

Many further cultural changes begin shortly after the end of our period, between the mid-1530s and the late 1540s; equally, aspects of earlier poetry persist into the mid-sixteenth century.[19] Nevertheless, patterns of vernacular poetic production and consumption suggest that the distinctive culture of late medieval poetic knowledge undergoes its first significant ruptures around 1530. It is then that a new culture starts to begin, even if it is not for some years that the old one stops ending.

17. Goyet, "Sonnet français."
18. Sturm-Maddox, *Ronsard;* Gendre, *Évolution,* 89; Fontaine, "Système."
19. Rothstein, *Charting Change,* addresses a number of major developments.

Bibliography

Primary Texts

Texts in Verse

Adam de la Halle. *Œuvres complètes*. Ed. and trans. Pierre-Yves Badel. Paris: Librairie Générale Française, 1995.

Arnaut Daniel. *Canzoni*. Ed. Gianluigi Toja. Florence: Sansoni, 1960.

Le Bâtard de Bouillon. Chanson de Geste. Ed. Robert Francis Cook. Geneva: Droz, 1972.

[Boethius. *Consolation;* French *prosimetrum* translation.] *Le Livre de Boece de Consolacion*. Ed. Glynnis M. Cropp. Geneva: Droz, 2006.

Bouchet, Jean. *Les Anciennes et modernes genealogies des Roys de France*. Poitiers: Jacques Bouchet, 1527 o.s.

——. *Œuvres complètes*. Vol 1, *Le Jugement poetic de l'honneur femenin*. Ed. Adrian Armstrong. Paris: Champion, 2006.

[Candie, Gauvain. *L'Advisement de Mémoire et d'Entendement.*] "*L'Advisement* de Gauvain Candie." Ed. Evelyn Mottard. Bachelor's thesis, Université de Liège, 1984.

La Chanson de Bertrand du Guesclin de Cuvelier. Ed. Jean-Claude Faucon. 3 vols. Toulouse: Éditions universitaires du Sud, 1990–1993.

Charles d'Orléans. *Ballades et rondeaux*. Ed. Jean-Claude Mühlethaler. Paris: Librarie Générale Française, 1992.

Chartier, Alain. *Le Livre de l'Espérance*. Ed. François Rouy. Paris: Champion, 1989.

——. *The Poetical Works of Alain Chartier*. Ed. James C. Laidlaw. Cambridge: Cambridge University Press, 1974.

——. *The Quarrel of the "Belle dame sans mercy."* Ed. and trans. Joan E. McRae. New York: Routledge, 2004.

Chartier, Alain, Baudet Herenc, and Achille Caulier. *Le Cycle de "La Belle Dame sans mercy."* Ed. and trans. David F. Hult and Joan E. McRae. Paris: Champion, 2003.

Chastelain, George. *Les Exposicions sur Verité mal prise / Le Dit de Verité*. Ed. Jean-Claude Delclos. Paris: Champion, 2005.

Christine de Pizan. *Cent ballades d'amant et de dame*. Ed. Jacqueline Cerquiglini-Toulet. Paris: Union Générale d'Éditions, 1982.

——. *Le Chemin de longue étude.* Ed. and trans. Andrea Tarnowski. Paris: Librarie Générale Française, 2000.

——. *Le Ditié de Jehanne d'Arc.* Ed. Angus J. Kennedy and Kenneth Varty. Oxford: Society for the Study of Mediæval Languages and Literature, 1977. Also available online at http://www.jeanne-darc.dk/p_multimedia/literature/christine_de_pisan.html.

——. *Epistre Othea.* Ed. Gabriella Parussa. Geneva: Droz, 1999.

——. *Le Livre du Duc des vrais amans.* Ed. Thelma S. Fenster. Binghamton, N.Y.: Medieval and Renaissance Texts and Studies, 1995.

——. *Le Livre de la Mutacion de Fortune.* Ed. Suzanne Solente. 4 vols. Paris: Picard, 1959.

——. *The Love Debate Poems of Christine de Pizan.* Ed. Barbara K. Altmann. Gainesville: University Press of Florida, 1998.

——. *Œuvres poétiques.* Ed. Maurice Roy. 3 vols. Paris: Firmin-Didot, 1886–1896.

Coudrette, *Le Roman de Mélusine ou histoire de Lusignan par Coudrette.* Ed. Eleanor Roach. Paris: Klincksieck, 1982.

La Cour amoureuse dite de Charles VI. Ed. Carla Bozzolo and Hélène Loyau. 3 vols. Paris: Le Léopard d'Or, 1982–1992.

Deguileville, Guillaume de. *Le Pèlerinage de l'âme.* Ed. J. J. Stürzinger. London: Nichols, 1895.

——. *Le Pèlerinage de Jésus-Christ.* Ed. J. J. Stürzinger. London: Nichols, 1897.

——. *Le Pèlerinage de vie humaine.* Ed. J. J. Stürzinger. London: Nichols, 1893.

De Ram, P. F. X., ed. *Documents relatifs aux troubles du pays de Liège sous les princes-évêques Louis de Bourbon et Jean de Horne 1455–1505.* Brussels: M. Hayez, 1844.

[Deschamps, Eustache.] *Œuvres complètes de Eustache Deschamps: Publiées d'après le manuscrit de la Bibliothèque nationale.* Ed. le marquis de Queux de Saint-Hilaire and Gaston Raynaud. 11 vols. Paris: Firmin-Didot, 1878–1903.

Destrées. *Œuvres poétiques.* Ed. Holger Peterson. [Helsinki, 1927]. Montreal: CERES, 1989.

[*Les Échecs amoureux.*] Raimondi, Gianmario. "*Les Eschez amoureux,* studio preparatorio ed edizione." *Pluteus* 8–9 (1990–1998): 67–241.

Florent et Octavien: Chanson de geste du XIVᵉ siecle. Ed. Noëlle Laborderie. 2 vols. Paris: Champion, 1991.

Froissart, Jean. *L'Espinette amoureuse.* Ed. Anthime Fourrier. Paris: Klincksieck, 1963.

——. *Le Joli buisson de Jonece.* Ed. Anthime Fourrier. Geneva: Droz, 1975.

——. *Méliador.* Ed. Auguste Longnon. 3 vols. Paris: Firmin-Didot, 1895–1899.

——. *La Prison amoureuse.* Ed. Anthime Fourrier. Paris: Klincksieck, 1974.

Geffroy de Paris. *La Chronique métrique attribuée à Geffroy de Paris.* Ed. Armel Diverrès. Paris: Faculté des lettres de l'Université de Strasbourg, 1956.

Gervais du Bus. *Le Roman de Fauvel.* Ed. Arthur Långfors. Paris: Firmin-Didot, 1919.

La Geste des ducs de Bourgogne. In *Chroniques relatives à l'histoire de la Belgique sous la domination des ducs de Bourgogne.* Ed. J. C. Kervyn de Lettenhove. 3 vols. 2:259–572. Brussels: Hayez, 1870–1876.

Girart d'Amiens. *Escanor.* Ed. Richard Trachsler. 2 vols. Geneva: Droz, 1994.

Gossuin de Metz. See *Image du monde.*

Gréban, Arnoul. *Le Mystère de la Passion.* Ed. Omer Jodogne. 2 vols. Brussels: Palais des Académies, 1965–1983.

Gringore, Pierre. *Les Entrées royales à Paris de Marie d'Angleterre 1514 et Claude de France 1517.* Ed. Cynthia J. Brown. Geneva: Droz, 2005.

——. *Le Jeu du Prince des Sotz et de Mere Sotte.* Ed. Alan Hindley. Paris: Champion, 2000.

——. *Œuvres polémiques rédigées sous le règne de Louis XII.* Ed. Cynthia J. Brown. Geneva: Droz, 2003.

Guillaume de Lorris. See *Roman de la rose.*

Hugues Capet. Chanson de geste du XIVe siecle. Ed. Noëlle Laborderie. Paris: Champion, 1997.

[*Image du monde.*] "*L'Image du monde,* une encyclopédie du XIIIe siècle." Ed. Chantal Connochie-Bourgne. Ph.D. diss., Université de Paris-Sorbonne, 1999.

[——.] Centili, Sara. "La seconda redazione in versi dell'*Image du monde:* Edizione et traduzione." Ph.D., diss., University of Florence, 2002.

Le Jardin de Plaisance, et Fleur de Rhétorique par Antoine Vérard vers 1501. Ed. Eugénie Droz and Arthur Piaget. 2 vols. Paris: Firmin-Didot, 1910–1925.

Jean de Meun. See *Roman de la rose.*

La Marche, Olivier de. *Le Chevalier délibéré.* Ed. Carleton W. Carroll, trans. Lois Hawley Wilson and Carleton W. Carroll. Tempe: Arizona Center for Medieval and Renaissance Studies, 1999.

La Vigne, André de. *Le Mystère de Saint Martin.* Ed. André Duplat. Geneva: Droz, 1979.

——. *La Ressource de la Chrestienté.* Ed. Cynthia J. Brown. Montreal: CERES, 1989.

——. *Le Voyage de Naples.* Ed. Anna Slerca. Milan: Vita e Pensiero, 1981.

Le Franc, Martin. *Le Champion des Dames.* Ed. Robert Deschaux. 5 vols. Paris: Champion, 1999.

Lemaire de Belges, Jean. *La Concorde des deux langages.* Ed. Jean Frappier. Paris: Droz, 1947.

——. [*Couronne Margaritique.*] In *Œuvres,* ed. Jean Stecher. 4 vols. 4:1–167. Louvain: Lefever, 1882–1891.

——. *La Plainte du Désiré.* Ed. Dora Yabsley. Paris: Droz, 1932.

——. *Le Temple d'Honneur et de Vertus.* Ed. Henri Hornik. Geneva: Droz; Paris: Minard, 1957.

Lion de Bourges: Poème épique du XIVe siècle. Ed. William W. Kibler, Jean-Louis G. Picherit, and Thelma S. Fenster. 2 vols. Geneva: Droz, 1980.

La Lumere as lais by Pierre d'Albernon of Fetcham. Ed. Glynn Hesketh. 3 vols. London: ANTS, 1996–2000.

Machaut, Guillaume de. *Le Confort d'ami (Comfort for a Friend).* Ed. and trans. R. Barton Palmer. New York: Garland, 1992.

——. *The Fountain of Love (La fonteinne amoureuse) and Two Other Love Vision Poems.* Ed. and trans. R. Barton Palmer. New York: Garland, 1993.

——. [*Jugement dou roy de Behaingne.*] "*Le Jugement du roy de Behaigne" and "Remede de Fortune."* Ed. and trans. James I. Wimsatt and William W. Kibler. Athens: University of Georgia Press, 1988.

——. [*Jugement dou roy de Navarre.*] *The Judgment of the King of Navarre.* Ed. and trans. R. Barton Palmer. New York: Garland, 1988.

——. *Le Livre du Voir dit.* Ed. and trans. Paul Imbs and Jacqueline Cerquiglini-Toulet. Paris: Librairie Générale Française, 1999.

——. *La Prise d'Alixandre.* Ed. and trans. R. Barton Palmer. New York: Routledge, 2002.

——. *[Remede de Fortune.] "Le Jugement du roy de Behaigne" and "Remede de Fortune."* Ed. and trans. James I. Wimsatt and William W. Kibler. Athens: University of Georgia Press, 1988.

Maistre Pierre Pathelin: Le Miroir d'Orgueil. Ed. Darwin Smith. Saint-Benoît-du-Sault: Tarabuste, 2002.

Margival, Nicole de. *Le Dit de la panthère.* Ed. Bernard Ribémont. Paris: Champion, 2000.

Marot, Clément. *Œuvres poétiques complètes.* Ed. Gérard Defaux. 2 vols. Paris: Bordas, 1990–1993.

Marot, Jehan. *Le Voyage de Gênes.* Ed. Giovanna Trisolini. Geneva: Droz, 1974.

——. *Le Voyage de Venise.* Ed. Giovanna Trisolini. Geneva: Droz, 1977.

Matfre Ermengaud. *Le Breviari d'amor.* Ed. Peter T. Ricketts. 5 vols. Vol. 5, Leiden: Brill, 1976. Vols. 2 and 3, London: Publications de l'AIEO, 1989, 1998. Vol. 4, Turnhout: Brepols, Publications de l'AIEO, 2004.

Meschinot, Jean. *Les Lunettes des Princes.* Ed. Christine Martineau-Génieys. Geneva: Droz, 1972.

Michault, Pierre. *Le Doctrinal du temps présent.* Ed. Thomas Walton. Paris: Droz, 1931.

——. *Œuvres poétiques.* Ed. Barbara Folkart. Paris: Union Générale d'Éditions, 1980.

——. *Le Procès d'Honneur Féminin.* Ed. Barbara Folkart. *Le Moyen Français* 2 (1978).

Michel, Jean. *Le Mystère de la Passion Angers 1486.* Ed. Omer Jodogne. Gembloux: Duculot, 1959.

Miracles de Nostre Dame par personnages. Ed. Gaston Paris, Ulysse Robert, and François Bonnardot. 8 vols. Paris: Firmin-Didot, 1876–1893.

Molinet, Jean. *Les Faictz et dictz de Jean Molinet.* Ed. Noël Dupire. 3 vols. Paris: Picard, 1936–1939.

——(?). *Le Mystère de Judith et Holofernés.* Ed. Graham A. Runnalls. Geneva: Droz, 1995.

Le Mystère de Saint Laurent. Ed. W. Söderhjelm and A. Wallensköld. Helsinki: Imprimerie de la Société de littérature finnoise, 1890.

Ovide moralisé: Poème du commencement du quatorzième siècle. Ed. C. de Boer and others. *Verhandelingen der Koninklijke Akademie van Wetenschapen te Amsterdam: Afdeeling Letterkunde.* Vol. 1, books 1–3. Ed. Cornelius de Boer, Nieuwe Reeks 15, 1915. Vol. 2, books 4–6. Ed. Cornelius de Boer, Nieuwe Reeks 21, 1920. Vol. 3, books 7–9. Ed. Cornelius De Boer, Martina G. De Boer, and Jeannette Th. M. van't Sant, Nieuwe Reeks 30, 1931. Vol. 4, books 10–13. Ed. Cornelius de Boer, Martina G. de Boer. and Jeannette Th. M. van't Sant, Nieuwe Reeks 37, 1936. Vol. 5, books 14 and 15 and Appendices. Ed. Cornelius de Boer, Nieuwe Reeks 43, 1938.

Palinodz, Chantz royaulx, Ballades, Rondeaulx, et Epigrammes, à l'honneur de l'immaculée Conception de la toute belle Mere de Dieu, Marie Patronne des Normans, presentez au Puy à Rouen. Paris: Pierre Vidoue, [1525].

[Peire Corbian.] "Le *Thezaur* de Peire Corbian." Ed. Alfred Jeanroy and Giulio Bertoni. *Annales du Midi* 23 (1911): 289–308, 451–71.

La Petite Philosophie. Ed. W. H. Trethewey. London: ANTS, 1939.

[Phillippe Mouskés.] *Chronique rimée de Philippe Mouskés, évêque de Tournay au treizième siècle.* Ed. le Baron de Reiffenberg. 2 vols. Brussels: Hayez, 1836–1845.

Pierre d'Albernon. See *La Lumere as lais.*

[Pierre de Beauvais. *La Mappemonde.*] Angremy, Annie. "La *Mappemonde* de Pierre de Beauvais." *Romania* 104 (1983): 316–50, 457–98.

Renart le Contrefait, Le Roman de. Ed. Gaston Raynaud and Henri Lemaître. 2 vols. Paris: Champion, 1914.

René d'Anjou, *Le Livre du Cœur d'amour épris.* Ed. and trans. Florence Bouchet. Paris: Librairie Générale Française, 2003.

——. *Le Mortifiement de Vaine Plaisance de René d'Anjou: Étude du texte et des manuscrits à peintures.* Ed. Frédéric Lyna. Brussels: Société des bibliophiles et iconophiles de Belgique, 1926.

Ritmes et refrains tournésiens. Poésies couronnées par le Puy d'Escole de rhétorique de Tournay. 1477–1491. Extraites d'un manuscrit de la Bibliothèque publique de Tournai. [Ed. Frédéric Hennebert.] Mons: Hoyois-Derely, 1837.

[*Le Roman de la rose.*] Guillaume de Lorris and Jean de Meun. *Le Roman de la rose.* Ed. Clément Marot. Paris: Jean Petit, [1526].

——. Ed. Félix Lecoy. 3 vols. Paris: Champion, 1965–1970.

Rutebeuf. *Le Miracle de Théophile.* Ed. and trans. Jean Dufournet. Paris: Flammarion, 1987.

Saint-Gelais, Octovien de. *Le Séjour d'Honneur.* Ed. Frédéric Duval. Geneva: Droz, 2002.

Seneschal, Jean le, *Les Cent Ballades.* Ed. Gaston Raynaud. Paris: Firmin-Didot, 1905.

[Taillevent, Michault.] Deschaux, Robert. *Un poète bourguignon du XVe siècle: Michault Taillevent (Édition et Étude).* Geneva: Droz, 1975.

Villon, François. *Poésies complètes.* Ed. Claude Thiry. Paris: Librairie Générale Française, 1991.

[William of Waddington. *Manuel des pechiez.*] *Roberd of Brunnè's "Handling Synne."* Ed. F. J. Furnivall. London: Roxburghe Club, 1862.

Texts about Poetics and Rhetoric

[Boccaccio, *Genealogia.*] *Boccaccio on Poetry; Being the Preface and the Fourteenth and Fifteenth Books of Boccaccio's "Genealogia deorum gentilium."* Trans. Charles G. Osgood. Indianapolis: Bobbs-Merrill, 1956.

Deschamps, Eustache. *L'Art de dictier.* Ed. and trans. Deborah M. Sinnreich-Levi. East Lansing, Mich.: Colleagues Press, 1994.

Du Pont, Gratien. *Art et science de rhétoricque metriffiée.* Geneva: Slatkine, 1972.

Fabri, Pierre. *Le Grand et vrai art de plei ne rhétorique.* Ed. Alexandre Héron. 3 vols. Rouen: Société des Bibliophiles Normands, 1889–1890.

Instructif de seconde rhétorique. In *Le Jardin de Plaisance et Fleur de Rhétorique par Antoine Vérard vers 1501,* ed. Eugénie Droz and Arthur Piaget. 2 vols. Vol. 1, fols. a$_{ii}$v–c$_{iii}$r. Paris: Firmin-Didot, 1910–1925.

Legrand, Jacques. *Archiloge Sophie/Livre de bonnes meurs*. Ed. Evencio Beltran. Paris: Champion, 1986.

Molinier, Guilhem. *Las Leys d'Amors*. Ed. Joseph Anglade. 4 vols. Toulouse: Privat, 1919–1920.

[Raimon Vidal, *Razos de trobar*.] *Las Razos de trobar of Raimon Vidal and Associated Texts*. Ed. J. H. Marshall. London: Oxford University Press, 1972.

Recueil d'arts de seconde rhétorique. Ed. Ernest Langlois. Paris: Imprimerie Nationale, 1902.

Other Premodern Works

Aristotle. *The Complete Works of Aristotle: The Revised Oxford Translation*. Ed. Jonathan Barnes. 2 vols. Princeton: Princeton University Press, 1984.

Bible des poetes, La. Paris: Anthoine Vérard, 1493 o.s.

Boethius. *De Consolatione Philosophiæ*. Ed. and trans. S. J. Tester. Cambridge: Harvard University Press, 1918.

[Boethius, *Consolation;* Jean de Meun's prose translation]. Dedeck-Héry, V. L. "Boethius' *De Consolatione* by Jean de Meun." *Mediæval Studies* 14 (1952): 165–275.

[anonymous; medieval French prose translation]. *Boeces: De Consolacion*. Ed. J. Keith Atkinson. Tübingen: Niemeyer, 1996.

Bouchet, Jean. *Annales d'Aquitaine*. Poitiers: For Enguilbert de Marnef and Jacques Bouchet, 1524.

Brunel, Clovis, ed. *Les plus anciennes chartes en langue provençale: Recueil des pièces originales antérieures au XIIIᵉ siècle*. Paris: Picard, 1926.

Brunetto Latini. *Li Livres dou tresor*. Ed. Spurgeon Baldwin and Paul Barrette. Tempe: Arizona Center for Medieval and Renaissance Studies, 2003.

Christine de Pizan. *Le Livre de l'advision Christine*. Ed. Christine Reno and Liliane Dulac. Paris: Champion, 2001.

——. *Livre des fais et bonnes meurs du sage roy Charles V*. Ed. Suzanne Solente. 2 vols. Paris: Champion, 1936–1940.

Conty, Evrart de, *Li Livre des eschez amoureux moralisés*. Ed. Bruno Roy and Françoise Guichard-Tesson. Montreal: CERES, 1993.

Le Débat sur le "Roman de la Rose." Ed. Eric Hicks. Paris: Champion, 1977.

——. Ed. and trans. Virginie Greene. Paris: Champion, 2006.

Froissart, Jean. *Voyage en Béarn*. Ed. A. H. Diverrès. Manchester: Manchester University Press, 1953.

L'Image du Monde de Maitre Gossouin: Rédaction en prose. Ed. O. H. Prior. Lausanne: Payot, 1913.

Laurent of Orléans. *La Somme le roi par frère Laurent*. Ed. Édith Brayer and Anne-Françoise Leurquin-Labie. Paris: Société des Anciens Textes Français, 2008.

Lemaire de Belges, Jean. *Les Illustrations de Gaule et singularités de Troie*. Vols. 1–2 of *Œuvres,* ed. Jean Stecher. Louvain: Lefever, 1882–1891.

The Mirroure of the Worlde: A Middle English Translation of the "Miroir du monde." Ed. Robert R. Raymo et al. Toronto: University of Toronto Press, 2003.

Molinet, Jean. *Le Roman de la Rose moralisé*. Lyon: Guillaume Balsarin, 1503.

Nicolas de Senlis. *Chronique dite Saintongeaise.* Ed. André de Mandach. Tubingen: Niemeyer, 1970.

Nicolay, Jehan. *Kalendrier des guerres de Tournay (1477–1479).* Ed. Frédéric Hennebert. 2 vols. *Mémoires de la Société historique et littéraire de Tournai* 2–3 (1853–1856).

Ovid. *Metamorphoses.* Ed. and trans. Frank Justus Miller, rev. G. P. Goold. Vols. 3–4 of *Ovid.* Cambridge: Harvard University Press, 1977 (Vol. 3, 3rd ed.) and 1984 (Vol. 4, 2nd ed).

Perceforest, Le Roman de: Première partie. Ed. Jane H. M. Taylor. Geneva: Droz, 1979.

Placides et Timéo ou Li secrés as philosophes. Ed. Claude Alexandre Thomasset. Geneva: Droz, 1980.

Quintilian. *The Orator's Education [Institutiones oratoriæ].* Ed. and trans. Donald A. Russell. 5 vols. Cambridge: Harvard University Press, 2001.

Sydrac le philosophe, Le livre de la fontaine de toutes sciences: Edition des enzyklopädischen Lehrdialogs aus dem XIII. Jahrhundert. Ed. Ernstpeter Ruhe. Wiesbaden: Reichert, 2000.

Modern Critical, Philosophical, Theoretical, and Other Secondary Works

Adams, Tracy. "Love as Metaphor in Christine de Pizan's Ballade Cycles." In *Christine de Pizan: A Casebook,* ed. Barbara Altmann and Deborah McGrady, 149–65. New York: Routledge, 2003.

Agamben, Giorgio. *The Coming Community.* Trans. Michael Hardt. Minneapolis: University of Minnesota Press, 1993.

——. *Stanzas: Word and Phantasm in Western Culture.* Trans. Ronald L. Martinez. Minneapolis: University of Minnesota Press, 1993.

——. *The End of the Poem: Studies in Poetics.* Trans. Daniel Heller-Roazen. Stanford: Stanford University Press, 1999.

Akbari, Suzanne Conklin. "The Movement from Verse to Prose in the Allegories of Christine de Pizan." In *Poetry, Knowledge and Community in Late Medieval France,* ed. Rebecca Dixon and Finn E. Sinclair, 136–48. Cambridge: D. S. Brewer, 2008.

Allen, Graham. *Intertextuality.* London: Routledge, 2000.

Allen, Peter. *The Art of Love: Amatory Fiction from Ovide to the Romance of the Rose.* Philadelphia: University of Pennsylvania Press, 1993.

Altmann, Barbara K. "Reopening the Case: Machaut's *Jugement* Poems as a Source in Christine de Pizan." In *Reinterpreting Christine de Pizan,* ed. Earl Jeffrey Richards, with Joan Williamson, Nadia Margolis, and Christine Reno, 137–56. Athens: University of Georgia Press, 1992.

——. "Last Words: Reflections on a 'Lay mortel' and the Poetics of Lyric Sequences." In *Christine de Pizan and Medieval French Lyric,* ed. Earl Jeffrey Richards, 83–102. Gainesville: University Press of Florida, 1998.

Armstrong, Adrian. "The Practice of Textual Transmission: Jean Molinet's *Ressource du Petit Peuple.*" *Forum for Modern Language Studies* 33 (1997): 270–82.

——. "Dead Man Walking: *Remaniements* and Recontextualisations of Jean Molinet's Occasional Writing." In *Vernacular Literature and Current Affairs in*

the Early Sixteenth Century: France, England and Scotland, ed. Jennifer Britnell
   and Richard Britnell, 80–98. Aldershot: Ashgate, 2000.

——. Technique and Technology: Script, Print, and Poetics in France, 1470–1550.
   Oxford: Clarendon, 2000.

——. "Versification on the Page in Jean Molinet's Art de Rhétorique: From Aesthetic
   to Utilitarian." TEXT 15 (2002): 121–39.

——. "The Manuscript Reception of Jean Molinet's Trosne d'honneur." Medium
   Ævum 74 (2005): 311–28.

——. "Prosimètre et savoir." In Le Prosimètre à la Renaissance, ed. Nathalie Dauvois,
   125–42. Paris: Éditions Rue d'Ulm/Presses de l'École normale supérieure,
   2005.

——. "Avatars d'un griffonnage à succès: L'Epitaphe du duc Philippe de Bourgogne de
   Jean Molinet." Le Moyen Âge 113 (2007): 25–44.

——. "Songe, vision, savoir: L'onirique et l'épistémique chez Molinet et Lemaire de
   Belges." Zeitschrift für romanische Philologie 123 (2007): 50–68.

——. "The Testament of François Villon." In The Cambridge Companion to Medieval
   French Literature, ed. Simon Gaunt and Sarah Kay, 63–76. Cambridge:
   Cambridge University Press, 2008.

——. "Yearning and Learning: Spaces of Desire in Jean Lemaire de Belges's
   Concorde des deux langages (1511)." In The Erotics of Consolation: Desire and
   Distance in the Late Middle Ages, ed. Catherine E. Léglu and Stephen J. Milner,
   79–94. New York: Palgrave Macmillan, 2008.

——. The Virtuoso Circle: Competition, Collaboration, and Complexity in Late
   Medieval French Poetry. Tempe: Arizona Center for Medieval and Renaissance
   Studies, 2012.

Attwood, Catherine, Dynamic Dichotomy: The Poetic "I" in Fourteenth- and Fifteenth-
   Century French Lyric Poetry. Amsterdam: Rodopi, 1998.

——. "Temps et lieux de Souvenir." In Comme mon cœur desire: Guillaume de Machaut,
   "Le Livre du Voir Dit," ed. Denis Hüe, 235–56. Caen: Paradigme, 2002.

——. Fortune la contrefaite: L'envers de l'écriture médiévale. Paris: Champion, 2007.

Aubailly, Jean-Claude. Le Monologue, le dialogue et la sottie. Paris: Champion, 1976.

Badel, Pierre-Yves. Le Roman de la rose au XIVe siècle: Étude de la réception de
   l'œuvre. Geneva: Droz, 1980.

Bagoly, Suzanne. "'De mainctz aucteurs une progression': Un siècle à la recherche
   du Parnasse français." Le Moyen Français 17 (1985): 83–123.

Banks, Kathryn. Cosmos and Image in the Renaissance: French Love Lyric and Natural-
   Philosophical Poetry. Oxford: Legenda, 2008.

Baumgartner, Frederic J. Louis XII. Stroud: Sutton, 1994.

Beam, Sara. Laughing Matters: Farce and the Making of Absolutism in France. Ithaca:
   Cornell University Press, 2007.

Beaune, Colette. Naissance de la nation France. Paris: Gallimard, 1985.

Beer, Jeanette. Narrative Conventions of Truth in the Middle Ages. Geneva: Droz, 1981.

——. Early Prose in France: Contexts of Bilingualism and Authority. Kalamazoo:
   Western Michigan University, Medieval Institute Publications, 1992.

Bennett, Philip. "Rhetoric, Poetics and History: Machaut's Prise d'Alixandre and the
   Anonymous Geste des ducs de Bourgogne." In Medieval Historical Discourses:
   Essays in Honour of Professor Peter S. Noble, ed. Marianne J. Ailes, Anne

Lawrence-Mathers, and Françoise H. M. Le Saux. *Reading Medieval Studies* 34 (2008): 53–76.

Bent, Margaret, and Andrew Wathey. Introduction. In *Fauvel Studies: Allegory, Chronicle, Music, and Image in Paris, Bibliothèque Nationale de France, MS français 146,* ed. Margaret Bent and Andrew Wathey, 1–24. Oxford: Clarendon, 1998.

Berger, Roger. *Littérature et société arrageoises au XIIIe sieècle: Les chansons et dits arteésiens.* Arras: Commission départementale des monuments historiques du Pas-de-Calais, 1981.

Berthelot, Anne. "Nicole de Margival lecteur d'Adam de la Halle: 'Tel qu'en lui-même….'" *Perspectives Médiévales* 20 (1994): 4–14.

Blanchard, Joël. "La Conception des échafauds dans les entrées royales 1484–1517." *Le Moyen français* 19 (1989): 58–78.

Blanchard, Joël, and Jean-Claude Mühlethaler. *Écriture et pouvoir à l'aube des temps modernes.* Paris: Presses universitaires de France, 2002.

Bliggenstorfer, Susanna. *"Castellani Georgii Opera Poetica Gallice:* Le recueil Chastelain de la Bibliothèque Laurentienne à Florence; description du manuscrit medceo-palatino 120." *Vox Romanica* 43 (1984): 123–53.

Blumenfeld-Kosinski, Renate. "The Scandal of Pasiphae: Narration and Interpretation in the *Ovide moralisé." Modern Philology* 93 (1996): 307–26.

Bolduc, Michelle. *The Medieval Poetics of Contraries.* Gainesville: University Press of Florida, 2006.

Bouchet, Florence. *Le Discours sur la lecture en France aux XIVe et XVe siècles: Pratiques, poétique, imaginaire.* Paris: Champion, 2008.

Boudet, Jean-Patrice, and Hélène Millet, eds. *Eustache Deschamps et son temps.* Paris: Publications de la Sorbonne, 1997.

Bouhaïk-Gironès, Marie. "Le Théâtre sur la place de marché: La représentation du mystère de sainte Catherine à Rouen en 1454." In *"Mainte belle œuvre faicte": Études sur le théâtre médiéval offertes à Graham A. Runnalls,* ed. Denis Hüe, Mario Longtin, and Lynette Muir, 29–38. Orléans: Paradigme, 2005.

———. "La *Sottie de l'Astrologue* (Paris, 1499?): Contextes et polémiques autour de la figure de l'astrologue à Paris à la fin du Moyen Âge." In *Le Théâtre polémique français 1450–1550,* ed. Marie Bouhaïk-Gironès, Jelle Koopmans, and Katell Lavéant, 65–75. Rennes: Presses universitaires de Rennes, 2008.

Boulton, Maureen. "Guillaume de Machaut's *Voir Dit:* The Ideology of Form." In *Courtly Literature: Culture and Context; Selected Papers from the 5th Triennial Congress of the International Courtly Literature Society, Dalfsen, The Netherlands, 9–16 August, 1986,* ed. Keith Busby and Erik Kooper, 39–47. Amsterdam: Benjamins, 1990.

———. *The Song in the Story: Lyric Insertions in French Narrative Fiction, 1200–1400.* Philadelphia: University of Pennsylvania Press, 1993.

———. "Digulleville's *Pèlerinage de Jésus Christ:* A Poem of Courtly Devotion." In *The Vernacular Spirit: Essays on Medieval Religious Literature,* ed. Renate Blumenfeld-Kosinski, Duncan Robertson, and Nancy Bradley Warren, 125–44. New York: Palgrave Macmillan, 2002.

Bourgain, Pascale. "Les Chansonniers lyriques latins." In *Lyrique romane médiévale: La tradition des chansonniers. Actes du colloque de Liège 1989,* 61–84. Liège:

Bibliothèque de la Faculté de Philosophie et Lettres de l'Université de Liège, 1991.

Bozzolo, Carla. *Manuscrits des traductions françaises d'œuvres de Boccace.* Padua: Editrice Antenore, 1973.

Brand, William. *The Shape of Medieval History: Studies in Perception.* New Haven: Yale University Press, 1966.

Britnell, Jennifer. *Jean Bouchet.* Edinburgh: Edinburgh University Press, 1986.

——. "Aspects de la 'propagande' au temps de Louis XII: Les textes courts." In *Les Écrits courts à vocation polémique,* ed. Barbara Ertlé and Martin Gosman, 99–111. Frankfurt am Main: Peter Lang, 2006.

Brooke, C. N. L. *The Twelfth-Century Renaissance.* London: Thames and Hudson, 1969.

Brown, Cynthia J. "The Rise of Literary Consciousness in Late Medieval France: Jean Lemaire de Belges and the *Rhétoriqueur* Tradition." *Journal of Medieval and Renaissance Studies* 13 (1983): 51–74.

——. *The Shaping of History and Poetry in Late Medieval France: Propaganda and Artistic Expression in the Works of the Rhétoriqueurs.* Birmingham, Ala.: Summa, 1985.

——. *Poets, Patrons, and Printers: Crisis of Authority in Late Medieval France.* Ithaca: Cornell University Press, 1995.

——. "From Stage to Page: Royal Entry Performances in Honour of Mary Tudor, 1514." In *Book and Text in France, 1400–1600: Poetry on the Page,* ed. Adrian Armstrong and Malcolm Quainton, 49–72. Aldershot: Ashgate, 2007.

Brownlee, Kevin. *Poetic Identity in Guillaume de Machaut.* Madison: University of Wisconsin Press, 1984.

——. "Transformations of the Couple: Genre and Language in the *Jeu de Robin et de Marion.*" *French Forum* 14 (1989): 419–33.

——. "The Image of History in Christine de Pizan's *Livre de la Mutacion de Fortune.*" In *Contexts: Style and Values in Medieval Art and Literature,* ed. Daniel Poirion and Nancy Freeman Regalado, 44–56. Special number of *Yale French Studies* (1991).

——. "Authorial Self-representation and Literary Models in the *Roman de Fauvel.*" In *Fauvel Studies: Allegory, Chronicle, Music, and Image in Paris, Bibliothèque Nationale de France, MS français 146,* ed. Margaret Bent and Andrew Wathey, 73–103. Oxford: Clarendon, 1998.

Bryant, Lawrence. *The King and the City in the Parisian Royal Entry Ceremony: Politics, Ritual and Art in the Renaissance.* Geneva: Droz, 1986.

Burgoyne, Linda. "La Rime mnémonique et la structuration du texte dramatique médiéval." *Le Moyen Français* 29 (1991): 7–20.

Burgwinkle, William. *Sodomy, Masculinity, and Law in Medieval Literature: France and England, 1050–1230.* Cambridge: Cambridge University Press, 2004.

Burrow, John. *The Ages of Man: A Study in Medieval Writing and Thought.* Oxford: Oxford University Press, 1988.

Butterfield, Ardis. "*Aucassin et Nicolette* and Mixed Forms in Medieval French." In *Prosimetrum: Cross-cultural Perspectives on Narrative in Prose and Verse,* ed. Joseph Harris and Karl Reichl, 67–98. Woodbridge, Suffolk: D. S. Brewer, 1997.

———. *Poetry and Music in Medieval France: From Jean Renart to Guillaume de Machaut*. Cambridge: Cammbridge University Press, 2002.

———. "Historicizing Performance: The Case of the *Jeu de Robin et Marion*." In *Cultural Performances in Medieval France: Essays in Honour of Nancy Freeman Regalado*, ed. Eglal Doss-Quinby, Roberta L. Krueger, and E. Jane Burns, 99–107. Cambridge: D. S. Brewer, 2007.

———. *The Familiar Enemy: Chaucer, Language, and Nation in the Hundred Years War*. Oxford: Oxford University Press, 2009.

Calin, William. "Intertextual Play and the Game of Love: The *Belle Dame sans mercy* Cycle." *Fifteenth-Century Studies* 31 (2006): 31–46.

Castor, Grahame. *Pléiade Poetics: A Study in Sixteenth-Century Thought and Terminology*. Cambridge: Cambridge University Press, 1964.

Cayley, Emma. *Debate and Dialogue: Alain Chartier in His Cultural Context*. Oxford: Clarendon, 2006.

Céard, Jean. "Encyclopédie et encyclopédisme à la Renaissance." In *Encyclopédisme: Actes du colloque de Caen, 12–16 janvier 1987*, ed. Annie Becq, 57–67. Paris: Aux Amateurs de Livres, 1991.

Centili, Sara. "La seconda redazione in versi dell'*Image du monde:* Una riscrittura didattica." *Cultura Neolatina* 66 (2006): 161–206.

Cerquiglini-Toulet, Jacqueline. "Le Clerc et l'écriture: Le *Voir dit* de Guillaume de Machaut et la définition du dit." In *Literatur in der Gesellschaft des Spätmittelalters*, ed. Hans Ulrich Gumbrecht, 151–68. Heidelberg: Winter, 1980.

———. "Le Lyrisme en mouvement." *Perspectives Médiévales* 6 (1980): 75–86.

———. "L'Écriture louche: La voie oblique chez les Grands Rhétoriqueurs." In *Les Grands Rhétoriqueurs: Actes du 5ᵉ colloque sur le moyen français, Milan, 6–8 mai 1985*, Vol. 1, 21–31. Milan: Vita e Pensiero, 1985.

———. *"Un engin si soutil." Guillaume de Machaut et l'écriture au XIVᵉ siècle*. Geneva: Slatkine, 1985.

———. "Écrire le temps: Le lyrisme de la durée aux XIVᵉ et XVᵉ siècles." In *Le Temps et la durée dans la littérature au Moyen Âge à la Renaissance: Actes du Colloque organisé par le Centre de Recherche sur la Littérature du Moyen Âge et de la Renaissance de l'Université de Reims, novembre 1984*, ed. Yvonne Bellenger, 103–14. Paris: Nizet, 1986.

———. "Des Emplois seconds de la rime et du rythme dans la poésie française des XIVᵉ et XVᵉ siècles." *Le Moyen Français* 29 (1991): 21–31.

———. "Fullness and Emptiness: Shortages and Storehouses of Lyric Treasures in the Fourteenth and Fifteenth Centuries." In *Contexts: Style and Values in Medieval Art and Literature*, ed. Daniel Poirion and Nancy Freeman Regalado, 224–39. Special number of *Yale French Studies* (1991).

———. *La Couleur de la mélancolie: La fréquentation des livres au XIVᵉ siècle*. Paris: Hatier, 1993.

———. "Un paradoxe mélancolique ou le lyrisme chez Jean Froissart." In *Perspectives Médiévales, Actes du Colloque International Jehan Froissart, Lille 3-Valenciennes, 30 septembre–1ᵉʳ octobre 2004*, ed. Marie-Madeleine Castellani and Jean-Charles Herbin, 53–62. Paris: Société de langues et de littératures médiévales d'oc et d'oïl, 2006.

———. "Introduction. L'Amour de Sophie: Poésie et savoir du *Roman de la Rose* à Christine de Pizan." In *Poetry, Knowledge and Community in Late Medieval France,* ed. Rebecca Dixon and Finn E. Sinclair, 1–15. Cambridge: D. S. Brewer, 2008.

Cerritto, Stefania. "Histoires de femmes, jeux de formes et jeux de sens." In *Nouvelles études sur L'Ovide Moralisé,* ed. Marylène Possamaï-Perez, 73–97. Paris: Champion, 2009.

Champion, Pierre. *Histoire poétique du XVᵉ siècle.* 2 vols. Paris: Champion, 1923.

Chatelain, Henri. *Recherches sur le vers français au XVᵉ siècle: Rimes, mètres et strophes.* Paris: Champion, 1907.

Chenu, M.-D. "Auctor, Actor, Autor." *Bulletin du Cange: Archivum Latinitatis Medii Ævi* 3 (1927): 81–86.

Cherchi, Paolo, "L'enciclopedia nel mondo dei trovatori: Il *Breviari d'amor* di Matfre Ermengau." In *L'enciclopedismo medievale,* ed. Michelangelo Picone, 277–91. Ravenna: Longo, 1994.

Le Choix de la prose XIIIᵉ–XVᵉ siècles. = *Cahiers de recherches médiévales* 5 (1998).

Clark, Robert L. A. "Community versus Subject in Late Medieval French Confraternity Drama and Ritual." In *Drama and Community: People and Plays in Medieval Europe,* ed. Alan Hindley, 34–56. Turnhout: Brepols, 1999.

Cojan-Negulescu, Maria. "Watriquet de Couvin, *sire de Verjoli:* Statut du poète et évolution de la poésie française à l'aube du XIVᵉᵐᵉ siècle." Ph.D. diss., Université de Paris–Sorbonne Paris IV, 1997.

Coleman, Janet. *Ancient and Medieval Memories: Studies in the Reconstruction of the Past.* Cambridge: Cambridge University Press, 1992.

Coleman, Joyce. *Public Reading and the Reading Public in Late Medieval England and France.* Cambridge: Cambridge University Press, 1996.

———. "The Text Recontextualized in Performance: Deschamps' Prelection of Machaut's *Voir Dit* to the Count of Flanders." *Viator* 31 (2000): 233–48.

Collison, Robert. *Encyclopaedias: Their History throughout the Ages.* New York: Hafner, 1966.

Compagnon, Antoine. *La Seconde main ou le travail de la citation.* Paris: Seuil, 1979.

Connochie-Bourgne, Chantal. "L'Œuvre exemplaire de la nature dans la première encyclopédie en langue française." In *Sciences, techniques et encyclopédies: Actes du colloque de Mortagne-au-Perche,* ed. Denis Hüe, 65–85. Caen: Paradigme, 1993.

———. "'Theorike' et 'théologie' dans le *Trésor* de Brunet Latin." In *Le Divin: Discours encyclopediques. Actes du colloque de Mortagne-au-Perche,* ed. Denis Hüe, 125–37. Caen: Paradigme, 1994.

———. "Pourquoi et comment réécrire une encyclopédie? Deux rédactions de *L'Image du monde.*" In *Discours et savoirs: Encylopédies médiévales,* ed. Bernard Baillaud, Jérôme de Gramont, and Denis Hüe, 143–54. Rennes: Presses universitaires de Rennes, 1998.

———. "*Miroir* ou *image:* Le choix d'un titre pour un texte didactique." In *Miroirs et jeux de miroirs dans la littérature médiévale,* ed. Fabienne Pomel, 29–38. Rennes: Presses universitaires de Rennes, 2003.

———. "La Tour de Boctus le bon roi dans le *Livre de Sydrach.*" In *"Furent les merveilles pruvees et les aventures truvees,"* ed. Francis Gingras, Françoise

Laurent, Frédérique Le Nan, and Jean-René Valette, 163–76. Paris: Champion, 2005.

Corbellari, Alain. *La Voix des clercs: Littérature et savoir universitaire autour des dits du XIIIe siècle.* Geneva: Droz, 2005.

Cornilliat, François. *"Or ne mens": Couleurs de l'éloge et du blâme chez les "Grands rhétoriqueurs."* Paris: Champion, 1994.

———. "Prosimètre et persuasion chez Jean Molinet, ou l'art de consoler à demi." In *Le Prosimètre à la Renaissance,* ed. Nathalie Dauvois, 51–74. Paris: Éditions Rue d'Ulm/Presses de l'École normale supérieure, 2005.

Cornilliat, François, Jean-Claude Mühlethaler, and Olga Anna Duhl. "La Poésie parmi les arts au XVe siècle." In *Poétiques de la Renaissance: Le modèle italien, le monde franco-bourguignon et leur héritage en France au XVIe siècle,* ed. Perrine Galand-Hallyn and Fernand Hallyn, 29–53. Geneva: Droz, 2001.

Courcelle, Pierre. *La Consolation de Philosophie dans la tradition littéraire: Antécédents et postérité de Boèce.* Paris: Études Augustiniennes, 1967.

Cropp, Glynnis M. "The Medieval French Tradition." In *Boethius in the Middle Ages: Latin and Vernacular Traditions of the "Consolatio Philosophiæ,"* ed. Maarten J. F. M. Hoenen and Lodi Nauta, 243–65. Leiden: Brill, 1997.

Dauvois, Nathalie. "L'Évolution des formes lyriques dans les pièces primées aux Jeux Floraux toulousains XVe–XVIe siècles." In *Première poésie française de la Renaissance: Autour des Puys poétiques normands. Actes du Colloque international organisé par le CÉRÉDI Université de Rouen, 30 septembre–2 octobre 1999,* ed. Jean-Claude Arnould and Thierry Mantovani, 555–74. Paris: Champion, 2003.

———, ed. *Le Prosimètre à la Renaissance.* Paris: Éditions Rue d'Ulm/Presses de l'École normale supérieure, 2005.

De Grazia, Margreta. "The Modern Divide: From Either Side." *Journal of Medieval and Early Modern Studies* 37 (2007): 453–67.

Delclos, Jean-Claude. *Le Témoignage de Georges Chastellain: Historiographe de Philippe le Bon et de Charles le Téméraire.* Geneva: Droz, 1980.

De Looze, Laurence. *Pseudo-autobiography in the Fourteenth Century.* Gainesville: University Press of Florida, 1997.

Delumeau, Jean. *Le Péché et la peur: La culpabilisation en Occident (XIIIe–XVIIIe siècles).* Paris: Fayard, 1983.

Desmond, Marilynn. "The *Querelle de la Rose* and the Ethics of Reading." In *Christine de Pizan: A Casebook,* ed. Barbara K. Altmann and Deborah McGrady, 167–80. New York: Routledge, 2003.

Desmond, Marilynn, and Pamela Sheingorn. *Myth, Montage, and Visuality in Late Medieval Manuscript Culture: Christine de Pizan's "Epistre Othea."* Ann Arbor: University of Michigan Press, 2003.

Devaux, Jean. *Jean Molinet, Indiciaire bourguignon.* Paris: Champion, 1996.

———. "Molinet dramaturge: Une moralité inédite jouée lors du chapitre valenciennois de la Toison d'Or 1473." *Revue du Nord* 78 (1996): 35–47.

———. "De l'amour profane à l'amour sacré: Jean Molinet et sa version moralisée du *Roman de la Rose.*" In *Image et mémoire du Hainaut médiéval,* ed. Jean-Charles Herbin, 21–32. Valenciennes: Presses universitaires de Valenciennes, 2004.

Dillon, Emma. "The Profile of Philip V in the Music of *Fauvel*." In *Fauvel Studies: Allegory, Chronicle, Music, and Image in Paris, Bibliothèque Nationale de France, MS français 146,* ed. Margaret Bent and Andrew Wathey, 215–31. Oxford: Clarendon, 1998.

Dinshaw, Carolyn. *Getting Medieval: Sexualities and Communities, Pre- and Postmodern.* Durham: Duke University Press, 1999.

Di Stefano, Giuseppe. "Nota sul Songe du Vieil Pelerin di Philippe de Mézières." *Le Moyen Français* 11 (1982): 129–32.

———. "Structure métrique et structure dramatique dans le théâtre médiéval." In *The Theatre in the Middle Ages,* ed. Herman Braet, Johan Nowé, and Gilbert Tournoy, 194–206. Leuven: Leuven University Press, 1985.

Dixon, Rebecca. "Conclusion: Knowing Poetry, Knowing Communities." In *Poetry, Knowledge and Community in Late Medieval France,* ed. Rebecca Dixon and Finn E. Sinclair, 215–24. Cambridge: D. S. Brewer, 2008.

Dixon, Rebecca, and Finn E. Sinclair, eds. *Poetry, Knowledge and Community in Late Medieval France.* Cambridge: D. S. Brewer, 2008.

Doudet, Estelle. "Aux frontières du prosimètre: George Chastelain et le théâtre." *Le Prosimètre à la Renaissance,* ed. Nathalie Dauvois, 21–50. Paris: Éditions Rue d'Ulm/Presses de l'École normale supérieure, 2005.

———. *Poétique de George Chastelain 1415–1475: Un cristal mucié en un coffre.* Paris: Champion, 2005.

———. "Statut et figures de la voix satirique dans le théâtre polémique français (XVᵉ–XVIᵉ siècles)." In *Le Théâtre polémique français 1450–1550,* ed. Marie Bouhaïk-Gironès, Jelle Koopmans, and Katell Lavéant, 15–31. Rennes: Presses Universitaires de Rennes, 2008.

Doutrepont, Georges. *Les Mises en prose des épopées et des romans chevaleresques du XIVᵉ au XVIᵉ siècle.* Brussels: Palais des Académies, 1939.

Dragonetti, Roger. "'La Poésie…ceste musique naturele': Essai d'exégèse d'un passage de l'*Art de dictier* d'Eustache Deschamps." In *Fin du moyen âge et Renaissance: Mélanges de philologie française offerts à Robert Guiette,* 49–64. Antwerp: De Nederlandsche Boekhandel, 1961.

Dulac, Liliane. "Travail allégorique et ruptures du sens chez Christine de Pizan: L'*Epistre Othea*." In *Continuités et ruptures dans l'histoire et la littérature: Actes du colloque franco-polonais, Montpellier, 1987,* ed. Michèle Weil, Halina Suwala, and Dominique Triaire, 24–32. Paris: Champion; Geneva: Slatkine, 1988.

Dull, Olga Anna. *Folie et rhétorique dans la sottie.* Geneva: Droz, 1994.

Dunbabin, Jean. "The Metrical Chronicle Traditionally Ascribed to Geffroy de Paris." In *Fauvel Studies: Allegory, Chronicle, Music, and Image in Paris, Bibliothèque Nationale de France, MS français 146,* ed. Margaret Bent and Andrew Wathey, 233–46. Oxford: Clarendon Press, 1998.

Dupire, Noël. *Jean Molinet: La vie—les œuvres.* Paris: Droz, 1932.

Earp, Lawrence. *Guillaume de Machaut: A Guide to Research.* New York: Garland, 1995.

Fasseur, Valérie. "Une expérience avec la lyrique: le *Perilhos Tractat d'amor de donas* de Matfre Ermengaud." In *L'Expérience lyrique au Moyen Âge: Actes du colloque tenu les 26 et 27 septembre 2002 à l'École normale supérieure lettres et sciences humaines de Lyon,* ed. Michèle Gally, 169–92. Paris: Société de langue et de littérature médiévales d'oc et d'oïl, 2003.

Fenster, Thelma S., and Daniel Lord Smail, eds. *Fama: The Politics of Talk and Reputation in Medieval Europe.* Ithaca: Cornell University Press, 2003.

Fleming, John. *An Introduction to the Franciscan Literature of the Middle Ages.* Chicago: Chicago University Press, 1977.

Floquet, Oreste. "Considérations sur la musique et la métrique des chansons d'Adam de la Halle dans le chansonnier La Vallière *W.*" *Romania* 131 (2005): 123–40.

Fontaine, Marie-Madeleine. "Le Système des *Antiquités* de Du Bellay: L'alternance entre décasyllabes et alexandrins dans un recueil de sonnets." In *Le Sonnet à la Renaissance: Des origines au XVIIe siècle,* ed. Yvonne Bellenger, 67–81. Paris: Aux Amateurs de Livres, 1988.

Ford, Philip, and Gillian Jondorf, eds. *Intellectual Life in Renaissance Lyon: Proceedings of the Cambridge Lyon Colloquium, 14–16 April 1991.* Cambridge: Cambridge French Colloquia, 1993.

Forhan, Kate Langdon. *The Political Theory of Christine de Pizan.* Aldershot: Ashgate, 2002.

Fragonard, Marie-Madeleine. *La Pensée religieuse d'Agrippa d'Aubigné et son expression.* Paris: Didier, 1986.

Françon, Marcel. "Humanisme, *bonæ literæ,* encyclopédie." *Romance Notes* 13 (1972): 523–28.

Freud, Sigmund. "Mourning and Melancholia." In *The Standard Edition of the Complete Psychological Works of Sigmund Freud.* Trans. James J. Strachey et al. Vol. 14, 243–58. London: Hogarth Press, 1953–1974.

Galderisi, Claudio. "Vers et prose." In *Histoire de la France Littéraire. Naissances, Renaissances: Moyen Âge—XVIe siècle.* Ed. Frank Lestringant and Michel Zink, 745–66. Paris: Presses Universitaires de France, 2006.

Galent-Fasseur, Valérie. "La Dame de l'arbre: Rôle de la 'vue' structurale dans le *Breviaire d'amour* de Matfre Ermengau." *Romania* 117 (1999): 32–50.

——. "Mort et salut des troubadours. Le *Breviari d'amor* de Matfre Ermengau." *Cahiers de Fanjeaux* 35 (2000): 423–41.

Gally, Michèle. "Poésie en jeu: Des jeux-partis aux fatrasies." In *Arras au Moyen Âge: Histoire et littérature,* ed. Marie-Madeleine Castellani and Jean-Pierre Martin, 71–80. Arras: Presses de l'Université d'Artois, 1994.

——. "Archéologie des arts poétiques français." *Nouvelle Revue du Seizième Siècle* 18 (2000): 9–23.

——. *L'Intelligence de l'amour d'Ovide à Dante: Arts d'aimer et poésie au Moyen Âge.* Paris: Éditions du CNRS, 2005.

Gaucher, Élisabeth. *La Biographie chevaleresque: Typologie d'un genre (XIIIe–XVe siècle).* Paris: Champion, 1994.

Gendre, André. *Évolution du sonnet français.* Paris: Presses universitaires de France, 1996.

Godzich, Wlad, and Jeffrey Kittay. *The Emergence of Prose: An Essay in Prosaics.* Minneapolis: University of Minnesota Press, 1987.

Goyet, Francis. "Le Sonnet français, vrai et faux héritier de la Grande Rhétorique." In *Le Sonnet à la Renaissance: Des origines au XVIIe siècle,* ed. Yvonne Bellenger, 31–41. Paris: Aux Amateurs de Livres, 1988.

——. "Encyclopédie et 'lieux communs.'" In *Encyclopédisme: Actes du colloque de Caen, 12–16 janvier 1987,* ed. Annie Becq, 493–504. Paris: Aux Amateurs de Livres, 1991.

Greene, Thomas M. *The Light in Troy: Imitation and Discovery in Renaissance Poetry.* New Haven: Yale University Press, 1982.

Griffin, Miranda. *The Object and the Cause in the Vulgate Cycle.* London: Legenda, 2005.

——. "Material and Poetic Knowledge in Christine de Pizan." Unpublished paper presented in Cambridge, 2007.

Gros, Gérard. *Le Poète, la vierge et le prince du puy: Étude sur les Puys marials de la France du Nord du XIVᵉ siècle à la Renaissance.* Paris: Klincksieck, 1992.

——. *Le Poème du Puy marial: Étude sur le serventois et le chant royal du XIVᵉ siècle à la Renaissance.* Paris: Klincksieck, 1996.

Grundriss der romanischen Literaturen des Mittelalters, Vol. 8 part 1 = La Littérature française aux XIVᵉ et XVᵉ siècles: Partie historique, ed. Daniel Poirion. Heidelberg: Winter 1988.

Guynn, Noah D. *Allegory and Sexual Ethics in the High Middle Ages.* New York: Palgrave Macmillan, 2007.

Hasenohr, Geneviève. "Traductions et littérature en langue vulgaire." In *Mise en page et mise en texte du livre manuscrit,* ed. Henri-Jean Martin and Jean Vezin, 229–352. Paris: Éditions du Cercle de la librairie/Promodis, 1990.

Heers, Jacques. *La Ville au Moyen Âge en Occident: Paysages, pouvoir et conflits.* Paris: Fayard, 1990.

Heller-Roazen, Daniel. *Fortune's Faces: The "Roman de la Rose" and the Poetics of Contingency.* Baltimore: Parallax, 2003.

Hill, Jillian M. L. *The Medieval Debate on Jean de Meung's "Roman de la Rose": Morality versus Art.* Lewiston: Edwin Mellen Press, 1991.

Hindman, Sandra L. *Christine de Pizan's "Epistre Othéa": Painting and Politics at the Court of Charles VI.* Toronto: Pontifical Institute of Medieval Studies, 1986.

Hochner, Nichole. *Louis XII: les dérèglements de l'image royale 1498–1515.* Seyssel: Champ Vallon, 2006.

Hoepffner, Ernest, "Les Poésies lyriques du *Dit de la panthere* de Nicole de Margival." *Romania* 46 (1920): 204–30.

Hüe, Denis. "Le Vers et le nombre: notes sur quelques théories poétiques." *Nouvelle Revue du Seizième Siècle* 18 (2000): 25–40.

——. *La Poésie palinodique à Rouen 1486–1550.* Paris: Champion, 2002.

——. "Le Prince chez Meschinot, mise en forme d'un objet poétique/politique." In *Poetry, Knowledge and Community in Late Medieval France,* ed. Rebecca Dixon and Finn E. Sinclair, 187–201. Cambridge: D. S. Brewer, 2008.

Hult, David. "Poetry and the Translation of Knowledge in Jean de Meun." In *Poetry, Knowledge and Community in Late Medieval France,* ed. Rebecca Dixon and Finn E. Sinclair, 19–41. Cambridge: D. S. Brewer, 2008.

Hunt, Tony. "Aristotle, Dialectic, and Courtly Literature." *Viator* 10 (1979): 95–129.

——. "The Christianization of Fortune." *Fortune and Women in Medieval Literature. Nottingham French Studies* 38 (1999): 95–113.

Huot, Sylvia. *From Song to Book: The Poetics of Writing in Old French Lyric and Lyrical Narrative Poetry.* Ithaca: Cornell University Press, 1987.

——. "Transformations of Lyric Voice in the Songs, Motets, and Plays of Adam de la Halle." *Romanic Review* 78 (1987): 148–64.

——. "'Ci parle l'aucteur': The Rubrication of Voice and Authorship in the *Roman de la Rose* Manuscripts." *SubStance* 56 (1988): 42–48.

——. "Chronicle, Lai, and Romance: Orality and Writing in the *Roman de Perceforest*." In *Vox Intexta: Orality and Textuality in the Middle Ages,* ed. A. Nick Doane and Carol Pasternak, 201–21. Madison: University of Wisconsin Press, 1991.

——. *The Romance of the Rose and Its Medieval Readers.* Cambridge: Cambridge University Press, 1993.

——. "Sentences and Subtle Fictions: On Reading Literature in the Later Middle Ages." In *What Is Literature? France, 1100–1600,* ed. François Cornilliat, Ullrich Langer, and Douglas Kelly, 197–209. Lexington, Ky.: French Forum, 1993.

——. "Bodily Peril: Sexuality and the Subversion of Order in Jean de Meun's *Roman de la Rose." Modern Language Review* 95 (2000): 41–61.

——. "The Writer's Mirror: Watriquet de Couvin and the Development of the Author-Centred Book." In *Across Boundaries: The Book in Culture and Commerce,* ed. Bill Bell, Philip Bennett, and Jonquil Bevan, 29–46. Winchester: St. Paul's Bibliographies/New Castle, Del.: Oak Knoll, 2000.

——. "Guillaume de Machaut and the Consolation of Poetry." *Modern Philology* 100 (2002): 169–95.

——. *Madness in Medieval French Literature: Identities Found and Lost.* Oxford: Oxford University Press, 2003.

——. "Reading the Lies of Poets: The Literal and the Allegorical in Machaut's *Fontainne amoureuse." Philological Quarterly* 85 (2006): 25–48.

——. "Re-fashioning Boethius: Prose and Poetry in Chartier's *Livre de l'Esperance." Medium Ævum* 76 (2007): 268–84.

——. *Dreams of Lovers and Lies of Poets: Poetry, Knowledge, and Desire in the Roman de la Rose.* Oxford: Legenda, 2010.

——. "'Finding-Aids' for the Study of Vernacular Poetry in the Fourteenth Century: The Example of the *Roman de la Rose*." In *Lesevorgänge: Prozesse des Erkennens in mittelalterlichen Texten, Bildern und Handschriften,* ed. Eckart Conrad Lutz, Martina Backes, and Stefan Matter, 263–82, 685–87. Zürich: Cronos, 2010.

Iser, Wolfgang. *The Implied Reader: Patterns of Communication in Prose Fiction from Bunyan to Beckett,* trans. David Henry Wilson. Baltimore: Johns Hopkins University Press, 1974.

Jeanneret, Sylvia. "Texte et enluminures dans l'*Epistre Othea* de Christine de Pizan: Une lecture politique?" In *Au champ des escriptures: IIIe colloque international sur Christine de Pizan, Lausanne, 18–22 juillet 1998,* ed. Eric Hicks, Diego Gonzalez, and Philippe Simon, 723–36. Paris: Champion, 2000.

Jodogne, Pierre. *Jean Lemaire de Belges, écrivain franco-bourguignon.* Brussels: Palais des Académies, 1972.

Jones, Catherine M. *Philippe de Vigneulles and the Art of Prose Translation.* Cambridge: D. S. Brewer, 2008.

Jung, Marc-René. "Poetria: Zur Dichtungstheorie des ausgehenden Mittelalters in Frankreich." *Vox Romanica* 30 (1971): 44–64.

——. "La Naissance de la ballade dans la première moitié du XIVe siècle, de Jean Acart à Jean de le Mote et à Guillaume de Machaut." *L'Analisi linguistica e letteraria* 8, no. 1–2 (2000): 7–29.

——. "Les plus anciennes ballades de Machaut et la tradition antérieure de la ballade: Aspects métriques." In *Convergences médiévales: Épopée, lyrique, roman. Mélanges offerts à Madeleine Tyssens,* ed. Nadine Henrard, Paola Moreno, and Martine Thiry-Stassin, 287–97. Brussels: De Boeck Université, 2001.

——. "La Ballade à la fin du XVe et au début du XVIe siècle: Agonie ou reviviscence?" In *Poétiques en transition: Entre Moyen Âge et Renaissance,* ed. Jean-Claude Mühlethaler and Jacqueline Cerquiglini-Toulet, special number of *Études de Lettres* 4 (2002): 23–41.

Kamber, Urs. *Arbor Amoris: Der Minnebaum; Ein Pseudo-Bonaventura-Traktat.* Berlin: Erich Schmidt, 1964.

Kay, Sarah. *Courtly Contradictions: The Emergence of the Literary Object in the Twelfth Century.* Stanford: Stanford University Press, 2001.

——. "Mémoire et imagination dans *Le Joli buisson de Jonece* de Jean Froissart: La fiction entre philosophie et poétique." *Francofonia* 45 (2003): 179–97.

——. *Žižek: A Critical Introduction.* Cambridge: Polity, 2003.

——. "*Le moment de conclure:* Initiation as Retrospection in Froissart's *dits.*" In *Rites of Passage,* ed. Nicola McDonald and Mark Ormrod, 153–71. Woodbridge, Suffolk: Boydell and Brewer, 2004.

——. "Grafting the Knowledge Community: The Purposes of Verse in the *Breviari d'amor* of Matfre Ermengaud." *Neophilologus* 91 (2007): 361–73.

——. *The Place of Thought: The Complexity of One in Late Medieval French Didactic Poetry.* Philadelphia: University of Pennsylvania Press, 2007.

——. "Touching Singularity: Melancholy and Consolation in the Medieval French *dit.*" In *The Erotics of Consolation: Desire and Distance in the Late Middle Ages,* ed. Catherine E. Léglu and Stephen J. Milner, 21–38. New York: Palgrave Macmillan, 2008.

——. "How Long Is a Quotation? Quotations from the Troubadours in the Text and Manuscripts of the *Breviari d'amor.*" *Romania* 127 (2009): 140–68.

——. "Knowledge and Truth in Quotations from the Troubadours: Matfre Ermengaud, Compagnon, Lyotard, Lacan." *Australian Journal of French Studies* 46 (2009): 178–90.

——. "Poésie, vérité, et le sujet supposé savoir: Citations des troubadours et poétique européenne." In *Pourquoi des théories,* ed. Denis Guénoun and Nicolas Doutey, 87–111. Paris: Les Solitaires Intempestifs, 2009.

——. "L'Arbre et la greffe dans le *Breviari d'amor* de Matfre Ermengaud: Temps du savoir et temps de l'amour." In *L'Arbre au Moyen Âge,* ed. Valérie Fasseur, Danièle James-Raoul, Jean-René Valette, 169–81. Paris: Presses de l'Université Paris-Sorbonne, 2010.

Kelly, Allison. "Christine de Pizan and Antoine de la Sale: The Dangers of Love in Theory and Fiction." In *Reinterpreting Christine de Pizan,* ed. Earl Jeffrey Richards, with Joan Williamson, Nadia Margolis, and Christine Reno, 173–86. Athens: University of Georgia Press, 1992.

Kelly, Douglas. "Imitation, Metamorphosis, and Froissart's Use of the Exemplary *Modus tractandi.*" In *Froissart across the Genres,* ed. Donald Maddox and Sarah Sturm-Maddox, 101–18. Gainesville: University Press of Florida, 1998.

——. *Christine de Pizan's Changing Opinion: A Quest for Certainty in the Midst of Chaos.* Cambridge: D. S. Brewer, 2007.

Kenny, Neil. *The Palace of Secrets: Béroalde de Verville and Renaissance Conceptions of Knowledge.* Oxford: Clarendon, 1991.

Kibler, William W. "*Le joli buisson de Jonece:* Froissart's Midlife Crisis." In *Froissart across the Genres,* ed. Donald Maddox and Sarah Sturm-Maddox, 63–80. Gainesville: University Press of Florida, 1998.

Knecht, Robert J. *Renaissance Warrior and Patron: The Reign of Francis I.* Cambridge: Cambridge University Press, 1994.

Knight, Alan E. *Aspects of Genre in Late Medieval French Drama.* Manchester: Manchester University Press, 1983.

——. "The Stage as Context: Two Late Medieval French Susanna Plays." In *The Stage as Mirror: Civic Theatre in Late Medieval Europe,* ed. Alan E. Knight, 201–16. Cambridge: D. S. Brewer, 1997.

——. "Processional Theatre and the Rituals of Social Unity in Lille." In *Drama and Community: People and Plays in Medieval Europe,* ed. Alan Hindley, 99–109. Turnhout: Brepols, 1999.

Kosta-Théfaine, Jean-François. "Le *Ditié de Jehanne d'Arc* de Christine de Pizan: Un modèle d'architecture fondé sur l'utilisation de la symbolique des nombres." *Cahiers de Recherches Médiévales* 3 (1997): 121–29.

Kovacs, Susan R. "Staging Lyric Performances in Early Print Culture: *Le Jardin de Plaisance et Fleur de Rethorique* c.1501–02." *French Studies* 55 (2001): 1–24.

Kristeva, Julia. *Powers of Horror: An Essay on Abjection.* Trans. Leon S. Roudiez. New York: Columbia University Press, 1982.

Krueger, Roberta L. *Women Readers and the Ideology of Gender in Old French Verse Romance.* Cambridge: Cambridge University Press, 1993.

——. "Christine's Anxious Lessons: Gender, Morality, and the Social Order from the *Enseignemens* to the *Avision.*" In *Christine de Pizan and the Categories of Difference,* ed. Marilynn Desmond, 16–40. Minneapolis: University of Minnesota Press, 1998.

Labarre, Albert, "Les Incunables: La présentation du livre." In *Histoire de l'édition française,* ed. Henri-Jean Martin and Roger Chartier. 4 vols. 1:195–215. Paris: Promodis, 1982–1986.

Lacan, Jacques. *Écrits.* Paris: Seuil, 1966.

——. *Le Séminaire de Jacques Lacan. Livre XV: L'Acte psychanalytique.* Unpublished seminar read on http://gaogoa.free.fr/.

Lacy, Norris J. "The Flight of Time: Villon's Trilogy of *Ballades.*" *Romance Notes* 22 (1982): 353–58.

Laidlaw, James C. "Christine de Pizan—A Publisher's Progress." *Modern Language Review* 82 (1987): 35–75.

——. "The *Cent balades:* The Marriage of Content and Form." In *Christine de Pizan and Medieval French Lyric,* ed. Earl Jeffrey Richards, 53–82. Gainesville: University Press of Florida, 1998.

——. "Christine and the Manuscript Tradition." In *Christine de Pizan: A Casebook,* ed. Barbara Altmann and Deborah McGrady, 231–49. New York: Routledge, 2003.

Laird, Judith, and Earl Jeffrey Richards. "*Tous parlent par une mesmes bouche:* Lyrical Outbursts, Prosaic Remedies, and Voice in Christine de Pizan's *Livre du Duc des vrais amans.*" In *Christine de Pizan and Medieval French Lyric,* ed. Earl Jeffrey Richards, 103–31. Gainesville: University Press of Florida, 1998.

Lalou, Élisabeth. "La Chancellerie royale à la fin du règne de Philippe IV le Bel." In *Fauvel Studies: Allegory, Chronicle, Music, and Image in Paris, Bibliothèque Nationale de France, MS français 146,* ed. Margaret Bent and Andrew Wathey, 307–19. Oxford: Clarendon, 1998.

Langer, Ullrich. *Divine and Poetic Freedom in the Renaissance: Nominalist Theology and Literature in France.* Princeton: Princeton University Press, 1990.

LeBlanc, Yvonne. *Va Lettre Va: The French Verse Epistle, 1400–1550.* Birmingham, Ala.: Summa Publications, 1995.

Lechat, Didier. "La Place du *sentement* dans l'expérience lyrique aux XIV^c et XV^c siècles." In *L'expérience lyrique au Moyen Âge,* supplement to *Perspectives Médiévales,* no. 28 (2002): 193–207.

——. "*Dire par fiction*": *Métamorphoses du "je" chez Guillaume de Machaut, Jean Froissart et Christine de Pizan.* Paris: Champion, 2005.

Lefèvre, Yves. *L'Elucidarium et les lucidaires: Contribution, par l'histoire d'un texte, à l'histoire des croyances religieuses en France au Moyen Âge.* Paris: Boccard, 1954.

Léglu, Catherine. "Memory, Teaching and Performance: The Two Versions of Peire de Corbian's *Thezaur.*" In *Études de langue et de littérature romanes offertes à Peter T. Ricketts à l'occasion de son 70ème anniversaire,* ed. Dominique Billy and Ann Buckley, 281–92. Brepols: Turnhout, 2005.

——. "Languages in Conflict in Toulouse: *Las Leys d'amors.*" *Modern Language Review* 103 (2008): 383–96.

——. "Performance and Civic Ritual in Toulouse." *e-France* (2011).

Léonard, Monique. *Le "dit" et sa technique littéraire, des origines à 1340.* Paris: Champion, 1996.

Levi, A. H. T. "Ethics and the Encyclopedia in the Sixteenth Century." In *French Renaissance Studies, 1540–1570: Humanism and the Encyclopedia,* ed. Peter Sharratt, 170–84. Edinburgh: Edinburgh University Press, 1976.

Le Vot, Gérard, "La Notation musicale et le chant dans les chansonniers et les recueils de motets français au XIIIe siècle." In *Théories et pratiques de l'écriture au Moyen Âge: Actes du colloque Palais du Luxembourg-Sénat, 5 et 6 mars 1987,* ed. Emmanuèle Baumgartner and Christiane Marchello-Nizia, *Littérales* 4 (1988): 155–89.

Libera, Alain de. *La Querelle des universaux de Platon à la fin du Moyen Âge.* Paris: Seuil, 1996.

Lods, Jeanne. *Les Pièces lyriques du "Roman de Perceforest."* Geneva: Droz, 1953.

Longtin, Mario. "Chercher l'intrus: Le roi de Chypre et le *Mystère de sainte Barbe cinq journées.*" In *Le Théâtre polémique français 1450–1550,* ed. Marie Bouhaïk-Gironès, Jelle Koopmans, and Katell Lavéant, 123–38. Rennes: Presses Universitaires de Rennes, 2008.

Lubienski-Bodenham, Henry. "The Origins of the Fifteenth Century View of
   Poetry as 'Seconde Rhétorique.'" *Modern Language Review* 74 (1979): 26–38.
Lukitsch, Shirley. "The Poetics of the *Prologue:* Machaut's Conception of the
   Purpose of His Art." *Medium Ævum* 52 (1983): 258–71.
Lütgemeier, Gertrud. *Beiträge zum Verständnis des "Jeu de la Feuillée" von Adam le
   Bossu.* Bonn: Romanisches Seminar des Universität Bonn, 1969.
Lyotard, Jean-François. *La Condition postmoderne.* Paris: Minuit, 1979.
Mallette, Karla. *The Kingdom of Sicily, 1100–1250: A Literary History.* Philadelphia:
   University of Pennsylvania Press, 2005.
Mantovani, Thierry. "Pierre Fabri et la poétique des Puys dans le second livre du
   Grand et vrai art de pleine rhétorique." *Nouvelle Revue du Seizième Siècle* 18
   (2000): 41–54.
Marchello-Nizia, Christiane. *La Langue française aux XIV* et XV* siècles.* Paris:
   Nathan, 1997.
Marenbon, John. *Later Medieval Philosophy.* London: Routledge, 1987.
———. *Boethius.* Oxford: Oxford University Press, 2003.
Margolis, Nadia. "Clerkliness and Courtliness in the Complaintes of Christine
   de Pizan." In *Christine de Pizan and Medieval French Lyric,* ed. Earl Jeffrey
   Richards, 135–54. Gainesville: University Press of Florida, 1998.
Mazouer, Charles. *Le Théâtre français du Moyen Âge.* Paris: SEDES, 1999.
McClelland, John. "Sonnet ou quatorzain? Marot et le choix d'une forme poétique."
   Revue d'Histoire Littéraire de la France 73 (1973): 591–607.
McGrady, Deborah. "What Is a Patron? Benefactors and Authorship in Harley 4431,
   Christine de Pizan's Collected Works." In *Christine de Pizan and the Categories
   of Difference,* ed. Marilynn Desmond, 195–214. Minneapolis: University of
   Minnesota Press, 1998.
———. *Controlling Readers: Guillaume de Machaut and His Late Medieval Audience.*
   Toronto: University of Toronto Press, 2006.
———. "Guillaume de Machaut." In *The Cambridge Companion to Medieval French
   Literature,* ed. Simon Gaunt and Sarah Kay, 109–22. Cambridge: Cambridge
   University Press, 2008.
———. "A Master, a *Vilain,* a Lady and a Scribe: Competing for Authority in a
   Late Medieval Translation of the *Ars Amatoria.*" In *Poetry, Knowledge and
   Community in Late Medieval France,* ed. Rebecca Dixon and Finn E. Sinclair,
   98–110. Cambridge: D. S. Brewer, 2008.
McGregor, Gordon Douglas. *The Broken Pot Restored: "Le Jeu de la Feuillée" of Adam
   de la Halle.* Lexington: French Forum, 1991.
Melczer, William. "Humanism and the Encyclopædic Tradition of the Fifteenth
   Century." *Cithara* 17 (1978): 13–19.
Ménager, Daniel. "Vers et prose dans le *Séjour d'Honneur* d'Octovien de Saint-
   Gelais." In *Grands Rhétoriqueurs,* 133–44. Paris: Presses de l'École normale
   supérieure, 1997.
Menegaldo, Silvère. "Théâtre et musique: Le cas exemplaire du *Jeu de Robin et
   Marion* d'Adam de la Halle." In *"Mainte belle œuvre faicte": Études sur le théâtre
   médiéval offertes à Graham A. Runnalls,* ed. Denis Hüe, Mario Longtin, and
   Lynette Muir, 389–405. Orléans: Paradigme, 2005.

——. "Amateurs et professionnels: La composition poétique selon le *Meliador* et les *dits* de Jean Froissart." *Perspectives Médiévales* 31 (2006): 179–201.

Mertens, Veronika. *Mi-parti als Zeichen: Zur Bedeutung von geteiltem Kleid und geteilter Gestalt in der Ständetracht, in literarischen und bildnerischen Quellen sowie im Fastnachtsbrauch vom Mittelalter bis zur Gegenwart.* Remscheid: Verlag Ute Kierdorf, 1983.

Meyer, Paul. "Prologue en vers français d'une histoire perdue de Philippe Auguste." *Romania* 6 (1877): 494–98.

——. "Matfre Ermengaud de Béziers, troubadour." *Histoire Littéraire de la France* 32 (1898): 16–56.

Miernowski, Jan. *Dialectique et connaissance dans "La Sepmaine" de Du Bartas: "Discours sur discours infiniment divers."* Geneva: Droz, 1992.

Minet-Mahy, Virginie. *Esthétique et pouvoir de l'œuvre allégorique à l'époque de Charles VI: Imaginaires et discours.* Paris: Champion, 2005.

Moisan, Jean-Claude. "La Naissance du monde dans la *Bible des poètes.*" In *Naissance du monde et l'invention du poème: Mélanges de poétique et d'histoire littéraire du XVIᵉ siècle offerts à Yvonne Bellenger,* ed. Jean-Claude Ternaux, 121–45. Paris: Champion, 1998.

Mombello, Gianni. *La tradizione manoscritta dell' "Epistre Othea" di Christine de Pizan: Prolegomeni all'edizione del testo.* Turin: Accademia delle Scienze, 1967.

——. "I manoscritti delle opere di Dante, Petrarca e Boccaccio nelle principali librerie francesi del secolo XV." In *Il Boccaccio nella cultura francese,* ed. Carlo Pellegrini, 81–209. Florence: Olschki, 1971.

Morin, Joseph C. "Jehannot de Lescurel's Chansons, Geffroy de Paris's *Dits,* and the Process of Design in BN fr. 146." In *Fauvel Studies: Allegory, Chronicle, Music, and Image in Paris, Bibliothèque Nationale de France, MS français 146,* ed. Margaret Bent and Andrew Wathey, 321–36. Oxford: Clarendon, 1998.

Morse, Ruth. *Truth and Convention in the Middle Ages: Rhetoric, Representation, and Reality.* Cambridge: Cambridge University Press, 1991.

Moss, Ann. *Ovid in Renaissance France: A Survey of the Latin Editions of Ovid and Commentaires Printed in France before 1600.* London: Warburg Institute, 1982.

——. *Poetry and Fable: Studies in Mythological Narrative in Sixteenth-Century France.* Cambridge: Cambridge University Press, 1984.

Mühlethaler, Jean-Claude. "Les poetes que de vert on couronne." *Le Moyen Français* 30 (1992): 97–112.

——. *Fauvel au pouvoir: Lire la satire médiévale.* Paris: Champion, 1994.

——. "Discours du narrateur, discours de Fortune: Les enjeux d'un changement de point de vue." In *Fauvel Studies: Allegory, Chronicle, Music, and Image in Paris, Bibliothèque Nationale de France, MS français 146,* ed. Margaret Bent and Andrew Wathey, 337–51. Oxford: Clarendon, 1998.

——. "Entre amour et politique: Métamorphoses ovideniennes à la fin du Moyen Âge. La fable de Céyx et Alcyoné, de l'Ovide moralisé à Christine de Pizan et Alain Chartier." *Cahiers de Recherches Médiévales* 9 (2002): 145–56.

——. "Vers statt Prosa: Schreiben gegen den Strom im Frankreich des ausgehenden Mittelalters." *Chloe: Beihefte zum "Daphnis"* 42 (2010): 163–82.

Murray, Alexander. *Reason and Society in the Middle Ages.* Oxford: Clarendon, 1978.

Mussou, Amandine. "Apprendre à jouer? Fonctions de la partie d'échecs des *Eschés amoureux.*" In *Poetry, Knowledge and Community in Late Medieval France,* ed. Rebecca Dixon and Finn E. Sinclair, 42–55. Cambridge: D. S. Brewer, 2008.

Nash, Jerry C. "The Literary Legacy of Pre-Pléiade Poetry." In *Pre-Pléiade Poetry,* ed. Jerry C. Nash, 9–14. Lexington, Ky.: French Forum, 1985.

Nicholson, Francesca M. "Branches of Knowledge: The Purposes of Citation in the *Breviari d'amor* of Matfre Ermengaud." *Neophilologus* 91 (2007): 361–73.

Noakes, Susan. *Timely Reading: Between Exegesis and Interpretation.* Ithaca: Cornell University Press, 1988.

Nouvet, Claire. "Pour une Économie de la dé-limitation: La *Prison amoureuse* de Jean Froissart." *Neophilologus* 70 (1986): 341–56.

Olson, Glending. "Making and Poetry in the Age of Chaucer." *Comparative Literature* 31 (1979): 272–90.

——. *Literature as Recreation in the Later Middle Ages.* Ithaca: Cornell University Press, 1982.

Paden, William D. "Christine de Pizan and the Transformation of Late Medieval Lyrical Genres." In *Christine de Pizan and Medieval French Lyric,* ed. Earl Jeffrey Richards, 27–49. Gainesville: University Press of Florida, 1998.

Pairet, Ana. *Les Mutacions des fables: Figures de la métamorphose dans la littérature française du Moyen Âge.* Paris: Champion, 2002.

——. "Les Formes qui muees furent: Figures et enjeux de la *mutacion* dans l'*Ovide moralisé.*" In *Nouvelles Études sur l'Ovide moralisé,* ed. Marylène Possamaï-Perez, 19–34. Paris: Champion, 2009.

Palmer, Nigel F. "Cosmic Quaternities in the *Roman de Fauvel.*" In *Fauvel Studies: Allegory, Chronicle, Music, and Image in Paris, Bibliothèque Nationale de France, MS français 146,* ed. Margaret Bent and Andrew Wathey, 395–419. Oxford: Clarendon, 1998.

Palonen, Kari. *Quentin Skinner: History, Politics, Rhetoric.* Cambridge: Polity, 2003.

Panofsky, Erwin. *Renaissance and Renascences in Western Art.* Stockholm: Almqvist and Wiksell, 1960.

Pantin, Isabelle. *La Poésie du ciel en France dans la seconde moitié du seizième siècle.* Geneva: Droz, 1995.

Paradis, Françoise. "Une polyphonie narrative: Pour une description de la structure des *Cent ballades d'amant et de dame* de Christine de Pizan." *Bien dire et bien aprandre* 8 (1990): 127–40.

Parkes, M. B. "The Influence of the Concepts of *Ordinatio* and *Compilatio* on the Development of the Book." In *Medieval Learning and Literature: Essays Presented to R. W. Hunt,* ed. J. J. G. Alexander and M. T. Gibson, 115–41. Oxford: Clarendon Press, 1976.

Pastoureau, Michel. *Figures et couleurs: Études sur la symbolique et la sensibilité médiévales.* Paris: Le Léopard d'Or, 1986.

Patch, Howard R. *The Goddess Fortuna in Mediæval Literature.* Cambridge: Harvard University Press, 1927.

Paterson, Linda. *Troubadours and Eloquence.* Oxford: Oxford University Press, 1975.

Pettegree, Andrew, Malcolm Walsby, and Alexander Wilkinson, eds. *French Vernacular Books: Books Published in the French Language before 1601.* 2 vols. Leiden: Brill, 2007.

Picone, Michelangelo, ed. *L'enciclopedismo medievale.* Ravenna: Longo, 1994.

Planche, Alice. *Charles d'Orléans ou la recherche d'un langage.* Paris: Champion, 1975.

———. "Du Tournoi au théâtre en Bourgogne: Le Pas de la Fontaine des Pleurs à Châlon-sur-Seine 1449–50." *Le Moyen Âge* 81 (1975): 97–128.

Poe, Elizabeth Wilson. *Compilatio: Lyric Texts and Prose Commentaries in Troubadour Manuscript H Vat. Lat. 3207.* Lexington, Ky.: French Forum, 2000.

Poirion, Daniel. *Le Poète et le prince: L'évolution du lyrisme courtois de Guillaume de Machaut à Charles d'Orléans.* Grenoble: Université de Grenoble, Faculté des Lettres et Sciences humaines, 1965.

———. "Lectures de la *Belle Dame sans Mercy.*" In *Mélanges de langue et de littérature offertes à Pierre Le Gentil,* 691–705. Paris: SEDES/CDU, 1973.

Polak, Lucie. "Plato, Nature and Jean de Meun." *Reading Medieval Studies* 3 (1977): 80–103.

Possamaï-Perez, Marylène. *L'"Ovide moralisé": Essai d'interprétation.* Paris: Champion, 2006.

Radden, Jennifer, ed. *The Nature of Melancholy.* Oxford: Oxford University Press, 2000.

Randall, Michael. *Building Resemblance: Analogical Imagery in the Early French Renaissance.* Baltimore: Johns Hopkins University Press, 1996.

Rasmussen, Jens. *La Prose narrative française du XVe siècle: Étude esthétique et stylistique.* Copenhagen: Munksgaard, 1958.

Rech, Régis. "La Culture historique de Jean Bouchet." In *Jean Bouchet, traverseur des voies périlleuses 1476–1557: Actes du colloque de Poitiers 30–31 août 2001,* ed. Jennifer Britnell and Nathalie Dauvois, 105–43. Paris: Champion, 2003.

Regalado, Nancy Freeman. "*Effet de réel, Effet du réel:* Representation and Reference in Villon's *Testament.*" *Yale French Studies* 70 (1986): 63–77.

———. "'En l'an de mon trentiesme aage': Date, Deixis, and Moral Vision in Villon's *Testament.*" In *Le Nombre du temps: En hommage à Paul Zumthor,* ed. Emmanuèle Baumgartner, Giuseppe Di Stefano, Françoise Ferrand, Serge Lusignan, Christiane Marchello-Nizia, and Michèle Perret, 237–46. Paris: Champion, 1988.

———. "The *Chronique métrique* and the Moral Design of BN fr. 146: Feasts of Good and Evil." In *Fauvel Studies: Allegory, Chronicle, Music, and Image in Paris, BnF MS fr. 146,* ed. Margaret Bent and Andrew Wathey, 467–94. Oxford: Clarendon, 1998.

———. "Villon's Legacy from *Le Testament* of Jean de Meun: Misquotation, Memory, and the Wisdom of Fools." In *Villon at Oxford: The Drama of the Text; Proceedings of the Conference Held at St. Hilda's College Oxford, March 1996.* Ed. Michael J. Freeman and Jane H. M. Taylor, 282–311. Amsterdam: Rodopi, 1999.

———. "Le *Romant de la Rose moralisé* de Jean Molinet: Alchimie d'une lecture méditative." In *Mouvances et jointures: Du manuscrit au texte médiéval,* ed. Milena Mikhaïlova, 99–118. Orléans: Paradigme, 2005.

———. "The Songs of Jehannot de Lescurel in Paris, BnF, MS fr. 146: Love Lyrics, Moral Wisdom and the Material Book." In *Poetry, Knowledge and Community in Late Medieval France,* ed. Rebecca Dixon and Finn E. Sinclair, 151–72. Cambridge: D. S. Brewer, 2008.

Ribémont, Bernard. "Avant-propos." In *Écrire pour dire: Études sur le dit médiéval.* Ed. Bernard Ribémont, 3–8. Paris: Klincksieck, 1990.

——. "Christine de Pizan: Entre espace scientifique et espace imaginé (*Le Livre du chemin de long estude*)." In *Une femme de lettres au Moyen Âge: Études autour de Christine de Pizan,* ed. Liliane Dulac and Bernard Ribémont, 245–61. Orléans: Paradigme, 1995.

——. *Les Origines des encyclopédies médiévales.* Paris: Champion, 2001.

——. "L'*Ovide moralisé* et la tradition encyclopédique médiévale: Une approche générique comparative." In *Lectures et usages d'Ovide,* ed. Emmanèle Baumgartner. *Cahiers de Recherches Médiévales* 9 (2002): 13–24.

——. "Dire le vrai et chanter des louanges: *La Prise d'Alexandrie* de Guillaume de Machaut." *Cahiers de Recherches Médiévales* 10 (2003): 173–90.

Richards, Earl Jeffrey. "Poems of Water without Salt and Ballades without Feeling, or Reintroducing History into the Text: Prose and Verse in the Works of Christine de Pizan." In *Christine de Pizan and Medieval French Lyric,* ed. Earl Jeffrey Richards, 206–29. Gainesville: University Press of Florida, 1998.

Richter, Reinhilt. *Die Troubadourzitate im "Breviari d'amor."* Modena: Mucchi, 1976.

Riffaterre, Michael. *Semiotics of Poetry.* Bloomington: Indiana University Press, 1978.

Rigolot, François. "Qu'est-ce qu'un sonnet? Perspectives sur les origines d'une forme poétique." *Revue d'Histoire Littéraire de la France* 84 (1984): 3–18.

Roccati, G. Matteo. "Guillaume de Machaut, 'Prologue' aux œuvres: La disposition du texte dans le ms. A Paris, B.N.F., fr. 1584." *Studi Francesi* 44 (2000): 535–40.

Rothstein, Marian, ed. *Charting Change in France around 1540.* Selinsgrove, Pa.: Susquehanna University Press, 2006.

Rouget, François. "Une forme reine des Puys poétiques: La ballade." in *Première poésie française de la Renaissance: Autour des Puys poétiques normands. Actes du Colloque international organisé par le CÉRÉDI Université de Rouen, 30 septembre— 2 octobre 1999,* ed. Jean-Claude Arnould and Thierry Mantovani, 329–46. Paris: Champion, 2003.

Rouse, Mary, and Richard Rouse. *Manuscripts and Their Makers: Commercial Book Producers in Medieval Paris, 1200–1500.* 2 vols. Turnhout: Miller, 2000.

Roussel, Claude. "L'Automne de la chanson de geste." *Cahiers de Recherches Médiévales* 12 (2005): 15–28.

Rouy, François. *L'Esthétique du traité moral d'après les œuvres d'Alain Chartier.* Geneva: Droz, 1980.

Roy, Bruno. "Eustache Deschamps et Évrart de Conty théoriciens de l'art poétique." In *Cy nous dient: Dialogue avec quelques auteurs médiévaux,* 25–40. Orléans: Paradigme, 1999.

Runnalls, Graham A. "The Staging of André de la Vigne's *Mystere de Saint Martin.*" *Trétaux* 3 (1981): 68–79.

——. "Towards a Typology of Medieval French Play Manuscripts." In *The Editor and the Text: In Honour of Professor Anthony J. Holden,* ed. Philip E. Bennett and Graham A. Runnalls, 96–113. Edinburgh: Edinburgh University Press, 1990.

——. "Un Siècle dans la vie d'un mystère: *Le Mystère de Saint Denis.*" *Le Moyen Âge* 97 (1991): 407–30.

——. "Les Mystères de la Passion en langue française: Tentative de classement." *Romania* 114 (1996): 468–516.

——. "Langage de la parole ou langage du geste? Le Mystère de Saint Laurent." In *Langues, codes et conventions de l'ancien théâtre: Actes de la troisième rencontre sur l'ancien théâtre européen,* ed. Jean-Pierre Bordier, 121–34. Paris: Champion, 2002.

Saltzstein, Jennifer. "Refrains in the *Jeu de Robin et Marion:* History of a Citation." In *Poetry, Knowledge and Community in Late Medieval France,* ed. Rebecca Dixon and Finn E. Sinclair, 173–86. Cambridge: D. S. Brewer, 2008.

Scheller, Robert W. "Ung fil tres delicat: Louis XII and Italian affairs, 1510–11." *Simiolus* 31 (2005): 4–45.

Schmitt, Charles B. *Aristotle and the Renaissance.* Cambridge: Harvard University Press, 1983.

Schoysman, Anne. "Prosimètre et *varietas* chez Jean Lemaire de Belges." In *Le Prosimètre à la Renaissance,* ed. Nathalie Dauvois, 111–24. Paris: Éditions Rue d'Ulm/Presses de l'École normale supérieure, 2005.

Segre, Cesare. "Le forme et le tradizione didattichi." In *Grundriss der romanischen Literaturen des Mittelalters,* Vol. 6 part 1: *La Littérature didactique, allégorique et satirique, Partie historique,* ed. Jürgen Beyer, 58–145. Heidelberg: Winter 1968.

——. *Teatro e romanzo: Due tipi di comunicazione letteraria.* Turin: Einaudi, 1984.

Shackleton, Robert. "The Encyclopedic Spirit." In *Greene Centennial Studies: Essays Presented to Donald Greene in the Centennial Year of the University of Southern California,* ed. Paul J. Korshin and Robert R. Allen, 377–90. Charlottesville: University Press of Virginia, 1984.

Short, Ian. Review of Gabrielle Spiegel, *Romancing the Past. Romance Philology* 51 (1997): 97–99.

Siciliano, Italo. *François Villon et les thèmes poétiques du Moyen Âge.* Paris: Armand Colin, 1934.

Simone, Franco. "La notion d'Encyclopédie: Élément caractéristique de la Renaissance française." In *French Renaissance Studies, 1540–1570: Humanism and the Encyclopedia,* ed. Peter Sharratt, 234–62. Edinburgh: Edinburgh University Press, 1976.

Simpson, James R. *Fantasy, Identity and Misrecognition in Medieval French Narrative.* Bern: Peter Lang, 2000.

Sinclair, Finn E. "Froissart and the Re-membering of Memory." *French Studies,* forthcoming.

——. "Poetic Creation in Jean Froissart's *L'Espinette amoureuse* and *Le Joli Buisson de jonece." Modern Philology,* forthcoming.

Singer, Julie. "Clockwork Genres: Temperance and the Articulated Text in Late Medieval France." *Exemplaria* 21 (2009): 225–46.

Sinnreich-Levi, Deborah M., ed. *Eustache Deschamps, French Courtier-Poet: His Work and His World.* New York: AMS Press, 1998.

Small, Graeme. *George Chastelain and the Shaping of Valois Burgundy: Political and Historical Culture at Court in the Fifteenth Century.* Woodbridge, Suffolk: Boydell Press, 1997.

——. "When Indiciaires Meet Rederijkers: A Contribution to the History of the Burgundian 'Theatre State.'" In *Stad van koopmanschap en vrede: Literatuur in Brugge tussen Middeleeuwen en Rederijkerstijd,* ed. Johan Oosterman, 133–61. Leuven: Peeters, 2005.

Smith, Darwin. "La Question du Prologue de la Passion ou le rôle des formes
    métriques dans la Creacion du Monde d'Arnoul Gréban." In *L'Économie du
    dialogue dans l'ancien théâtre européen: Actes de la première rencontre sur l'ancien
    théâtre européen en 1995,* ed. Jean-Pierre Bordier, 141–65. Paris: Champion, 1999.
Smith, Margaret M. "Medieval Roots of the Renaissance Printed Book: An Essay
    in Design History." In *Forms of the "Medieval" in the "Renaissance": A
    Multidisciplinary Exploration of a Cultural Continuum,* ed. George Hugo
    Tucker, 143–53. Charlottesville: Rookwood Press, 2000.
Solterer, Helen. "Fiction versus Defamation: The Quarrel over *The Romance of the
    Rose.*" *Medieval History Journal* 2 (1999): 111–41.
———. "Theatre and Theatricality." In *The Cambridge Companion to Medieval French
    Literature,* ed. Simon Gaunt and Sarah Kay, 181–94. Cambridge: Cambridge
    University Press, 2008.
Somers, Margaret R., and Gloria D. Gibson. "Reclaiming the Epistemological
    'Other': Narrative and the Social Constitution of Identity." In *Social Theory
    and the Politics of Identity,* ed. Craig Calhoun, 37–99. Oxford: Blackwell, 1994.
Speer, Mary B., and Alfred Foulet. "Is *Marques de Rome* a Derhymed Romance?"
    Romania 101 (1980): 336–65.
Spiegel, Gabrielle M. *Romancing the Past: The Rise of Vernacular Prose Historiography
    in Thirteenth-Century France.* Berkeley: University of California Press, 1993.
Staub, Hans. *Le Curieux Désir: Scève et Peletier du Man poètes de la connaissance.*
    Geneva: Droz, 1967.
Stock, Brian. *The Implications of Literacy: Written Language and Models of
    Interpretation.* Princeton: Princeton University Press, 1983.
Stoneburner, Michelle. "*Le Miroir de Mariage:* Misunderstood Misogyny." In
    Eustache Deschamps, French Courtier-Poet: His Work and His World, ed.
    Deborah M. Sinnreich-Levi, 145–62. New York: AMS Press, 1998.
Strubel, Armand. *"Grant senefiance a": Allégorie et littérature au Moyen Âge.* Paris:
    Champion, 2002.
Sturm-Maddox, Sara. *Ronsard, Petrarch, and the "Amours."* Gainesville: University of
    Florida Press, 1999.
Suard, François. "Y a-t-il un avenir pour la tradition épique médiévale après 1400?"
    Cahiers de Recherches Médiévales 11 (2004): 75–89.
Symes, Carol. *A Common Stage: Theater and Public Life in Medieval Arras.* Ithaca:
    Cornell University Press, 2007.
Taithe, Bertrand, and Tim Thornton. "Propaganda: A Misnomer of Rhetoric
    and Persuasion?" In *Propaganda: Political Rhetoric and Identity, 1300–2000,*
    ed. Bertrand Taithe and Tim Thornton, 1–24. Stroud, Gloucestershire:
    Sutton, 1999.
Taylor, Jane H. M. "The Lyric Insertion: Towards a Functional Model." In *Courtly
    Literature: Culture and Context; Selected Papers from the 5ᵗʰ Triennial Congress of
    the International Courtly Literature Society, Dalfsen, The Netherlands, 9–16 August,
    1986,* ed. Keith Busby and Erik Kooper, 539–48. Amsterdam: Benjamins, 1990.
———. "Inescapable Rose: Jean le Seneschal's *Cent Ballades* and the Art of Cheerful
    Paradox." *Medium Ævum* 67 (1998): 60–84.
———. *The Poetry of François Villon: Text and Context.* Cambridge: Cambridge
    University Press, 2001.

——. "Embodying the Rose: An Intertextual Reading of Alain Chartier's *La Belle Dame sans Mercy.*" In *The Court Reconvenes: Courtly Literature across the Disciplines; Selected Papers from the Ninth Triennial Congress of the International Courtly Literature Society, University of British Columbia, 25–31 July 1998,* ed. Barbara K. Altmann and Carleton W. Carroll, 325–33. Cambridge: D. S. Brewer, 2003.

——. *The Making of Poetry: Late-Medieval French Poetic Anthologies.* Turnhout: Brepols, 2007.

Thiry, Claude. "La Jeunesse littéraire de Clément Marot." *Revue des langues vivantes* 34 (1968): 436–60, 567–78.

——. "Rhétorique et genres littéraires au XVᵉ siècle." In *Sémantique lexicale et sémantique grammaticale en moyen français: Colloque organisé par le Centre d'Études Linguistiques et Littéraires de la Vrije Universiteit Brussel 28–29 septembre 1978,* ed. Marc Wilmet, 23–50. Brussels: V. U. B. Centrum voor Taal- en Literatuurwetenschap, 1979.

——. "La Poétique des grands rhétoriqueurs." *Le Moyen Âge* 86 (1980): 117–33.

——. "Au Carrefour des deux rhétoriques: Les prosimètres de Jean Molinet." In *Du mot au texte: Actes du IIIᵉ Colloque International sur le Moyen Français, Düsseldorf, 17–19 septembre 1980,* ed. Peter Wunderli, 213–27. Tübingen: Narr, 1982.

——. "Le vieux renard et le jeune loup: L'évolution interne de la *Recollection des merveilleuses advenues.*" *Le Moyen Âge* 90 (1984): 455–85.

——. "Débats et moralités dans la littérature française du XVᵉ siècle: Intersection et interaction du narratif et du dramatique." *Le Moyen Français* 19 (1986): 203–44.

——. "Historiographie et actualité: XIVᵉ et XVᵉ siècles." In *Grundriss der romanischen Literaturen des Mittelalters,* Vol. 11 part 1: *La Littérature historiographique des origines à 1500,* ed. Armin Biermann et al., 1025–63. Heidelberg: Winter 1987.

——. "La Poésie de circonstance." In *Grundriss der romanischen Literaturen des Mittelalters,* Vol. 8 part 1: *La Littérature française aux XIVᵉ et XVᵉ siècles, Partie historique,* ed. Daniel Poirion, 111–38. Heidelberg: Winter 1988.

——. "Stylistique et auto-critique: Georges Chastelain et l'Exposition sur Verité mal prise." In *Recherches sur la littérature du XVᵉ siècle: Actes du VIᵉ Colloque international sur le moyen français,* ed. Sergio Cigada and Anna Slerca. 3 vols. 3:101–35. Milan: Vita e Pensiero, 1991.

——. "Rhétoriqueurs de Bourgogne, rhétoriqueurs de France: Convergences, divergences?" In *Rhetoric—Rhétoriqueurs—Rederijkers,* ed. Jelle Koopmans, Mark A. Meadow, Kees Meerhoff, and Marijke Spies, 101–16. Amsterdam: North-Holland, 1995.

——. "Prospections et prospectives sur la Rhétorique seconde." *Le Moyen Français* 46–47 (2000): 541–62.

——. "La *Fantasie subit ymaginée* de Simon: Analyse d'un prosimètre inédit destiné à Marguerite d'Autriche." In *Le Prosimètre à la Renaissance,* ed. Nathalie Dauvois, 75–86. Paris: Éditions Rue d'Ulm/Presses de l'École normale supérieure, 2005.

Tilliette, Jean-Yves. "Éclipse de la fortune dans le haut moyen âge?" In *Fortune: Thèmes, representations, discours,* ed. Yasmina Foehr-Janssens and Emmanuelle Métry, 93–104. Geneva: Droz, 2003.

Tilliette, Jean-Yves, Jacqueline Cerquiglini-Toulet, and Jean-Claude Mühlethaler. "Poétiques en transition: *L'Instructif de la seconde rhétorique,* balises pour un chantier." *Poétiques en transition: Entre Moyen Âge et Renaissance,* ed. Jean-Claude Mühlethaler and Jacqueline Cerquiglini-Toulet, special number of *Études de Lettres* 4 (2002): 9–22.

Trachsler, Richard. "Cent Sénateurs, neuf soleils et un songe." *Romania* 116 (1998): 188–214.

Tucci, Patrizio. "Modes de la citation dans la poésie du XVᵉ siècle: Charles d'Orléans, Jean Regnier, François Villon." *Poétique* 150 (2007): 199–215.

Tucker, George Hugo, ed. *Forms of the "Medieval" in the "Renaissance": A Multidisciplinary Exploration of a Cultural Continuum.* Charlottesville: Rookwood Press, 2000.

Vale, Malcolm. "The World of the Courts: Content and Context of the *Fauvel* Manuscript." In *Fauvel Studies: Allegory, Chronicle, Music, and Image in Paris, Bibliothèque Nationale de France, MS français 146,* ed. Margaret Bent and Andrew Wathey, 591–98. Oxford: Clarendon, 1998.

Vaughan, Richard. *Philip the Good: The Apogee of Burgundy.* London: Longman, 1970.

Wack, Mary. *Lovesickness in the Middle Ages: The "Viaticum" and Its Commentaries.* Philadelphia: University of Pennsylvania Press, 1990.

Wallace, David. *Chaucerian Polity: Absolutist Lineages and Associational Forms in England and Italy.* Stanford: Stanford University Press, 1997.

Walters, Lori. "*Translatio Studii:* Christine de Pizan's Self-portrayal in Two Lyric Poems and in the *Livre de la mutacion de Fortune.*" In *Christine de Pizan and Medieval French Lyric,* ed. Earl Jeffrey Richards, 155–67. Gainesville: University Press of Florida, 1998.

Wathey, Andrew. "Gervès du Bus, the *Roman de Fauvel,* and the Politics of the Later Capetian Court." In *Fauvel Studies: Allegory, Chronicle, Music, and Image in Paris, Bibliothèque Nationale de France, MS français 146,* ed. Margaret Bent and Andrew Wathey, 599–613. Oxford: Clarendon, 1998.

Winn, Mary Beth. "In Pursuit of the *Acteur* in *La Chasse et le Départ d'Amours.*" *Le Moyen Français* 7 (1980): 92–117.

Woledge, Brian, and H. P. Clive. *Répertoire des plus anciens textes en prose française depuis 842 jusqu'aux premières années du XIIIᵉ siècle.* Geneva: Droz, 1964.

Wolf-Bonvin, Romaine. "L'Art de disparaître: La métamorphose d'Arachné." In *Nouvelles Études sur l'Ovide moralisé,* ed. Marylène Possamaï-Perez, 181–210. Paris: Champion, 2009.

Zink, Michel. *La Subjectivité littéraire autour du siècle de saint Louis.* Paris: Presses universitaires de France, 1985.

———. "L'Amour en fuite: *L'Espinette amoureuse* et *Le joli buisson de jeunesse* de Froissart ou la poésie comme histoire sans objet." In *Musique naturele: Interpretationen zür französischen Lyrik des Spätmittelalters,* ed. Wolf-Dieter Stempel, 195–209. Munich: Fink, 1995.

———. *Froissart et le temps.* Paris: Presses universitaires de France, 1998.

———. "Nature et sentiment." *Littérature* 130 (2003): 39–47.

———. *Nature et poésie au Moyen Âge.* Paris: Fayard, 2006.

Zsuppán, C. M. "An Early Example of the Renaissance Themes of Immortality and Divine Inspiration: The Work of Jean Robertet." *Bibliothèque d'Humanisme et Renaissance* 28 (1966): 553–63.

Zumthor, Paul. *Essai de poétique médiévale.* Paris: Seuil, 1972.

———. *La Mesure du monde: Représentation de l'espace au Moyen Âge.* Paris: Seuil, 1993.

Index

abject, the, 174
abridgment, 187
absences, 203
abstraction, intellectual, 21, 142
Achilles, 162
Actaeon, 86
acteur. See narrator, first-person
actors, theatrical, 191, 193–94, 196, 199
Adam de la Halle, 152–53, 155; *Jeu de la Feuillée,* 168–69, 195; *Jeu de Robin et Marion,* 152
adaptation, 145
Adolphe de Gueldre, 59
Agamben, Giorgio, 20–21, 67, 180, 198n2, 204; *Stanzas,* 20–21, 60–61; *The End of the Poem,* 21
Aimeric de Peguilhan, 6
Alan of Lille, 4; *Anticlaudianus,* 80; *De planctu naturae,* 73, 77
Alcyone, 81, 86–88
Alexander the Great, 162
Al-Farabi, 10
allegoresis, 19, 80–81, 97, 202. *See also* interpretation
allegory, 9–13, 19, 147–49, 152–54, 160, 162–63, 169, 173, 187–90, 202
allusion, 135, 142–50, 171, 176, 180, 186, 188. *See also* intertextuality; quotation
anamnesis, 91. *See also* memory
anamorphosis, 189
Angers, 194
Anglo-Norman, 33
Anjou, house of, 152

anthologies, anthologization, 3–4, 136–39, 141, 146, 154, 156, 170, 176, 179, 181, 186–88, 206–7; *chansonniers,* 157. *See also* manuscripts
antiquity, classical, 4, 10–11, 15, 180, 200–202, 205–7
Arachne, Araigne, 82–84
Aristotle, 12, 64, 66, 73, 112, 200; Aristotelianism, 16, 21; *Metaphysics,* 77; natural philosophy, 77; *Physics,* 77–78, 95; *Problemata,* 128
Armstrong, Adrian, 95
Arnaut Daniel, 118–19
Arras, 142, 152, 166–69, 195, 200, 204; Abbey of Saint-Vaast, 167; Petit Marché, 168
arts de seconde rhétorique, 8–10, 137–40, 205n9
astrology, 187
Attwood, Catherine, 72–73, 96
Aubailly, Jean-Claude, 46
Aubert, David, 53
audiences, 7–9, 23, 135–36, 138, 164, 166–67, 172–78, 182, 185, 190, 192–96, 199; theatrical, 191–93. *See also* readers; reception
Augustine, Saint, 107; on music, 141
authenticity, 3
authority, 2–3, 15, 20, 150–51, 152–53, 158, 162, 165–66, 170, 174–75, 192, 207

ballade, 5, 11, 37–39, 61–63, 66, 76, 128, 138–39, 144, 147, 153, 156–57, 159,